Language
Development
and Intervention
With the Hearing
Impaired

Language Development and Intervention with the Hearing Impaired is a volume in the PERSPECTIVES IN AUDIOLOGY SERIES—Lyle L. Lloyd, series editor. Other volumes in the series include:

Published:

Communicating with Deaf People: A Resource Manual for Teachers and Students of American Sign Language by Harry W. Hoemann, Ph.D.

Noise and Audiology edited by David M. Lipscomb, Ph.D.

The Sounds of Speech Communication: A Primer of Acoustic Phonetics and Speech Perception by J. M. Pickett, Ph.D.

Supervision in Audiology by Judith A. Rassi, M.A.

Hearing Assessment edited by William F. Rintelmann, Ph.D.

Auditory Management of Hearing-Impaired Children: Principles and Prerequisites for Intervention edited by Mark Ross, Ph.D., and Thomas G. Giolas, Ph.D.

Introduction to Aural Rehabilitation edited by Ronald L. Schow, Ph.D., and Michael A. Nerbonne, Ph.D.

Acoustical Factors Affecting Hearing Aid Performance edited by Gerald A. Studebaker, Ph.D, and Irving Hochberg, Ph.D.

American Sign Language and Sign Systems by Ronnie Bring Wilbur, Ph.D.

Aging and the Perception of Speech by Moe Bergman, Ed.D.

In preparation:

Principles of Speech Audiometry edited by Dan F. Konkle, Ph.D., and William F. Rintelmann, Ph.D.

Forensic Audiology edited by Marc B. Kramer, Ph.D. and Joan M. Armbruster, M.S.

Acoustic Amplificaton: A Unified Treatment by Harry Levitt, Ph.D.

The Development of Special Auditory Testing: A Book of Readings edited by Jay Sanders, Jr., Ph.D., and M. Richard Navarro, Ph.D.

Publisher's Note

Perspectives in Audiology is a carefully planned series of clinically oriented and basic science textbooks. The series is enriched by contributions from leading specialists in audiology and allied disciplines. Because technical language and terminology in these disciplines are constantly being refined and sometimes vary, this series has been edited as far as possible for consistency of style in conformity with current majority usage as set forth by the American Speech-Language-Hearing Association, the *Publication Manual of the American Psychological Association,* and The University of Chicago's *A Manual of Style.* University Park Press and the series editors and authors welcome readers' comments about individual volumes in the series or the series concept as a whole in the interest of making **Perspectives in Audiology** as useful as possible to students, teachers, clinicians, and scientists.

A Volume in the Perspectives in Audiology Series

LANGUAGE DEVELOPMENT AND INTERVENTION WITH THE HEARING IMPAIRED

by
Richard R. Kretschmer, Jr., Ed.D.
Department of Special Education and School
  Psychology
University of Cincinnati
and
Laura W. Kretschmer, Ed.D.
Department of Communication, Speech, Theatre
University of Cincinnati

with contribution by
Roberta R. Truax
Department of Special Education and School Psychology
University of Cincinnati

University Park Press
Baltimore

UNIVERSITY PARK PRESS
International Publishers in Science, Medicine, and Education
233 East Redwood Street
Baltimore, Maryland 21202

Typeset by American Graphic Arts Corporation
Manufactured in the United States of America by the Maple Press Company

Library of Congress Cataloging in Publication Data

Kretschmer, Richard R.
Language development and intervention with the hearing impaired.

(Perspectives in audiology series)
Includes index.
1. Deaf—Means of communication.   2. Deaf—Education
—English language.   I. Kretschmer, Laura W., joint
suthor.   III. Title.   IV. Series.

HV2471.K73   362.4'2   78-8186
ISBN 0-8391-0993-8

We dedicate this book to two women who were a great influence in the authors' lives, Louise F. Wilcox and Margaret T. Kretschmer.

CONTENTS

TABLES

FIGURES

PREFACE TO PERSPECTIVES IN AUDIOLOGY

Audiology is a young, vibrant, dynamic field. Its lineage can be traced to the fields of education, medicine, physics, and psychology in the nineteenth century and the emergence of speech pathology in the first half of this century. The term "audiology," meaning the science of hearing, was coined by Raymond Carhart in 1947. Since then, its definition has expanded to include its professional nature. Audiology is the profession that provides knowledge and service in the areas of human hearing and, more broadly, human communication and its disorders. As evidence of the growth of audiology as a major profession, in the 1940s there were no programs designed to prepare "audiologists," while now there are over 112 graduate training programs accredited by the Education and Training Board of the American Board of Examiners in Speech Pathology and Audiology for providing academic and clinical training designed to prepare clinically competent audiologists. Audiology is also a major area of study in the professional preparation of speech pathologists, speech and hearing scientists, and otologists.

Perspectives in Audiology is the first series of books designed to cover the major areas of study in audiology. The interdisciplinary nature of the field is reflected by the scope of the volumes in this series. The volumes currently in preparation (see p. ii) include both clinically oriented and basic science texts. The series consists of topic-specific textbooks designed to meet the needs of today's advanced level student. Each volume will also serve as a focal reference source for practicing audiologists and specialists in many related fields.

The **Perspectives in Audiology** series offers several advantages not usually found in other texts, but purposely featured in this series to increase the practical value of the books for practitioners and researchers, as well as for students and teachers.

1. Every volume includes thorough discussion of all relevant clinical and/or research papers on each topic.
2. Every volume is organized in an educational format to serve as the main text or as one of the main texts for graduate and advanced undergraduate students in courses on audiology and/or other studies concerned with human communication and its disorders.
3. Unlike ordinary texts, **Perspectives in Audiology** volumes will retain their professional reference value as focal reference sources for practitioners and researchers in career work long after completion of their studies.
4. Each volume serves as a rich source of authoritative, up-to-date information and valuable reviews for specialists in many fields, including administration, audiology, early childhood studies, linguistics, otology, psychology, pediatrics, public health, special education, speech pathology, and speech and hearing science.

Language Intervention with the Hearing Impaired, by Richard W. Kretschmer and Laura R. Kretschmer, represents a major thrust in the series. The series covers many approaches to habilitation, and language and communication are major problems in the habilitation of hearing-impaired persons. This volume exemplifies the series in that it offers both basic information on linguistics and language problems and practical information that can be applied to intervention methods.

There is a good deal of lively controversy over approaches to language intervention with severely hearing-impaired persons. On the one hand is the emphasis on the manual system and on the other are the advocates of the aural-oral approach. *Language Intervention with the Hearing Impaired* provides an introduction to the linguistic basis of language teaching of the hearing impaired along with information concerning the nature of language differences found in the hearing impaired, and combines these into practical application. Thus, this volume is applicable to either language intervention approach.

Lyle L. Lloyd, Ph.D.
Chairman and Professor
of Special Education
Professor of Audiology and
Speech Sciences
Purdue University

PREFACE

The task we have undertaken in this book is to consider once again the issues and strategies for helping hearing-impaired children and youth to learn fluent uses of language. We believe that educators of deaf children have no reason to be satisfied with the present status of most deaf persons' ability to communicate with a range of individuals in contemporary society.

As a consequence, during the past ten years, we have seriously considered the problems, the successes, and the efforts that have fallen short of the mark in the area of language teaching and learning. Deaf children, their parents, and finally teachers and university students have all helped us to make a decision that a developmental approach to language learning was the most reasonable one for our purposes. We think it is reasonable to take advantage of the linguistic and cognitive potential that is the human heritage of any deaf child. To this end, we have developed and refined the notions about language that are expressed in this book, leaning heavily on the literature in language acquisition, child development, and linguistics to guide us. The unfortunate consequence of such an approach is that the disciplines from which we strive to learn are in such rapid and exciting stages of growth that many of our conclusions seem stale by the time they are committed to paper.

We have tried to provide reasonable contemporary summaries of language description, of child language first, moving to consideration of the state of knowledge about the linguistic capabilities of deaf persons, to suggestions on assessment of those capabilities, and finally to the outline of approaches to intervention, including our own, which seem to grow naturally from an understanding of language, children, deafness, and learning.

Attention in this book is focused on syntactic and semantic issues, but always within the context of communication. It is our clear conviction that all three aspects need to be considered in developing intervention programs for hearing handicapped persons. It is the very absence of integration of these factors that has failed to occur in many educational programs, to the detriment of language growth in hearing-impaired children.

We hope what we have written will interest, stimulate, or even irritate others enough that they will take a fresh look at deaf children with language learning problems, or with less than fluent language usage, to determine if any of our ideas or suggestions have merit. More important, they may implement their own ideas and make them work. Within the space of a single book it has not been possible to enumerate in sufficient detail the contributions of the various disciplines from which we have drawn. It is left to each reader to pursue the vitality and excitement of the literature in child language.

A variety of persons could be thanked for their contributions to our thinking. To avoid an endless list we would simply like to extend our thanks to Ms. Maureen Flynn, who provided the majority of the typing of the final manuscript. Without her support and patience, we would have failed to meet the deadlines for completion of this book.

Richard R. Kretschmer, Jr., Ed.D.
Laura W. Kretschmer, Ed.D.

Language Development and Intervention With the Hearing Impaired

CHAPTER 1

LANGUAGE—AN OVERVIEW

CONTENTS

BACKGROUND INFORMATION

For the purpose of this book, language is defined as an organized set of symbolic relationships, mutually agreed upon by a speech community to represent experience and facilitate communication. Within this definition, there are several assumptions, both implicitly and explicitly stated, that need clarification.

Language may be expressed through speech, but not in all cases. Speech is the audible production of language, the result of manipulation of the vocal tract and oral musculature. Language, on the other hand, denotes the intended messages or meanings contained in the speaker's utterances. It is possible to have speech without language, as with parrots or mynah birds, or language without speech, as with deaf persons who express language in a manual mode, or children with severe neuromuscular disorders who may use communication boards or machines for expression.

Language is encompassed by the broader concept of communication. Communication is any attempt by the speaker to exchange information with another person in his speech community. Tapping a person on the shoulder to obtain his attention can be considered an example of a communicative act. If language is used to establish communication between individuals, verbal messages may be exchanged between them, but it is important to realize that not all communication is verbal.

These three concepts, *language, speech,* and *communication,* are so interwoven in actual dialogues between speakers and listeners that it is difficult to determine where one process begins and another ends. In general, communication can be seen as the framework through which language is utilized to exchange information. Speech can be seen as the most common manifestation of communication employed by the majority of individuals.

Language is arbitrary. The specific linguistic units selected by a particular speech community for use within their language have no inherent relationship with what they are selected to represent. For instance, there is no reason why in English a sleeping platform is called a *bed* and not a *sheep*. A bed is a *bed* only because that is what previous English language speakers decided to call it. As the demands of society dictate the need for new words, their selection will be arbitrary. Likewise, syntactic conventions in any language are equally arbitrary. In English, plurality may be signaled by the use of the regular suffix /-s/ attached to words designated as nouns. English could just as easily have been organized to indicate plurality by use of a variety of other word endings or linguistic devices. All aspects of linguistic usage, including syntactic conventions, semantic understandings, and communication correlates, are arbitrarily established by the society that uses them.

Language is an organized set of symbolic relationships. Language is composed of a set of consistent, regularly recurring patterns that can be shown to be generated through a finite set of rules (Chafe, 1970; N. Chomsky, 1957, 1965, 1971, 1972; Fillmore, 1968, 1971a,b; Jacobs and Rosenbaum, 1968). Language has a prescribed number of underlying rules or regulations that govern the comprehension and production of utterances. Language is not just a process of stringing words together; instead words are organized in a systematic fashion with permissable word and meaning arrangements. These regularities are referred to as symbolic relationships.

We know that we do not say *Car the had wreck a* in English, because word order constraints specify that articles such as *the* and *a* must precede, not follow, their nouns in sentences. The meanings of words are also dictated by their use and function within sentences: in the sentence *I have a run in my stocking, run* functions in the noun sense, not the verb sense. The listener knows this because of a sense of how word order interfaces with the meanings of lexical items. There are also rules that dictate the ways in which words and sentences are used to convey information in conversations. In the organized sentence *The car had a wreck,* we know that the article *a* indicates that the word following is new information, whereas the article *the* is used to signal information that is old or already known information (Clark and Clark, 1977). The listener would be expected to know something about the car, but not the wreck.

Mastery of the symbolic relationships that exist within language gives any person the potential to produce and comprehend all the possible sentences of his language. This capacity is referred to as the generative capacity of language. To say that language is rule governed and that there is a finite set of these rules should not imply that a language user can articulate such systematic underlying representations. Instead he probably knows them only to the point of being able to understand and produce sentences he has never heard before or produced himself.

Appreciation of the contemporary notion of underlying symbolic relationships or rules in language is vital, because they form the core of current linguistic theory whether the theory focuses on syntax, or meaning, or communication. Linguistic theories, because of their adherence to the concept of symbolic relationship or linguistic rule, make two distinctions important to any discussion of language. These distinctions are between linguistic competence and linguistic performance, and between deep structure and surface structure (N. Chomsky, 1972).

Linguistic competence is defined as the sum of knowledge that a particular speaker has about his language. It involves word arrangement or syntactic knowledge, meaning or semantic knowledge, and communication or pragmatic/conversational knowledge. Use of this knowledge in actual communication exchanges is referred to as linguistic performance. Linguistic performance is subject to all the foibles inherent in speaking and understanding, such as motivational issues, slips of the tongue, and misperception of sounds. People often make errors in linguistic performance even though they have linguistic competence for a particular aspect of language. That this is true is evidenced by the number of times people reconstruct utterances when they perceive that they have violated some underlying syntactic, semantic, pragmatic, or phonological rule (Fromkin, 1973).

Deep structure refers to the mental operations presumed necessary to produce and comprehend a particular sentence. Surface structure refers to the actual sounds and sound combinations that are produced or comprehended in making deep structures available to others. Surface structures must be used to theorize about deep structure. It could be argued that only when one ascertains the deep structure of a sentence can one truly understand or use a sentence effectively, but most people happily pass their lives without explicit awareness of deep structure relationships, and more importantly, communicate daily and effectively without such knowledge.

Deep structure is usually represented by linguists through diagrams that indicate the major components of the sentence, the words to be inserted, and the uses for which the sentence is to be employed. Figure 1 presents such a diagram for the sentence *The girl tore the dress*. The lines ranging from Sentence (S) point to the syntactic portions of the sentence, the words at the bottom of the diagram represent the semantic portion of the sentence, and the words *I tell you that* suggest the pragmatic or conversational intent of the sentence. Not all linguists would agree with the

(I tell you that)

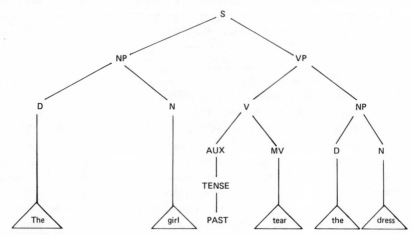

Figure 1.   Tree diagram for the sentence *The girl tore the dress.*

structure of this diagram, but any linguistic theory must somehow account for each of these three components if deep structure is to be adequately described.

Syntax refers to word order and word choice, semantics concerns the meanings intended by the use of particular syntactic forms and vocabulary, and pragmatics involves the intended uses for the syntactic forms. The final component of deep structure is considered to be the phonological one, which is concerned with the actual production of language through the sound system. It is through mastery of the interactions of syntactic, semantic, pragmatic, and phonological components that individuals are capable of producing and understanding sentences. The most informative disciplines concerning these matters are linguistics and its cousins psycholinguistics and sociolinguistics. The next chapter contains discussion of the components of language to show how each may contribute to the establishments of linguistic competence and to the formulation of sentence deep structures.

Language is systematic.   Linguistic rules or regularities as described previously are applicable across all sentences within a language and do not randomly vary according to the idiosyncratic whims of the language user. Although language units may be arbitrary in their initial selection by a speech community, once a decision is made to refer to or to use a particular symbolic relationship, it ceases to be arbitrary and must be adhered to systematically by language users. For instance, if we invent a new word *glub* to mean little things that run through wires, from that moment on the word *glub* must be used as a noun that is countable, and as a real object that can be measured in some fashion. Thus we could not say *some glub* or *he glubbed,* because each of these constructions violate the restraints that English places on countable nouns and their uses within a sentence.

Language is mutually agreed upon by a speech community. The term speech community means any group of individuals who adhere to the same set of linguistic conventions or rules (Fishman, 1973). Implicit in the notion of a speech community is the concept of group membership. It is now generally accepted that there is no universal language deserving the undisputed label of English, rather there are variations on English. These variations or dialects can be regionally determined, as in New England or Southern English, or nationally determined, as in British or American English, but more importantly they can be class determined, as in middle-class (Standard) English or poor English (Shuy, 1965). Although these variations share many characteristics, they are different enough to be identified as dialects. When considering any language remediation, one must decide which dialect one wishes to hold as the standard. It is important to consider the target dialect to be used with hearing-impaired children. This becomes a particularly important issue in those instances where the dialect used in school may be at variance with the dialect used in the home. If a hearing-impaired child and his family are part of a preschool program that emphasizes parent participation, such as those programs outlined by Horton (1974), Northcutt (1977), and Simmons-Martin (1976), and that program's personnel use a dialect that differs substantially from the one used by the clients, language learning could be even more difficult than it is ordinarily. Such situations do exist with deaf children, as shown by Boutte (1975) and Walton (1972), who found that poor Black hearing-impaired children were exposed to a dialect at home that differed substantially from the teacher's dialect. In this book the focus is on the General American dialect, which is the most extensively studied English dialect in this country.

Language is used to represent experience and to facilitate communication. This statement lists two important uses of language. First, we use language to convey our ideas, messages, and thoughts to others. To generate ideas or represent experience we must involve the cognitive substrates of language. Language has cognitive underpinnings that are clearly necessary to children learning language. Language is also useful for communicating information; as a system it allows for maximum efficiency in this task. Clearly, it is not possible to discuss language and its emergence in children apart from consideration of children's cognitive growth and their development of communication usage.

We know that children do not instantly produce mature language forms. We know instead that they learn approximations to adult linguistic usage that over time come closer and closer to the adult model. Language forms can be shown to be tied to children's cognitive growth and to their development of social awareness. In consideration of language instruction programs for hearing-impaired children, a full understanding of how language is learned by normally hearing children is mandatory. This is particularly important if one agrees with Lenneberg (1967) that hearing-impaired children demonstrate the same potential for developing language as other children. Chapter 3 is devoted to an examination of contemporary information on child language and its development.

LANGUAGE AND DEAFNESS

Two distinct traditions have emerged relative to teaching and learning in education of the hearing impaired. On the one hand, some researchers (Myklebust, 1960) have suggested that the experiential base of hearing-impaired children is altered significantly by the absence of audition from an early age. The absence of auditory input produces a reorganization of processing abilities that results in developmentally different cognitive and psychological strategies as compared to children born with normal hearing. Language learning with an altered cognitive base might reasonably result in language usage or understanding that is necessarily different from that of children with normal hearing.

A second and contrasting tradition insists that hearing-impaired children are normal children in all respects except for auditory processing. This latter tradition would argue that the cognitive, nonverbal capabilities of hearing-impaired children are such that if adequate linguistic experience is acquired, then normalized, but perhaps delayed, language development will result. By adhering to this view, parents and professional workers in deafness are seen as developing an unrealistic expectation of "normalcy," which may produce differences in social or cognitive performance in deaf children because of environmental stress (Furth, 1966). Different or divergent linguistic patterns of deaf children might be attributed in this view to restictions placed on children by their environments rather than on the different cognitive functions that result from deafness.

In Chapter 4, the literature on the language performance of hearing-impaired persons is reviewed. Whether this language performance is deviant, or different, or simply delayed when compared to normally hearing children is considered. Underlying language rule systems of deaf persons and the deviance, delay, or difference of these language patterns are important, because educational programs are considered on the basis of the language capabilities of the particular deaf child. If deaf children are cognitively different, as is suggested by the organismic shift point of view, then such differences should be documented and planned for in any educational and language instructional program. On the other hand, if deaf children have cognitive organization similar to that of children who hear, then information about the development of normal children could be used to assist in promoting language growth in hearing-impaired children.

Although the focus of this book is on the establishment of interpersonal communication such as oral language and American Sign Language, there is another important aspect of language to be considered: use of the printed page, or reading. Reading is a language comprehension process that is normally learned after reasonable mastery of listening or talking (or watching and signing in the case of some deaf children). Educators have urged the use of reading as a primary input system for deaf children (Fitzgerald, 1943). To examine the role of reading in a language intervention program, Roberta Truax has developed Chapter 7 on reading: what it is, how it interfaces with spoken language, how it seems to develop in children, and how it can be integrated meaningfully into language instructional programs with hearing-impaired children.

Chapter 5 concerns the assessment of linguistic capabilites in children, normally hearing or not. Educational programming efforts are successful only if they are built upon accurate knowledge of children's abilities and needs.

Chapter 6 is devoted to discussing educational programming and teaching strategies, including those the authors have found to be most reasonable, based on personal experiences and those of others in classroom settings.

Because the authors' experiences have not been restricted to the language instruction of deaf children, the suggestions herein have important implications for the management of children with language disorders, with autistic-like children, and with other developmentally delayed children who have communication problems. The authors are well aware, however, that deaf children have the most classic kinds of language learning problems; problems that have resisted efforts of parents and educators to bring deaf children into the linguistic mainstream for well over 400 years. As a consequence, the present concerns and interests are with the linguistically nonfluent deaf child.

This book is devoted to language and its development in deaf children. It should be kept in mind, of course, that language intervention, although a vital aspect of the development of hearing-impaired persons, should not constitute the total educational effort in programs for persons with significant hearing loss. There are important areas of knowledge besides communication and language function. It should be recognized that after a certain age, language and communication can never be taught apart from content, even though the child may have limited language and communication skills. Rather, language should become the instrument through which content is taught and the process by which content is mastered by the deaf child.

Last, it cannot be emphasized too often that language must be learned and then generated within context, whether it is the context of mother-child dialogue, or parent-child communication, or peer rap sessions, or teacher-student exchanges. The authors repeatedly point out the contexts of language learning and usage, so that if no other message is obtained from this book, at least the relation of language to its dynamic context will be appreciated.

CHAPTER 2

THE NATURE OF LANGUAGE

CONTENTS

In 1957, Noam Chomsky enunciated a theory of language description that revolutionized the study of the relationship between Man and his language. Chomsky's theory is referred to as the generative-transformational grammar approach, and it has dominated much of linguistic thought for the past 20 years. This theory has undergone significant revision since 1957. It has generated both complementary and opposing systems of language analysis, a process that has continued the revitalized study of language. Much of recent linguistic research has focused on adult uses of language, but the area of child language acquisition for both normal children and for children with sensory, intellectual, or psychosocial handicaps has certainly not been quiescent. Child language research has drawn from traditional linguistics, but also from cognitive psychology, sociolinguistics, and psycholinguistics, disciplines that have all been deeply influenced by Chomsky's formulations. This exchange of interests developed an exciting view of the child's role in language acquisition, and stimulated interest in reexamining the contributions of adults as well as the environment to the language development process.

In order to appreciate the significance of contemporary child language research, it seems necessary to consider first the contemporary views of the nature of the language system itself, including some ideas on how adults seem to process this unique symbol system. A prerequisite for productive intervention with children who have inadequate language fluency, particularly deaf children, is the coherent knowledge of the nature and uses of language, for both internal and environmental purposes.

From Chapter 1 we learned that language can be described as consisting of four aspects or dimensions: pragmatics, semantics, syntax, and phonology. Language involves comprehension and use of a variety of conversational constraints, meanings, word order arrangements, and classes of sounds. The interrelationships of these four components constitute the linguistic competence possessed by a speaker of any language. Simultaneously, the interaction between these four components allows for the deep structure of a sentence to be brought to the surface for the benefit of other members of the speech community. Each of the components is discussed in turn herein; the discussion concludes with suggestions as to how these components interface with one another in the comprehension and production of sentences.

One could embark on consideration of the nature of language by examining the current theories of language description as each relates to the four components of language. Summarizing the salient points of the important theories might be of interest to some, but this would not show how integration of contemporary linguistic information can form a base for interpreting the child language research, or how knowledge of language can lead to a rationale for the instruction and diagnosis of language capacities in hearing-impaired children. In this book the choice is to describe language, its components, and their relationships from the point of view that can lead most productively to improved instruction. The risk exists that this idiosyncratic approach is not reasonable to all readers. However, unless some basic notion of language as a system and of children's development of language are agreed to, subsequent suggestions on instructional approaches will not be theoretically defensible.

PRAGMATICS

Pragmatics concerns the role of context in the execution and comprehension of sentences. The content and form of language cannot be properly understood outside the context of communication. People say things that they expect to be used by the listener in certain ways. This expectation shapes the types of decisions the speaker makes about the requirements of a communication situation, which in turn affects the syntactic/semantic forms that he will use in dialogue, or even in monologue. In addition, judgments concerning the nature of conversation and how one can legitimately enter into a conversation also play significant roles in shaping the choice of sentence constructions. Discussion of language apart from its communication correlates fails to present a complete picture of language usage. A child must master both communication competence as well as linguistic competence to become a fluent, mature language user. Five major concepts should be considered in discussing pragmatics: speech acts, sentence utilization, presupposition, informational organization, and conversational constraints. Each of these concepts have added provocative new dimentions to the understanding of linguistic processing in human beings.

Speech Acts

Speech act theorists (Austin, 1962; L. Cohen, 1974; Searle, 1969, 1975; Strawson, 1964) begin with the premise that each sentence produced by a speaker has an underlying communicative intent, which is referred to as the *illocutionary force* of the sentence. Some linguists, such as Ross (1970, 1975), have suggested that the illocutionary force of the sentence represents higher level sentences into which lower level sentences are embedded. The illocutionary force of a particular sentence is determined by identifying the performative verb that appears before the content statement of the sentence. For instance in the sentence *I promise you that I will go home.*, the performative verb is *promise*, and the content portion of the sentence is *I will go home.* As indicated by Ross (1970), in many cases the performative is not expressed in the surface structure of the sentence, but is rather implied—exists within the deep structure. In the sentence *What time is the party?* the performative implied in the deep structure would be the higher order sentence *I ask you something.* If the performative was brought to the surface structure, the sentence *I ask you what time is the party?* would have emerged. The performative indicating the illocutionary force of the sentence may be either explicitly or implicitly stated, but for each sentence generated a performative exists within the speaker's deep structure. This is an important concept because the performative in effect tells the listener what is expected from him with regard to a particular sentence. If the performative is *tell*, the expectation is that the listener will listen to the speaker; if it is *order*, the expectation is that the listener will be compelled to accomplish the directive of the sentence, and so forth.

According to Clark and Clark (1977), the most common speech acts in English are the declarative (tell), interrogative (ask), request (order), expressive (feel), and commissive (promise). Declarative speech acts are telling or relating acts; interrogative speech acts are questioning or information gathering acts; request or imperative acts ask the listener to accommodate himself to the speaker's demands; expressive acts are verbalized thoughts or feelings; commissive acts are those that permit or allow behavior, as in permission or promise. Examples of each act follow: declarative speech acts, (*I tell you that*) *The Allies won the war.*; interrogative speech acts, (*I ask you*) *Why did you buy that suit?*; request or imperative speech acts, (*I order you to*) *Go home!*; expressive speech acts, (*I think that*) *I will go to the party.*; commissive speech acts, (*I promise that*) *I will stop eating all the time.*

The surface structure of many sentences allows for a clear interpretation of which speech act is intended by the use of a performative verb, through the syntactic construction of the sentence, or through the semantic content of the information portion of the sentence. There are other instances in English in which the intended speech act can only be inferred from contextual cues such as intonational patterns or facial expressions, because the surface structure of the sentence adheres to that expected for one speech act, but is actually intended to be interpreted as another (Davidson, 1975; Searle, 1975). These latter speech acts are referred to as indirect speech acts. An example of an indirect speech act might be production of a surface structure such as *Wouldn't you like to go home?* The surface structure of the sentence seems to suggest an illocutionary force of interrogative, or asking, but the intent of such a statement, if one is trying to clear the room, is not one of soliciting information but rather an imperative or request that individuals actually leave. Indirect speech acts are used in General American when uttering verbal manipulations such as imperatives and requests by casting them into "polite" verbal forms that allow for peaceful social exchange.

Speech acts facilitate the ongoing conduct of communication and social interchange. Without mastery or understanding of the concept of speech acts of both the direct and indirect variety, communication would be seriously disrupted, or could occur only in situations in which illocutionary force is always explicitly stated. Thus the child, whether developing language normally or not, must master this aspect of communication competence in order to understand how to communicate with others or how to interpret the utterances directed toward him by other speakers.

Sentence Utilization

When a speaker produces a sentence, he intends for it to have a certain effect upon the listener; he utilizes sentences to fulfill certain purposes. The intent may have a one-to-one correspondence to the performative, but not necessarily (Clark and Clark, 1977). Each type of speech act, declarative, interrogative, and so on, is utilized in special ways for communication. Question forms offer an example of how intended use may be implied other than by the performative itself. Questions may be asked for at least two purposes: to solicit new information or to verify existing facts. For instance, if it is not clear who broke the tumbler, Mother might say *Who broke the glass?* On the other hand, if Mother is quite certain of the culprit, she might say *Dan, did you break the glass?*, asking him to verify the content of the question. It should be noted, however, that even wh-questions can be used for verification purposes, such as saying *WHO broke the glass?* even when we are quite certain that we know who did it. We wish the listener to verify what we already know by officially admitting his guilt.

Under normal communication situations, declarative speech acts are utilized to assert new information about old information. The purpose of the declarative sentence is to say to the listener *I am talking about something you know about. Identify the old information, locate it in your memory, and then integrate the new information I have uttered with what you know about the old information.* By changing the stress pattern, one can change the function of a declarative speech act so that the intention is to verify existing information rather than just telling. For instance one can say *You DID hit the ball.* with the intention that the listener will answer either *yes* or *no* in verification of the sentence. There are even circumstances in which declarative sentences can be utilized in a directive way. If a guest in your house says *It's COLD in here,* it is probably a statement requiring immediate action with the thermostat rather than a statement of fact.

As indicated previously, interrogative forms are often utilized to encourage speakers to provide new information or to verify existing information. Because of the phenomenon of indirect speech acts, the interrogative form can be utilized to encourage action on the part of the listener with sentences such as *Wouldn't you like to close the door?*

Request or imperative speech acts are generally uttered to activate listeners. Instructions are the classic example of such request or imperative speech acts. Even the imperative format can be utilized in verification, as in the sentence *Follow YOUR instructions!*, which certainly could be responded to with *yes* or *no.*

Thus, each sentence uttered by a listener contains a speech act and, simultaneously, it points out an intended action for the listener. To be an effective communication partner, each person must be able to understand both of these conditions. Otherwise conversations fail or individuals must resort to forms that may not be totally acceptable to others, such as direct orders.

Presuppositions

When initiating communication a speaker makes certain assumptions about the listener and about the communication situation. These assumptions are referred to by linguists as *presuppositions* or *implicatures* (Grice, 1975; Jackendoff, 1972). These presuppositions determine the type of syntactic/semantic constructions the speaker will select for use, as well as the sophistication of the information content of the sentence. The notion of presupposition or implicature is important because it allows adjustments to occur in conversational exchanges as the speaker ascertains the legitimacy of his assumptions about the listener and the listener's awareness of the topic of conversation. If the speaker presupposes that the listener knows that reference will be made to a vacation spot both visited recently, the conversation will probably start on that supposition. If the first few exchanges show that this assumption was unwarranted, the speaker will normally adjust both his assumption and his linguistic structures in order to clarify communication.

Contemporary literature (Bates, 1976a; Gordon and Lakoff, 1971; Grice, 1975; Katz, 1972; Kempson, 1975; Kiefer, 1973) argues for three types of presuppositions: psychological presupposition, pragmatic presupposition, and semantic presupposition.

Psychological Presupposition Psychological presupposition refers to the assumptions the speaker makes about the level of information possessed by the listener relative to the topic under discussion. This type of presupposition is tied to the issue of topicalization within discourse. In order for one individual to hold an intelligent discussion with another, it requires that both individuals agree on the topic. Conversations seem to be a process of establishing mutually agreed upon topics and then making comments about these topics. The amount of time the speaker spends in establishing the topic depends upon what assumptions he makes concerning the listener's awareness and understanding of the topic. If the speaker assumes that the listener has intimate knowledge of the topic, he may choose a single word to establish the topic, such as the word *Mother*. On the other hand, if the speaker makes the presupposition that the listener has little knowledge, he may embark upon an extended explanation using relative clauses or coordination to establish the important dimensions of the topic so that the listener knows precisely what they are to be talking about.

The degree of topicalization depends upon a principle of conversation exchange, the cooperative principle (Grice, 1975). The cooperative principle states that speakers tacitly agree to provide only that degree of information that will allow for the continuation of efficient communication. The cooperative principle seems to operate under four constraints: quantity (the speaker is to contribute no more or no less information than the listener requires to understand the conversation); quality (the speaker is expected to make his contribution as genuine as possible);

relation (the speaker is expected to make contributions appropriate to the immediate needs of each verbal transaction); and manner (the speaker is expected to make clear what contribution he is making and to execute his tasks with reasonable dispatch). If any one of these constraints is violated, then communication and discourse are affected, either on the basis of the enormity of the verbiage presented, or on the basis of the distrust of the information being provided.

Psychological presupposition can also refer to the judgments a speaker makes about the listener's ability to process information. If the speaker makes the assumption that the listener has considerable capacity to process multiple levels of information, he will increase the syntactic/semantic complexity of the sentence. If, on the other hand, the listener is judged incapable of processing complex linguistic units, the speaker may elect to break his utterances into small units to reduce its complexity. This phenomenon is frequently at work when the ways adults speak to children are compared to the ways they speak to other linguistically competent adults (Farwell, 1975; Landes, 1975). Another example of how this type of presupposition can influence conversation levels can be seen in speech addressed to less competent individuals, such as mentally retarded adults.

Pragmatic Presupposition   Pragmatic presupposition refers to the extraneous conditions that shape the intention and grammatical structure of a sentence, the decisions a speaker makes about the communication needs of a situation. The communication situation itself can dictate the types of syntactic/semantic constructions that should be used. For instance, the use of adjectives within sentences is dominated by the need of the speaker to identify which specific noun-topic is under consideration. If a speaker hands an apple to the listener, he need not say *Take the red apple*. On the other hand, if the speaker gives the listener a choice among a variety of apples, the listener might indicate his choice by saying *Give me the red apple*. Only in the latter situation would it be communicatively important to include the adjective. Use of any linguistic principle seems related to communicative constraints within conversations, and the child, whether normally developing or hearing impaired, must learn these communication constraints in order to know when or where one need not use linguistic principles.

Pragmatic presuppositions also seem to be related to the speaker's impression of the listener's social status. Depending upon the perceived social station of a listener, the speaker will adjust his linguistic structures to observe conventions relative to issues of authority and solidarity (Brown and Ford, 1961; Brown and Gilman, 1960). The form of address and the number of indirect speech acts increases in degree according to the speaker's perception of the authority level of the listener. For instance, one might speak of *Joe Brown* to a friend, but might refer to *Mr. Brown* when with a person perceived as having authority. Likewise, one is more likely to use direct imperative forms such as *Close the door.* with close friends, and to choose indirect speech acts with parents, teachers, ministers, and law enforcement officials. In addition, if the speaker feels that a listener is not informed about the speaker's personal style, he might limit the use of humor or sarcasm, or make their employment explicit in the surface structure when first introduced.

Semantic Presupposition   Semantic presupposition involves issues of asserted meaning; entailed meaning; and implicature, or presumed meaning. Every statement produced by a speaker has content that can be deemed either true or false. This apparent meaning within the sentence is referred to as asserted meaning, or obvious meaning. Every statement produced also entails additional information that is implicit and presumed by the speaker to be within the information bank of the listener. For instance if the speaker says *A baby dog is called a puppy.*, he can presume that if the listener understands the sentence, he also understands that *Puppies are small* and that *Puppies are young.* These presumed understandings are labeled "entailments to the original sentence." The level at which a speaker decides to begin a sentence depends solely upon the presuppositions he can make about the listener's informational resources. If his assumption about the level of the listener's understanding proves inaccurate, as in conversations with persons for whom English is a second language, then entailment statements must be uttered explicitly either as separate statements or perhaps as relative clauses attached to the original sentence.

Implicature, or presumed meaning, refers to those information notions that the speaker presumes the listener is making in order to be able to follow a conversation. As speakers move from sentence to sentence, they often assume that listeners can carry certain meanings from previous sentences that will allow them to accurately calculate the intended meaning of subsequent sentences. Such shifts in meaning are often referred to as "bridging assumptions that are carried over from one sentence to another" (Clark and Clark, 1977; Clark and Haviland, 1974). For example, a speaker can say *She was fast asleep. The open bottle of sleeping pills lay on the night stand next to her bed.* knowing that if the listener understands the first sentence, he will have little difficulty in handling the second because it is an obvious extension from the first sentence, namely, that she probably took a sleeping pill to fall asleep. In this way speakers do not have to make constant references to previous sentences in discourse. If there are too many bridging assumptions or if the bridging assumptions require too much work for the listener, communication can be disrupted. The degree to which the speaker performs implicatures depends exclusively upon his assessment of the listener's ability to handle these shifts in meaning and his additional perceptions concerning the conduct of the conversation. The moment speakers perceive a breakdown in communication, most will try to reorganize their utterances to resolve what they perceive to be the cause of the breakdown. Of course there are speakers who are poor at perceiving when they have contributed to conversation breakdown, and at solving conversational problems.

Presuppositions can be seen as involving general assumptions made by the speaker relative to the capabilities of the listener, the nature and conduct of the communication act itself, and the clarity of the message to be conveyed.

Informational Organization

According to some psycholinguists (Clark and Clark, 1977), there is an implicit contract in English conversation that governs the informational organization of sentence productions. This contract essentially requires that one begin each sentence with given or known information and end it with new or unknown information. This organizational convention is followed to enable listeners to focus quickly on the important information components within the sentence, so that the new or informative content can be compared with previous information and integrated into already stored information. The following example illustrates this convention, labeled the given-new contract: Johnny's mother is sitting in the living room and hears a crash in Johnny's room. She might say *Johnny probably broke something.*, in which *Johnny* is the known information and *broke something* is the new information. If she heard a crash when Johnny was with her, she might utter *That sounds like something broke.* In both instances the sentence starts with information that is given or known, *Johnny* or *that* (sound). The new information would be *broke something* or *something broke.*

The reality of the given-new distinction was demonstrated nicely by Hornby (1974). He presented subjects with sentences and then showed them a picture expressed at one twentieth of a second, which was to be judged as conforming or not conforming to the stimulus sentence. In all cases one of the sentence nouns was inaccurately portrayed in the picture. For instance, the picture for the stimulus sentence *The boy petted the cat.* might be of a girl petting a cat or a boy petting a dog. If the picture of a girl petting a cat was paired with the example sentence, the subjects generally said the sentence and picture matched. On the other hand, if the picture was of a boy petting a dog, the subjects said the sentence and picture did not match. The results were directly related to the notion that *cat* was identified as the new information and became the focal point for picture matching. These same results were found for sentences such as *It is the cat that the boy is petting.* In this case the new information was shifted to the beginning of the sentence, disputing any claim that the results were a function of the position in the sentence rather than the informational status of the new information. The organization of information within a sentence clearly plays a role in the interpretation and retention of that information.

Of course new information can be given at the beginning of a sentence, but if so, the sentence needs to be marked by intonation or syntax to cue the listener that the normal given-new organizational convention has been violated. For instance after answering the phone one could say *It's Bill on the phone.*, or *BILL is on the phone.* with the primary stress on *Bill*, rather than *phone.* In both instances the new information is placed at the beginning of the sentence, in one instance indicated by the addition of the syntactic filler *it was*, and in the other by a change of intonation to emphasize the new information. The original contract, if observed, would have resulted in a sentence such as *The person on the phone was Bill.*

The given-new contract influences the use of some aspects of language to such an extent that they must be seen not as sentence-controlled, but as discourse-controlled linguistic units. Among such linguistic units are articles and pronouns (Clark and Clark, 1977; Wilbur, 1977). The use of articles and pronouns within discourse is directly related to assumptions the speaker makes about the informativeness of the content of the sentence. If the speaker uses a particular noun as a new information, use of that noun is accompanied by the restriction that its determiner be an article that conveys the notion of indefiniteness. In contrast, selection of definite articles depends upon information being viewed as known or given information. Pronominalization occurs only when information is old; noun usage is reserved for new information or to clarify reference. Once a noun has been introduced into a discourse, the speaker must decide whether to use pronouns, which streamline the conduct of discourse, or to continue using nouns and their accompanying definite articles, a decision made necessary if the speaker supposes that the listener will have difficulty with extensive pronominalization or will be confused by pronoun reference.

Knowledge of the given-new contract is important for members of the English speech community. Without it, information processing would be very difficult. New information that is presented unpredictably would

force a listener to attend to all aspects of a dialogue in order to understand, which would certainly be tiring. A lack of adherence to the given-
new convention would probably increase grammatical complexity as
well, another potential hindrance to information processing.

Conversational Constraints

Language is normally used in the communication unit of conversation,
an exchange between two or more speakers. As with the use of linguistic
forms, conversations have social conventions that are rule governed and
are known by most mature fluent speakers in the speech community
(Ervin-Tripp, 1976; Sacks, Schegloff, and Jefferson, 1974; Schegloff,
1968; Schegloff and Sacks, 1973). These rules are referred to as the conversation constraints of discourse. They regulate such issues as turn-taking within discourse, the opening of conversations, the techniques used to
change topics within discourse, and the closing of conversations.

   One of the keys to successful conduct of dialogue is proper turn-taking by all members of the conversation unit. It is important that each
partner know when it is his turn to talk. Otherwise, conversations could
deteriorate into verbal sparring matches between partners, with little
actual communication occurring. Sacks, Schegloff, and Jefferson (1974)
have suggested that there are three rules governing conversation turn-
taking. When a speaker relinquishes the lead, the next speaker is the one
whom is given permission by the first person to take a turn, usually
through a question. These question and answer exchanges often result in
adjacency pairs. If the initial speaker fails to indicate who should talk
next, the turn is assumed by the first person to speak up in the conversation unit. The next turn reverts to the current speaker, if he resumes talking before anyone else begins to speak. Interruptions are permitted only
if there is a logical break in the discourse. Without such implicit regulations about turn-taking it would be difficult to conduct organized, well-
mannered verbal exchanges.

   Openings in conversations are usually initiated by a summons-
answer sequence. For instance, Speaker 1 may say *Hi, how are you?* (a
summons to conversation), to which Speaker 2 can reply *I'm fine. How
are you?* Such a sequence permits the initiation of conversations if both
partners so desire. If not, the summons-answer sequence is aborted to
end the conversation.

   Changes of topics within conversations are usually signaled by specially designed grammatical devices such as *Oh, by the way . . . , I don't
mean to change the subject, but . . .* , or *Remember when . . . .* Without
such signaling devices it would be very difficult to follow most conversations, which typically change freely from topic to topic. Conversations

also have certain conventions relative to their closure. Schegloff and Sacks (1973) indicate that most conversations end with a pre-closing statement and, depending upon the listener's response to that, a closing statement. If Speaker 1 decides that he has nothing more to contribute, he may say *All right, I'll call you when I get there. Okay?,* which serves as an indicator that he is ready to bring the conversation to an end if Speaker 2 agrees. Speaker 2 now has an opportunity to continue the conversation if there is anything more he wishes to say. If Speaker 2 does not elect to continue the conversation, Speaker 1 can close the conversation by simply saying *Good-bye.*

It is important that both normally hearing and hearing-impaired children learn these conversational constraints. Without them they cannot easily enter into dialogue with others, and more importantly, others cannot easily establish meaningful conversations with them.

SEMANTICS

Meaning is said to exist on at least two levels in language: sentences are meaningful and words are meaningful. Linguistic theory has tended to address meaning at both the sentence and word level, which are discussed in turn.

Sentence Meaning

Each sentence in any language contains information a speaker wishes to represent or convey to a listener(s). This information can be thought of as being arranged in mental statements that stipulate the intents to be conveyed by and within each sentence. Some linguists contend that these mental statements or primary units of meaning should be designated as propositions (Cartwright, 1962). The processing of language would then involve procedures whereby sentences are comprehended and stored in memory according to their individual propositions (Bever, 1970; Fodor and Bever, 1965; Fodor and Garrett, 1967; Garrett, Bever, and Fodor, 1966; Kimball, 1973; Kintsch, 1972, 1974; Watt, 1970).

Formal propositions consist of statements that indicate how the action (predicate) of a sentence relates to the nouns (arguments) of that sentence. In other words, each proposition contained within a sentence encompasses an elementary state or action accompanied by one or more nouns involved in that state or action. Each proposition consists of a single bit of information. A particular sentence can contain any number of propositions from one to infinity. The number of propositions actually used is determined in part by the speaker's linguistic facility, by his presuppositions concerning the listener's ability to understand the content, by the needs of the communication exchange, and finally by the coding potentials or limitations of the language system itself.

Propositions are ordinarily represented in a special form that differs from formal sentences. For instance, the sentence *The girl tore up the letter.* would be written propositionally as (tear up, girl, letter) to emphasize that the notions underlying any sentence are not actual sentences, but major predicate-argument relationships presumed to be organized in a particular fashion. In this book propositions are shown as real sentences, but the reader is cautioned to remember that the propositional predicate-argument relationships, not the surface structure sentence, are presumed to be understood, processed, and stored by the speaker/listener.

An example is provided to gain a clearer picture of the range of propositions that can be included in a sentence. From *The white dog with the brown nose is gnawing the bone that I got for him from behind the bush.,* the following propositions could be derived: (1) a dog is gnawing the bone, (2) the dog is white, (3) the dog has a nose, (4) the nose is brown, (5) the bone was from behind the bush, and (6) I got the bone for the dog.

Case grammarians (Anderson, 1971; Bach, 1968, 1974; Chafe, 1970, 1972, 1976; Fillmore, 1968, 1971a, 1971b; McCawley, 1968) postulate that sentences are composed of case relationships that specify the underlying semantic intent of the sentence, or the predicate-argument relationships of propositions. Case grammarians posit that the existence of these propositional relationships within the deep structure dictates the types of syntactic forms that will appear in the surface structure through the application of generative semantic-based rules. Each proposition in the deep structure is seen to consist of a verbal unit with appropriate noun-arguments. As can be seen from the dog-bone example, the verbal unit may consist of traditional verbs such as *gnawing,* or of larger stative units such as *is brown* or *was from behind* (Propositions 4 and 5). To determine the verbal units contained in propositions, it is important not to be tied to the traditional position that the verbal unit of any proposition must be the verb. This is not true for stative conditions, for example, which can include verbal units such as adjectives and propositions.

Case grammar theories specify that verbal units and potential arguments carry contextual features that specify the types of case assignments for specific lexical items contained within propositions. When a speaker chooses a particular verbal unit or argument, that choice establishes the germ of the case relationship for that sentence. Any lexical entries subsequently combined with the original selection must contain contextual features that are compatible with, but not duplicative of, the first lexical choice.

There is controversy about how case relations are determined (Chafe, 1970; Fillmore, 1968). The authors support the tradition that the main determinant of case assignments in the sentence is the verb. Verbs specify the types of case assignments that exist within the sentence, stated either implicitly in the deep structure or explicitly in the surface structure.

English verbs are seen to be of three types: stative, process, and action verbs, with intermediate types being common—that is, stative-process and action-process verbs. Stative verbs specify that an object is in a certain state or condition. Verbs such as *is, become, seem,* and *remain* are stative verbs. Process verbs specify the event whereby an object undergoes a change of state or condition. Verbs such as *think, change,* and *forget* are process verbs because they indicate change in states or conditions for specific objects. Action verbs specify activity that can be seen or heard. Since verbs such as *run, skip* or *cry* are verbs of activity, they are members of the action verb class.

In some instances verbs can occur without meaningful arguments being present. Ambient-stative verbs specify conditions in the absence of a noun, as in *It was fun.* Ambient-action verbs specify an activity in the absence of a specific argument, as in *It was raining.*

The verb *have* exemplifies English intermediate verbs. *Have* can at times be an action-process verb, as in the sentence *I have the ball now.,* in which it is a synonym for *picked up* or *took physical possession.* Used in this sense, *have* is simultaneously expressing a physical activity (picking up an object) and a change in condition (in this case, a sense of possession). There are instances, however, when the verb *have* is representative of stative-process verbs. This occurs in sentences such as *I have a red shirt.,* where *have* is a synonym for *ownership.* In this instance the verb indicates a state in which an object exists in a location with other objects belonging to the owner, as well as a process, which in this case is the feeling that the owner has toward the object, possession or ownership. *Have* may also exist as a purely stative verb in part-to-whole sentences, such as *I have a nose.* In this sentence, all that is being reported is a state of being: *I* is made up of at least one part, *a nose.* This discussion should suggest that learning the appropriate use of intermediate verbs such as *have* can be very challenging for children, particularly if they demonstrate language-learning difficulties.

Each verb case determines the number and types of argument cases that may appear in a proposition. Action verbs imply the presence of an actor, a performer of action. In some instances the verb also signals that the actor used an instrument to perform the action. If the speaker uses the action verb *cut*, it is understood that the actor must have used an instrument such as a *knife* to accomplish this act. The arguments a speaker chooses to use in the surface structure depend upon his presuppositions concerning the knowledge base of the listener and the needs of the conversation.

The three types of verb cases consistently identifiable have been listed, but the number of argument cases is less clear. Table 1 presents a compilation of the various argument cases that have been identified in child language research. Because no single research effort has yet generated this list of argument case designations, their compilation was felt to be helpful in understanding the contemporary semantic development literature that is presented in Chapter 3.

In order to comprehend or to produce any particular sentence, it can be argued that the speaker or listener must be able to decipher the sentence and identify its various propositions, so that the information can be integrated into memory and related to other information from the discourse. To this end, some propositions may be more important than others, and some may be more difficult to understand than others (Clark and Clark, 1977)—not all propositions have equal status within sentences. For instance in the previous dog-bone example, the most important proposition from an information viewpoint is *the dog is gnawing the bone* rather than *the dog is white* or *the dog has a nose*. The proposition *the dog is gnawing the bone* is probably easier to process from a content point of view than *the bone is from behind the bush.*

In developing a sentence the speaker must also decide on the core proposition for the sentence, and then determine how to articulate all other propositions with the core so that the sentence is coherent, but the lesser propositions do not obscure the comprehensibility of the core proposition. For instance if, in the previous example, the speaker had said *The dog with the brown nose who is gnawing on the bone that I got for him from behind the bush, is white.,* the result gives one of the minor propositions major status but relegates the core proposition to secondary importance.

Propositions constitute the basic unit of linguistic meaning. Inability to handle propositions could be a significant deterrent to facile use of any language system. However, meaning cannot be described using case grammar alone. Specific words must still be selected for use as verbal units and as arguments. Lexical or dictionary meaning must thus be dealt with, as well as the semantics of the lexical forms selected for the surface structure.

Table 1. Compilation of noun (argument) cases identified in child language research

Case	Definition	Examples
Mover (Bloom, Miller, and Hood, 1975)	Objects that perform actions that affect themselves	*The boy* ran. *The girl* cried.
Agent (Bloom, 1970)	Objects that perform actions that have an effect on another object	*The boy* ate the apple. *The girl* spanked her doll.
Patient (Bloom, 1970)	Objects that receive the effects of action or process verbs	The boy pushed *the girl*. Jack thought about *Mary*.
Complement (D. Edwards, 1973)	Objects that come into being as a result of the action or process verb	Mother made *the dinner*. Mary thought up *the idea*.
Experiencer (Brown, 1973)	Objects that perform process verbs	*Jack* thought. *Jack* forgot about Mary.
Instrument (D. Edwards, 1973)	Objects that agents or experiencers use to bring about action or process verbs	The boy cut the bread with *the knife*. Jackie thought up the idea with *his own mind*.
Beneficiary-dative (Schlesinger, 1971)	Objects that benefit from action or process verbs	Harriet gave *Mark* a present. *Harriet* got a thrill from Mike's idea.

Term	Definition	Examples
Possessor (Bloom, 1970)	Objects that own or have possession of other objects	*Ken* has a car. *Mike's* car.
Location (Schlesinger, 1971)	The place where verbs occur	Henry played the game in *Somerset Park.* Larry gave Mary her present at *home.*
Time (Kretschmer, in preparation)	The time when verbs take place	Mary cried during *the wedding.* Margaret got her letter on *Friday.*
Entity (Brown, 1973)	Objects that are in a state of being	*The apple* is red. *The party* is fun.
Part (Kretschmer, in preparation)	Objects that are parts of entities	The clown had *a funny nose.* The spider only has *four legs.*
Notice-designator (Schlesinger, 1971)	Objects that are indicated or named	That's *a ball.* There's *Mary.*
Source (D. Edwards, 1973)	Objects from which action verbs emanate	We walked from *the house.* Ideas come from *the mind.*
Goal (D. Edwards, 1973)	Objects where verbs end	We walked to *Mary's House.* I put the ball *in the box.*

Word Meaning

The most popular theoretical model relating to the semantic underpinnings of individual words assumes that word meaning comprises
components or semantic features that detail the semantic roles or functions a word can play when used in sentences (Bierwisch, 1970; Katz,
1972; Leech, 1974). It is presumed that within each natural language
there is a finite set of semantic or componential features that, when
variously arranged, yield lexical entries that differ from each other in
meaning by at least one feature, but simultaneously share many other
features. The task of the speaker is to decide which set of features he
wishes to express. The semantic features chosen dictate the first word
inserted into the sentence frame. After this selection has been made, the
semantic expectations for the remainder of the lexical items in the
sentence are set; the other words selected must contain features compatible with those of the first item selected.

Semantic components have traditionally been viewed as being either
present or absent as meaning attachments to words, notated in a binary
system as (+) feature present or (−) feature absent. Unfortunately,
because of the underlying assumptions this notational system has two
serious drawbacks. First, not all semantic features are merely present or
absent within the meaning of a word—each may be present to some
degree. This can be demonstrated with the features of *more* and *less*,
which signify comparison to another object or a given standard. Relational concepts such as these cannot be completely captured in a binary
notational system. Second, some features demand to be viewed as hierar-
chically related rather than as simply present or absent. Consider the
sentence *A baby cow is a calf*. To say that *calf* carries the feature of
smallness, making it compatible with *baby*, does not clearly indicate how
calf also relates to the class *bovine*, of which *cow* is a member. *Calf* has
to be seen as having a simultaneous relationship with both baby and
bovine. Conversely, *bovine* can entail the concept of baby. The notions of
entailment and relation are not easily captured using a presence-absence
notional system.

To account for these difficulties, contemporary semantic theory has
tended to shift to a notational system that emphasizes specification of the
possible constellation of relationships that can exist for semantic features
(Miller and Johnson-Laird, 1976). Such notational systems involve defining words as a series of propositional-like statements that delineate the
characteristics surrounding each word's function within the feature
system of English. This latter notational approach allows for a clearer

picture of how lexical selection interfaces with the sentence level propositional generation discussed previously—the ways in which semantic features determine which words will be chosen for use in specific sentence propositions. Component or feature notion systems of the relation type specify for each word the arguments or dimensions of importance that it signifies. The predicates appear as an open notation signal ($\times$). *Calf*, thus, can be defined as having the following argument-predicate relationships: baby (calf), animal (calf), and bovine (calf), which translated mean that *calf* is some type of baby, some type of animal, and some type of bovine, and can only be used with words that interface meaningfully with at least one of these dimensions. In the description of the word *calf*, the features can be ordered so that higher level features entail or subsume lower level features. In the case of *calf*, the features already listed can be reordered so that they appear in a hierarchy: animal ($\times$), bovine, ($\times$), and baby ($\times$), which would be read that in considering a baby cow or calf, the dimensions of animal and bovine are entailed. If, on the other hand, one starts at the animal feature level, as in a game of 20 questions, it is still necessary to specify the bovine and baby features to arrive at precise meaning components for *calf*.

By specifying more than presence or absence of features, it is possible to consider relational characteristics or dimensions such as size, quantity, or comparison as part of a meaning hierarchy.

In summary, selection of meaningful lexical items for use in sentences must satisfy two semantic requirements, namely, the case relationships contained within the sentence and the presence of a compatible feature matrix.

SYNTAX

Syntax refers to the orderly or systematic arrangement of word orders permissible in English. In his original work on generative-transformational grammar, N. Chomsky (1957) declared that although semantics formed an important aspect of language, it was possible to deal with syntactic forms without recourse to semantic description. It would be contemporary consensus that syntax cannot be considered entirely apart from meaning, although current generative-transformational theory continues to have a strong syntactic bias (N. Chomsky, 1965, 1966, 1971; Francis, 1973). Knowledge of English syntax is an important component to the formulation and understanding of language, but knowledge of word order constraints alone will not ensure fluent linguistic comprehension or use in hearing-impaired children.

Because syntactic theory has changed drastically in recent years, it is felt that the best approach to its discussion is to distinguish between old and new syntactic theory.

Early Syntactic Theory

In his original theory, N. Chomsky (1957) postulated that language description must differentiate between deep and surface structures, definitions of which were presented in Chapter 1. Within one's deep structure, a speaker was felt to hold phrase structure rule understandings. Phrase structure rules were defined as the rules that allow for the generation of basic sentence patterns or kernel sentences. Kernel sentences were seen as fundamental to all language understanding and production. Phrase structure rules were represented by branching diagrams, with the first point of the diagram designated Sentence (S). The diagram showed how each focal point within the sentence could be rewritten or redefined into more basic components. The focal points of the branching diagram were called nodes, with each node dominated by the node or nodes that came before it in the diagram. The sentence node could be resolved into a noun phrase (NP) node and a verb phrase (VP) node. The noun phrase could be resolved into the sub-nodes of determiner, (D) + noun (N), and the verb phrase could be resolved into tense + auxiliary, (AUX) + verb (MV) + the remainder of the sentence.

Branching diagrams, although useful, were not felt to adequately convey the character of generative-transformational theory. As a consequence, N. Chomsky (1957) decided to show each step within the branching diagram as a formal rule of language. These so-called rewrite rules were not to be interpreted as equations that indicated additive processes. Instead it seemed to be Chomsky's intention that a particular sentence be considered not merely as the sum of its individual parts, but rather conceived of as a whole with individual parts working in concert. This is why he utilized the symbol ($\rightarrow$) rather than ($=$). Sentence (S) could be rewritten to contain NP (noun phrase) and VP (verb phrase). NP could be rewritten to include D (determiner) and N (noun), the traditional definition of noun phrase. In those instances where the noun phrase contained no determiner, as in the case of proper nouns, a zero or null indicator ($\emptyset$) was used in lieu of the determiner node. D could be rewritten to show a specific determiner, such as *the, a,* or *some*; this represents the lexical insertion stage of rewrite rules. N could be rewritten to represent a specific noun, such as *boy* or *elephant*. The VP could consist of auxiliary to include tense, main verb, or any other appropriate grammatical unit. The end result for each of these categories is the terminal string, where real lexical items are presumed to be inserted into their appropriate slots. Figure 2 presents an example of one such branching diagram with its accompanying phrase structure rewrite rules. Through such a process, Chomsky felt one could describe the basic or kernel sentences of English.

In applying Chomsky's concepts, Streng (1972) suggested that English had five basic sentence patterns: the intransitive verb sentence, the transitive verb sentence, the predicate nominal sentence, the predicate adjective sentence, and the predicate adverbial sentence. Examples of each of these types of sentences and their rewrite rules are presented in Table 2.

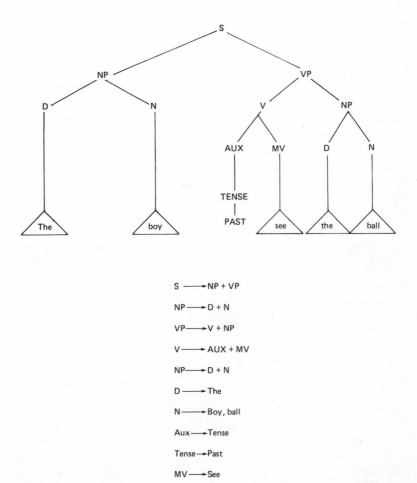

Figure 2. Example of branching diagram accompanied by rewrite rules appropriate to the nodes shown.

Table 2.   Examples of Streng's (1972) five basic sentence types

Sentence pattern	Rewrite rule	Rewrite
1: NP + VP	VP → AUX + V_i	Jack ran. Mary cried.
2: NP + VP	VP → AUX + V_t + NP	Jack hit the ball. Mary cooked the dinner.
3: NP + VP	VP → AUX + be + NP	Jack is the president. Mary is a mother.
4: NP + VP	VP → AUX + be + ADJ	Jack is sad. Mary is beautiful.
5: NP + VP	VP → AUX + be + ADV	Jack is in the park. Mary is near the store.

Chomsky utilized the notion of transformation to account for the generation of more complex sentences. Transformations were viewed as grammatical operations employed to alter kernel or basic sentence abstractions into more complex sentence forms. These operations ranged from adding, omitting, and substituting linguistic units within the kernel sentence frame to rearranging the word order of the sentence, and conjoining and/or embedding kernel sentences into one another. Table 3 presents examples of each of these types of transformational operations. By applying these transformations, structurally more complex sentences could be derived.

In traditional generative-transformational theory, transformations were generally considered to be one of two types, either simple or single-based tranformations, which acted on one kernel sentence at a time, or

Table 3.   Examples of transformational operations using the kernel sentence *Mark can hit the ball.*

Operation	Rearrangement	Rewrite
Adding constituents	T/Negation	Mark cannot hit the ball.
Omitting constituents	T/Imperative	Mark, hit the ball!
Substituting constituents	T/Pronominalization	He can hit the ball.
Rearranging constituents	T/Yes-no question	Can Mark hit the ball?
Conjoining kernel sentences	T/Coordinating conjunction	Mark can hit the ball, and Alvin can catch it.
Embedding one kernel sentence in another	T/Relative clause	Mark can hit the ball that Alvin has in his hand.

complex or double-based transformations, which acted on two or more kernel sentences simultaneously. Examples of single-based transformational operations would be question formation, application of negation, or imperative forms. Application of double-based transformational operations might result in conjunctive or relative clause sentences.

Syntactic derivation resulted from establishment of kernel sentences through the application of phrase structure rules, and the creation of complex sentences through application of transformations on kernel sentence notions. Transformed sentences were seen as being derived from kernel sentences. These assumptions have been challenged by researchers, including Chomsky himself (Francis, 1973). It is now argued that early transformational theory cannot account for semantically unacceptable sentences such as *Loveliness desires Laurene*. Application of a phrase structure syntactic model does not completely explain how or why specific words are inserted into the phrase structure. In addition, application of transformational rules often gave an impression of non-reversibility; complex sentences could be derived from kernel sentences, but it was not always possible to break complex sentences into their kernel sentence derivations.

Current Syntactic Theory

Linguistic theory now postulates three constructs to explain the transformation in a sentence from deep to surface structure (Akmajian and Henry, 1975; N. Chomsky, 1965; Jacobs and Rosenbaum, 1968; Katz and Postal, 1964; Langacker, 1973; Langendoen, 1969, 1970; Stockwell, Schachter, and Partee, 1973). These constructs are base structure, lexicon insertion rule, and transformational rule.

Base Structure The base structure of a sentence represents the underlying rules that govern the constituents and their ordering for that sentence. Sentences are not seen as being derived from kernel or basic sentences, but from deep structures that encode the entire sentence frame at one time. The speaker decides upon an entire sentence frame rather than formulating single components and then combining them into complex frames. This approach does not completely negate the consideration of some sort of "kernel" sentences. Kernel sentences might now be defined as the various predicate-argument propositions underlying the sentence, not as grammatical derivations. Branching nodes that serve as focal points for the formulation of sentence constituents such as noun phrase and verb phrase, as well as the application of rewrite rules, remain essentially unaltered in contemporary syntactic theories. The primary differences are in the number and elaboration of the nodes thought to exist within the deep structure.

To explain the derivation of complex sentences, current linguistic theory argues that some base structure strings are seen to carry nodes that specify modality changes that need to be applied to constituents within the sentence. Modality nodes describe, for example, question formation, imperative formation, or negation formation. These nodes, which are presumed to exist in the deep structure, dictate how constituents need to be ordered to produce question, imperative, or negation forms, respectively. The addition of modality nodes to the deep structure implies that the speaker intends to produce a negation sentence immediately, rather than producing a kernel sentence first and then negating it. The modality node seems to short circuit deep structure manipulations at the appropriate time, with the result of a fully formed complex sentence. For all practical purposes the addition of modality node accounts for most of the single-based transformations of traditional generative-transformational theory.

Double-based transformations such as complements, relative clauses, coordination, and nominalization are seen as being derived by elaboration of the appropriate node within the deep structure. An example of a contemporary branching diagram for a relative clause sentence is presented in Figure 3. The sentence node is divided into its appropriate NP and VP nodes; the NP node, in turn, is divided into its NP and an S node, with the latter representing the insertion of a relative clause into its appropriate place within the sentence. Linguistic theory now stresses the initial complexity of base structures in the execution of complex sentences, rather than assuming that deep structure is merely a simple abstraction (kernel sentence) that is changed into complex forms by the application of other linguistic operations such as transformations.

Structure Operations   Contemporary generative-transformational theory provides several mechanisms by which propositions are supposed to be incorporated into meaningful deep structures. For those propositions considered minor, the primary operations that permit their integration into core or major propositions is through deep structure operations such as adjective preposing or genitive formation. For instance the propositions *The dress is red* and *Frances bought a dress.* could be combined into the following sentence: *Frances bought a red dress.*, an example of adjective preposing. The propositions *The car belongs to Ms. Jones* and *Frances bought the car* can be integrated using a genitive formation rule, resulting in the sentence *Frances bought Ms. Jones' car.*

There are instances when propositions need to be combined so that they complement each other or coordinate with one another. In coordination, the speaker's intention is that the listener interpret the content of the propositions as having somewhat equal value, or as following a tem-

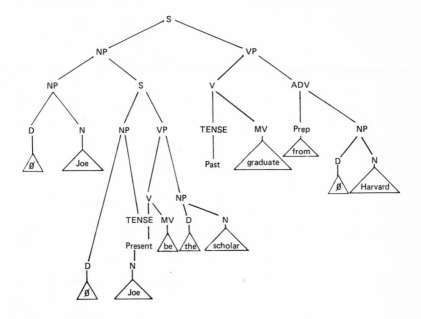

Sentence: Joe, who is the scholar, graduated from Harvard.

Figure 3.   Example of branching diagram containing elaborated node.

poral sequence. In complementation, some propositions need to be tagged so that the listener will recognize these propositions as being secondary, but complementary to the primary or core proposition. In English, the mechanisms that allow these operations to occur are coordination, relativization, complementation, and nominalization.

Coordination involves the linking of two propositions into a single deep structure string, which results either in conjunctive relationships, conditioned relationships, or disjunctive relationships. Conjunctive relationships occur when two propositions exist either concurrently physically, or consecutively in time. The surface form *and* usually signals such relationships. Disjunctive relationships can be identified when one proposition exists in contradiction to another, or when a choice must be made between the truth of two competing propositions. Disjunctive relationships are usually signaled by the surface forms *but* or *or* (*nor*). Conditional relationships occur when one proposition acts as a qualifier of the core or primary proposition, usually along dimensions such as cause-effect, time, conclusion, or summation. Surface forms such as *because, therefore, since, after, before,* and other subordinate conjunctions commonly signal conditional relationships in sentences.

A second mechanism for interrelating propositions in the deep structure is relativization, which consists of embedding one proposition into another in order to restrict or clarify specific arguments contained within the core proposition. The insertion of a second proposition into a core proposition serves to specify which aspect of the argument, or which specific argument, is being referred to by the speaker. In the sentence *John's dog, a champion Miniature Schnauzer, won first place at the Belmont Dog Show.*, the initial argument of the core proposition, *John's dog*, is clarified by the insertion of the second proposition *The dog is a champion Miniature Schnauzer.* The second proposition would be unnecessary if John possessed only one dog and the listener knew this fact, or if the speaker assumed that the listener had no interest in the type of dog John possessed. Use of relativization is only warranted when the precise nature or status of some argument within the proposition is likely to be unclear and it is necessary to the conduct of conversation that the listener be privy to this information.

A third process, complementation, involves insertion of a proposition into an empty or null argument slot. In some propositions, an argument slot that may be unspecified can be filled by another proposition that acts organizationally as the argument within the core proposition. The core proposition in the sentence *Mary wanted to go to Chicago.* is *Mary wanted something. Something* in this case is used to indicate that the second argument slot is null within this proposition. In order to complete this sentence, the insertion of a second proposition at that node is required; in this case it would be *Mary go to Chicago.* If the speaker had intended the core proposition to have contained a specific object as the second argument, the slot in the original proposition would have been filled with a specific argument, such as *trip*, and not with an empty slot indicator, such as *something*. If the speaker's intention had been to retain the information about going to Chicago, as well as Mary's embarking on a trip, he could have generated the sentence *Mary wanted a trip to Chicago.*, which incorporates the propositions *Mary wanted a trip* and *the trip was to Chicago* through the process of relativization. A speaker must decide ahead of time what he wishes the core proposition to be, which arguments are to be specified, and which slots are to be left empty in order to be filled by other propositions through complementation if he wishes to perform the complementation operation. The choice of complementation over the previous process of relativization depends entirely upon what the speaker wishes to communicate and upon his assessment of the communication situation at a particular moment.

The fourth process useful in relating propositions is called nominalization, which can be considered a special form of complementation. Nominalization usually, although not exclusively, functions as the grammatical subject of a sentence. Consider the sentence *Japan's destruction of China was a tragic event.* The word *destruction* can carry two meanings: a synonym for debris or the act of destroying an object. When destruction carries the latter definition, the agent who produced the act and the patient or receiver of the action need to be signaled. It is obvious in the example that destruction means the act of destroying. The proposition *Japan destroyed China* best completes the core proposition *Something was a tragic event,* rather than just the word *destruction.* In other words, it was the agent's (Japan) action (destruction) on the patient (China) that was tragic in this instance. This is an example of nominalization. Nominalization can also be expressed by gerunds, both progressive and perfect forms, as per the examples *running down* or *turned down,* respectively.

At times the combination of several propositions into a single deep structure can result in highly complicated surface structure realizations. English allows for operations that streamline the inclusion of propositions in one another. The most important of these linguistic operations are labeled ellipsis and pronominalization. Ellipsis refers to the elimination of extraneous information to make the surface structure manifestation of the sentence more manageable. The two underlying propositions in the sentence *The teacher dyed the egg green.* are *the teacher dyed the egg* and *the egg became green.* In combining the two propositions, a conjoining linguistic operation would yield the sentence *The teacher dyed the egg so that the egg became green.* A more economical way to convey the content is to perform an ellipsis, which suppresses the old information in the second proposition to yield the target sentence *The teacher dyed the egg green.* Before a speaker elects to perform an ellipsis, he must assure himself that the listener is capable of understanding the sentence content in its reduced form, an application of presupposition discussed previously in this chapter. Ellipsis is applied only to information that can be deemed as old or given information, never to new information.

Constant repetition of the same argument in proposition after proposition can make potential discourse difficult. In order to facilitate sentence comprehension, the speaker may elect to pronominalize repetitious arguments instead of using the full noun form. Pronominalization is used only to simplify known information, never new information. English also has mechanisms for pronominalizing verbal units, as in *John hit Mary, and so did Peter.,* where *so did* is obviously a pronominalization of the verbal unit *hit Mary.* Matters are complicated somewhat by the fact that pronominalization can be used to express not only single-word argument, but may also be applied to propositions that are used as arguments within complex sentence patterns. A speaker can say *Japan's destruction of China was a tragic event. It resulted in the death of millions of people.*, in which the referant for *it* is the nominalized predicate-argument *Japan destroyed China.*

Contemporary generative-transformational theorizing has particular significance in considering child language studies, especially in trying to account for descrepancies or uneveness in developmental patterns that are often observed in children. If language is viewed as being generated by kernel sentences transformed into complex sentences, then one could expect kernel sentence forms to develop before transformed forms, and simple transformational sentences to develop before more complex forms—a situation that rarely occurs in children. If language forms are seen to be generated from deep structures that are independent, although perhaps related in some particulars to each other, each with their own set of nodes and deep structure manipulations, then observed descrepancies in the developmental literature could be explained. The child may be focusing on a variety of deep structures at the same time rather than developing one set of deep structures before moving onto other sets. The order or motivation for actual consideration of some operations before others or at the same time as others may be both pragmatically and cognitively determined (Bates, 1976b; Bloom, 1973; Bowerman, 1976; Brown, 1973).

Lexical Insertion Rules   The second aspect of current generative-transformational theory that is of particular value in understanding language competence is the addition of explanations for lexicon insertion into the deep structures of sentences (N. Chomsky, 1965; Friedman and Bredt, 1968; Katz, 1972; Katz and Fodor, 1963; Kintsch, 1974; Ruwet, 1973; Stockwell, Schachter, and Partee, 1973). Early generative-transformational theory either did not address itself to the issue of lexical choice, or assumed that decisions about lexical items came after the establishment of both basic sentence frames and the application of transformational operations, with no explanation of how such selection was accomplished. It is now argued that the speaker decides upon the propositions he wishes to convey and then the appropriate sentence frame he wishes to employ, which automatically restricts the range of words permissible for use within that sentence (Clark and Clark, 1977). Restated, if the first decision is the type of sentence to be employed, then the speaker must adjust his lexical choices to conform to both the semantic and lexical constraints imposed by this sentence frame.

As previously stated, each speaker in forming a sentence must consider the choice of lexical items for any given sentence. Lexicon is a term that refers to the specific words known to the speaker of a particular language. The mature speaker must know thousands of words and how each can be meaningfully and grammatically used in his language. Every lexical item has constraints imposed upon its use within the various base structures of language. These constraints are features carried by lexical entries that dictate how these items can be used. There are contextual features, inherent features, strict subcategorization features, selectional features, and transformational restriction features. These five sets of features seem to determine the permissible deep structures into which lexical items can be inserted, and suggest which other lexical items are permitted to occur at the same time.

Features that designate the grammatical category to which the lexical item belongs are called contextual (categorical) features—is the word a noun, a verb, and so on. Inherent features define a lexical item quite apart from any reference to a particular sentence frame. Features such as gender, animacy, or humanness would be examples of inherent features.

Features that specify the constituent frame into which a word can be inserted would be strict subcategorization features. Whether a verb is transitive or intransitive would be an example of such a constraint. If the verb is transitive, it can only be inserted into a verb + noun phrase frame. Theorists (Ruwet, 1973) have suggested that the best notational system for representing such strict subcategorization features would be one that designated permission in terms of the constituent frame into which a lexical unit could be inserted, i.e., instead of noting +transitive, write (+ _____ NP) instead.

Selectional features refer to those characteristics that determine which word or words are compatible with one another, such as (+animate subject). Selectional restrictions combine inherent and strict subcategorization features to designate the constraints imposed on the remaining lexical entries that are decided upon for the sentence frame. By virtue of selectional features, decisions concerning the choice of one lexical item in one deep structure node determine the range of words that can appear in subsequent deep structure nodes. If the speaker selects *boys* as the lexical item for the noun node in the noun-phrase node, then the speaker is constrained to use lexical items in subsequent nodes that adhere to the features of plurality, maleness, and humanness. The verb that the speaker inserts into the verb node of the verb-phrase node must share the selectional restrictions of the word *boys.*

Transformational restriction features refer to the constraints placed on the types of transformations that can be applied to lexical items. For instance, some adverbs carry with them the feature of extraposition placement, which means they must be shifted into the body of the sentence frame if they are to be used. Such adverbs in English would include *never, ever,* and *often.*

The speaker must understand and adhere to all five of the foregoing sets of features in their choice of lexical items for the various nodes within the deep structure. If correct lexical choices are made, it can be said that a coherent feature matrix has been built for all lexical entries in the sentence frame.

Errors in lexical selection can and do occur, of course. Three primary types of errors are of interest: violations of subcategorization restrictions, violations of selectional restrictions, and violations of transformational restrictions. If the speaker violates strict subcategorization features, he might be heard to produce a sentence such as *John liked never*. In this case he has violated the constraint that the node following the transitive verb should be filled with an item that carries the strict subcategorization of *object of transitive verb*, which *never* does not.

Selectional restriction violations occur when selectional features are ignored or improperly matched. If the word *stone* is selected to fill the noun node, its accompanying determiner node must be filled with a determiner that carries the selectional features of inanimate and singular, such as *a, the,* or *each*; selection of *some* would represent a selectional restriction violation.

Finally, if the speaker uses a lexical item in a transformational operation that is inappropriate, he has violated a transformational restriction. Application of a past tense marker to the grammatical subject of a sentence would be an example of a transformational restriction violation.

Transformational Operations   As emphasized earlier, old generative-transformational theory argued for transformational operations that converted kernel sentences into more complex syntactic constructions. With the expansion of the concept of base structure to include modality and expanded nodes, transformational operations have been redefined as well. In contemporary terms, transformations tend to be arranged into three categories: generalized transformations, local transformations, and lexically based transformations (N. Chomsky, 1965; Ruwet, 1973). Transformations are still defined as those steps that the speaker goes through to bring deep structures to the surface, but transformational operations are now confined only to the manipulations of addition, omission, substitution, and word order change.

Generalized transformations refer to steps that establish basic constituent (sentence) frames that are properly ordered and syntactically appropriate to the propositional intents to be conveyed by the speaker. Lexical transformations refer to adjustments in generalized transformations that occur when specific lexical items are inserted appropriately into sentence frames. Local transformations are the finer grammatical changes such as plurality, tense, contraction, or insertion of the *to* with infinitive constructions that are applied to specific constituents. Bringing deep structure to surface structure is then seen as application of generalized transformations to establish sentence frames, application of lexical transformations to adjust the lexical requirements of those frames, and finally, local transformations that result in the finer forms required to make the sentence syntactically acceptable.

Errors in sentence production can also occur in application of transformations. A generalized transformation error could be defined as use of inappropriate word order, or failure to order the nodes available in the deep structure sentence frame appropriately. A lexical transformational error would be exemplified by use of an infinitive complement following *enjoy* rather than a participle form resulting in *The boy enjoyed to play.* A local transformational error could be a failure to apply tense to the verb node of the sentence.

Syntactic theory today is seen to favor the notion of the application of generalized transformations to establish basic sentence frame in the deep structure. The frames contain all the elements of the sentence before the application of any additional transformational operations. Each sentence frame is seen to exist independently of all others, although it shares many of the same characteristics. The number of nodes and the number of transformational operations required to bring these nodes to the surface determines the complexity level of a sentence.

Even with the significant changes that have occurred within generative-transformational linguistic theories, emphasis in these theories has been and continues to be on seeking an explanation for the operation of the syntactic aspects of language. The role of semantics within generative-transformational theory continues to be relegated to that of monitoring syntactic appropriateness rather than directly influencing the generation of syntactic forms. However, language forms depend upon meaning, both semantically and pragmatically; indeed, language description is only complete if meaning is the central factor in any theory of linguistic performance. Syntactic theory should be viewed as an adjunct to semantic and pragmatic descriptions of language.

PHONOLOGY

The fourth aspect of language that has been considered extensively is phonology. Once the speaker has planned his sentence frame based on the pragmatic, semantic, and syntactic requirements of the moment, he still must articulate these sentence frames in auditory sequences that can be interpreted by others. To achieve this goal, the speaker must develop articulatory programs that allow for the actual production of sentence frames (Clark and Clark, 1977).

When discussing phonology several important concepts need to be examined: phonetic distinctions, phonological distinctions, and suprasegmental distinctions. Phonetic distinctions are concerned with the raw speech sounds and how they are produced. Phoneticians study the acoustic properties of speech sounds and how the vocal tract behaves in the production of speech. Phonological distinctions, on the other hand, are concerned with speech sounds as part of the system of language. Phonologists have attempted to provide abstract representations of the sound system that will explain how sounds are added, changed, and omitted in the formation of words. For example phonologists attempt to explain why the final sound in *electric* /k/ is changed into an /s/ sound in electricity. Suprasegmental distinctions refer to the rhythm and stress patterns that exist within the language and interface with phonetic and phonologic rules.

Speech sounds can be represented on two levels. The phonetic level considers all the characteristics that go into making up the audible acoustic event, the places and manners of articulation. The more abstract phonological level, on the other hand, considers sounds of speech in a meaningful context—the significant differences that distinguish one class of sounds from another. Consider *sip* and *sips*. At the level of pronounciation these two words are phonetically different. The final /p/ in *sip* is accomplished by a slight release of air, an aspiration, whereas the /p/ in *sips* is not. The two /p/ sounds, then, are distinct phonetic entities. At the phonological level, however, these two /p/ sounds are said to be manifestations of the same underlying segment, or phoneme, which is the technical name given to a class of sounds treated as one sound. Thus the /p/ in *sip* and the /p/ in *sips* are said to be two phonetic segments, or allophones, derived from the same phonological segment, or phoneme /p/.

Suprasegmental aspects of speech refer to intonational, stress, and time patterns, which stretch over more than one phonological segment at one time. Intonation contours are defined as extra-segmental variations in the pitch of the voice. Most English assertions begins with a raised pitch and conclude with a falling pitch at sentence end. With questions, on the other hand, the pitch rises slightly at the end of the sentence, giving the question contour. Closely tied to intonation is stress, the difference in emphasis given to different syllables in words or sentences. Stress is produced by making the vowel in the syllable louder, higher in pitch, or longer, and thus is a property of the vocalic center of the syllable. These two suprasegmental features—intonation and stress—are important in speech because they tie the individual segments and syllables together, and serve to cue pragmatic and semantic concerns as well.

Chomsky and Halle (1968) initiated a procedure by which phonological differences between sounds could be described using a distinctive feature matrix procedure. They postulated a series of characteristics that seemed to differentiate sound categories from one another within a language. These distinguishing characteristics were designated as the distinctive features of the phonological system. The closer the sounds were from a production standpoint, the fewer the differences in distinctive features between them. Traditional phonological theory has tended to produce descriptions that emphasize motor production aspects (Chomsky and Halle, 1968; Jakobson, 1968; Jakobson and Halle, 1956). Recent attempts have been made to tie these motorically based distinctive features to actual changes in auditory messages that produce changes in auditory perception, thus emphasizing the fact that phonemes have a motor and auditory component (W. Cooper, 1975; Liberman, et al., 1967; Lisker and Abramson, 1964).

The second concern of phonological theory is word formation. Phonologists work to uncover rules for the addition of prefixes and suffixes, particular rules governing the application of local transformations such as past tense or plurality. These rules are referred to as morphophonemic rules.

It is interesting to note that the notion of speech distinctive features is similar to phenomena described in sign language and in identification of printed letters (Bellugi, Klima, and Siple, 1974; Gibson and Levin, 1975). Bellugi, Klima, and Siple, for instance, found that hearing-impaired person fluent in American Sign Language tended to make errors in short-term memory tasks along four dimensions, all related to formational characteristics of signs. These dimensions were place of articulation, location of articulation, hand configuration, and direction away or toward the body. It was argued that perhaps these dimensions are similar in their organizational effect to distinctive feature differences in phonological processing.

It is generally now agreed that the production unit planned within the deep structure is the constituent, not the entire sentence, or conversely, not just a single sound at a time. It is argued that the stress and timing patterns of speech play a significant role in this articulatory planning stage (Fromkin, 1973; MacKay, 1976; MacNeilage, 1970). Words and their prefixes and suffixes are filed into articulatory programs separately, with individuals tending to work out the articulatory aspects of words first, then prefixes and suffixes. Stressed words tend to be coded before non-stressed words, and more precisely. Content word articulatory planning may take precedence over function word articulatory planning. This strategy may change only when the stress patterns seem to favor informational emphasis on the function word. Those aspects of the sentence and/or constituent that seems to be more clearly articulated are those that are highly stressed within the sentence. This makes sense if one accepts the notion that ongoing speech involves the task of establishing and hitting one articulatory target after another. It is not possible, nor is it necessary, to strike every target precisely within continuous speech, particularly when speaking very rapidly or attempting to enlarge constituents to include more information than the normal English intonational contour can handle. For instance when saying *He ran down the street* or *The big boy ran down the street.,* one tries to fit both phrases into approximately the same intonational and time envelope. To accomplish this, one must take some articulatory shortcuts in the second sentence in order to make it fit within the target time frame. Part of such shortcuts includes emphasizing precise articulation of stressed items, because these items are often the very words or constituents that carry the topic and new information of the sentence frame. Even pragmatic considerations can be seen to play a definite role in phonological theory and speech production.

UNDERSTANDING AND PRODUCING SENTENCES

This brings us to a proposed model for how listeners may try to understand what someone says to them and how speakers may proceed to produce sentences that conform to the expectations of English listeners. It is easy to fall into the trap of conceiving comprehension as merely the reverse of production, but the two processes are separate. Comprehension involves auditory processing skills, whereas production involves the mobilization of the speech (or sign) motor system. Although comprehension and production share many common processes and mechanisms, they are organized differently in order to achieve the different tasks that are involved. Consequently each does include processes and mechanisms unique to that system and not shared with the other system. With this in mind, we turn to a description of how one comprehends and produces a sentence. Much of the model proposed in this discussion is drawn from the model developed by Clark and Clark (1977).

Comprehension

Because comprehension involves incoming auditory patterns, the first task may be to identify the speech sounds one is hearing. Identification of speech sounds may occur roughly in three stages: an auditory stage, a phonetic stage, and a phonological stage (Pisoni and Sawusch, 1975; Studdert-Kennedy, 1974, 1975). During the auditory stage, listeners take in short stretches of the raw acoustical signal reaching the ear, make a preliminary auditory analysis of the signal, and place the result in auditory memory. So far no speech segments have been identified. In the phonetic stage of identification, listeners examine the content of their auditory memory for acoustic cues, put these cues together, and identify each pattern of cues as a particular phonetic segment, such as /s/. These identifications are placed into a phonetic memory that is categorical in nature. It preserves the identification of a sound, but does not preserve the acoustic cues upon which the identification was made. During the phonological stage, listeners consult the constraints English places on sequences of phonetic segments and adjusts preliminary identifications to conform to these constraints. The final product is stored in the working memory for use in constructing propositions.

Listeners seem to construct the underlying representations for a sentence in roughly four steps. First, they take in raw speech and retain a phonological representation of those signals in the working memory. Second, they immediately attempt to organize the phonological representation into constituents, identifying their content and function. Third, as they identify each constituent, they use it to construct underlying propositions, building continually toward a hierarchal representation of propositions. Finally, having identified the propositions for a sentence, they are retained in the working memory, which at some point allows for a memory purge of the previously resolved phonological representations. In doing this, listeners tend to forget exact sentence wording, retaining instead the meaning of the sentence. Throughout this process, syntactic and semantic knowledge is brought to bear in the identification of both the constituents and the underlying representations of the sentence.

At the same time, listeners are attempting to identify the pragmatic constraints, such as the speaker's intended speech act, the informational organization of the sentence, and the contextual cues derived from the environment and the discourse. In addition they are drawing upon knowledge of the conduct of discourse to determine the weight they should place on certain utterances, while giving appropriate attention to those other aspects of the conversation that require attention, such as recognizing the topic and sorting the comments made about that topic. Listeners attend not only to the underlying representation of the sentence, but also to how the sentence is to be utilized from the speaker's point of view and the role of the sentence within the overall conversation.

Production

When a speaker decides to produce a particular sentence, he must enter into two activities, a planning stage and an execution stage. First the speaker needs to establish discourse plans; he must decide on the type of discourse in which he is participating. As previously indicated, each kind of discourse has a different structure, and he must plan his utterances to fit into the particular discourse. Each utterance should contribute to the discourse by conveying the right message, at just the right time. When the speaker has identified the discourse requirements and his intention (speech act) to produce a sentence with the right message, the speaker must then select a sentence that will accomplish this feat. This task involves sentence planning, which consists of selecting the correct speech act, the appropriate propositions, the sentence frame, and the correct organization of given-new information. The speaker must also decide how he wants to convey the message: directly or indirectly. Once the speaker has decided upon the global characteristics of a sentence, he needs to plan its constituents. He must pick the right words, phrases, or idioms to inhabit each constituent, all in proper order. During this process the speaker brings to bear his semantic and syntactic knowledge about sentence frames and lexical use. Although the speaker may have planned the global form of a sentence, he normally selects words and constituents on a phrase-by-phrase basis, perhaps one to three phases ahead in the sentence frame. As specific words and constituents are selected, they are formed into articulatory programs in memory, which is capable of holding all the words of a planned constituent at once. Memory can be argued to contain a representation of the actual phonetic segments, stresses, and intonational patterns that are to be executed at the final step, which is the audible articulation of the sentence. This final step involves the addition of sequence and timing to the articulatory program, which in turn tells the articulatory muscles and air stream valves what they should do. This final step results in externalized surface structures—sounds in the case of speech, signs in the case of American Sign Language, and printed or script strings in the case of writing.

The processes underlying comprehension and production must be mastered by any child, whether normally hearing or hearing-impaired. Chapter 3 considers the issue of how normally hearing children learn to comprehend and produce language, and Chapter 4 examines the success of hearing-impaired children in learning Standard English.

CHAPTER 3

CHILD LANGUAGE

CONTENTS

Consideration of contemporary literature on child language acquisition is a prerequisite to productive assessment of the problems of hearing-impaired persons with regard to the mastery of spoken, signed, read, or written English. The authors would be the first to admit that the rich array of information on the acquisition of language forms and functions in young children cannot be completely summarized here. Witness, for instance, the recent publication of an annotated bibliography (Abrahamson, 1977) containing more than 1500 references, a bibliography that may double in the number of entries in one year, considering the explosion of research in child language.

Within the confines of this disclaimer, this chapter provides first a discussion of the probable prerequisites (or co-requisites) for language acquisition: the biological-cognitive bases within the child and the nature and rate of caregiver language input to the child. The chapter concludes with consideration of developmental stages of English language acquisition and the data generated about each of these stages. This section should aid the reader in appreciating the ways in which children seem to actualize or map knowledge about language as they strive to become mature language users.

FOUNDATIONS OF LANGUAGE ACQUISITION

The biological foundations of language acquisition are well documented (Jacobson, 1975; Lenneberg, 1967; Nottebohm, 1975). The human infant is acknowledged to have predilection, even predisposition, for acquisition of language based on unique cognitive organization and perceptual-motor skills, which shape the ability to pay attention to language and to abstract out the regularities or irregularities of the system as the bases for communication with others (Bates et al., 1977; Bloom, 1973; Morehead and Morehead, 1974; Slobin, 1973). Cognitive abilities are clearly related to the acquisition of language in children, and many researchers are inclined to argue that cognitive understandings and skills are actually prerequisites to language development. The biological-cognitive underpinnings of language are discussed later in this section, with particular reference to the concept of linguistic universals and the factors involved in cognitive development from the perspective of Piagetian theory.

The second foundation of language learning is the language imparted to the child by his communication environment. Research on mother language (motherese) and caregiver-child verbal interactions indicates that caregivers talk to and interact with infants and very young children in ways that are uniquely different from their encounters with older children and adults (Farwell, 1975; Landes, 1975). Although a direct link between the content of adult-child interactions and resultant stages in language acquisition of children has not been forged, there are indications that adults do shape children's language within the limitations imposed on language learning by children's cognitive and perceptual readiness. Despite the role of adults as just outlined, it should be stressed that it is accepted that children actively learn language, rather than having adults teach it to them (Menyuk, 1971). This attitude is particularly critical to subsequent arguments about deaf children and their language learning experiences and abilities.

Biological-Cognitive Foundations

It has been established by contemporary researchers (Jacobson, 1975; Lenneberg, 1967; Nottebohm, 1975) that the biological make-up of human beings permits the natural acquisition of language. The physiological, neurological, and biochemical dimensions of human behavior are particularly adapted to the easy acquisition of symbol systems.

Language has traditionally been deemed as species-specific. Humans have the physical equipment and central nervous system organization to acquire and produce language because of genetic predispositions, whereas it has been argued that other species lack these necessary biological adaptations. Such an argument may now be highly questionable in light of the accomplishments of great apes such as Washoe and Lana (Fouts, 1972; Gardner and Gardner, 1971, 1974, 1975a,b; Gill and Rumbaugh, 1974; Rumbaugh and Gill, 1976, 1977). It is now apparent that Man may not be the only species capable of producing connected, rule-governed language. The upper limits of linguistic sophistication are probably different from ape to human, but even the ease with which language is mastered cannot be said to favor humans over chimpanzees. Man's superior position is still tenable only if one defines linguistic usage in oral or spoken language terms.

A second issue needs to be mentioned here. Maximum language growth apparently does occur normally during a critical period characterized by rapid development of neurological maturity, the so-called period of *resonance* between the ages of 2 and 12 years (Lenneberg, 1967). If a child exceeds this time period without mastery of some rudiments of a language system, the probability of adequate mastery of any language system is felt to be greatly reduced. However, experience with some children indicates that language growth is possible even when the upper limit of the critical resonant period has been passed. Studies that describe the language growth of Genie, a severely environmentally deprived child who only began language learning in early adolescence, indicate that the extent of language function may be restricted, that acquisition processes may be slower and more tediously learned than if initiated during the optimum period, but that learning does occur (Curtiss, 1977). The question of the reality of an optimum period for language acquisition is of special concern with many older deaf children, adolescents, and adults who have not had the benefit of systematic education at early periods of their life.

Linguistic Universals   The exact nature of the child's biological inheritance has served as a major point of disagreement in recent years. Some researchers (McNeill, 1970a,b) have suggested that children are born with inherent linguistic understandings expressed as linguistic universals, those commonalities among language and language users that seem to be a function of linguistic endowment. Linguistic universals have been divided into strong and weak universals. Weak linguistic universals are defined as those commonalities that seem tied to factors that are other than purely linguistic, such as cognitive limitations or social conditions. Strong linguistic universals, on the other hand, are those commonalities that are completely language dependent or language specific. These universals are seen as the inherent basis of language learning in all children. Concepts such as *nounness* and *verbness* have been argued to be genetically coded understandings known by human infants at birth; these are examples of strong linguistic universals. Once the language acquisition process is initiated, weak linguistic universals are thought to come into play to ensure the continuation of the process leading to eventual mastery of language. Such contentions are highly speculative, even improbable, given the variety of encoding proclivities of languages around the world.

Recently those aspects of language deemed good candidates for definition as strong linguistic universals have been explained as being cognitively determined with regard to their order and rate of acquisition. The foremost proponent of cognitively based linguistic universals is Slobin (1973), who has suggested that children possess operating principles or strategies of cognitive organization that allow them to make sense of the flow of language surrounding them. Two basic types of strategies can be differentiated: semantically based operations and surface structure-attentional operations.

Semantically based operations involve strategies such as seeking grammatical markers that encode meaningful distinctions, avoiding exceptions, and seeking systematic modifications of exceptions to make them conform to a single form. In other words, Slobin argues that children attempt to find those linguistic units that are semantically relevant and to internalize a single feature to represent these meaningful units. Once children have accomplished this feat, they can direct their attention to alternate ways of dealing with the same semantically meaningful units, in accordance with the variety of devices available in their mother tongue. They can learn exceptions to a general rule they have just formulated. A frequently used example of this process would be the acquisition of past tense markers in English, which semantically encode the concept of time completed. Children will tend to learn the /-ed/ suffix rule first, which they overgeneralize to irregular verbs. Once the regular verb system is mastered reasonably well, children can turn their attention to acquisition of the exceptions to the past tense system, namely, irregular verbs.

Surface structure-attentional operations refer to those operating principles that allow children to note and treat surface structures for the purpose of segmentation. This latter skill allows a child to develop an appreciation of the elements of language from which he can deduce regularities and then formulate rules governing their production. Children are observed to follow certain perceptual-cognitive strategies when paying attention to streams of language directed to them. They tend to remember ends of strings, to pay attention to word order constraints, and to disallow interruption of continuous linguistic units. This means, for example, that children seem to have more difficulty producing and comprehending relative clauses or similar constructions when they occur medially in a language set than when such constructions occur at the end or beginning of a sentence. Children seem to prefer sentences such as *The boy hit the girl who lives across the street.*, more than sentences like *The apples that are on the kitchen table are rotten.* In the latter example, the relative clause disrupts the continuity of the main sentence, which makes processing that sentence more difficult for the child language learner.

In summary, Slobin's semantic operating principles are oriented toward meaning abstraction, whereas his surface structure-attentional operations involve perceptual organization.

Piagetian Theory Researchers interested in the relation of cognition to language acquisition have suggested a need to formulate a detailed theory of cognitive acquisition that will relate to or explain linguistic development in children. To fulfill this need, appeals to an already existing theory of cognition such as that of Piaget have been made (Bates, 1976b; Bloom, 1973; D. Edwards, 1973; Moerk, 1975a; Morehead and Morehead, 1974; Wells, 1974). Piagetian theory views language development as part of the more general process of cognitive development (Piaget, 1926, 1951, 1952, 1954; Piaget and Inhelder, 1969). Cognitive development begins at the moment of birth and proceeds through the adolescent years and beyond. It is considered to be a continuous, fluid process, although certain stages of development have been identified and described. These stages of development are characterized by application of cognitive strategies and description of cognitive structures. During development of cognition, the child is establishing strategies that he will use as an adult to solve problems. The content of these cognitive strategies, or cognitive structures, is referred to as schemas, those internal cognitive frameworks that give meaning to experience and that provide the child with tools to solve problems.

As a biologist, Piaget tends to approach developmental problems from that perspective. Cognitive growth is thought to occur as the child establishes a balance between the processes of assimilation and accommodation, which lead to the acquisition of operative and figurative knowledge. Assimilation is the process of modifying reality so that it matches internal organizations the child has developed. Accommodation consists of the child's modifying his internal structures in order to make them correspond with environmental influences; as the child interacts with his environment, he is developing internal representations about that environment. This is accomplished in part by adjusting his internal understandings in accordance with the information he is receiving about the environment. Simultaneously he is adjusting his information about the environment to make it conform with what he thinks reality is all about. These two processes yield, in the extreme, fantasy as an expression of assimilation and imitation as an expression of accommodation. Although both assimilation and accommodation are important, researchers (Bates, 1976b) feel that accommodation processes relate most to the acquisition of symbolic behavior, which by definition includes both language and symbolic play.

Assimilation and accommodation shape internal representations, which become separated from external reality to exist as mental representations or the foundations of symbolic behavior. Internal representations are seen to exist on the levels of operative knowledge and figurative knowledge. Operational knowledge can be described as the process of reorganization that individuals apply to internal representations to produce higher level conceptual frameworks. Figurative knowledge, on the other hand, consists of the end products, or schemas, that have developed as a result of the application of operative knowledge. For instance, recognition or knowledge of an end would be figurative knowledge, whereas the knowledge or application of different means to achieve that end would be an example of operative knowledge. This distinction is important, because investigators of child language acquisition differ over whether operative or figurative knowledge is the primary cognitive prerequisite for language development.

Piaget speculates that in order to develop operative and figurative knowledge children pass through stages of cognitive development. Each major stage is characterized by certain types of knowledge acquisition. The four major Piagetian stages in cognitive development are designated the sensorimotor stage, the pre-operational stage, the concrete operational stage, and the formal operational stage.

The sensorimotor stage is that period of time when the infant acquires and masters basic knowledge about the world in order to lay foundations for symbolic and logical development. During the sensorimotor stage the child learns about the figurative aspects of the environment: object constancy and transivity and basic notions about the operative aspect of the environment, namely, end-means, causality, and the use of instrumentation.

The pre-operational stage is characterized by the evolution of symbolic behavior and the development of pre-logical thought, which is dominated by the child's perceptual limitations. The evolution of pre-logical thought into logical thought characterized by the properties of reversibility, class inclusion, and part-whole relationships of concrete objects occurs during the so-called concrete operational stage. The last or formal operational stage is characterized by the child's use of logical thought by employing mental operations rather than his depending upon environmental constraints, which was true through the concrete operational stage.

Because the most vigorous application of Piagetian theory to language acquisition research findings has involved the sensorimotor stage, it might be useful to describe this particular stage in greater detail. The sensorimotor stage is seen as consisting of six sub-stages, all of which have been argued to be important determinants in the development of early language forms, forms actually produced by children who are considered to be at the end of the sensorimotor stage and at the beginning of the pre-operational stage.

Sub-stage 1, occurring during the first month of life, is thought to consist of reflexive behavior, in which accommodative and assimilative tendencies are virtually absent. The sensory and motor systems, suggests Piaget, lack any coordination. However, even within this earliest stage, reflexes are being modified through interaction with the environment to be the beginning expressions of accommodation. Refinement of knowledge concerning Sub-stage 1 is being gained through description of infant sensory and cognitive capabilities during the first hours and days of life. Infant competence is being demonstrated most impressively in research such as that by Bower (1974), Eimas (1974), Lipsitt (1977), and Morse (1974). A particularly exciting expression of these capabilities is discussed in the section of this chapter devoted to comments about early speech acquisition.

Sub-stage 2, which lasts from approximately 2 to 4 months of age, is described in the Piagetian framework as the period for developing primary circular reactions. As the child interacts with the environment, he begins to perform actions that initially have unpredictable results, but with learning he keeps repeating his actions to produce recurring results. In his constant repetitions, the young infant produces actions that differ slightly from his previous efforts. These repetitions and resultant changes become incorporated, through accommodation, into action schemas. Sensory schemas and motor schemas become coordinated during this period so that the infant can engage in motor and sensory behavior simultaneously, an important change in processing that allows for the eventual acquisition of symbolic behavior.

Sub-stage 3, the period from approximately 4 to 8 months, is the period of development of secondary circular reactions. In previous sub-stages, Piaget believes that the child has been concerned primarily with his own actions; during this stage, however, the child becomes interested in the events that are produced by his actions. This means that his actions have become externalized toward objects in the environment rather than being merely confined to an egocentric concern with his own actions per se. This externalization of the infant's interests leads to the notion of separation of agent from action from object acted upon, a distinction that is of interest relative to early language acquisition. Externalization of action toward objects is presumed to lead to the development of object constancy, or the understanding that objects remain the same regardless of the viewer's perspective or the object's shape. Imitations at this period are confined to physical activities. Auditory events or their schemas, such as babbling, are seen to be tied in part to physical schemas, such as the ability to localize sounds within the environment.

Sub-stage 4, the period from approximately 8 to 12 months, is the time when the infant begins to develop a sense of means to a goal. It is at this point that the infant can adjust his activities to introduce different means to attain a specific goal. Up to this point the means have been inextricably tied to a goal, but now they begin to develop as separate entities. The infant begins to link causality attributes to other social objects within the environment, including people. This latter development is important, because it provides the infant with a basis for initiating communication to persuade others to effect changes in the environment on his behalf. This is also the period when understanding of part-to-whole relationships begins to emerge, that is, parts of an object can signify the entire object. This development is seen as a precursor to the establishment of symbols or signifiers for objects.

Sub-stage 5, the period ranging from about 12 to 18 months, is described as a period of active experimentation in which the infant attempts to combine his schemas to produce novel means to achieve his goals. The infant in Sub-stage 4 needs to keep social and nonsocial action and personal schemas separate, whereas in Sub-stage 5 he can combine these internal representations to achieve goals. It is during this period that object experimentation by the infant is prevalent. The infant is discovering the various characteristics and functions governing objects. This is the period when the idea of instrumentation may be introduced. The infant learns that objects can be used in a variety of ways to achieve desired goals. The notions of novelty and instrumentation are crucial components of this stage.

Sub-stage 6, the final division in the sensorimotor stage, lasts from approximately 18 to 24 months. It is seen as the period of representation, the time for the internalization of action and object schemas developed during Sub-stage 5, as well as the time when the sensorimotor schemas developed in both Sub-stages 4 and 5 are transformed into symbolic representations through the action of signifiers. These are referred to as tertiary circular reactions.

In summary, Piaget sees cognition emerging from the coordination of reflex behavior into organized patterns, patterns that are transformed into sensorimotor knowledge schemas. These schemas are the basis for representational thought, which in turn seems to be the basis for symbolic activity represented by both symbolic play and language development. The ability to use schemas to solve problems, e.g., employment of means to a goal relationship, constitutes operative knowledge. The knowledge of specific object schemas is termed figurative knowledge. This conceptual framework has led child language researchers to postulate that the cognitive bases of language acquisition are rooted in the earliest periods of infant sensorimotor development.

Environmental Foundations

When individuals communicate, they normally do not use exactly the same style with each person they contact, nor do they interact in precisely the same way each time they meet the same person. Instead, speakers vary their language syntactically, semantically, phonologically, and pragmatically, depending upon the communication circumstances. Such variations in style are referred to as changes in register. In the literature there is ample suggestion that adults change to parent or caregiver register when talking with very young children (Broen, 1972; Drach, 1969; Ferguson, 1964; Holzman, 1974; Kobashigawa, 1969; Moerk, 1972, 1974; Nelson, 1973; Pfuderer, 1969; Phillips, 1973; Snow, 1972; Snow and Ferguson, 1977; Snow et al., 1976). Not only is communication register adjusted to a young child's communication level, but adult patterns of social interaction also seem to be reconstructed to aid the infant in paying attention to communication (Bruner, 1974, 1975, 1977; Collis, 1977; Collis and Schaffer, 1975; Freedle and Lewis, 1977; Jaffe, Stern, and Peery, 1973; Kaye, 1976, 1977; Murphy and Messer, 1977; Pawlby, 1977; Scaife and Bruner, 1975; Schaffer, Collis, and Parsons, 1977; Trevarthen, 1977). In this respect mother-child interactions have been most extensively studied. They can be characterized by changes in both linguistic input and social interaction, which are apparently related to enhancement of communication growth in young children. Although mother language has been the focus of most research efforts, it should be noted that older siblings (Berko-Gleason, 1973; Gelman and Shatz, 1977; Sachs and Devin, 1976; Shatz and Gelman, 1973), nursery school teachers (Berko-Gleason, 1975; Granowsky and Krossner, 1970), and fathers (Berko-Gleason, 1975; Giattino and Hogan, 1975), to a lesser degree, all employ modifications in their communication behaviors with very young children.

Studies of mother interactions with young children focus on or revolve around three general topics: the manner of communication, how a parent catches a child's attention for communication; the topics that parents and children consider; and the complexity and stimulation characteristics of adult language directed to young children.

Conduct of Mother-Child Interactions   The essential ingredient for communication is the establishment of exchange through joint activities initiated either by the mother or at later stages by the infant himself (Bruner, 1974, 1975).

Interactions between adults and children can be seen to be highly coordinated, with a parent providing visual and vocal information simultaneously (Bruner, 1977; Collis, 1977; Collis and Schaffer, 1975; Freedle and Lewis, 1977; Jaffe, Stern, and Peery, 1973). In addition, the caregiver uses a variety of techniques to establish and maintain the child's attention. As a mother interacts with her baby, the baby may express interest in particular objects or activities, which the mother notes. She may imitate the child's efforts (Pawlby, 1977; Trevarthen, 1977) in an attempt to establish turn-taking communication patterns (Bruner, 1977; Kaye, 1976, 1977; Schaffer, Collis, and Parsons, 1977). For instance the baby might vocalize or grab for a particular object. The mother reacts by repeating the vocal event, or by making a game of grabbing, and then she waits for the child to respond or react to her activity. If the child fails to react properly, the mother will often induce communication by further engaging the child or by providing a response for the child. In the earliest months of life, mothers are quite content with minimal communication attempts by infants themselves, but they do identify the child's role for him. Interplays between mother and child lead to awareness and eventual exercise of turn-taking communication, a vital component of language acquisition and development.

Mothers also establish communication by focusing the child's attention visually on some aspect of the environment. Pointing or visual cuing coupled with verbal attention getters such as *Hey, look here.* or the child's name are a coordinated part of establishing common ground for considering objects or events (Murphy and Messer, 1977; Scaife and Bruner, 1975).

Often mothers change vocal quality or intonational patterns as part of the strategy for establishing and maintaining attention (Garnica, 1977). For instance sing-song modulation of speech patterns and high pitched voices are often used with very young children. Whispering also seems highly effective in maintaining the attention of infants and young children.

Topics in Mother-Child Interactions   Communication in normal mother-child pairs does not appear in isolation from joint activities and social interactions. Mothers engage their children in topics that are seldom if ever removed from the immediate situation (Bruner, 1977).

They tend to hold discussions on the here and now, making comments about ongoing activities, apparently with the expectation that the child will respond with comments appropriate to the situation. The child's comments initially may be nothing more than a look in the right direction. Newport, Gleitman, and Gleitman (1977) describe the initial conversations between children and adults as consisting predominantly of action-directives. The response of the child is one of action to comply with the directives. As the child matures linguistically, mother conversation tends more toward declaratives or comments. In all these cases it is generally agreed that immediate context must be supportive of the ongoing conversation.

At later ages, the joint activity exchanges allow the mother to monitor her own linguistic and social input to the child as well as lend meaning to the child's early utterances, which may lack clarity of form or reference. Through communication exchanges the child comes to understand that words and sentences have reference, that they communicate propositions and information (Bruner, 1975, 1977). In these contexts the child learns that language involves topics and comments about these topics (Bates, 1976b; Greenfield and Smith, 1976). Topics can be conceived to be the given information, whereas comments can be conceived to be any new information about the topic. Eventual understanding of the given-new contract discussed in Chapter 1 arises from such exchanges. It is likely, however, that the first organized aspects of communication that the child learns are speech acts, turn-taking, and communication exchanges, all of which are critical to appreciation of language functions.

Syntactic Complexity of Mother-Child Language The form of mothers' speech to infants is simple and correct both syntactically and semantically (Drach, 1969; Moerk, 1974; Pfuderer, 1969; Phillips, 1973; Snow, 1972). Her utterances are characterized by few hesitations within phrases, but longer than normal pauses between sentences (Broen, 1972; Drach, 1969). The rate of mother's utterances is slower, containing fewer disfluencies than found in her speech with adults (Broen, 1972; Drach, 1969). Mothers tend to use single proposition sentences in highly redundant conversational forms (Holzman, 1974; Snow, 1972). Lexical items are generally consistent from exchange to exchange with some simplification of phonological and morphological aspects (Ferguson, 1977). This simplification results in use of so-called baby words and phrases. The assumption apparently made by most mothers while talking to very young children is that unless there is some change in propositional and syntactical levels, the child will fail to understand what is being said. This may or may not be a valid assumption, but descriptions of mothers' talk certainly discredit the traditional notion that the language provided to children is highly complex, disorganized, and replete with hesitations, rewordings, false starts, and syntactic inaccuracies.

Linguistic input to children who are preverbal does seem to differ in character from motherese used with verbal children. For instance Phillips (1973) found that speech addressed to children of about 8 months showed a greater variability in utterance length, ratio of function to content words, number of verbs per utterance, and percentage of weak verbs than speech addressed to older children. Phillips interpreted her findings as support for the notion that mothers adjust their speech to their children's linguistic level, but that no adjustment is considered to be called for before the child has language. Other research supports this diversity in adjusting language input to children's presumed levels of understanding (Cross, 1977; Newport, Gleitman, and Gleitman, 1977). In contrast, Snow (1977), although observing a significant change in linguistic input to infants at about 7 months of age, accounts for the change not on the basis of presence or absence of language in the child, but as a reflection of mothers' confidence in their children's growing ability to function as conversation partners, to show communication competence. This argument seems to be reasonable, particularly because researchers do not report dramatic changes in motherese when children begin to produce actual speech, a time when it would seem appropriate for parents to alter their input if they were concerned exclusively with adjustment of their language on the basis of the linguistic sophistication of their children.

Studies of language of older children (Berko-Gleason, 1973; Gelman and Shatz, 1977; Sachs and Devin, 1976; Shatz and Gelman, 1973), of nursery school teachers, whether male or female (Berko-Gleason, 1975; Granowsky and Krossner, 1970), of women with no children (Snow, 1972), and of fathers (Berko-Gleason, 1975; Giattino and Hogan, 1975), when directed to young children, indicate that modifications such as those just described for mothers are common to these groups, also. There are differences, however, in the conversational constraints that different partners impose on dialogues with very young children. For instance 4-year-old children who are instructed to talk with a much younger child tend to use imperatives almost exclusively, particularly when there are no adults present in the environment. Apparently they do not wish to be alone with a very young child or to have responsibility for his actions (Gelman and Shatz, 1977). These same children switch to polite indirect speech forms with adults when asking them to perform various activities. Fathers, too, impose some unique constraints on conversational exchanges with young children (Berko-Gleason, 1975). They tend to use many more imperative forms, forms that could be described as indicative of threats or authority, and to choose words with higher conceptual complexity than do mothers. These differences in behavior seem to be a function of a societally determined paternal role rather than a sex difference in performance. Male nursery school teachers, for example, are observed to provide linguistic input that is more similar to that of female nursery school teachers and mothers than to fathers (Berko-Gleason, 1975).

Language Stimulation Techniques Used By Mothers As a child begins to demonstrate some understanding and use of language, maternal language stimulation techniques also change (Moerk, 1975b). Mothers with children who as yet demonstrate little linguistic understanding tend to employ expansion and modeling techniques, whereas mothers with children who have demonstrated language understanding and use shift to prodding (completion) and questioning techniques. Of course mothers, regardless of the age of their children, actually use all four techniques—expansion, modeling, completion or prodding, and questioning—but certain strategies predominate in mother talk at certain stages of a child's language development.

Expansion consists of expanding what the child says into the appropriate linguistic form presumed to be intended by the child. If the child says *ball* while pointing to a picture of a ball, the mother might expand his production by saying *Yes, that's a ball.*, which provides the child with a mature form of the utterance he might have been striving to produce. Modeling refers to the presentation of additional comments about the child's production. If, in the above example, mother had said *Yes, the ball is on the table.*, she is encoding the form attempted by the child, but by providing additional information rather than just an expansion. A common pattern among mothers is to alternate between expansion and modeling techniques, which has the decided advantage of providing models while simultaneously presenting new information to the child.

Prodding or completion techniques involve the mother's providing the stem of a sentence that the child is encouraged to complete. The mother might say *Mother gave you a (   )?* to which the child can add *ball*. A more sophisticated variation on this approach is termed questioning, which is in many cases the most commonly used strategy employed by mothers to encourage children's linguistic usage and to check their comprehension. Questions can take the form of properly formulated or less well formulated strings, such as *What did you throw?* or *You threw what?* respectively.

STAGES IN LANGUAGE DEVELOPMENT

Descriptions of child language can be divided according to the following stages: (1) preverbal stage, (2) single-word stage, (3) two-word stage, (4) three-word stage, (5) refinement stage, and (6) complex form stage. For each of these stages, research concern has been directed predominately toward explaining acquisition of language forms, with attempts to tie form development to cognitive maturation, and more recently to communication competence. The remainder of this chapter is devoted to a discussion of language development stages in consideration of how each stage relates to the foundations already outlined.

Preverbal Stage

Within recent years, the question of whether there is such a being as a prelinguistic child has been posed (Kaplan and Kaplan, 1971). The answer must be a resounding *no,* particularly if one pays attention to the demonstrated sensory capabilities of infants related to language events. The notion of the infant as a passive receptor of sensory information or as an organism unrelated or discontinuous with the communication competence shown by older children or adults is no longer tenable. Language performance must, of course, be considered in its broadest sense. Spoken languages, indeed all forms of language, involve understandings that transcend formal syntactic, semantic, or even morphophonemic distinctions, including the functions of language that are learned and expressed through social interaction. The preverbal infant operates primarily as a social being—hedonistic to be sure, strongly concerned about his comforts, but certainly social. His social preferences include interest in communicators and communication.

In fact within the first few days and weeks of life, infants can be shown to have a preference for listening to, and responding with, speech events (Morse, 1972, 1974; Turnure, 1971). As early as the fourth to sixth week of life, infants can distinguish as fine a phonetic distinction as the voice onset time difference between cognate phoneme pairs (Eimas, 1974, 1975; Eimas et al., 1971; Moffitt, 1971; Trehub, 1973; Trehub and Rabinovitch, 1972). Although it can be argued that such auditory resolving power is of no practical use to the infant at such an early age, the baby's capabilities certainly are impressive. If contemporary research on infant vocal behavior in early life (Oller, 1977; Oller et al., 1976) is correct, however, these auditory capacities are as critical to acquisition of phonetic controls during the first year of life as they are to acquisition of language during the second year. To reiterate, normal newborn and very young infants have the sensory equipment to resolve any feature of spoken communication, although it clearly takes them a year or so to separate critical aspects of the language system. That is, by the end of the first year of life, the child must somehow learn what the basic units of the language are in order to begin an assign meaning to these units.

The child must learn to segment environmental language into units, units in which word boundaries can be identified, even though the child rarely hears just words alone. How does the child know where one word begins and another ends within this mass of continuous dialogue?

Early Phonological Acquisition   It has been suggested that during the preverbal stage the child is learning about segments that exist within words, segments that tend to concentrate around syllabic differentiations (M. Edwards, 1974; Garnica, 1973; Shvachkin, 1973). Infants begin by defining syllables within English as consonant + vowel or consonant + vowel + consonant strings. As they differentiate one form from another, they also learn that sounds usually appear in one or the other position of a syllabic frame, either in the consonant or vowel slot. Discrimination of sounds seems to be learned in an orderly fashion. Certain sounds may be learned before others because of the ease of their discriminations; e.g., bilabial sounds such as /b/, /p/, and /m/ would be perceptually less complicated and thus expressively less complicated when compared to sibilants such as /s/, /z/, or /sh/. In addition to learning the general discrimination of English sounds within syllables, children also need to learn about acceptable sequence arrangements within English (Messer, 1967). If such order could be established early in the young child, he could begin to determine which meanings are attributed to the segments that he has deduced from the language being directed at him. Baby register or motherese must surely aid in this process because of the organization features described previously, such as phonological simplification.

Although there are some indications that children learn the general role of stress and intonational patterns rather early (Berko, 1958; Kaplan and Kaplan, 1971; Lieberman, 1967; Menyuk, 1971, 1974), there is also evidence to suggest that complete mastery of the stress and intonational system is not accomplished until children are much older (Cruttenden, 1974; Gleitman and Gleitman, 1970). Some rudimentary mastery of so-called suprasegmental information would still seem to be important however, for at least three reasons. First, it should aid in deciphering the given-new information contract, because intonational patterns are frequently used to cue which is given information and which is new information (Halliday, 1967). Second, it should aid in interpreting which speech act is to be responded to. Indirect speech acts, for instance, can be best interpreted when it is understood that the accompanying intonational pattern directs one to disregard the surface structure and pay attention to contextual and situational cues (Clark and Lucy, 1975; Gordon and Lakoff, 1971; Searle, 1975). Last, intonation should aid in the establishment of linguistic units. Intonation and stress patterns do cue listeners to the major constituents within a dialogue, most importantly to sentences and clause boundaries (Martin, 1972; Shields, McHugh, and Martin, 1974). Attention to the intonation and stress patterns would give the child valuable aids in segmenting discourse, as well as individual sentences into meaningful units.

Preverbal Utterances Vocalizations of infants during the preverbal stage, if viewed as speech practice and not language practice, can be seen as strikingly similar to the speech of older children in some ways, clearly different in others, and certainly related or continuous in a general way to mature speech.

The model suggested by Oller and his associates (Oller, 1975, 1977; Oller et al., 1976) to explain the development of phonetic control by normal infants is particularly intriguing and satisfying because it emphasizes the infant's active auditory processing role as well as his dynamic expressive capabilities, capacities that have been increasingly documented by infant researchers in the past few years (Eisenberg, 1976; Stark, Heinz, and Wright-Wilson, 1976; Stark, Rose, and McLagen, 1975; Zlatin, 1975, 1976).

Basically Oller's argument is that during the first year of life the infant abstracts and practices what he terms metaphonological and concrete phonological features of speech, those features that could be described as underlying any spoken language. These features include normal phonation, use of the full resonance capacity of the vocal tract, volume and pitch variation, opposition of high and low amplitude vocal tract openings, and constraints on timing relationships of vocal tract openings and closures. In mastering these metaphonological features, Oller suggests a series of stages in which the infant is observed to highlight practice of particular metaphonological features on his way to development of one aspect of oral language, namely, speech. Note that Oller is not suggesting mastery of phonemic elements during the first year of life, only the abstraction and practice of some universal phonetic or metaphonological elements.

For example the feature of voluntary control of phonation is highlighted during the first month of life in a period that Oller terms the Phonation Stage. The characteristic type of vocalization usually heard during this stage is the Quasi Resonant Nucleus, which serves as the basis for the phonetic characteristic of normal phonation in mature speech systems. This stage contains infant utterances that are not fully resonated elements, but increasingly show the normal infant to be gaining control of voluntary, rather than purely reflexive vocalizations.

All of Oller's stages of infant vocalization are detailed in Table 4, but an additional explanation of the Canonical Stage might be of interest

Table 4.   Stages of infant vocalization[a]

Infant age (months)	Infant vocal behavior	Metaphonological trait
0–1	Quasi-resonant nucleus	Normal phonation
2–3	Quasi-resonant nucleus plus velar consonant-like element	Open and close vocal tract contrast
4–6	Fully resonant nuclei	Resonance contrast
	Raspberry	Front and back closure contrast
	Squeal; growl	Pitch contrast
	Yell	Loudness contrast
	Marginal babble	Full open and close vocal tract contrast
7–10	Reduplicated babbling	Timing contrast
11–12	Variegated babbling	Vocalic and consonantal contrasts

[a] Taken from Oller, D., 1977. Infant vocalization and the development of speech.

here. From ages 7 to 10 months, Oller observes normal infants to be engaged in practice of the critical aspect of timing constraints in a reduplicated framework. Contrary to other researchers, he suggests that the infant will practice only a limited number of consonant-mid vowel combinations (perhaps as few as seven) in focus on reduplication of acceptable syllable time or length. Other previously practiced features such as volume or pitch change will certainly be heard, but infants may be remarkably single-minded about timing practice, with a decided preference for single consonants in initial position, particularly unaspirated initial stops, similar to the preferences of 12- to 13-month-old infants (Oller et al., 1976).

This brief description has not exhaustively explored Oller's well-reasoned position, and is certainly not intended to suggest that other points of view regarding vocal activity in the first year of life are not also of value. However, any person interested in development of speech skills in hearing-impaired children, particularly as they interface with language acquisition, would do well to consider how clearly Oller's description of the vocal business of normal infants supports Ling's (1976) concerns about the need to develop phonetic prerequisites for speech in deaf children.

If Oller's position is correct, early onset of deafness prevents normal speech sampling and practice from the first moments of life, and unless systematic early intervention in vocal tract skills is initiated, the outcome will never be satisfactory for the deaf child.

Preverbal Communication Development   In addition to being able to decode phonetic and intonational patterns, the preverbal child is developing internal referential and pragmatic skills that act as the framework into which formal language is inserted as it is learned. Bruner (1974, 1975, 1977) has demonstrated that as a result of joint activities, the child learns very early about reference (that words represent externalized reality); about predication (continuous dialogue consists of a series of topic-comment relationships); and about language function (the manner in which language can be used).

Working from an orientation similar to Bruner's, Bates (1976b) suggests that the foundations of language emerge as a result of the acquisition of knowledge about conversation constraints and language context, termed hereafter as pragmatic knowledge. Pragmatic knowlege serves as the frame into which symbolic language is inserted for use in communication.

During the preverbal period, according to Bates (1976b; Bates et al., 1977), the child develops an elementary knowledge of performatives, propositions, and presupposition, but this knowledge exists only at the sensorimotor level, as defined in Piagetian terms. Pragmatic knowledge emerges during the fifth sensorimotor sub-stage because of the acquisition of some important operative knowledge: agency and instrumentation are possible through the development of tool-making abilities, and ends can be achieved through the introduction of innovative means. The child uses this knowledge to develop gestures that function as imperative and declarative performatives, but on a sensorimotor level. Imperative sensorimotor performatives are expressed as pointing gestures coupled with eye contact or an outstretched hand performing the open-and-shut *give-me* gesture. Such gestures are seen to indicate a child's notion of the request performative on a sensorimotor rather than a symbolic level.

A second or proto-declarative performative also emerges during this period. The declarative sensorimotor performative begins by the child simply exhibiting objects in front of an adult, showing something to the adult, rather than demanding that something be done. This displaying behavior eventually evolves into a pointing gesture, which clearly differs from the aforementioned proto-imperative *give-me* gesture. Now the child points the proto-declarative turning to the adult for validation of his point, for confirmation of what he is showing, not as a request for action.

With the advent of sensorimotor Sub-stage 6, Bates (1976b) suggests that the child is ready to develop symbolic behavior or referential function, which may be confirmed by observation of his play and communication behavior. The roots of reference come from sensorimotor performative frames, with gradual development toward greater sophistication. The first stage identified in the development of reference involves word-like utterances that have no discernible referential value. They are used solely as part of a performative routine. Bates cites the example of a child who used *Mmm* as part of an imperative performative routine, that is, as he performed the imperative gesture he uttered the sound *Mmm*. If an adult failed to respond appropriately, the child would point again and make the *Mmmm* sound louder and more intonationally varied.

The next stage involves the use of referential words, but in very restricted situations. For instance, the child might say *Bam,* but only when knocking over blocks. Such words are not seen as true symbolic forms, but merely vocalizations considered part of the sensorimotor task being completed, such as knocking blocks down.

The next and last stage is the use of single words in a consistent referential sense. Thus, referential language in very young children is seen as a gradual transition from gestures to vocalizations used in conjunction with sensorimotor frames, to genuine symbolic speech used initially within declarative and imperative performative frames.

In the preverbal stage, presupposition seems to be related to the quality of information. Young children tend to express that aspect of a proposition that seems most informative to them, informative in the sense of new or novel. Bates (1976b) argues that these relationships emerge from proto-declarative pointing activities that children engage in as they become aware of new objects in the environment. As the child begins to develop referential speech, he will first encode new or novel information moving at the two-word stage and beyond to topic-comment utterances.

Bates (1976b) shows early language development emerging from cognitive prerequisites, specifically from the notions of agency and instrument, from awareness of new means to attain old goals, and from internalization of action schemas to be re-represented in symbolic form. These features evolve into performatives, propositions (reference), and presuppositions, respectively, the three language aspects essential to the establishment of conversation and discourse.

Single-Word Space

From the preverbal stage the child moves into a period of speaking almost entirely in single words. Both comprehension and production of language are of interest during this stage.

Comprehension At Single-Word Stage   Studies of children's comprehension during the single-word stage of language development are few in number; the most comprehensive study was reported by Huttenlocher (1974). She devised procedures that she felt assessed comprehension, but minimized the influence of contextual cuing. Words for which comprehension could be confirmed were shown to be understood rather precisely by very young children. This observation on the precise definition of words seems somewhat contradictory to some reports about children in the one-word stage. Many instances of overgeneralized use of words are offered as typical of young children rather than narrow application of word meanings (Bowerman, 1976; Clark, 1973a,b,c).

In Huttenlocher's study, early meaning acquisition tended to focus on proper nouns, although some common nouns attained this status, such as animal names, word class representatives, and actions. Noun understanding always outdistanced action word understanding. This response pattern in children relative to word meaning acquisition tended to support the notion that young children have fairly distinct, albeit generalized, semantic fields. Her subjects seemed to organize their words into units that were clustered along definite categorical lines. For instance the words *bear* and *dog* were treated similarly, whereas *dog* and *bottle* were not, indicating that the first two words were members of a related semantic field but the latter two words were not. Words do not seem to be stored in the young child's memory in a haphazard manner. Confusions that did occur in subjects' comprehension were typically within, rather than between, domains of objects.

The semantic fields seem to parallel those found in adults, but the basis upon which such categories are organized do not seem to be the same as for adults. For example children are aware of semantic notions such as recipient, possessor, and patient, but not their accompanying aspects in the stimulus sentence. Some semantic aspects of connected language generally seem to be comprehended before any of the syntactic components.

From these results, Huttenlocher (1974) concluded that children in the single-word stage do not possess the degree of language understanding often attributed to them. Instead she was forced to conclude that understanding at 12 to 15 months of age heavily depends on contextual cuing rather than on verbal comprehension. Furthermore, she concluded that young children's language productions are limited by their inability to retrieve the correct spoken form, but they may still exhibit precise understanding of more words than they can say. This accounts for the overgeneralization of word use found by Bowerman (1976) and Clark (1973a,b,c). This study of Huttenlocher, as well as the work of Bates (1976b), suggest that the earliest understandings of language are semantic in nature, with precise or narrow delineation of knowledge being the rule rather than the exception.

Production At Single-Word Stage   Production studies of children at the single-word level, as well as at more advanced levels, generally consist of descriptions of a language corpus from one or more children, with extrapolation from these data to the probable cognitive understandings motivating their production.

From the preverbal section of this chapter we learned that children develop performative frames from sensorimotor bases. These frames begin as gestures that eventually include vocalizations as part of the performative routine. Eventually these vocalizations become real words that serve important functions within the performative. The words fitted into the proto-declarative frame act as labels for *indicative* objects, objects being designated for attention by the child. Words for *volitional* objects, objects desired by the child, serve as the semantic bases for words used in the proto-imperative frame. To have true referential function, however, words must become separated from performative routines and must show referential application by themselves within a variety of communication situations, rather than serving merely to designate or request objects.

Bloom (1973) argues that the earliest spontaneous word productions of young children are function words that express the concepts of existence, nonexistence, and recurrence. She suggests that these words proceed out of the development of the figurative knowledges outlined in the section on Piagetian theory: the concepts of object constancy, coordinated space, causality, and time. As children interact with their environments, they come to understand that objects remain constant regardless of changes in form or removal from the situation; that objects are ordered within the environment in relation to each other; that some objects can effect change on other objects; and that these processes of change occur as a function of movement through space or time. As part of linguistic and cognitive interactions, the child begins to learn and express notions of existence, nonexistence, and recurrence of objects, locations, and actions. Use of words such as *there, up, uh-oh, no, away, gone, stop,* and *more* are characteristic of this development.

Bloom (1973) observed that function words not only come early in the single-word stage, but that such words tended to be the most stable of the child's productions over time. This is a sensible finding if one considers that the meaning of function words is generally the same across a variety of situations and objects. As a consequence, function words do not have a limited life span. They persist through the entire single-word stage and are used throughout the two-word stage quite frequently.

After the appearance of functional words, young children tend to express immediate aspects of the causality-locative relationship (Bloom,

1973; Bowerman, 1976; D. Edwards, 1973; Greenfield and Smith, 1976; Wells, 1974). As they encounter situations they wish to talk about, children tend to describe various aspects of these situations. Initially focus is on the agent; the action or state of the agent; the object of the action; the action or state of the object; and the recipient of the action or object. Greenfield and Smith (1976) have suggested that action and object encoding appear much earlier than agent encoding during the development of the causality-locative components. Early actions that are verbalized by the child are typically performed by the child himself, so that naming of the agent would be a conversationally and cognitively redundant act for the child. Verbs describing the actions of others occur much later than verbs describing the child's own actions, an observation consistent with the emergence of agent encodings in single-word utterances.

Unlike function words, according to Bloom (1973), words employed to express causative-locative aspects tend to have a limited life span in the spontaneous productions of children. This phenomenon is also sensible if one recognizes that causative-locative words have limited potential for reference, in sharp contrast to function words. Thus it is not particularly surprising to find such lexical items appearing in a corpus for a limited time and then disappearing, only to reappear in later language developmental stages. This phenomenon has particularly interesting implications for deaf children, implications that are reconsidered in a later chapter.

It should be stressed that single-word utterances are probably not based on syntactic knowledge, but rather they are verbal expressions of conceptual understandings. Children know about objects and how they relate as a result of figurative knowledge derived from earlier sensorimotor stages, so it is not surprising when such knowledge is expressed early in the language development process. It should be acknowledged that, although instances of indicative (verbal declarative pointing) and volitional (verbal request pointing) verbalizations can be observed during the single-word stage, most utterances at this stage express sensorimotor figurative concepts (Greenfield and Smith, 1976).

Nelson (1973), in a study of the first 50 words, enumerated the semantic categories of these words and found that they were quite restricted, confined primarily to labels of objects and persons that had particular meaning in the child's immediate environment. Her content words included instances of the following categories: food, body parts, clothing, animals, household items, vehicles, instruments, and people. These categories are compatible with early expressions of causality-locative relationships, thus confirming indirectly the findings outlined previously, even though Nelson did not concern herself with the issue of the functions served by the words she recorded.

Immediately after acquisition and use of elementary notions relating to the causality-locative relationship, the acquisition of more remote concepts can be observed. Greenfield and Smith (1976) found that possessor, attribution, and stative-location usage tended to be late developing semantic notions in the single-word stage. In addition, expressions of internal experience (experiencers) have also been found to emerge late during this stage of language development (Leonard, 1976).

The single-word stage can be seen as the period extending from development of basic concepts such as existence, non-existence, and recurrence through expression of notions of the causality-locative relationship, and ending with more sophisticated usage, including experiencer, possessor, and stative-locations. Leonard (1976), in a comprehensive study of the development patterns of several children during the entire single-word stage, confirmed that this pattern of development was generally consistent from child to child.

Although children encode basic notions about reality, it also seems that children are focusing on pragmatic issues, particularly the given-new contract. According to Greenfield and Smith (1976), young children encode through their single word the aspect of the environment that contains the greatest level of uncertainty from their perspective. When an object or patient in the child's possession undergoes a change of state, it would be considered given information. Thus, from the child's point of view, only the new action-state needs to be articulated, that aspect of the situation that is the most uncertain. If the child is not holding an object, he will probably use the object word to indicate the most uncertain aspect of the situation for him. If the child continues to talk about the situation, he will probably state the second most uncertain aspect of the situation next, in this case the action-state change. The previously described aspect, the object, is now given information and need not be referred to again. The primary exception to this strategy occurs when an adult asks about the object by presupposing the action-state, which makes that action-state the given information while the object becomes the new information.

Maternal-Child Interaction Styles Up to this point the focus has been on the development of basic semantic categories in the single-word stage. Obviously, from within the general semantic categories, children are selecting specific words to express specific concepts, as are adults. What do we know about these lexical items and their use in presenting conceptual notions about the world, such as objects and locations?

Nelson (1973), as indicated previously, found that the first 50 words could be divided into several categories. She further suggested that these categories could be sorted based on whether the child specialized in so-called "referential" or "expressive" learning. Referential learners seemed interested in learning about things, which caused them to use more object words, leading to a large single-word vocabulary before they proceeded to combine words. Expressive learners, on the other hand, seemed more interested in themselves and other people, which caused them to learn more non-object words, thus facilitating the operation of putting words together at a much earlier age than for referential learners. The rate of language development was apparently influenced by each child's interests, as well as the functions that each chose to elaborate.

There are at least two other factors that influence the rate of language development according to Nelson (1973). The first is maternal communication focus. Maternal communication focus can also be classified as expressive (socially oriented) or referential (object oriented). In such a case it is conceivable that a child's approach to language usage will not match his mother's language usage preferences. When matches in style or focus occur, language growth seems likely to be facilitated; when mismatches occur, language growth might be necessarily slowed until the child shifts his style to match that of his mother, the reverse of which almost never happens.

The other factor that is supposed to influence language development rate is the willingness of the mother to accept language from her child. Rejection of children's communication attempts can deter language growth. Those instances of a language usage match between mother and child that entail a mother who is also accepting of her child's utterances showed language growth rates to be the quickest and showed the most complete end product. All other possible combinations would slow language growth to some degree, with a communication mismatch coupled with rejection being the most destructive to the rate of language acquisition.

Lexicon Development Development of the reference function, development of a word as a symbol, has been the focus of considerable attention. Disagreement about the conceptual bases of symbolic reference continues. Some researchers (Nelson, 1974) argue that children first learn words because of their functionality, whereas others (Anglin, 1977; Bowerman, 1976; Clark, 1973a,b,c, 1974) contend that words are learned to express perceptual differences noted among objects. It is unclear if either position is correct or if a middle ground incorporating aspects of both positions would be closer to the truth. There is at least one situation where perceptual saliency seems more important than function—in the phenomenon of overgeneralization (Clark, 1973a,b,c).

The classic example of expressive overgeneralization in young language learners is that of the 18-month-old who calls every man he sees *Daddy*. In this case classification based on size, voice pitch, and hairness are probably at work to yield this overgeneralization. Dimensions of size, shape, movement, texture, and taste do seem to be critical classification dimensions for young children. One could speculate that these are the visual/tactual dimensions that children might utilize in the sensorimotor stage when internalizing the notion of object constancy.

Bowerman (1976) reported not only overgeneralization, but underextension. In the latter instance children seem to fixate on a characteristic or set of characteristics that is relevant only to a sub-set of the object class, or perhaps even unique to a single instance of that class. In this instance a word is used only for a limited set of objects rather than for all objects that adults would classify as sharing a label. Underextension is often difficult to identify because the child's use of a word will be correct on the surface, but can be shown to be inaccurate if other members of the class in question are examined: the class name will not be extended to all the correct instances of that class. Underextension, like overgeneralization, seems more related to perceptual rather than to functional characteristics of objects.

In summary, the child's task during the single-word stage is to master basic components of language, such as semantic categories, that will lead to the development of propositions. Lexical items that eventually can be used in performative and propositional frames are developed as well. Of course, simply assigning case grammar designations to young children's utterances does not mean that such adult definitions are actually possessed by children; rather, the child's categories should be thought of as generalized semantic understandings that eventually become converted into the grammar-oriented cases used to establish formal propositions. All the foregoing arguments are based on the premise that the single-word stage is semantically, not syntactically, bound.

Two-Word Stage

The child moves next to a stage in which two-word utterances, or two words framed in a cohesive proposition unit, begin to appear. The transition from the single- to the two-word stage does not occur fully blown, without additional learning on the child's part.

Successive Utterances It has been observed by some researchers (Bloom, 1973; Greenfield and Smith, 1976) that there is a period of linguistic activity intermediate to the two-word stage in which the child strings words together that do not yet function as cohesive units; the child produces consecutive words that articulate related aspects of an event, but are best called successive utterances, or utterances in which each word is produced with accompanying downward intonational contour. Successive utterances continue to encode the same aspects of the environment critical to the causality-location relationship seen in the single-word stage, such as action, agent, and patient, suggesting a simple transition to a new level of language performance. However, successive utterances do not follow Standard English word order as later utterances do, which gives credence to the assertion that successive utterances, like single words, are semantically rather than syntactically motivated.

Successive utterances do show that the child is becoming more aware of the given-new information dichotomy, because the least certain aspect of the event (new information) usually occurs first in a successive string, followed by articulation of other aspects that apparently are more certain or obvious to the child (Greenfield and Smith, 1976).

Presyntactic Devices Some researchers (Bloom, 1973; Dore et al., 1976; Leonard, 1975c) have also identified what seem to be grammatical or presyntactic devices in use during the transition to two-word combinations. Five examples of presyntactic or dummy elements have been reported. They may be single, phonetically unstable units preceding a conventional word; a nonsense syllable preceding any genuine lexical item; reduplicated productions consisting of a single word produced successively within one intonational envelope; empty form productions composed of phonetically stable units in conjunction with conventional words, such as Bloom's (1973) report of the /wide/ phenomenon; or rote memorization of a conventional two-word combination, the items of which do not occur in other combinations, although each member may occur alone. Presyntactic devices seem to be employed by the child to show that he is at work on syntactic stringing before he has the necessary conceptual-semantic bases to accomplish such stringing with real lexical items.

From the successive utterance stage, children normally begin to join two words together in functionally meaningful ways. The most obvious difference between two-word combinations and successive utterances is that the former contain no hesitations or downward intonation contour on each word (Bloom, 1973). The two words are to be interpreted now as a single unit, a most important step forward in the development of connected language.

Semantic Development at Two-Word Stage The word combinations encode the same semantic information that could be identified in the single word stage (Bloom, 1973). Indeed, it is argued that children's two-word formulations contain only those semantic notions expressed previously in the single-word or successive utterance stages (Greenfield and Smith, 1976). In other words, children in this stage can express old or previously mastered knowledge while attempting to gain mastery of new forms.

Two-word combinations can be described as expressing either functional (linear) relationships or grammatical (hierarchal) relationships (Bloom, 1973; Bloom and Lahey, 1978; Brown, 1973; Leonard, 1976). Functional relationships express the semantic notions of existence, non-existence, and recurrence, whereas so-called grammatical relationships tend to express variations on the agent-action-patient-location construction. Meanings expressed through functional combinations tend to be the sum of the individual meanings of each word, whereas grammatical combinations tend to include some relational concept or meaning in addition to the specific meanings of the words employed. These extra meanings generally describe relationships that exist between actors, actions, objects, and locations. For example, in the functional combination *no ball,* the meaning is non-existence (*no*) plus *ball,* whereas in the grammatical combination *hit ball,* the overriding relational concept of some action on some object is expressed, in this case *hit* (the action upon) and *ball* (the object), a meaning that cannot be extracted from the dictionary meanings of *hit* and *ball* alone. Both functional and grammatical relationships can be observed in the oral language productions of children at the two-word stage. If children develop normally, grammatical relationships become the dominant force in the child's language by the end of the two-word stage.

Within the refinement of grammatical and functional relationships, children tend to emphasize either a nominal or pronominal strategy (Bloom, Lightbown, and Hood, 1975). Children who favor use of pronominals tend to use what seem to be functional relation frames to code action, location, and possessor relations. For instance they may use the pronouns *I* and *me* as agent or mover, *it, this one,* or *that* as affected-object, *my* as possessor, and *here* and *there* as location, resulting in utterances such as *play it, I do, up there, my truck,* which consist of different verb or noun forms with a small number of constant prenominal forms, such as *it, my* or *there.* Pronominally inclined children are able to talk about a great variety of objects within action and location relationships, but they do not depend greatly upon lexical variety when making reference to different objects or locations. Pronominal children apparently know the names of many objects and persons, although they tend to use these labels only in single-word utterances or in functional relations, such as expressions of nonexistence or recurrence.

Nominal usage, the alternative strategy to a pronominal usage, stresses use of nominal forms for agent, affected object, location, and possessor instead of the constant pronominal form, resulting in utterances such as *read book, touch milk, sit on piano, sheep ear.*

A major shift in coding and integration of pronominal and nominal reference occurs when mean length of utterances passes 2.0 morphemes. As mean length of utterance (MLU) approaches 2.5 morphemes, the variation among children in the choice of reference is greatly reduced. Nominal children have learned a primitive system of pronominal substitution for nominal categories, and pronominal children are learning to use categories of nominal forms to code action, location, and possession. By 2.5 morphemes, children seem to conform to a common rule: affected object must always be expressed in the nominal form and agent described in the pronominal form. Such behavior is particularly interesting because it demonstrates that children may vary considerably in their attempt to master the language system, but that they eventually arrive at comparable performance at critical stages of change in language development.

Investigations of the order of acquisition of both types of relational combinations in children have occurred. Bloom, Lightbown, and Hood (1975), for example, found that the development of functional relations of existence, non-existence, and recurrence preceded the development of verb relations. When verb relations did appear, knowledge of action events (action and location-action relationships) were expressed before knowledge of state events (location-stative, state-process, and notice relationships). Two of their four subjects expressed action statements before location-action statements. Other categories observed after the emergence of the basic verb relation, which tended to include possession and attribution statements, were specification of instrument, recipient, wh-questions, and infinitival forms, called matrix verbs.

Syntactic Development at the Two-Word Stage   A second issue of interest regarding children at the two-word stage concerns the question of whether two-word utterances can be taken to reflect any comprehension of adult syntactic conventions such as subject and predicate. Based on the observation that children in their study had developed fairly stable word order behavior, Bloom, Lightbown, and Hood (1975) concluded that children have learned superordinate categories such as sentence-subject, consisting of agents, movers, and possessors; predicate-object, consisting of affected objects, locative-actions, and possession; and predicate-complements, consisting of locative-states. Bowerman (1975) takes exception to this position, insisting that observation of word order alone is not sufficient to credit a young child with knowledge of grammatical categories.

Braine (1976) insists on a third point of view, namely, that children learn a number of positional or word-order formulas through which they map components of meaning into positions in the surface structure. Each formula is seen to account for the expression of a specific narrow range of conceptual relations. However, these formulas are not supposed by Braine to indicate any syntactic understanding beyond positional rules. Many two-word combinations are found to violate standard word orders. Braine accounts for such exceptions by introducing the concept of groping patterns, or those positional formulas in which the components may seem to be unordered. The lack of order is presumably a result of the child's groping for patterns to express meaning before he has learned a rule for appropriate word order arrangement to assist in consistent expression of meaning.

Pragmatically oriented theorists (Bates, 1976b; Greenfield and Smith, 1976) have suggested yet another notion concerning the uses of word order by young children that explains, in part, the variation from standard order frequently noted. It is argued that children establish a word-order rule based on the given-new contract, namely, the first word of the combination is the comment and the second word is the topic, expressed as verb-argument, rather than the standard English order of argument-verb unit. Young children have also been noted to use contrastive stress patterns to indicate differences between comment and topic within their two-word productions.

Clearly there is significant disagreement concerning the possible presence of syntactic knowledge at the two-word stage. Occurrences of standard word order as well as exceptions to standard arrangement have been reported. A satisfactory explanation of the syntactic knowledge of children at the two-word stage is still being developed.

Communication Development at the Two-Word Stage In the preverbal and single-word stages of language development, children, regardless of sex and family socioeconomic status, show similar types of communication patterns. Beginning at the two-word stage, however, differences in pragmatic expression and understanding have been observed that are apparently related to variables such as the child's sex (Lewis and Cherry, 1977). For instance the number of questions and directives used by mothers is highly correlated with proximity of the child. Proximity is dictated in middle-class English speaking homes by the sex of the child. Mothers tends to encourage their female children to stay close to them, which promotes the adult's use of questioning types of behaviors; male children are encouraged to be independent, which prompts the need for greater use of directives with boys.

In summary, the two-word stage can be seen as a continuation from the single-word stage. It is during the two-word stage that the child begins to combine the semantic notions developed during the single-word stage into meaningful relations. He proceeds from simple semantic concepts such as functional relations to more complex concepts embodied by so-called grammatical relations. Whether use of two-word combinations reflects genuine syntactic understanding is still subject to considerable debate.

Refinement and Complex Sentence
Development—Three Words and Beyond

As witnessed in the transition from the single-word to the two-word stage, children employ some interesting syntactic devices in the transition from the two- to three-word stage also (Dore et al., 1976; Menyuk, 1969). When producing two-word combinations, children will often insert a schwa-type vowel between the two words in a position where additional nodes might be expected to develop next, such as determiners or prepositions.

In describing the three-word stage, two important operations should be highlighted (Brown, 1973). First, children exhibit development of an embedding process that involves the insertion of a functional relationship into a grammatical relationship. For instance the child might insert the functional relation *no ball* into the grammatical relation *hit ball,* yielding the three-word combination *hit no ball.*

The second operation is one of conjoining, in which two grammatical relations that share a common term are merged with reduction of the overlapping term. The child in the two-word stage may say both *Bobby hit* and *hit ball.* These utterances are conjoined in the three-word stage into the combination *Bobby hit ball,* with the redundant *hit* being reduced. The linguistic operations of embedding and conjoining can be viewed as a step toward the development of propositions in which predicate-argument relations are established through conjoining, and in which two propositions are merged through embedding.

Children who have passed through the two-word stage may begin to adhere rigidly to noun-verb-noun word order in their comprehension of utterances, even when it seems inappropriate, as in passive-like constructions (deVilliers and deVilliers, 1972). This rigidity in comprehension is interpreted by researchers as the overlearning of a syntactic rule that had not been used with great certainty during the two-word stage. Other researchers (Sinclair, 1973; Sinclair and Bronckert, 1972) have found that when children of increasing linguistic sophistication are presented with strings of words of which differing interpretations are possible, they begin by interpreting the strings as if the first noun was the subject. Then children change to interpret the first noun as the object, and finally, they are seen to adhere to a rigid subject-verb-predicate interpretation, in spite of contrary semantic expressions in some instances, such as *box opened boy*. These research findings conform with recent observations in pragmatics that children establish topic-comment relations, which results in adherence to rigid word-order patterns. The intermediate stage of first noun as object identification mentioned previously could be viewed as recognition by the child of the basic nodes within the proposition predicate, namely, verb and object, a possible precursor to real word order comprehension. Bates (1976b) cites the evolution of the pronominal system as the only semantic/syntactic precursor to the development of word order. Development of pronominal usage in her view is the child's recognition that the basic nodes within the proposition need not be coded nominally to establish their semantic reference.

Refinement Processes   As the child moves into and beyond the three-word stage, he begins to work on both linguistic refinement and linguistic complexity. There is a tendency for refinements to appear at earlier ages than operations that increase complexity levels. Refinements are defined as linguistic units that semantically explicate basic linguistic relations. The most comprehensive study of the dimensions involved in refinement in normal children was conducted by Brown (1973), who investigated the acquisition of modulations of various morphophonemic endings in young children. Table 5 contains a listing of the order of modulation development suggested by Brown as taken from his and other research findings (Brown and Fraser, 1963; Cazden, 1968; deVilliers and deVilliers, 1973a,b; Menyuk, 1963a,b, 1964a,b; Miller and Ervin, 1964). A review of this table reveals several trends. Initially semantic complexity seems to take precedence over syntactic complexity, but once some initial sorting has taken place, syntactic complexity determines acquisition rate. For instance present progressive, designated in English by /-ing/, is a straightforward, semantically based acquisition that codes action occurring in the here and now. It is a simple form to use syntactically because it involves only the application or addition of /-ing/ to the end of a verb. In contrast, the copula, as it appears in predicate nominative, adjective, or adverbial sentences, has little semantic value because the transitivity of the sentence is carried by the second noun, adjective, or adverb of the sentence. In other words, the copula is essentially a place holder or linguistic convention inserted into the verb node of the predicate in order to structurally complete the sentence. The copula is quite complex to master syntactically because its application requires knowledge of number, person, and tense constraints. Articles also involve a variety of syntactic distinctions, but their semantic contribution to a sentence is potentially much greater than the copula, so it is not surprising to find articles mastery preceding the copula, but occurring after development of the progressive form.

Imitation   Children seem to accomplish the goal of modulation acquisition by establishing general rules governing the application of these language forms. Traditional psychological theory has viewed language acquisition, particularly the syntactic aspects, as the result of direct imitation by the child of adults. It is clear, however, that direct imitation is not sufficient to explain the rapid and fluent acquisition of complex language (Berko-Gleason, 1967; Menyuk, 1971). Instead the child seems to take an active role in the process, in part by deducing the regularities from samples of language provided to him by others, and by formulating hypotheses about the application of a rule (Berko, 1958; Brown and Bellugi, 1964; Menyuk, 1971). As the child tests his hypotheses, his performance will match or mismatch the adult model, which aids the child in revising his hunches. In the quest for hypotheses, certain stages in modulation acquisition have been noted that detail children's progress toward syntactic mastery (Cazden, 1968). Children begin by using some form of the modulation correctly, but in a sporadic fashion. Next they overgeneralize the appropriate and most common form to all situations, even if their application is incorrect. This stage is

Table 5.   Examples of and the developmental sequence for the 14 grammatical morphemes identified by Brown (1973)[a]

Linguistic unit	Example
Present progressive	Johnny go*ing*.
In-on	put *in* box; put *on* table
Plural	some boy*s*
Past irregular	he w*ent*
Possessive	Johnny*'s* book
Uncontractible copula	Johnny *was* sick
Articles	See *the* dog.
Past regular	He jump*ed*.
Third person regular	He jump*s*.
Third person irregular	He *has* eyes.
Uncontractible auxiliary	The boys *are* going.
Contractible copula	He*'s* running.
Contractible auxiliary	He*'s* nice.

[a] Based on Brown, R. A First Language. Harvard University Press, Cambridge, Ma., 1973.

generally followed by the final situation, in which the child sorts out the exceptions to the most common form and begins to employ the exceptions correctly. As suggested previously, past tense offers a good example of these stages. The child begins to apply the most common modulation /-ed/ to a few verbs appropriately. Then the child applies the /-ed/ form in all past tense situations, including irregular verb forms. After this, the child learns the exceptions to the /-ed/ form or the irregular verb forms, and begins to use all forms correctly. From this example it can be seen that the process of rule learning often results in overgeneralizations. The child's expression of such rules are quite resistive to change or modification by adults, particularly in a direct imitation format (Berko-Gleason, 1967).

Brown (1973) also examined the frequency with which certain forms were used with children to determine whether the amount of exposure would affect the rate and order of acquisition of the modulations summarized in Table 5. He found little correspondence between the amount of exposure and the order of development of forms, which seems to indicate that the semantic and syntactic complexity of a linguistic principle can do more to determine its acquisition than the amount of exposure to that principle. This finding gives additional support to the notion that direct imitation is not the primary factor in acquisition of more complex modulation forms.

Certainly it has been observed by many researchers (Bloom, Hood, and Lightbown, 1974; Ervin-Tripp, 1964) that children do imitate, but imitation of forms that are not within the linguistic repertoire of the child seldom occur spontaneously, nor does imitation occur with forms that are firmly established in the language of the child. Instead imitation has been observed primarily in the acquisition of new vocabulary; children tend to imitate new words, not new syntactic constructions. Imitation can be seen to have a role in practice of forms that are emerging in a child's language, but it does not seem to play a role in use of forms that are well established. Exactly how imitation aids in this learning process is still uncertain, because there are children who do not imitate extensively in spite of the fact that they have been studied during periods of rapid language learning (Bloom, Hood, and Lightbown, 1974).

Moerk (1977) studied imitative behavior in two young children as they interacted with their baby-sitter. His findings confirmed the report of Bloom, Hood, and Lightbown (1974) with regard to lexical imitation and the use of imitation to master new vocabulary items. In addition to lexical imitation, Moerk observed that certain constituent rules were also subject to imitative learning, namely, morphophonemic organization, an issue not addressed by the Bloom, Hood, and Lightbown (1974) report.

This type of imitation occurred only after a sentence frame appeared within the spontaneous productions of the child. The adult would then replace a particular morphophonemic construction within the child's utterance, prompting the child to imitate her substitution. This was termed a replacement strategy. Because such exchanges occurred within the same interactive sequence, Moerk's descriptions were somewhat different from those of Bloom, Hood, and Lightbown (1974), who tended to take the imitative responses out of context to analyze them.

Modality Refinement   While children are working on modulation elaborations, they are also learning about modality nodes, specifically, negation, question, and imperative forms. The syntactic development of these forms occurs in stages that are invariant across children (Klima and Bellugi, 1966; Menyuk, 1971). In each case the child first selects a single form of the modality and then affixes it in front of or in back of the word combination, resulting in utterances such as *no me go* or *want car no*. Next the child tends to embed the modality marker in the middle of the combination, which in effect serves as the syntactic frame with which the child can work in learning the selectional restrictions related to the modality. In these ways the child gradually approximates the adult syntactic form.

The rate of acquisition of modalities seems strongly related to semantic issues as well. For instance negation can encode three semantic intents: non-existence, rejection, and denial (Bloom, 1970). Non-existence refers to the proposition that an action, attribute, or object does not exist, either permanently or temporarily; rejection refers to the proposition that a person refuses to participate in an ongoing activity; and denial refers to the proposition that a person can recognize the reality of an object within his immediate environment, but denies some statement made about it. Although the syntax of non-existence and denial propositions is quite similar, namely, the insertion of *not* into the modality node, non-existence appears, and is developed by children, before denial. Not only does the expression of non-existence appear first in children's language, it also appears in its completed form first. This developmental trend is attributed to the idea that non-existence is a less complex semantic structure than denial or rejection. The same trend is said to hold for the acquisition of wh-question forms, because so-called semantically simpler forms such as *what* and *where* develop before more complex forms such as *who, why, how,* and *when* (Ervin-Tripp, 1970).

Refinement of Communication Competence   Refinement of language involves not only the acquisition and development of more sophisticated semantic and syntactic forms, but acquisition of conversational skills as well, such as knowledge of how to enter into dialogue with others. This particular ability involves the acquisition of a variety of cues that inform a speaker that you have understood what has been previously said and are responding to those comments. As with most aspects of language development, children seem to pass through several stages in mastery of conversational skills, each of which evidences greater sophistication both syntactically and socially than the previous ones (Bates, 1976b).

The first stage is characterized by the child's use of numerous directives—the child makes direct requests of the listener rather than employing more polite forms. During this stage the child uses few if any personal pronouns or connectives such as *therefore,* preferring demonstrative pronouns (this, that) and spatial locatives instead. The initial absence of personal pronouns and connectors is noteworthy, because these are devices that are used to indicate to others that one has been paying attention. Connectors are used to indicate that one expects to take a turn in the conversation, or that it is not time for another participant in the conversation to interrupt. Personal pronoun usage signals to others that the new information contained within the conversation has been presented and is now deemed as old information. If the new information is not understood, a speaker continues to use the nominal form until he is sure that his intentions are clear, at which time pronoun representation can be initiated.

The next stage of dialogue competence that seems to correspond with the initial acquisition of complex sentences is characterized by tense and time differentiations, along with the acquisition of additive connectors such as *and* and *and then.* Mastery of these forms aids considerably in the establishment of turn-taking and discourse exchange.

The last stage corresponding to the acquisition of relative, adverbial clauses and other embedded sentence forms, such as indirect discourse, includes the use of dimensional time as well as place adverbials, establishment of the pronoun system, and the use of conditional terms such as *if, because,* and other subordinate constructions, including *if not.* By this last stage, dialogues may be quite mature, especially because by now children have usually mastered most polite forms or indirect speech acts.

Bloom, Rocissano, and Hood (1976) studied discourse competency in children by exploring adult-child interchanges. Child utterances were identified in this study as adjacent (immediately preceded by an adult utterance) and as nonadjacent (not immediately preceded by an adult utterance). Adjacent utterances were either contingent (shared the same topic and added new information relative to the topic of the prior utterance) or noncontingent (did not share the same topic) in nature.

From the beginning adjacent speech was greater than nonadjacent speech. Contingent speech increased over time. In particular, linguistically contingent speech, speech that expanded the verb relation of the prior adult utterance with added or replaced constituents within a clause, showed the greatest developmental increase. Linguistically contingent speech recurred most often after questions as compared to non-question forms. These results would seem to demonstrate that over time children develop greater facility in maintaining and contributing to conversations with adults.

The foregoing discussion is meant to emphasize that while semantic and syntactic development is occurring, understanding of language use, such as how conversations are conducted, is also developing. All these aspects of language development are interwoven in normally developing children. It is not always clear which comes first, pragmatic use understandings or syntactic/semantic understandings, if either. In fact, the simultaneous emergence of performance in both language forms and language use is the only reasonable definition of normal language development.

Development of Complex Sentence Operations   Complex sentence development may be entered simultaneously with or slightly after initiation of refinement of basic nodes within the deep structure. The child begins to develop complex operations such as coordination, relativization, and complementation.

The first appearance of complex sentence frames is usually signaled by the use of the coordinating conjunction *and* acting as a conjoiner of constructions of equal value, resulting in child sentences such as *He like apples and pears.*, or as a temporal conjoiner indicating the order of occurrence of events, to yield early sentences such as *He go movie and then go home.* (Brown, 1973; Limber, 1973; Menyuk, 1971). With the development of a coordinating conjunction sentence frame, the rapid appearance of infinitival, what, relative, and adverbial clauses occurs.

Limber (1973, 1976), in a series of investigations on the acquisition of complex sentence forms, found that complement constructions appeared early, particularly in those instances when the subject of the matrix sentence and the complement were the same. The coordinating conjunction *and* and the adverbial conjunction *when* also were observed early in complex sentence frame acquisition. Complement forms tended to be used with a restricted number of verbs, such as *want* and *like*. Sentences such as *I want go.* or *I like play.* are examples of early complement utterances. It was Limber's contention that these early forms are the syntactical frames into which the child can insert a whole sentence instead of just a single word. Limber's suggestion could be evidence that children may establish a node such as direct object, and then elaborate on that node by incorporating a sentence rather than just an expanded phrase. A second finding by Limber (1973) of interest was that most of the complex forms observed appeared in object position rather than subject position, which adheres to the general principle already mentioned, that one does not interrupt sentences when constructing main propositions. In a subsequent report, however, Limber (1976) suggested that object position elaboration may be more a function of the extensive pronominalization of the subject position, which makes elaboration of that node difficult. If this finding is accurate, it would seem that discourse demands may take precedence over development of syntactic/semantic frames in language acquisition.

A wide variety of other semantic and syntactic forms develop during later complex sentence refinement. A discussion of the acquisition of only three aspects—complements, relative clauses, and subordinate conjunctions—closes this chapter.

Complement Development   Complements may consist of subjects that are shared with the main sentence into which they have been inserted, or subjects that are different from the subject of the main proposition. In addition, complements may be cued with the infinitive marker *to* or with the indirect discourse question form *what*. Within most complement frames, the noun immediately preceding the embedded verb is the subject of the verb. This is not always the case, of course, as in the sentence *Mark promised Maria to go*. In this case, *Maria* is not the subject of *go*, but rather *Mark* is, an example of a violation of the minimal distance principle, stated above.

Complements that conform to the minimal distancing principle are acquired early, as would be expected (Limber, 1973). In those instances in which the subject of the embedded complement differs from the matrix sentence, the complement introducer (*to* or *what*) is often omitted by children, resulting in the production of sentences such as *She wanted he read the book*. When children are asked to interpret sentences that violate the minimal distance principle, they frequently persist in treating such sentences as if they adhered to this principle. This behavior persists through early adolescence and even beyond in many normal children and adults (C. Chomsky, 1969; Reed, 1977; Sanders, 1971).

Relativization Development   A second complex sentence frame, relativization, occurs when two propositions, such as *John is my friend* and *John lives on Maple Street,* are combined to yield the final sentence *John, who is my friend, lives on Maple Street.* The pragmatic use of relative clauses seems to be to assist in the establishment of the topics of discourse; the relative clause provides the information that allows the listener to determine what the topic of conversation is.

Limber (1973) found that children began to use relative clauses by attaching them to the object of main clauses. He recorded sentences such as *I want the ones you got,* but did not observe utterances such as *The ones you got are bigger,* which would be an example of medially interrupted relativization. The earliest clauses tended to be attached to empty nouns such as *kind, one,* or *thing,* but they were attached without any relative pronoun. Children merely juxtaposed the two clauses. Within a month or two they began to employ the relative pronoun *that,* attaching it to objects such as *ball, dog,* or *chair. Who* or *which* did not appear as relative pronouns until several months later, and only after their being used as wh-words in question forms.

Slobin and Welsh (1973) found that in one imitation task, their subject (Echo) had considerable difficulty handling medially placed relative clauses, as well as relative clauses that were not marked overtly. This particular child was having difficulty with relative clauses that interrupted the natural integrity of sentences and that were not overtly marked in the surface structure. Brown (1971) also found that unmarked relative clauses were more difficult for children to process than those that were overtly marked; Sheldon (1977) found that both adults and children had more difficulty processing medially placed rather than terminally placed relative clauses.

Subordinate Conjunction Development   Subordinate conjunctions, a third type of complex sentence frame, tend to join sentences in order to express relational concepts. For instance the use of *when* tends to indicate the concept of *the time at which something occurs; because* tends to mean *for the reason that something occurs.* Every subordinate conjunction carries its own semantic distinctions. Some conjunctions traditionally appear at the beginning of the sentence, such as *since,* whereas others appear medially in the sentence, such as *because.* Both *since* and *because* can carry the same semantic meaning, so the question becomes which one would be selected for use in a particular sentence. The selection seems to be related to the informational organization of the sentence. If the given information serves as the main clause, then *because* is used. If, on the other hand, the given information is contained in the dependent clause, then *since* is selected. Use of subordinate conjunctions is related to the semantic intent and to the informational organization of the sentence.

Examination of children's use and mastery of subordinate conjunctions reveal that there is a developmental sequence that could be deemed semantically and organizationally based (Clark, 1970, 1971, 1973a,b,c; H. Johnson, 1975). The first adverbial clauses children use are consistently attached to the end of the main clause. The most frequently used conjunctions are *when, if,* and *'cuz* (because). Only a few children have been reported to use *before, after,* and *until* during the early stages of adverbial conjunction acquisition. Even though children occasionally use the early forms in first position within sentences, the main-clause first principle takes precedence over order of mention, which would dictate initial position use in some communication situations. Before using adverbial clauses, children describe events in their order of occurrence with a separate sentence for each event, or even a series of clauses joined by *and* or *and then.* This reliance on order of mention gives way to the main-clause first principle with each new conjunction acquired. Later, children start to use adverbial clauses in first position as well, and thus regain the option of using an order of mention that coincides with the other occurrence. This pattern of acquisition also occurs in comprehension tasks that employ acting out techniques.

SUMMARY

Language development in children involves acquisition of the comprehension and use of three aspects: syntax, semantics, and pragmatics. Language development is predictable across children, and can be described with reference to each of the aforementioned aspects of language behavior. Language development is intertwined with social and cognitive development. Language acquisition commences with the moment of birth and continues throughout childhood and adolescence, if not beyond.

This chapter has been a modest presentation of contemporary research on early child language development. The concepts expressed here are subject to continuing revision and modification. The appearance of new research information on the linguistic capabilities of young children is occurring at an astonishing rate, which is a particularly encouraging and exciting development for children with handicaps. The reader is advised that monitoring of the child language literature is a requirement for any serious student of language intervention with children who demonstrate language learning problems, particularly those with significant early onset of hearing impairment.

CHAPTER 4

LANGUAGE AND DEAFNESS

CONTENTS

The development of fluent language performance in deaf children has long been a central concern in education of the hearing impaired. This is attested to by the innumerable articles that have appeared over the years pleading for improvement in the language instruction of hearing-impaired children or outlining strategies for enhancing the language development process in deaf children. It is unfortunately true that despite 150 years or more of concern, quality research that specifies in detail the nature of linguistic problems associated with childhood deafness is still lacking.

This chapter reviews research on the language performance of hearing-impaired children—a review that was difficult to organize because the literature on language acquisition and performance cannot be neatly tied to any one communication mode in deaf persons. Because of the diverse opinions about communication held by educators and others interested in deafness, hearing-impaired children are often presented simultaneously with a variety of linguistic acquisition modalities, many of which are not well understood in terms of their linguistic features. Among the various systems through which deaf children can be expected to be taught a first language, one can include oral language, gesture language, signed and/or fingerspelled language, read, and written language. Although some might argue that language is language, so that the types of linguistic structures and processes that children learn in one system are transferable to any other system, such an assumption is unwarranted, especially when the nature of spoken, manual, and printed language systems are compared. Spoken language has been discussed in Chapter 2. Reading is considered in Chapter 7. Sign language is not reviewed extensively because there are many fine volumes on that subject now available, especially in this *Perspectives in Audiology* series (Friedman, 1977; Schlesinger and Namur, 1978; Wilbur, 1978). The literature on the acquisition of sign language is considered, however, to assist the reader in understanding the language acquisition capabilities of deaf children.

A discussion of the relative merits of instructional methods in education of the deaf has also been omitted from this book. There are a variety of reports and critiques of reports that compare deaf children who are receiving oral educations or who have a social history of oral education with manually instructed deaf children. These usually employ standardized educational achievement scores (Balow and Brill, 1975; Denton, 1966; Hester, 1964; E. Johnson, 1948; Meadow, 1968; Montgomery, 1966; Nix, 1975; Owrid, 1975; Quigley, 1969; Schlesinger and Meadow, 1972; Stuckless and Birch, 1966; Vernon and Koh, 1969, 1970). Such studies are potentially meaningful in understanding success or lack of it in language intervention, but there are at least four methodological difficulties that make in depth discussion of these studies unproductive.

First, most comparative studies on communication methodology do find statistically significant differences between sets of formal test scores obtained on the two groups of children just mentioned. Unfortunately, examination of the real scores often reveals that regardless of group tendencies, all subjects are still significantly below the performance of normally hearing children of the same chronological ages, which only points out that most of our strategies for helping deaf children learn English are not generally successful. There are at least two studies that found noteworthy differences, but of a somewhat opposing nature. Brasel and Quigley (1977) showed children instructed in signed English to be achieving significantly above children instructed in American Sign Language or children instructed by so-called traditional oral methods. Luterman (1976) reported that children exposed to visually oriented oral instruction were educationally inferior to children instructed by an auditorily based oral approach. The fact of the matter, however, is that the linguistic and educational potential of most deaf children continues to be unrealized regardless of the communication mode employed.

A second difficulty with comparative studies on communication modes is that many purport to use children exposed to certain communication modes when in fact these modes are, at best, only employed in the classroom. For example many investigators draw their orally educated deaf children from state residential settings, where total communication, or even manual communication, usually predominates in every setting except the classroom. Such a definition of oral education is certainly not the atmosphere advocated by educators supportive of so-called oral educational methods.

Third, there are widely quoted comparative studies involving comparison of deaf children of deaf parents who communicate manually with deaf children of hearing parents who have been instructed to utilize oral modes with their children. The superiority of manual-trained children, which again is usually a statistical and not necessarily a real difference, is attributed to the communication mode employed. Such a generalization is simplistic, and evidences ignorance of the variety of influences, including social and linguistic interactions of family life, that can often have profound influences on children's learning. This fact is amply demonstrated by a study completed by Corson (1973), in which he compared achievements in deaf children of manual deaf parents, deaf children of oral deaf parents, and deaf children of normally hearing parents. The latter group actually consisted of two sets of subjects, one set of children being educated orally and one set from a total communication educational background. Results of an extensive test battery found the performance of all the subjects with deaf parents to be indistinguishable, and found that deaf children of hearing parents from the oral tradition were educationally superior to deaf children of hearing parents from a total communication tradition. One conclusion was that communication mode alone could not account for the observed differences; instead, factors such as parental acceptance of the child and of his deafness, which might be expected from parents who are themselves deaf, may be as important in shaping the performance of deaf children as education through a particular communication mode.

Last, although these comparative studies focused on aspects of language performance, they tended to employ quantitative measures rather than to describe children's performance on specific linguistic tasks. Consequently, quantitative differences may be reported that ignore learning styles or specific linguistic rule development that may occur as a result of training in specific communication modalities.

This and subsequent chapters concentrate on the acquisition and use of specific linguistic rules in hearing-impaired children from different communication mode backgrounds in an attempt to delineate the linguistic capacities and developmental trends in deaf children's learning of language, no matter which communication system is employed.

Unfortunately the linguistic heritage of most deaf persons continues to be denied them, perhaps because of educational bigotry, ineptitude in instruction, family handicaps, or factors within deaf individuals themselves that might prevent normal language acquisition even if they were not hearing handicapped.

The authors' position from the beginning of this book has been that the majority of deaf children have potential for normal language learning, which should include fluency in interpersonal communication, ability to read a range of printed materials, and ability to write a coherent sentence. This chapter is written in an attempt to understand what progress we are making toward that goal.

LANGUAGE ACQUISITION IN HEARING-IMPAIRED CHILDREN

The literature on language acquisition and development in hearing-impaired children deals either with early language acquisition, emphasizing the effects of preschool experience on hearing-impaired children, or the linguistic performance of older deaf children. There have been some studies in each of these two categories that consider personal expression, whether spoken or signed performance, and a sizable number that focus on written language, especially with older children. These studies on language performance are considered here both by age of subjects and by mode of performance in an effort to clarify if deaf children seem to show deficiencies of language competence, develop a unique *deaf* English, employ dialectical variations of English, or if some combination of these features apply to a majority of deaf children.

Studies of Younger Deaf Children

Studies of younger deaf children have tended to focus on three modalities: gesture systems, spoken language systems, and manual language systems. In addition there has been research in the areas of development of communication competence and the types and amount of interactions that occur between deaf children and their primary caregivers. This section is devoted to an exploration of each of these topics.

Gesture Language Acquisition   It is well documented that many hearing-impaired children develop a gesture system for communication if spoken language is prevented from developing normally. Myklebust (1954) mentions the phenomenon of an elaborated gesture system as one of the distinguishing characteristics of deaf children as opposed to other types of language-impaired children. Heider, Heider, and Stykes (1941), evaluating the functional uses of vocalizations in a group of preschool hearing-children, compared gestures and gestures plus vocalization intents. They found that gestures were used almost exclusively in questioning others, but that explanation interchanges were evenly divided between use of gesture only and gestures plus vocalization. Desire or wish statements were most often communicated through gesture plus vocal surface form realizations. Carr (1971) explored the communicative behavior of 3- and 4-year-old deaf children and observed that the most frequent communication behaviors were vocalizations usually produced in conjunction with gestures, whole body actions, facial movements, and looking behaviors. She noted that facility in the use of gestures increased with chronological age, and that there were increases in other communication modes as well. Grewel (1963) also commented that gesture systems seem to develop in advance of verbalizations in hearing-impaired children. In the beginning, many deaf children develop a restricted range of stylized gestures that become more and more elaborated. As children learn a formal language system, they presumably combine formal symbols into their own gesture systems.

Although the presence of gesture behavior was acknowledged, the forms and functions of deaf children's gesture systems were not detailed until recently. Studies now confirm that, as alluded to by Heider, Heider, and Stykes (1941), deaf children's gesture systems are generally highly organized and possibly rule governed to a point that such systems must be considered as functioning in a symbolic way for the user.

In a most interesting pair of studies, Feldman (1975) and Goldin-Meadow (1975) examined the gesture output of five congenitally hearing-impaired children ranging in age from 17 to 49 months. Feldman investigated the relationships between the forms and the meanings of individual gestures, and Goldin-Meadow studied the semantic relations expressed by the subjects. The data were derived from informal visitations with the subjects in their homes over a period of several months. Observation of children's communication involved presentation of the same toys to all subjects in an effort to encourage comments. Unfortunately the studies were somewhat weakened by the fact that the number of visits was not held constant across all children, and that observations did not occur at the same ages for all children, so that commonalities of developmental patterns could not be generated; however, the analyses in these studies were particularly inventive.

The subjects' gestures were defined as those movements of the body that seemed to communicate meaning that transcended the specific situation in which the child found himself. Pointing could constitute a part of the child's gesture system, its status being analogous to that of demonstrative pronouns, as well as other syntactic functions. An examination of the subjects' parents' gestures revealed that their system was less complex than the structures used by their children. In fact the hearing-impaired children seemed to initiate advances in gesture communication complexity that the parents later incorporated in communication interchanges.

Feldman (1975) found that subjects' gestures could be divided into two categories: deictic and specific gestures, which seemed to function in different ways in the subjects' gesture systems.

Deictic gestures, the most commonly used and apparently the first acquired, functioned in a manner similar to that of deictic proforms and adverbials (*this* and *that*) of spoken language. They consisted of some variation on pointing at an object either explicitly, with an extended index finger, or implicitly, as in tapping the object or performing a swinging motion toward the referent.

As in the early verbalizations of normally hearing children, Feldman found that given the broad possibilities within any child's environment, the subjects chose to use deictic gestures to identify small objects rather than larger objects or locations, usually embedding the gesture in an action expression. This observation offers a striking parallel to Nelson's (1973) work on early word usage in normally hearing children. Likewise, the subjects used deictic gestures to indicate who was doing or giving what to whom, rather than simply to indicate that an object existed. This also parallels normally hearing children's early use of words, namely, to identify the agents, patients, or recipients within a given action sequence rather than the mere identification of objects apart from their activities or interactions. Nelson (1973) observed that normally hearing children also employ deictic gestures before they develop verbalizations. Gestures of this type seem to be a normal precursor to spoken language development (Bates, 1976b).

Specific gestures, which were observed most often at older ages or with older subjects, appeared first as action forms, then as non-action forms. The subjects tended to use specific gestures that identified action sequences in preference to forms that commented on attributes of entities in their world. Again, this seems to parallel the trend observed for normally hearing children, that first symbols are produced exclusively within action contexts.

Feldman's subjects utilized act-on specific referent gestures before act-by gestures. Act-on gestures were defined as entailing actions that indicated transitivity or action on objects, such as the gesture for *give*, whereas act-by gestures showed actions that indicated intransitivity or actions performed by agents on themselves, such as the gesture for *laugh*. If transitive gestures develop before intransitive forms in gesture systems, it would be contrary to normal language development sequences. The reasons for the difference in use of action categories seem to be related to formulation restrictions of a gesture system as compared to a spoken symbol system. For example act-on or transitive forms are expressions of actions that change the state or location of objects. Deaf children can employ act-on gestures by simply removing the action from the object; they only need to perform the action near, not necessarily with the object. An example would be the gesture *hit*, which could involve a hitting gesture next to the object rather than directly contacting it. In contrast, act-by or intransitive actions are more difficult to gesture because they do not involve an external object; the child, as agent, must generate forms in such a manner that they represent communication about an act rather than merely the performance of the act itself. The act-by gesture is probably cognitively and formationally more complex than the act-on gesture.

Understanding of the characteristics of different language modes is critical because different expressive modalities can impose limitations on the formation of symbols, thereby influencing the type and rate of symbolic forms that may develop in a particular system. Modality choice can produce differential effects on the growth of symbolic formation and processing, which should not be interpreted as a value judgment, but only as a statement affirming diversity among expressive modalities, such that signed, spoken, and written language vary in their strategies for expressing ideas.

In the non-action specific gesture category there also seemed to be a developmental trend. Pose gestures tended to precede the appearance of trait gestures. Pose gestures were defined as gestures that emulate some distinguishing body position or facial characteristic of an animate object, such as a person or animal; trait gestures, on the other hand, described a salient perceptual characteristic of an object, such as color, shape, or size. Pose gestures should be easy to generate because all the child has to do is mimic any posture or facial expression of the target object to produce them. For trait gestures, in contrast, the child must capture a single, salient feature to convey to others, a more difficult task than imitating poses or facial expressions.

Goldin-Meadow's (1975) investigation of the semantic relations expressed by these young deaf children considered only multi-gesture phrases that conveyed propositions, rather than productions in which a gesture was simply repeated over and over again. She classified the observed gestures into two basic classes of propositions: actions and attributes. An action proposition was usually employed to request the execution of an action or to comment on an action that was being, had been, or would be executed. An attribute proposition was defined as one used to comment on the perceptual characteristics of an object. As would be expected, action propositions or phrases were produced with greater frequency and at earlier ages than attribute propositions or phrases. This behavior has a parallel in spoken language, in which action two-word verbalizations are produced with greater frequency and at earlier ages in the developmental process than two-word adjectival (attribute) utterances.

Analysis of the observed attribute propositions revealed definite ordering rules that could be defined along three dimensions: those ordered by the nature of their referents, those ordered by their semantic roles, and those ordered by the formative characteristics of the gestures. Referentially, children usually pointed to a picture before making a gestured comment about it. In terms of semantic roles, children were observed to produce the entity form first and then the descriptor gesture, or to produce a picture identifier (pointing) gesture first and then an entity sign. If the subject was looking at a picture of a cow, the child might point to the cow and then make a gesture for *big*. If he saw a picture of a dog that seemed to remind him of the family pet, he would point to the picture of the dog first and then to his pet, or if the pet was not available, make an appropriate gesture for the dog. Deictic gestures always preceded characterizing gestures, that is, a subject always pointed to objects before performing more symbolic-like gestures, which seems to be a function of the formational characteristics of pointing as compared with other types of gestures. This latter observation was in line with Feldman's previously reported findings.

Analysis of action propositions revealed that all the deaf subjects combined the same roles to convey similar types of action proposition types. Moreover, semantic roles were organized in similar ways, specifically, patient + act and act + recipient. Subjects tended to omit from their action sequences any gestures indicating the agent of the sentence. This usage was subject to modification depending upon the predicate frame in which the agent appeared. Gesture agents were divided into subclasses: causatives, or agents that cause actions that occur to objects, and affectives, or agents that produce actions affecting themselves. Causative agents occurred in transfer (agent-action-patient-recipient) and transform (agent-action-patient) predicate frames; affective agents appeared in transport (agent-action-recipient) and perform (agent-action) predicate frames. Causative relationships tended to emerge in gesture systems before affective relationships. The agent position was not filled, however, until the child began to use affective relationships, and then agents were employed only in the latter circumstances; apparently, when the child only had the capability to produce two gestures, the agent node in the causative predicate frame was sacrificed.

An additional factor that emerged from the analysis of the agent gesture was that the affective-agent functioned within action proposition phrases identically to the patient gesture, an observation that would seem to support the notion that affective agent and patient may constitute a category apart from causative agent. Thus deaf children's gestural systems contain syntactic groupings that seemingly are semantically determined, as found in ergative languages, rather than determined by word order constraints. Spoken English is classified as an accusative, not an ergative, language because all agents are considered to be similar—they occupy the same syntactic slots within sentence frames, rather than being grouped together based on semantic similarity. If deaf children at early ages communicate with gesture systems having conceptual/syntactical categories that differ systematically from spoken English, it is probable that making a transition from one system to the other would be difficult. Learning spoken English for a child with a well entrenched gesture system might in effect be second language learning.

The findings of Feldman and Goldin-Meadow are tentative, of course, and certainly require substantiation, but they do seem to indicate that there are probable parallels between gesture language development and the development of spoken English. There are also points of difference caused by the formational and/or conceptual predispositions of the gesture modality. These differences are most important, especially for persons who work with young deaf children.

Skarakis and Prutting (1977) applied a sociolinguistic approach in describing the semantic-pragmatic component of the spontaneous communication acts of four hearing-impaired children. Communicative acts, in this case, were defined as gestures, descriptions of facial expressions, and actions, as well as vocalizations and verbalizations. Analysis of a set of 1000 acts was derived from the description procedures developed by Greenfield and Smith (1976) for semantic functions and by Dore (1974) for communication intents. The system of semantic functions provided for the identification of 13 categories, including performatives (greetings and action requests), volitional acts, some aspect of the agent-action-patient-location relation, and modification of events employing either time, or manner, or quantity modifiers. Communicative intent was classified into eight categories (labeling, response, request, greeting, protesting, repeating, describing, and attention getting) that were also coded according to the expressive mode employed by each child. Results indicated that across all subjects three of the four preverbal semantic functions—performative, indicative object, volition, and its sub-type, negative volition—occurred most frequently. Two linguistic functions, action/state of an action and action/state of an object, were also among the most frequently occurring semantic functions for these four hearing-impaired children. With regard to communicative intent, labeling, request, description, attention, and response occurred most frequently in communication, although all intents appeared in one form or another in the sample. The authors concluded that although their subjects were older than the subjects employed by Greenfield and Smith (1976) and by

Dore (1974), they were utilizing communicative intents and semantic functions that would normally be considered prerequisite to mature communicative competence. Hearing-impaired children were apparently on the same continuum with normally hearing children with regard to language development, being delayed rather than divergent from the normal expectations for language development and growth.

These studies on the development of symbolic gesture systems in hearing-impaired children, although limited in number, do suggest the following trends. Contrary to previous thinking, the deaf child does adapt his gestures to function symbolically in communication situations. There are indications that gesture usage parallels but diverges somewhat from the expectations set up by the literature on normal language development. Points of similarity are shown by a strong emphasis upon action strings rather than attribute strings; these action strings reflect understanding of semantic characterizations known to very young normally hearing children: causative and affective agents, patients, causative and affective verbs, and recipients. There are indications that the gesture systems of deaf children tend to be organized with semantic rather than word order focus, which may confound the learning of spoken English in hearing-impaired children identified at older chronological ages.

Oral Language Acquisition   In an application of generative-transformational analysis to oral production, Juenke (1971) examined the spoken language of two hearing-impaired children enrolled in an auditorily oriented preschool program. One child was in the formative stage of language development and the other was in the refinement stage, in the process of adding modulations and modalities. The data revealed that both children had developed many of the primary semantic categories evidenced in the language of normally hearing children.

Randy, the child in the formative stage, had developed a N + V + N frame, with the first N position filled almost exclusively with pronominal constructions. This strategy is reminiscent of the pronominal strategy described by Bloom, Lightbown, and Hood's (1975) study on variation in language learning. Randy seemed partial to D + N or M + N constructions, which translate into the semantic functions of nominalization and attribute. Unlike normally hearing children, however, he was not displaying the early emergence of functional relationships other than nomination, thus showing behaviors both similar and dissimilar from normal language development patterns.

Terri, the second child in Juenke's study, was more advanced linguistically than Randy at the initiation of the study. Her language performance also included a pronominal strategy in that the first noun phrase of the N + V + N frame was usually filled by pronouns rather than noun constructions. Other language usage was similar to that subsequently reported by Limber (1973, 1976), such as the employment of complement type relationships, specifically, infinitive clauses, factive clauses, and some embedded questions. The omissions evidenced in Terri's language were also similar to those reported by Limber: omission of appropriate transformational markers such as the *to* in infinitive clauses, and failure to permutate the word order of an embedded sentence to make *to* syntactically acceptable. Again, Terri's language was highly consistent with data on normally hearing children's language development.

In an extension of the Juenke study, Hess (1972) examined the language patterns of a hearing-impaired child over a 5-month period, choosing to compare this child's performance not against the developmental literature, but against the language output of a normally hearing child matched on the basis of language age. She collected spontaneous language samples from mother-child play sessions. Analysis of the data revealed that there were very few differences between the deaf subject and the normally hearing subject in the development of syntactic structures, as determined by ability to perform linguistic operations during the observation period.

Hess concluded that when the delay factor in the deaf subject's language was controlled by initially matching both children according to their linguistic rather than their chronological ages, the deaf child evidenced a sequence of acquisition comparable to the normally hearing child with two exceptions: (1) the hearing-impaired child had comparatively less differentiation of the subject form class, and (2) the hearing-impaired child exceeded the normally hearing child over the 5-month period in the acquisition of structures leading to a negative sentence frame. At the completion of the study, both children had expanded the NP node to include $D + N$ and $M + N$, the VP node to include $V + NP$ and tense/auxiliary position, and the notion of S to include embedding S_2 in S_1, the essential operations for generating unique, indefinitely long utterances. These findings were consistent with the developmental data reported by Bloom (1970), as well as subsequent reports by Brown (1973) and Limber (1973, 1975) on spoken language development in normally hearing children.

The present authors recently reanalyzed Hess's data employing a semantic case grammar approach, as suggested by Bloom (1970) and Brown (1973), to determine whether the two children differed substantially in semantic generative performance. Both children emphasized action sequences over functional sequences. Approximately 80% of each child's linguistic output could be adequately described using the Brown categorical system. The remainder of the productions tended to be early emergences of more complex forms, such as complements, which were compatible in form with Limber's (1973, 1976) reports on early language acquisition.

Smith (1972) investigated oral language comprehension of orally trained hearing-impaired children at three stages of language development, and in a comparable group of normally hearing children. Three groups of three normally hearing and three hearing-impaired children each were formed within the experimental subjects sorted by mean length of utterance (MLU). Group I had MLUs from 1.00–1.25; Group II from 1.50–2.00; and Group III from 2.00–2.50. The children were presented with subject-verb, verb-object, subject-verb-object, and fully grammatical strings, and were asked to identify the appropriate picture from a four-choice picture set.

The results of the study indicated no significant difference for deaf vs. normally hearing subjects by stage of development or by test sentence type. The deaf children performed in the same manner as the normally hearing on error types as well as correct responses. However, there was a significant interaction between test sentence type and stage of language development. This finding was interpreted as indicating that children, whether deaf or normally hearing, performed differently at each stage of language development depending upon the specific sentence presentation. Group I children seemed to comprehend more subject-verb and verb-object than subject-verb-object and fully grammatical strings. Group II children comprehended approximately half of the stimulus strings correctly on each sentence type, whereas Group III comprehended more subject-verb-object and fully grammatical strings than subject-verb and verb-object strings. The younger children seem to have treated the test sentences as work strings; the older children were using an actor-action-object strategy to process the sentences. In other words, the youngest children focused on the semantic content of the string, whereas older children were using not only this information, but also semantic/syntactic information such as word order. These results are certainly consistent with the findings of Sinclair (1973) on the effect of word order on comprehension of language, which again attests to the comparability of some deaf children's performance as compared to linguistically comparable normally hearing children.

West and Weber (1974) reported on the spoken language of a 4-year-old hard-of-hearing child. The emphasis of the description was syntactic rather than semantic. Analysis of the child's output indicated that it could be described by using seven rules: (a) verb + adverb, (b) noun + verb or verb + noun, (c) verb + noun + adverb, (d) verb + noun

+ verb or verb + verb +noun, (e) noun + noun, and (f) demonstrative pronoun + noun. They considered that the child had some awareness of basic constructions such as noun phrases and verb phrases. Semantic interpretation of the raw data that accompanied West and Weber's article shows most of this child's utterances to be consistent with previous studies on both normally hearing and on hearing-impaired children. The utterances fall into the categories of action + patient, nomination, and actor + action. The actor + action sequences are similar to the affective category identified in Goldin-Meadow's (1975) gesture study. There were no instances noted of actor-causative use, which is consistent with Goldin-Meadow's findings on gestures.

These studies on oral language development in young hearing-impaired children, although limited in number, do suggest the following trends. Early linguistic efforts of deaf children can be described using contemporary semantic/syntactic systems. Such descriptions show syntactic knowledge and semantic usage that is consistent in some ways with reports on normally hearing children. In most of the studies just reported, however, the agent category is underdeveloped, existing primarily on a pronominal level. There are also indications that affective-actors tend to be expressed more frequently than causative-actors, which was also reported in use of gestures.

Sign Language Acquisition   Recent interest in the characteristics of sign language as a symbol system has been reflected in the organization of studies on the acquisition of sign language.

Collins-Ahlgren (1974, 1975) observed two preschoolers' efforts in learning sign language as part of a total communication program. The subjects' first signs were simplifications of the adult model and were in some ways analogous to the emergence of "baby" words. Confusions tended to occur on the basis of hand configuration, movement, placement in relation to the signer's body, and the relation of each hand with respect to the other when two hands were needed for a sign. All these timing and spatial parameters have been identified by researchers (Bellugi, Klima, and Siple, 1974; Friedman, 1977) as primary discriminating features in American Sign Language. Like spoken language, signs seem to be learned through a process of feature discrimination.

Analysis of the vocabulary acquisition of Collins-Ahlgren's subjects showed patterns also seen in normally hearing children. The deaf subjects tended to acquire instances of the noun, verb, and adjective categories, with specific words initially representing the whole class, an example of the overextension phenomenon described for spoken language development. In addition, words were found to develop multiple meanings as a function of their semantic intent. For instance the sign *more* developed to first express quantitative meanings, as *more food,* then temporal meanings, as *more play*; next spatial meanings, as *more sock* (meaning higher up on the leg); and finally, qualitative meanings, as *knock more.*

Analysis of the semantic and syntactic functions of two-sign combinations showed that the deaf subjects tended to use communication in a fashion similar to normally hearing children and that they tended to encode the same communication intents. They used signs to demand, describe, negate, inquire, and modify. Collins-Ahlgren concluded that these two children were advancing linguistically in a manner predicted by literature descriptions of the early language of normally hearing children.

Winslow (1973) studied the acquisition of American Sign Language in a group of hearing-impaired children, ages 4 to 5 years, from a residential facility. The study focused primarily on two children and their performance in spontaneous communication situations and on an imitative task. The imitation task allowed for production of deictic (pointing) and specific reference signs, categories also employed by Feldman (1975) and Goldin-Meadow (1975) to differentiate gestures they observed.

In the analysis process, repetition of the same sign within the same utterance caused some difficulty. It was decided that if the gesture or sign referred in context to the same concept, it should be counted only once. Another analysis problem was the issue of simultaneous production of signs, which indicated different aspects of the same topic. In these cases the events were bracketed together as a single production. What to consider as signs also posed a problem. It was decided that if iconic or pointing gestures conveyed information, they were to be included for analysis, even though they may not have been "formal" signs.

Using these segmentation guidelines, 203 utterances with a deictic or point gesture and 269 utterances without a deictic or point sign were observed. Two and three sign sequences constituted 51% of the experimental sample.

Point statements proved to be the most prevalent forms used. Points tended to be employed initially for the purpose of specific reference, for indicating the presence of objects within the environment. Purely nonpoint utterances were few in number, but increased significantly with the introduction of two-sign combinations, behavior that was subsequently also observed in gesture systems by Feldman (1975) and Goldin-Meadow (1975).

Developmentally, semantic intents for point utterances proliferated from simple reference statements to include indications of location, possession, plurality, conjunction, and personal/demonstrative pronominalizations, which were usually included as functors and syntactic markers within sentences. Most syntactic markers that appeared in early productions were point signs, with the sole exception of the distinct sign *more,* which, is one of the earliest and most consistently used vocabulary items observed by Bloom (1973) in normally hearing children. The semantic differentiation of the point gesture to include other meanings besides specific reference is consistent with previous findings on gesture systems.

Semantic expressions that include the point sign fit nicely into Brown's (1973) classification of reference operations and semantic relations. In other words, Winslow's deaf subjects used a sign (symbol) system in essentially the same semantic fashion as normally hearing children use spoken symbols. However, it should be noted that there were certain constraints imposed by the sign system on the production of non-point units, as attested to by the low incidence of agent + action strings, as well as the absence of action + agent strings. These forms tended to appear only as point strings, with the point representing the agent category. It seems, therefore, that some of the subjects had developed early a semantic difference between point and non-point strings, a difference not prevalent in spoken English, but a distinction that seems basic to the acquisition of fluent sign language in young deaf children.

Winslow also found that her subjects tended to develop rigid surface structure orders as expressions of specific semantic meanings. Many of these word orders were found not to commonly exist within spoken English. The sole exception to this finding occurred on the repetition task, when subjects were directed to modify their sign system to make it conform to a model established by the examiner. Deaf children learning signs, not surprisingly, adhere to surface structures that seem consistent with sign language, not spoken English, which offers still another indication of the potential interference sign language can have on the acquisition of spoken English forms.

The acquisition advantage seems to be with sign language because it is apparently easier to initiate than spoken language. For example McIntire (1974) reported a vocabulary of about 20 signs in a deaf child at 10 months of age, the age at which hearing children in spoken language environments may be producing only proto-imperative and proto-declarative gesture frames. McIntire also reported two-sign productions at 16 months of age, which is 8 months earlier on the average than the appearance of similar constructions in spoken language. He attributed this early emergence and growth of signs to greater control of the hand as an expressor and to the complete visibility of the features of signs as compared to speech sounds.

Sign Language Acquisition in Normally Hearing Children The developmental sequence of sign language as compared to spoken language and the influence of each system on the other has some interesting expression in studies completed on hearing children of deaf parents. For example, there are studies indicating detrimental short and long-term effects of sign language on the language acquisition skills of hearing children, such as Critchley's (1967) report on problems with spelling or Schiff and Ventry's (1976) finding of prevalent undetected language disorders. Others observe that hearing children of deaf parents develop most satisfactory spoken language skills along with the acquisition of manual language (Lenneberg, 1967; Mayberry, 1976). Schiff (1976) observed that even by the age of 2 years, normally hearing children of deaf, non-oral parents recognized and employed register differences in communication with normally hearing adults as compared to their hearing-impaired parents. Specifically, although the children were generally developing normal spoken language, they tended to: (1) use proportionally more signs when conversing with deaf adults, (2) shorten their utterances, (3) produce more spoken utterances without voice, and (4) employ more "deaf-like" articulation patterns. Whether the children were communicating with normally hearing or with hearing-impaired adults, they did follow normal developmental strategies, the use of some imitation of adult patterns and the use of syntactic and lexical information from prior adult utterances to formulate their own sentences.

Register differences are present early in the communication repertoire of the normally hearing child of deaf parents, and apparently without corresponding interference in spoken language acquisition strategies, although there is evidence that the systems are not learned simultaneously by these children, but sequentially. Wilbur and Jones (1974) reported that the first sign of a hearing child of deaf parents emerged several months before that child's first spoken word, with the child's spoken vocabulary eventually complementing his signed vocabulary. There was only a small overlap in words that were both spoken and signed. This was taken by Wilbur and Jones as an indication that the child was neither simply learning spoken words to correspond to signs already known, nor learning signs to correspond to spoken language already mastered.

It seems that when spoken language is taught primarily through speechreading, it is likely to be interfered with or even dominated by the more clearly organized visual system of sign language. Unless the auditory features of spoken language are capitalized on, or the two visual systems are clearly separated in learning, interference seems bound to result. Sign language is a symbol system that can be acquired by young children, whether deaf or normally hearing. Sign has not been shown to interfere substantially with oral language acquisition in children whose two major sensory modalities are intact, perhaps because its features are clearly distinguishable, and can be sorted and stored without the confusion often apparent in situations where a child first learns two separate spoken language systems, such as English and Spanish, and especially when these languages are not clearly separated by the environment (Asher and Garcia, 1969; Dato, 1972, 1975; Dulay and Burt, 1972, 1974a,b, 1975; Hakuta, 1974, 1975; Larsen-Freeman, 1975, 1976; Milon, 1974; Natalicio and Natalicio, 1971; Rosansky, Schumann, and Cancino, 1975; Selinker, Swain, and Dumas, 1975).

There is, in fact, at least one study that suggests that sign language as a visual system does interfere with early acquisition of structural components in spoken language development. Todd (1976) noted reduplication, word order changes, and the overuse of holophrastic stringing in the early utterances of a hearing child of deaf parents. These phenomena are not common in normally hearing children who are learning spoken language, but are quite common in the sign language models provided to a child. It was Todd's contention that the child was learning two languages simultaneously, resulting in the kind of interference just referred to in bilingual children at early stages of their language development.

There is no indication that interference is a permanent condition, because when register and environment are properly sorted for the bilingual child, for example, he generally learns both languages most satisfactorily. Indeed Jones (1976) demonstrated that the acquisition of question-forms in both spoken and sign language in normally hearing children of deaf parents followed a parallel course to that reported for normally hearing children learning only spoken language.

Although there is considerable need for further work on the acquisition of manual language in young deaf children, the data already generated would seem to support a conclusion that it parallels in some ways the development of spoken language, but, like gesture systems, differs from spoken language acquisition patterns. These potential points of divergence would seem to serve as possible points of interference in the acquisition of mature spoken English forms. The data on the effects of manual acquisition on normally hearing children's ability to acquire spoken language seems somewhat contradictory, although all studies seem to indicate that the effects, if any, are not long-term, except in academic areas such as spelling. To say that the effects on normally hearing children are negligible does not rule out the possibility that the effects on a deaf child's ability may be more pervasive. The normally hearing child's ability to sort out differences and maintain two language systems may not be paralleled in the deaf child.

Communication Patterns of Young Deaf Children   From Chapter 1 we learned that language must be seen as part of a more general category, communication. Thus it would seem important that research consider not only language usage, but communication competence. Unfortunately, the number of studies devoted to this topic is minimal.

Gorrell (1971) investigated the social interactions of triads of hearing-impaired children interacting in a simulated preschool setting as compared to closely matched triads of normally hearing subjects. All interactions were videotaped for evaluation of the types and quality of the communication behaviors that occurred.

Deaf children attempted less direct influences and responded less favorably to them. Hearing children were more likely to direct their attention to objects than were deaf children. Vocalizations as well as other non-active behavior were employed much more frequently by hearing children. Self-directed behaviors were exhibited almost solely by the deaf group. In other words, at early ages, deaf children acted differently than their normally hearing counterparts by approaching one another less, responding to each other's overtures less, vocalizing less, and attending more to themselves. Deaf children seemed to be less outward and less capable of communicating effectively even with other deaf children. These observations may have been a function of the situation—an unfamiliar setting—but the situation was the same for all the subjects. The environment seemed to have little effect on the normally hearing subjects, who could, of course, receive direct or indirect assurance from their parents about the ensuing activity in contrast to most of the hearing-impaired children's ability to be secure and assured when separated from their parents.

Communication Environment of Young Deaf Children   The effects of a child's hearing impairment on his parents' ability to communicate with him, whether by talking or signing, are not yet fully understood, but some intriguing notions are being suggested from studies such as those that follow.

Mothers whose children have handicapping conditions such as language delay and mental retardation seem to show some differences in the amount, type, and situations under which they communicate with impaired children as compared to the data on normal children and their caregivers (Bondurant, 1977; Buium, Rynders and Turnure, 1974; Wulbert et al., 1975).

Research with hearing-impaired children suggests that knowledge of the presence of deafness can have a deleterious effect on parent-child communication patterns, and perhaps on subsequent language growth in the children.

Using an interaction analysis scale, Gross (1970) found that mothers of normally hearing children, as compared to mothers of hearing-impaired children, used more questions, asked for more opinions and suggestions rather than giving them, and used more language showing solidarity and agreement with their children. They were less likely to use humor as tension release, but demonstrated less use of tension and antagonism in their interactions with their children. Mothers of deaf children, on the other hand, were observed to use more atypical intonation contours than mothers of normally hearing children. All in all, Gross saw these results as indicating that mothers of deaf children were less likely to use teaching strategies and to give verbal praise than mothers of normally hearing children, perhaps an expression of the frustration encountered by mothers in communicating with their hearing-impaired children.

In a comparable study, Collins (1969) found that mothers of deaf children communicated mainly to direct the activities of their children, whereas their children's main purpose for communication seemed to be to inform their mothers about things or events in their environment. In Collins's sample, non-oral modes such as gestures, demonstration, and combined speech and gestures were used primarily by the children. Their mothers used an oral mode most often, but relied on non-oral modes as well. The communication between the mother subjects and their children was observed to be bound to events and ideas related to the immediate environment. The mothers were not able to describe accurately the communication between themselves and their children according to mode, but they did have a fairly good perception of the purposes of this communication. Generally, Collins found that what the mothers wanted from the communication situation did not necessarily correspond to or match with what their children wanted from communication.

If Nelson (1973) is correct about the impeding effects of communication style mismatching on oral language development of normally hearing children, then it is certainly possible that communication mismatching between deaf children and their parents could have serious repercussions for language development. The language acquisition process seems to be more difficult for the deaf child than for the normally hearing child, even through the visual mode. The communication between parent and deaf child is a most fragile link, broken easily by time, space, or distance from events or feelings to be communicated about.

Greenstein et al. (1975) investigated parent-child interactions of mothers whose deaf children had slow language development and mothers whose deaf children had so-called rapid language development. Children who showed consistently high language scores across the length of the study tended to look at their mothers more frequently and to move away from their mothers more often. Their mothers tended to look more frequently at them, resulting in more eye contact, but showed correspondingly less touching and appoaching. More contact behaviors on the part of mothers were associated with poorer language competence in their deaf children; more distal behaviors, such as exchanging looks, were associated with greater competence.

This could reflect two factors, both of which are crucial in language learning. First, proximity behaviors could reflect negative parental feelings about the child's competence and his need for more external control. Such attitudes have been found to have deleterious effects on language growth (Wulbert et al., 1975). Second, it might also reflect misunderstanding of the communication problems imposed by hearing impairment, namely, that although direct experience may be critical at some stages of language development, direct experience need not always be equated with direct physical contact.

Parental communication style is related in some important ways to language growth in children, but all the relationships are not yet clear. It is likely for example, that attention to parental style in communication may be vital if one is trying to coach that parent in the use of rules for talking—especially if those rules are contrary to their strategies for communication or the expectations that they have about communication with children who are deaf or otherwise communication impaired.

The influence of sibling linguistic input should not be overlooked either. C. Bennett (1973), for instance, has shown that a 4 1/2-year, normally hearing child could be trained to help teach her 3-year-old hearing-impaired sibling the use of a /-s/ allomorph. Although additional studies into sibling influence have not been reported, this is certainly an area worthy of investigation.

Summary   Studies on younger deaf children seem to indicate that: (1) spoken language development can be similar to that of normal hearing children, although it is often slower to appear, (2) development of organized gesture systems can be documented in young deaf children, systems that seem to be based on symbolic organization distinct from that of spoken English, (3) manual language acquisition shares many of the characteristics of spoken language acquisition, but like gesture systems, may come from symbolic bases quite different from spoken English, (4) normally hearing children of deaf parents seem to develop manual and spoken language systems that are relatively independent of one another; with regard to some structural issues there may be direct but temporary confounding influences of manual language on spoken language acquisition, (5) communication competence seems to be poorly developed in preschool hearing-impaired children, and (6) parental communication style with their hearing-impaired children is noticeably different from interactions with normally hearing children, especially among the mothers of deaf children with slow developing language performance.

Studies of Older Deaf Children

Studies on language acquisition and usage in hearing-impaired children beyond the preschool years are difficult to place in proper perspective. Chapter 3 provided evidence that language performance has a strong cognitive base that effects the scope and rate of linguistic development. Furth (1964, 1966, 1971) has pointed out repeatedly that many hearing-impaired children, in spite of a lack of verbal encoding skills, can and do progress to age-appropriate cognitive behavior, as measured by their ability to perform Piagetian tasks.

The observation that cognitive growth occurs in spite of the lack of a normal verbal symbol system was reinforced by Spence (1973), who found that deaf children deficient in verbal expression still performed as well as normally speaking children on various transposition and seriation tasks adapted from Piaget. Some linguistic skills in normally hearing subjects proved good predictors of test performance, such as comprehension of the negative pole of comparative and superlative forms predicting performance on transposition tasks, or ability to express superlative forms as an important factor in predicting seriation task performance. However, Spence argued that linguistic knowledge of relational or comparative concepts was neither necessary nor sufficient to account for the successful use of comparison in cognitive tasks. Thus older deaf children must be seen as cognitively more mature than the young normally hearing children with whom they are frequently compared linguistically.

Assuming comparable linguistic capabilities of older but cognitively more mature deaf children with younger normally hearing children may be highly questionable, especially if it is true that older deaf children are actually cognitively more sophisticated. Under such circumstances, it is possible that deaf children will not develop comparable linguistic patterns because of their ability to understand and deal more maturely with the underlying semantic-pragmatic bases of language presented to them. Older deaf subjects might show kaleidescoping of developmental stages, or even unusual variation in linguistic stages, thereby producing behaviors not usually seen in young normally hearing children. If such behaviors are noted, they cannot legitimately be considered atypical, or nondevelopmental. Instead they must be seen as the result of the interaction of mature cognitive understandings with linguistic information.

On the other hand, if one accepts Piagetian theory as fundamental to an understanding of language acquisition, it must be recognized that cognition and linguistic usage are highly intertwined at the formal operational stage (Furth and Youniss, 1971), so that the linguistic processing deficiencies of older deaf children may prevent them from cognitively organizing linguistic input as would a linguistically competent person of the same chronological age. Deaf children generally do not approximate the linguistic/cognitive sophistication of normally hearing persons of their own age, but they certainly are cognitively different from normally hearing children who are first learning language. The issue of how cognitive maturity actually affects language growth in older deaf children needs greater clarification, making interpretation of data on older deaf children somewhat uncertain.

Examination of the literature on language of older deaf children is useful, even if the factors that produce the behaviors observed are not yet completely understood. Such descriptions should provide the opportunity to evaluate the linguistic end products of both educational and natural influences. Understanding and describing the forms and functions of language in older deaf children should also assist us to understand how language changes as the deaf child matures, a particularly critical issue for those persons in intermediate, secondary, and adult education programs, or engaged in preparing older multihandicapped persons for employment or deinstitutionalization.

The research on older deaf children has tended to center on written language, but there have been some efforts to explore oral language, manual language, and pragmatic/communication competence. Each of these areas is considered in the final section of this chapter.

EFFECTS OF MILD HEARING
IMPAIRMENT ON LANGUAGE ACQUISITION

Although the focus of this book is on severe to profound hearing impairment and its effects on language acquisition, it is reasonable to digress to review the effects of less severe hearing impairments on language/speech development.

Hearing losses classified as moderate to mild can have an effect on language performance. Studies by Goetzinger (1962), Holm and Kuntze (1969), Keller (1944), Peckham, Sheridan, and Butlert (1972), and Quigley and Thomure (1968) focus on language measurements that, although providing little specific information about the areas of syntactic, semantic, or pragmatic dysfunctioning, give evidence that both slight sensorineural and early onset conductive hearing loss can have an effect on speech and language development well into the school years. In addition, Needleman and Menyuk (Needleman, 1977) found that children with recurrent otitis media had identifiable delays in phonologic acquisition that were usually resolved by the age of 7 years in some, but not all children. Although some children may eventually catch up phonologically, Ling (1972) reported that academic difficulties experienced by children with mild fluctuating conductive hearing loss were not necessarily outgrown. He found that delays in phonologic acquisition affected the acquisition of spelling and reading fluency at later ages.

The influence of mild or fluctuating hearing loss cannot be denied. There continues to be a need, however, to explore the ways in which children with mild losses relate to normally hearing and to severely hearing-impaired children with regard to the language acquisition process. Such data would provide valuable information concerning practical issues such as educational treatment of hearing-impaired children in regular classrooms as well as adding greatly to our understanding of the role of hearing in the acquisition of all aspects of spoken language.

STUDIES OF OLDER DEAF CHILDREN

Oral Language Performance

As frequently pointed out, when describing the oral language of deaf persons, one must establish techniques for differentiating between problems of language form or function and those related to poor speech clarity. The literature in education of the hearing-impaired focuses repeatedly on assessment of the intelligibility of speech, but there is surprisingly little description of older deaf children's spoken language, especially with regard to how it is organized syntactically, semantically, and pragmatically. This lack of information is all the more interesting when considered in light of the premium placed by some segments of the educational profession on the development of oral language skills in deaf persons.

In spite of the dearth of information about oral language development in older deaf children from a contemporary linguistic viewpoint, there is literature of interest that can be interpreted in a contemporary linguistic framework.

Early Studies of Oral Language   Bown and Mecham (1961) attempted to account for the verbal deficiency in hearing-impaired children by comparing performance on the Verbal Language Development Scale (Mecham, 1959) with their intellectual performance, as measured by the Wechsler Intelligence Scale for Children (WISC), with chronological age, and with degree of hearing impairment. It was found that language quotients did not change significantly with increments in Intelligence Quotients over a base score of 85. This relationship of language scores to scores within the normal IQ range could be considered supportive of Lenneberg's (1967) contention that within the normal population, linguistic achievement cannot be differentiated by the use of general measures of intellectual performance. Language performance quotients increased with chronological age, but so did verbal discrepancy scores (the difference between language age and chronological age), so that an increase in verbal performance was still not supportive of normalizing linguistic capabilities in older deaf children. Last, and not surprisingly, the amount of hearing loss had the most significant relation to Verbal Language Quotients. The greater the hearing impairment, the greater the probability of linguistic dysfunctioning in a subject.

Roach and Rosecrans (1971) conducted a study in which oral language skills were assessed by the Verbal Scale of the WISC. This study was designed to explore the relation between oral language proficiency and auditory sensitivity at discrete frequencies from 250 to 4000 Hz, as well as for various frequency bands of hearing, for children with high frequency impairment. The primary finding was that there was a significant relationship between reduced hearing levels at 1000, 1500, 2000, and 3000 Hz and lowered Verbal Scale scores. Of particular interest was the observation that this relationship proved to exist even in subjects whose hearing levels averaged 25 dB HTL, or whose hearing losses were undetected well into elementary age. In other words, even mild hearing impairments, particularly with a sloping configuration, had an adverse effect on general oral language development, the repercussions of which are obvious for classroom and for mainstreaming management.

In a study of oral language facility, Elliott, Hirsh, and Simmons (1967) used measurements such as total number of understandable words, frequency of word usage, and word class occurrence, as well as ratings of structural sophistication, syntactic accuracy, creativity, and content, in evaluating a sample of orally trained deaf children. The results indicated that all aspects of linguistic performance were intercorrelated. Uses of syntactic and semantic forms by deaf children were developing in a fashion similar to normally hearing children, who in early stages of language development show equivalent capabilities in the semantic and syntactic areas. It was Elliott, Hirsh, and Simmons's opinion that the lack of fractionation in linguistic performance usually shown with deaf children was a result of the instructional techniques used with their subjects, techniques that emphasized a global approach to learning. The accuracy of this opinion awaits further verification.

Lowenbraun and Affleck (1970), employing a repetition task, found that deaf subjects who were producing only single words expressively were unable to benefit from the use of syntactic cues in reproducing adult sentence patterns through speechreading. In other words, receptive oral language ability as measured by immediate recall was found not to exceed expressive language development in deaf children. With even older subjects, there seemed to be greater syntactic sophistication, but the subjects still did not demonstrate adequate immediate recall of sentences. It could be argued that such findings suggest spoken language performance whether comprehension or expression stems from a unitary linguistic base.

Several studies have used frequency count approaches in evaluating the oral language proficiency of older hearing-impaired children. For example, Brannon (1968) used the Jones, Goodman, and Wepman (1963) procedure of classifying words into word class groups to evaluate vocabulary sophistication in normally hearing, partially hearing, and deaf subjects. He evaluated both token distribution, or the number of times a particular set of words was used, and type distribution, or the number of different items used within a particular word class. Significant hearing impairment was found to reduce productivity of both tokens and types of words across all word classes. Moderate hearing impairments tended to result in the use of fewer adverbs, pronouns, and auxiliaries, whereas profound hearing impairments reduced nearly all classes. In proportion to total word output, the deaf subjects overused nouns and articles, rarely employing prepositions, quantifiers, and indefinite pronouns. This was felt to be caused by the relatively concrete nature of nouns and extensive exposure to the article forms associated with particular nouns. Reinterpreted, these findings seem to indicate that moderately hearing-impaired children had mastered many of the base structure nodes, whereas profoundly hearing-impaired children were having difficulty with almost all nodes. It also seemed to be the case that profoundly deaf children showed restricted semantic fields for spoken vocabulary.

Goda (1964) employed Fries's (1952) word class classification system in a comparison of the spoken language of deaf, normal, and retarded adolescent populations. Goda's deaf subjects, like Brannon's (1968), displayed inferior performance with respect to all word classes. Seventy-five percent of their verbal output was composed of two word classes—Class 1, or noun-like words, and Class 2, or verb-like words. There was a virtual absence of functor words such as conjunctions and prepositions. This would seem to argue again that many deaf children have developed an awareness of key nodes contained in basic sentence frames used in spoken language, but few resources beyond that.

Simmons (1962) compared the word class use of deaf children in their oral and written language productions by developing type/token ratios (TTR) for each part of speech. A TTR is derived by dividing the number of different words used by the total number of words to yield a proportion. It was found that hearing-impaired children's TTRs in all categories were lower than those of normally hearing children of comparable age. This was interpreted to mean that deaf children lack the lexical flexibility evidenced by normally hearing children. The most diverse TTRs for the deaf subjects appeared with verbs; the adverb and preposition categories were the next most variable. In other words, there tended to be greater variability of verb appearance in the language of hearing-impaired children than of any other word classification.

Brannon and Murry (1966) compared normally hearing, partially hearing, and deaf children's total spoken language output and syntactic accuracy by obtaining the number of addition, omission, substitution, and word order errors observed in a spoken sample. The partially deaf group resembled the normal hearing group in total output, but the deaf subjects again were significantly lower on these measures. The differences between syntactic accuracy scores were significant among all three groups. As hearing level decreased, the accuracy of syntactic production decreased accordingly. Unfortunately, as indicated by Cooper and Rosenstein (1966), the value of this type of study is somewhat diminished because of the lack of specification of types of difficulty experienced by the deaf subjects. By lumping errors together under general categories such as additions or omissions, it is not possible to determine the nature of problems any subject might be having. For instance, there may be difficulty with phrase structure constructions shown by omission of verbs, nouns, articles, or higher level difficulties as indicated by omission of conjunctions or relative adverb introducers. Totaling of errors may show quantities of differences, but only through description of actual performance can we progress toward understanding of how spoken language is understood or used by deaf children.

Contemporary Studies of Oral Language   Recently, studies motivated by generative-transformational theory have tried to shed light on the specific difficulties evidenced by deaf speakers. Stoutenburgh (1971) evaluated the utterances of hearing-impaired and normally hearing children generated by asking them to use certain words in sentences. There was a significant difference of over 46% between the two groups in the production of acceptable sentences. The hearing subjects showed a 20% increase in their ability to produce grammatically correct sentences between the ages of 9 and 14 years, which was not true of the hearing-impaired subjects. Within the deaf sample, there was a definite preference for simple sentence patterns with a low production of double-base sentences. This finding was taken as indication of the deaf subjects' failure to comprehend fully the general transformational rules of addition or blocking. Semantic content and use of optional and obligatory forms did not differ significantly between the two groups of children. The normally hearing sample employed a larger range of lexical items than did the hearing-impaired subjects. Deaf children tended to repeat the same word choices regardless of age, indicating a failure to develop increasingly sophisticated and diversified semantic fields.

Deaf subjects were shown to employ words from a one-dimensional, concrete reference point of view. This observation was supported by the finding that the deaf subjects arranged syntax around the noun-verb phrase axis, and not within the noun-verb phrase. Consequently deaf children produced, almost exclusively, sentence frames similar to the format found in the Fitzgerald Key (Fitzgerald, 1949)—subject-verb-object. In other words, deaf children tended to rigidly approach use of even simple sentence patterns, confining themselves to the repetitious subject-verb-object sentence frame.

Based on results from a sentence repetition task that included items exemplifying active, passive, negative, and passive-negative sentences, Sarachan-Deily and Love (1974) found that both normally hearing and hearing-impaired adolescents made many errors in recalling test sentences. Normally hearing subjects in the study rarely violated English sentence structure. If errors occurred, they usually consisted of the substitution or use of a synonym in the sentence, deletion of a modifying adjective, or changing the transformational complexity of the sentence to make it either transformationally more or less complex. On the other hand, approximately one-half of all deaf subjects produced deletions of major sentence nodes, incorrect derivational or inflectional endings, agrammatical word orders, or inappropriate substitutions for the verb, which caused gross violations of English sentence structure. These last findings were interpreted as evidence of the lack of a stable syntactic competence for the basic rules of spoken English.

Wilcox and Tobin (1974) also used a repetition task, but found that hard-of-hearing as well as normally hearing children tended to use grammatical constructions rather than nongrammatical ones, which is in contrast to the findings of Sarachan-Deily and Love (1974). However, two mitigating factors weigh against direct comparison of these studies. First, the deaf subjects' degree of hearing loss differed: Wilcox and Tobin's sample had better hearing levels. Second, the areas of investigation differed: Wilcox and Tobin confined their attention primarily to active sentences with single instances of passive and passive-negative constructions, whereas Sarachan-Deily and Love carried out detailed investigation of more complex forms such as negation and passives. In any event, Wilcox and Tobin's hard-of-hearing subjects tended to have significantly lower correct averages for each form tested, substituting simpler forms in most cases.

Wilcox and Tobin employed a direct repetition and a recall task. The strategies employed by the two groups of children on the recall portion of the task clearly showed differences in linguistic fluency. Both groups did poorly on the recall task. The normally hearing subjects' approach was to select one form and to use it repeatedly throughout the task, whereas the hard-of-hearing subjects' strategy was to repeat or recall only the preceding response, and in doing so produced repeated error patterns. This lack of verbal strategizing must be taken as a reaffirmation, even within a hard-of-hearing sample of a lack of command of oral language.

Presnell (1973) assessed the performance of hearing-impaired children using the Northwestern Syntax Screening Test (Lee, 1969) and the Developmental Sentence Scoring Procedure (Lee and Canter, 1971). As expected, the deaf children's performance was significantly below that of normative data on both the receptive and expressive portions of the NSST, as well as the overall score on the DSS. Examination of the DSS profile and of the accuracy of production of each form revealed particular difficulty with verbal constructions, especially progressive and perfect forms as compared to modal forms. In all other categories there seemed to be consistency of performance. Difficulty with verbal forms would, of course, be in concert with the findings by Wilcox and Tobin (1974) and Brannon (1968).

A study of morphological forms was conducted by Garber (1967), who utilized reading, speechreading, and speechreading with taction to present morphologic tests identical to those reported in Newfield and Schlanger (1968) and Berko (1958). Deaf children were inferior to normally hearing children in their ability to generate morphological forms. Reading yielded higher performance scores than speechreading, or speechreading supplemented by taction. Ability to use noun inflections was age related, whereas verb and possessive inflections were not. This last finding is of interest in confirming the difficulties that deaf children face in learning to employ the verb forms of spoken English.

Romanik (1976) studied the development of question forms in hearing-impaired children. She utilized controlled test situations in which various types of spoken question forms were elicited. Her findings were in concert with those obtained by Klima and Bellugi (1966) on normally hearing children, namely, that yes/no questions developed earlier than wh-questions; that there was semantic confusion between varying wh-questions, particularly *where* and *why*; and that there was a developmental pattern seen in the acquisition of the auxiliary position and the preposing rule. This latter developmental pattern began as an absence of the do-support and auxiliary position, proceeded to the filled auxiliary position that was not preposed to its correct position, and ended in mastery of the form in all circumstances. Romanik gives a clear-cut report of the development of spoken language in hearing-impaired children that seems to parallel that of normally hearing children. She also showed that linguistic rule application can be studied in the oral modality of deaf speakers if appropriate structure is utilized.

D. Holmes (1972), in an attempt to evaluate generative-transformational rule acquisition in the spoken language of hearing-impaired children, divided his sample into those children who displayed positive Bender-Gestalt results and those who did not. He found that the latter, "neurologically intact group" demonstrated mastery of the 24 linguistic rules under study by the age of 12 years, whereas the former, "neurologically impaired group" had acquired fewer rules and had never attained the level of proficiency that the intact deaf subjects demonstrated. This was interpreted as indicating that neurologically intact deaf children develop certain rules similarly to normally hearing children, but at later ages. One could question whether these differences should be attributed to neurological integrity alone or whether there are other factors that may influence spoken language as well, such as the natural variability of children in acquiring oral language, varying degrees of hearing loss, or differences in parental involvement in the learning process.

Luterman (1976) indicates one possible source of variation that is not clearly understood, namely, the quality of educational experiences provided to deaf children. In comparing auditorily trained and visually trained oral deaf children, he found a pronounced difference in educational and linguistic functioning in favor of the former group, which reinforced for him the importance of auditory processing in the acquisition of spoken language skills. However, it should be noted that even within the auditory group there was variability in linguistic acquisition, which did not seem to be directly related to simple differences in levels of hearing.

Walton (1972) and Boutte (1975) present another possible influence on linguistic fluency. After investigating the linguistic environment available to Black hearing-impaired adolescents and comparing their linguistic productions to those of Black normally hearing adolescents, they concluded that: (a) Black hearing-impaired adolescents are exposed to two linguistic environments, a home dialect similar in construction to Black Vernacular described in linguistic literature (Shuy, 1965) and to a school dialect comparable to General American, and (b) Black hearing-impaired adolescents display linguistic forms that are definitely consistent with Black Vernacular, but that might be considered by teachers of the hearing-impaired to be defective usage rather than acceptable dialectical variation.

One might summarize by saying that, although educators of the deaf have emphasized repeatedly the importance of developing spoken language in hearing-impaired children, there continues to be a lack of information concerning the success of these efforts. At present, evidence shows that: (a) spoken language attainment is still related to degree of hearing loss, which should not be interpreted to mean that profoundly hearing-impaired children are incapable of attaining oral language proficiency, although a high degree of success in this area is still to be awaited, (b) mastery of basic syntactic rules such as base structure frames and transformational operations are generally lacking in many deaf youngsters' spoken language, and (c) all the sources of variation influencing the acquisition of spoken language skills in deaf children have not been identified.

It is obvious from the research reviewed in this section that too little is known about the oral language capabilities of older hearing-impaired children. Most of these studies, of course, were completed using hearing-impaired children enrolled in self-contained classrooms and may not be representative of the full range of oral language capabilities found within the hearing-impaired population. Studies of communication competence in use of spoken language are also lacking, a curious situation given the heavy premium placed on oral language expression by many teachers of the hearing impaired.

Written Language Performance

As with spoken English, there is ample evidence that hearing-impaired children have difficulty in acquiring fluency in other modes of English language understanding and expression such as reading, self-generated written language, and varieties of pencil and paper tasks. Indeed, it is generally true that deaf children with difficulty in personal language expression are frequently deficient in other verbal language modes such as reading and writing. The issues of reading performance and instruction are covered in Chapter 7. The successes and problems of the acquisition of written expression are reviewed in this section.

Acquisition of writing skills has been shown to be a developmental process, the roots of which can be seen in normally hearing 4- and 5-year-old children (C. Chomsky, 1971; Ganschow, 1974; Read, 1975), as well as in young deaf children, although deaf children have less opportunity to develop written capabilities. Writing depends upon mastery of a printed symbol system of graphemes and of the spelling patterns in a particular language. However, as with articulation in speech development, overemphasis upon spelling accuracy can have the net effect of deterring the development of spontaneous written language forms.

Writing should be viewed as a way of expressing what is already known about the world, and what can already be expressed in at least one other mode such as speaking, gesturing, or signing. This is not to say that the conventions for writing are the same as the conventions for speaking or signing, but for fluent language users, they should simply be variations on the same theme.

Unfortunately, for many deaf children, there is no written equivalent for ASL, and, as a consequence, they must become literate in English, a second language for most, if we are to believe that the syntactic/semantic conventions of the visually/spatially oriented system of ASL is not similar to the auditorily/temporally oriented system of spoken English (Friedman, 1977; Wilbur, 1976). It is precisely this issue of literacy, however, that requires deaf persons to develop reasonable proficiency in read and written language in order to assume their rightful place in society.

Written language of hearing-impaired children has been studied extensively, presumably because it provides a static, relatively unambiguous sample for the researcher, as well as for the writer himself. With printed instructions and written responses, the misinterpretation probable in speech tasks and the hazards of understanding deaf speakers are presumably eliminated. A variety of strategies utilizing writing as a response have been employed to explore deaf children's linguistic function, such as word association and cloze techniques. Analysis of self-generated written samples have also occurred, with earlier studies employing structural approaches and more recent studies stressing models based on generative-transformational theory. In an attempt to understand more completely the linguistic difficulties of hearing-impaired children, some researchers have turned to the study of specific linguistic rules, usually resorting to some sort of paper and pencil task. Each of these types of research efforts is examined.

Word Association Research Word association techniques have been used to explore the scope and depth of deaf children's understanding of semantic categories (Hughes, 1961; Koplin et al., 1967; Nunnally and Blanton, 1966). These studies used printed test words to which subjects responded by either writing the first word that came into their mind (Koplin et al., 1967; Nunnally and Blanton, 1966), or sorting the words into categories in which all items were felt to have the same or similar meaning (Hughes, 1961). The collective findings seemed to indicate that older deaf children's semantic fields are not as extensive or differentiated as those of the normally hearing subjects employed. Although the deaf subjects seemed to understand the meaning of many words, they did not appreciate the interrelationships among words that would have allowed them to properly place words into larger conceptual categories.

Cloze Procedure Research Cloze procedures are employed to explore deaf children's understanding of the syntactic/semantic constraints that apply in English sentences. The subject is usually directed to supply words that have been deleted in ongoing printed texts of varying complexity. Hart and Rosenstein (1964), MacGinitie (1964), and Odom, Blanton, and Nunnally (1967), all of whom employed cloze techniques, found deaf children's performance to be consistently inferior to that of normally hearing subjects. This was interpreted to mean that deaf subjects' awareness of the syntactic/semantic requirements of grammatical sentences was less well developed than that of normally hearing children. However, when correctness was defined in terms of correct form class restoration rather than exact word restoration, deaf children achieved in a similar way to that of normally hearing subjects (MacGinitie, 1964), with their performance on substantive words better than on functor words (Odom, Blanton, and Nunnally, 1967). Marshall (1970) found that the degree of contextual support aided in deaf children's performance on cloze procedures, although even when maximum contextual cuing was provided to deaf subjects they were still inferior to normally hearing subjects in filling in blanks.

In an interesting variation on the cloze procedure, S. Cohen (1967) required deaf and hearing children to reconstruct, through writing, passages that had previously been read. Deaf writers' paraphrases contained a higher proportion of ungrammatical sentences than did normally hearing writers' paraphrases. Both subjects' paraphrases and the original text was then presented to deaf and normally hearing children and to a sample of normally hearing adults, using cloze procedures. All the hearing subjects found the deaf subjects' stories much less predictable than either the original story or the normally hearing children's stories; deaf subjects found all three materials equally unpredictable. Deaf stories were less cohesive, which was attributed to idiosyncratic usage, random errors in structures and content, and the presence of so-called deafisms.

Cloze procedures seem to indicate that deaf children have difficulties that are syntactically based for materials that are familiar to the child, but both syntactically and semantically based for materials that are not familiar to the child. Although deaf children profit from contextual cues, their performance still tends to be inferior to that of normally hearing children. Cloze procedures are useful in pointing to the existence of linguistic problems, but they fail to indicate in detail the types and sources of the linguistic difficulties that underlie the productions of hearing-impaired children.

Research with Spontaneously Produced Written Samples   Motivated by an attempt to specify in more precise terms the full extent of linguistic capabilities of hearing-impaired children, many researchers have turned to an examination of self-generated writing of deaf children. Many such studies have employed counting techniques emphasizing general error categories, or have used categories of description generated from models based on traditional English grammar or structural linguistics. Subsequent studies have employed more contemporary procedures based on generative-transformational theory; these have tended to emphasize the notion that productions generated by deaf children may not be errors in standard forms, but products derived from different grammatical bases. If so, the task of the researcher is then to describe the underlying rule system governing the deaf child's understanding and control of language, which can show how closely the grammars or linguistic rule systems of deaf persons parallel or diverge from those of normally hearing persons.

Early Studies of Spontaneously Written Language   Thompson (1936), Reay (1946), and Schulze (1965) all employed quantitative descriptions of deaf children's writings, such as identifying addition, omission, and substitution of words or syntactic units, or tallying of verb and noun usage only. Results suggested that deaf writers were generally restricted in their form and vocabulary choices, but they did demonstrate growth in linguistic sophistication over time. Verb restrictions were particulary pronounced in the written mode, which is somewhat contradictory to studies on spoken vocabulary such as that by Simmons (1962), who found verb usage to be the most diversified of the form classes she examined.

The vocabulary normative study reported by Silverman-Dresner and Guilfoyle (1972) confirm the general restriction in vocabulary knowledge for deaf children from all parts of the country, suggesting that compared to 1936 there has been relatively little change in this aspect of linguistic functioning.

Myklebust (1965) devised an instrument for assessing written language, *The Picture Story Test*, that included measures of output, syntactic control, and abstractness of the composition. Linguistic output involved totaling the number of sentences and words and computing *a* words per sentence score; syntactic control involved totaling numbers of omissions, substitutions, additions, and word order changes, categories essentially identical to those employed by Thompson (1936); abstractness evaluation involved classification into categories (abstract-concrete scale) commenting on varying levels of conceptual sophistication. As expected from previous studies, deaf children proved to be inferior in all three aforementioned areas of evaluation. Unfortunately, such categories, with the possible exception of the abstract-concrete score, tend to obscure important qualitative differences among children's compositions. For instance if a child were to produce the sentences *Boy is hitting the ball.* and *The boy is the ball.*, the two errors produced would be classified together as omissions, even though it is obvious that the errors demonstrated are not of equivalent value. Omission of verbs within sentences must be considered somewhat more serious than the omission of determiners. Likewise, although sentences such as *John is playing with the red balls.* and *John plays with dolls, cars, and trucks.* are of equal length, it does not seem reasonable to assume that these two sentences are of comparable linguistic complexity or express equivalent linguistic sophistication. Studies that are purely quantitative in approach and emphasize gross categories such as omissions or additions do not do justice in describing the linguistic capabilities actually possessed by deaf writers.

An early and very comprehensive descriptive study of syntactic usage employing a traditional English grammar model was reported by Heider and Heider (1941) on the writings of both deaf and normally hearing children. Although length of composition and quantity of certain forms such as infinitives and prepositions were not different, the deaf subjects preferred simpler, shorter, and less flexible word order usages. When faced with a choice between using a phrasal construction or a more complex subordinate clause construction, deaf children would elect to use the phrasal construction. Deaf children also tended to select surface structures that could be utilized in subject-verb-object sentence frames, with preference for complex constructions that fit the predominate sentence order, such as infinitive clauses or indirect discourse. When a particular semantic concept could be encoded using a variety of syntactic constructions, deaf children had the tendency to select one form and to use that form consistently throughout the sample. Normally hearing children, on the other hand, varied their use among the several options available to them.

Operating from a structural linguistic model involving the identification of word classes and sentence types, Walter (1955, 1959) sampled the writing of deaf children from two different English speaking countries, sorting the sentences generated into five developmental stages characterized by increasing fluency in the mastery of simple and compound sentences. The compositions progressed gradually from mastery of basic noun phrases to the subject-verb-object sentence frame, to compounding either the subject, verb, or object to production of compound sentences, with varying degrees of accuracy of course. In this study, deaf children demonstrated increase in syntactic complexity over age, a finding consistent with Heider and Heider (1941) for written language and Stoutenburgh (1971) for oral language.

Contemporary Studies of Spontaneous Written Language In an application of early generative-transformational theory, Taylor (1969) evaluated deaf children's spontaneous written compositions. Her deaf subjects showed understanding of two subcategorical rules quite early: that a sentence is made up of a noun phrase and a verb phrase and that verb phrases are either copula plus X (something) or main verb plus X. Determiners and auxiliaries appeared after the former subcategorical rules had been established. Sentence combining transformations appeared only after some phrase structure mastery had occurred. When sentence coordination and embedding operations were attempted, coordinating conjunctions tended to be employed earlier that nominalization, relative clauses, or adverbial clauses. Again, deaf children's linguistic efforts seemed to be partially shaped by the syntactic complexity of the construction under consideration.

Using a more contemporary generative-transformational approach, Ivimey (1976) studied a variety of written language samples from a single hearing-impaired child. The subject's sentences were clearly rule governed and orderly, but bore little resemblance to the spoken language to which she was exposed. For example, there was no consistent use of number, tense, or time indicators on the verb constituent; time was encoded consistently through the use of adverbial constructions rather than the more conventional use of tense; negative elements were inserted before time indicators within sentence frames, never after; copulas and prepositions were not functionally available to the child; determiners appeared only in the subject, not the object position; the features of possession and plurality were carried by the determiner system rather than by addition of word endings to nouns. Although the subject's writings were idiosyncratic in this single instance, the child's focus on a subject-verb-object sentence frame is consistent with previous reports. The study itself is an example of the detailed description needed on large samples of deaf children if we are to progress in understanding their rule acquisition strategies.

Interest in the application of generative-transformational descriptions to the writings of hearing-impaired children led R. R. Kretschmer (1972a) to study compositions of 90 deaf and 90 normally hearing adolescents, ages 12 to 18 years, elicited by use of the test picture from Myklebust's *Picture Story Test* (Myklebust, 1965).

There proved to be no statistical differences in quantity of sentences produced, as had also been shown by Goda (1959) and Waldon (1963), but as might be expected, there were clear differences in the complexity and variety of sentences actually produced. Generally, the deaf subjects produced less well-formed and less syntactically complex compositions, preferring single proposition sentences or simple transformational variations on these types of sentences rather than double-based constructions such as complementation or nominalization. Deaf children were seen to increase complexity by inserting new constituents such as adverbials or adjectives into the single proposition, subject-verb-object relationship rather than producing more complex constructions, a finding in concert with previous studies by Heider and Heider (1941), Walter (1955, 1959), and Ivimey (1976). Phrase structure difficulties proved the most common problem in deaf compositions, probably a function of the deaf child's preference for single proposition and simple transformational sentences. Phrase structure difficulties for deaf subjects centered around use of verbs, articles, and prepositions. At least some normally hearing subjects exhibited these same difficulties, however, as well as instances of all the atypical syntactic patterns for more complex constructions written by deaf subjects, but always to a lesser degree. Semantically based analysis was recommended as the next area of exploration for differences or similarities between deaf and normally hearing writers, because syntactic surface structure analysis did not reveal startling differences, other than complexity level, between the samples studied.

In a continuation of that study, Kretschmer (in preparation) has collected an additional 3000 compositions from both deaf and normally hearing children and adolescents, ages 7 through 18 years, as well as samples of young adults. A generative-transformational/case grammar approach is being used for analysis. Preliminary findings relative to syntactic usage have revealed many of the same areas of difficulty already reported. For example, a very sizable number of hearing-impaired subjects lack ability to generate any connected written language, whereas only two normally hearing subjects out of more than 1500 could not produce a sentence. Deaf writers have difficulty with general transformations because they do not establish complete sentence frames, even in very simple single proposition sentences. Within these sentence frames deaf writers display fewer elaborated nodes, which would indicate comparatively less complex language mastery than normally hearing writers. In addition, there are many strict subcategorization rule violations, such as filling sentence nodes with forms that are not grammatically appropriate, as using a verb in a noun node. Deaf writers tend to omit local transformations, or when applying them, to violate selectional restrictions such as plurality, possession, or correct tense. Finally, deaf writers produce a number of transformational restriction errors, such as applying transformations to surface structures when previous lexical insertions dictated the use of different transformations, i.e., use of infinitives instead of participle forms after verbs such as *enjoy*.

Classification of test sentences through appropriate case relationships has shown some interesting and new results. For example deaf writers select a restricted number of cases for expression, with actor-action-attribute-patient and entity sentences predominating even through the adolescent period. There is noticeable confusion among deaf subjects regarding the use of appropriate case indicators, such as difficulty with use of prepositions for bridging verbal and adverbial constructions. They favor using locative forms to represent adverbials other than location to such a point that one must assume either that adverbials other than location are not a functional part of these persons' linguistic repertoire, or that deaf writers do not truly understand the semantic role that case markers such as prepositions play within language.

Component feature problems are also evident. Deaf subjects select appropriate word class entries, entries that even share several important features with the appropriate vocabulary item, but too frequently the lexical entry actually used differs on one or two critical features, which caused the resulting sentence to "miss the mark" in meaning. It is almost as if deaf persons learn a general meaning for words, but not all the critical dimensions that govern their use with other words.

At this stage, self-generated compositions of deaf subjects can be said to be uniformly rigid and simple, with myriads of problems ranging from formation of simple sentence frames to incomplete mastery of the lexical items inserted into these sentence frames. As observed previously (Kretschmer, 1972a), deaf children demonstrate difficulty with base structure, particularly with use of articles, verbs, and prepositions.

Wilbur (1977) makes a strong case for many of the problems or "errors" observed being related to the deaf writer's approach to writing as a sentence-by-sentence task, rather than as a discourse task. Appropriate use of articles, pronouns, or verb tense is tied to understanding how sentences are related in comprehensible discourse. When one first writes about an object, it is generally assumed that the reader has no knowledge of it, and the object is tagged with an indefinite article. Once identified, the object tag is automatically shifted to a definite article, or is pronominalized, assuming normal retention on the reader's part. If Wilbur's contention is accurate, and it seems to be, considering that written language is frequently taught to deaf children apart from its discourse function, then some of the problems of language usage in hearing-impaired children should not be unexpected, nor attributed solely to the influence of deafness itself.

Study of self-generated compositions can provide some interesting information about deaf subjects' linguistic resources and about their performance fluency, but such compositions do not always reveal the full extent of the person's knowledge about language, because it is subject to a variety of performance errors such as spelling breakdown, carelessness in execution or proofreading, or even visual or motor impairments that may prevent mature written expression. As one technique for exploration of deaf children's ability to employ knowledge of linguistic rules in actual generation of language, however, the gathering and study of spontaneous compositions is useful, if not mandatory, for a complete understanding of linguistic performance, and for this reason its continued use is recommended and encouraged.

Studies of Specific Linguistic Rule Knowledge   Another important segment of information on the language understanding of hearing-impaired children and youth has been derived from application of contemporary linguistic theory to evaluation of deaf subjects' knowledge or intuitions about specific linguistic rules. Most often these studies have employed reading and the use of paper and pencil tasks, the latter to write responses, correct test copy, or draw answers. Studies that employed reading and response modes of pointing or picture arrangement are also of interest. The underlying theme of these studies is their use of contemporary linguistic and/or psycholinguistic orientation in development of test strategies and in the evaluation and interpretation of subjects' performance.

Evidence is accumulating that many deaf children have limited intuitive grasp of the organization of English, specifically, base structures for generating simple sentences frames. O'Neill (1973) developed a test of receptive language competence to explore the ability of normally hearing and deaf children to understand phrase structure rules. The test required each subject to decide which sentences were correct from choices that included syntactically inacurate sentences as well as some altered to resemble patterns presumed to contain common "deafisms." Deaf subjects were consistently poorer than normally hearing subjects in recognizing instances of both correct and incorrect productions generated from base structure rules. Especially difficult for deaf subjects to detect were patterns of omission, redundancy, and selectional restrictions. In view of the repeated finding that deaf writers have difficulty in producing sentences that contain accurate base structures, it is important, but not surprising, to know that deaf subjects have considerable difficulty in recognizing the same kind of pattern when produced by someone else.

Recall tests have also been used to investigate deaf children's awareness of base structure. For instance when Odom and Blanton (1967) presented deaf children with sets of four-word units that ranged from orderly phrases (*paid the tall lady*) to fractured phrases (*lady paid the tall*) to scrambled units (*lady tall the paid*), they showed limited recall of all the test sentences. Normally hearing children, on the other hand, showed facilitated recall of phrases when they were logical or fractured, but interference on the scrambled segments. The deaf children were apparently neither aided nor confused by contextual or organizational cues derived by phrase structure rules.

Another example of deaf children's inability to profit from language organization to aid recall of words can be found in the study reported by Fremer (1971). His deaf and normally hearing subjects were directed to recall words from lists that were organized in increasing approximations to grammatical English sentences. Deaf subjects from two groups remembered the lists of essentially unrelated words as well as or better than normally hearing subjects of equivalent ages. However, on lists with words arranged in groups or clusters, or even in sentence-like constructions, deaf children regardless of age did not appear to be able to take advantage of contextual cues provided by base structure understandings, which normally hearing subjects apparently could employ to succeed at the recall task.

To investigate whether Chomsky's contention that understanding of base structure selectional restrictions contributes to an individual sense of what is comprehensible linguistically, R. E. Kretschmer (1976) studied deaf and hearing adolescents' choices of sentences and of pictures that contained a single selectional restriction contrast.

The following display (R. E. Kretschmer, 1976) presents the types of sentences employed. The picture pairs that served to check the validity and reliability of the subjects' performance in the study showed the same type of selectional restriction contrasts as did the sentences, but did not employ the same lexicon. The task consisted of presenting pairs of sentences or pairs of pictures and having the subjects select the sentence or picture that was the best, that is, the most appropriate or most sensible.

Intransitive sentences:
1. Tall boys speak with pretty girls.
2. Purple boys speak with pretty girls.
3. Tall boys speak with purple girls.
4. Big dogs speak with pretty girls.
5. Tall boys speak with big dogs.
6. Thin pencils speak with pretty girls.
7. Tall boys speak with thin pencils.
8. Warm bread speaks with pretty girls.

9. Tall boys speak with warm bread.
10. Quiet fun speaks with pretty girls.
11. Tall boys speak with quiet fun.
12. Tall boys speak poor men.
13. Tall boys speak old.

Transitive sentences:
14. Fat brothers thank little sisters.
15. Purple brothers thank little sisters.
16. Fat brothers thank purple sisters.
17. Big dogs thank little sisters.
18. Fat brothers thank big dogs.
19. Thin pencils thank little sisters.
20. Fat brothers thank thin pencils.
21. Warm bread thank little sisters.
22. Fat brothers thank warm bread.
23. Quiet fun thanks warm bread.
24. Fat brothers thank quiet fun.
25. Fat brothers thank for beautiful presents.
26. Fat brothers thank old.

Random string:
27. Sit bears orange children hot.

Whether through reading or picture identification, both deaf and normally hearing subjects showed internal consistency or reliability in their choice of what was deemed more sensible or appropriate. The solutions employed by the normally hearing adolescents ranged from the idiosyncratic, or semantically oriented, ease of completion strategies of the youngest age group to a syntactically based approach, which approximated the predictions of Chomskian theory concerning the hierarchy of base component selectional restriction rules. Although almost 30% of the deaf subjects used either a semantic or syntactic strategy like those employed by the hearing subjects, the majority utilized highly unique or esoteric approaches that were based on something other than meaning or word order aspects of English. Some 11- and 14-year-old deaf subjects failed altogether to distinguish between well- and ill-formed rule conforming sentences, again demonstrating deficiency in knowledge about base component rules of simple English sentence frames.

One is forced to conclude from these studies that many deaf children do not master the base structures necessary to generate even simple English sentence frames. Studies on deaf children's abilities to master transformations, as defined by either early or late transformational theory, have also been subject to intensive investigation.

Studies by R. Cooper (1967) and Perlman (1973) investigated deaf children's ability to apply local transformations (morphophonemic rules) to yield properly inflected verbs and nouns. Whether nonsense words (R. Cooper, 1967), real lexical items, or both (Perlman, 1973) were utilized, deaf subjects were noticeably less proficient in inflecting words than normally hearing subjects even of much younger age. The kinds of errors made by the two groups were qualitatively similar, and both groups found real words easier to inflect than nonsense words.

Employing drawing as the response mode, Morrison (1970) presented printed contrastive sentence pairs representing 15 types of transformations to deaf and normally hearing subjects. A larger percentage of hearing-impaired subjects incorrectly portrayed sentences for every contrast tested, but patterns of errors were similar for both groups, as was the nature of the errors themselves. In this study, deaf subjects showed delayed but not deviant patterns of performance.

The most comprehensive exploration of specific transformational rules to date has been conducted by Quigley and his associates (Quigley, Montanelli, and Wilbur, 1976; Quigley, Smith, and Wilbur, 1974; Quigley, Wilbur, and Montanelli, 1974, 1976; Wilber, Montanelli, and Quigley, 1976; Wilbur and Quigley, 1975; Wilbur, Quigley, and Montanelli, 1975).

A Test of Syntactic Ability (Steinkamp and Quigley, 1976) was developed by this research group to explore understanding and use of negation, conjunction, question formation, pronominalization, verbal units, complementation, disjunction, and alternation. The receptive portion of the test requires a subject to differentiate between correct and incorrect instances of a particular transformation; in the expressive portion, the subject is instructed to generate a correct sentence when he finds an incorrect expression of a syntactic rule.

By all reports, deaf children's performance has not equaled that of any normally hearing subjects except for use of personal pronouns, even though the normally hearing subjects are chronologically much younger than their hearing-impaired counterparts. In several instances, Quigley et al.'s 18-year-old deaf subjects have approached the performance of younger normally hearing children, especially in mastery of negation, conjunctions, and wh- and yes-no questions. Deaf subjects have shown unusual difficulty with disjunction and alternation tasks, whereas normally hearing children have shown only moderate difficulty. Essentially, deaf subjects show more difficulty in identifying and correcting items that require the most syntactic manipulation.

Some instances of productions that are thought to have no analogue in child language literature or in the target language of mature English are shown in Table 6, reproduced by permission of the *Volta Review* from Quigley, Power, and Steinkamp (1977, p. 80). An examination of these productions suggests that they may result from the already well-

Table 6. Examples of distinct syntactic structures generated by deaf children[a]

Structural environment in which structure occurs	Description of structures	Example sentences
Verb system	Verb deletion	The cat under the table.
	Be or have deletion	John sick. The girl a ball.
	Be-have confusion	Jim have sick.
	Incorrect pairing of auxiliary with verb markers	Tom has pushing the wagon.
	By deletion (passive voice)	The boy was pushed the girl.
Negation	Negative outside the sentence	Beth made candy no.
Conjunction	Marking only first verb	Beth threw the ball and Jean catch it.
	Conjunction deletion	Joe bought ate the apple.
Complemention	Extra for	For to play baseball is fun.
	Extra to in POSS-ing complement	John goes to fishing.
	Infinitive in place of gerund	John goes to fish.
	Incorrectly inflected infinitive	Bill like to played baseball.
	Unmarked infinitive without to	Jim wanted to go.

Relativization	NPs where *whose* is required Copying of referent	I helped the boy's mother was sick. John saw the boy who the boy kicked the ball.
Question formation	Copying Failure to apply subject-auxiliary inversion Incorrect inversion	Who a boy gave you a ball? Who the baby did love? Who TV watched?
Question formation, negation	Overgeneralization of contraction rule	I amn't tired. Bill wiln't go.
Relativization, conjunction	Object-object deletion Object-subject deletion	John chased the girl and he scared. (John chased the girl and he scared the girl.) The dog chased the girl had on a red dress. (The dog chased the girl. The girl had on a red dress.)
All types of sentences	Forced subject-verb-object pattern	The boy pushed the girl. (The boy was pushed by the girl.)

[a] From Quigley, S., Power, B., and Steinkamp, M. 1977. The Language Structure of Deaf Children. *Volta Rev.* 79: 80.

established tendency of deaf children to adhere to a subject-verb-object sentence order, even when the pattern clearly is not appropriate, as in realization of passive voice or expression of some forms of relativization. Similar tendencies were identified by Tervoort (1970) in an investigation of the use of passive voice by deaf children.

Another strong inclination of deaf children suggested by Table 6 is related to SVO adherence, the tendency in reception to connect the noun phrase and the verb phrase nearest to one another, leading to misinterpretation of sentences such as those containing embedded relative clauses. As is probably already apparent, deaf subjects are influenced and frequently confused by sentence surface structure, with a concomitant lack of understanding of the deep structure implications of certain word order arrangements.

The question of the comparative ability of deaf and normally hearing children to interpret passive and active sentences was examined by Burrough's (1969) through replication of a strategy reported with normally hearing children (Huttenlocher, Eisenberg, and Strauss, 1968; Huttenlocher and Strauss, 1968). Each subject was given a fixed and a movable object. In this case trucks and dogs were employed to represent four sentence conditions: (a) active sentences with the movable toy as the syntactic and logical subject, (b) active sentences with the movable toy as the syntactic and logical object, (c) passive sentences with the movable toy as logical subject, but the syntactic object, and (d) passive sentences with the movable toy as syntactic subject, but logical object. The deaf subjects took longer to construct these sentences than the normally hearing subjects, but both groups found the tasks equally difficult when trucks were used; active subject portrayal was easiest to arrange and passive logical object sentences the most difficult.

The semantic problems involved with arranging dogs were easy for deaf subjects to overcome, leading Burroughs (1969) to suggest that syntactic structures cannot really be investigated apart from their pragmatic and semantic constraints.

Jarvella and Lubinsky (1975) observed that deaf children adhered to a "first mentioned is first event" strategy when interpreting both picture sequences and descriptions employing temporal clauses to describe those pictures. The left-to-right approach was satisfactory for picture ordering because deaf subjects were comparable to normally hearing subjects used in the study, but it resulted in sizable difficulties in sentence interpretation, causing deaf subjects' linguistic performance to resemble much younger hearing children, such as those described by Clark (1970, 1971) and Sinclair and Ferriero (1970).

Hargis, Evans, and Masters (1973) investigated the ability of deaf children in the earliest stages of reading to complete direct and indirect discourse sentences. Their subjects had more difficulty in filling indirect discourse segments, perhaps because surface structure cues as to appropriate pronoun and tense usage are generally unavailable if the sentence stem consists only of *John said . . . .* Clearly, as indicated by Wilbur (1977), knowledge of discourse constraints, what comes before and after a sentence, plays a role in meaningful interpretation of much of written or spoken language, including direct and indirect discourse sentences.

Summary In this section we have reviewed a variety of findings about the relative abilities of deaf and normally hearing children to generate spontaneous compositions, and to understand and/or produce meaningful English sentences through reading, writing, drawing, or pointing.

A few results are most consistent in their appearance. First, deaf subjects' written language, whether spontaneously produced or generated in a structured reading/writing format, is consistently immature when compared to normally hearing subjects who have completed the same tasks.

Second, although deaf children's linguistic efforts are generally less accurate than those of normally hearing children, both in production of base structures and of more complex forms, their restricted forms or pattern deviations generally parallel those of subjects without hearing loss. Normally hearing children make errors in written language or in paper and pencil tasks. Deaf children just make more of the same kinds of errors.

Third, deaf children depend highly upon surface structure organization in both comprehension and production of English written sentences. The simple active declarative subject-verb-object syntactic arrangement is the best mastered and most influential order apparent in their language performance. In this context it is reasonable to suggest that inadequate experience with read and written English may be responsible for this rigidity rather than deviant symbolic organization per se. It is apparent that deaf children do produce very esoteric word arrangements, but their reasons are as much related to limited exposure to and lack of experience with generating base structure and subsequent transformational operations as to disordered language learning potential.

Fourth, syntactic problems of deaf children have received considerable research attention, which is appropriate if general descriptions of their written abilities are to be gathered. It seems to be time now, however, to try to understand the semantic/pragmatic knowledge acquired by deaf children so that semantic field differentiation and other aspects of meaning may be brought into congruence with the majority of English language users.

Fifth, the paucity of English deep structure intuitions of most deaf children can be clearly seen in tasks that test grammatical sensitivity. Their ability to use language to aid memory or to understand the implications of discourse organization is impaired by their routinely superficial knowledge of the organization and functions of English. The poverty that deaf children show in their understanding and use of English, especially in light of their rich linguistic potential as human beings, is most distressing.

Manual Language Performance

In recent years there has been considerable study and linguistic description of sign or manual language as used by deaf adults (Bellugi and Fischer, 1972; Bellugi and Klima, 1975; Bellugi, Klima, and Siple, 1974; Fischer, 1973, 1975; Friedman, 1975, 1976, 1977; Grosjean and Lane, 1975; Hoemann, 1976; Wilbur, 1976; Woodward, 1971, 1973a,b, 1976). These efforts to define the linguistic dimensions of this symbol system have generated several important facts about American Sign Language (ASL): (a) ASL is a language in its own right and should not be viewed as a system piggybacked onto or a dialectical variation of spoken English, (b) ASL shares some characteristics with all languages, but also contains many unique features because of its visual/spatial orientation, and (c) many deaf children must be viewed as bilingual, if they are systematically exposed to ASL with or before spoken English.

As has been suggested, it is important that attention be paid to the acquisition of ASL because such attention should give clear indication of deaf children's potentials for acquisition of a symbol system. Because sign language has been viewed as a pale reflection of spoken English, insufficient attention has been paid to both the roots of ASL acquisition and to its development in hearing-impaired persons. The literature on the emergence of sign and gestures systems has been considered in the first portion of this chapter. Now we return to a consideration of the processes that seem to be in operation in the development of ASL fluency in older children and youth.

Grammatical Function in Sign Language Acquisition   One of the earliest efforts to explore manual communication and/or gesture systems was reported recently by Tervoort (1975). Over several years he observed the communication interactions of dyads of hearing-impaired children in Dutch, Belgian, and American schools for the deaf. Unfortunately his report is marred by his assumption that signed systems, which he labels esoteric systems, are derived from or are modifications of spoken languages. In spite of this limitation, his observations that deaf children depend heavily upon visual communication cannot be denied. This dependency is attributed to the fact that such systems are visually and spatially oriented, and because deaf children are essentially visual learners, an assumption that can be challenged with the advent and application of improved amplification systems, it is logical that they should turn to the system most resonant with their learning modes. It is Tervoort's contention that dependence upon "ungrammatical" forms from visual symbol systems leads to faulty acquisition of spoken language forms, although with age he observed a drift toward development of more "correct" spoken language.

Charrow (1976; Charrow and Fletcher, 1974) attempted to clarify the language dominance of deaf children systematically exposed to ASL as well as the question of the influences of ASL on the development of English fluency.

Charrow and Fletcher (1974) administered the Test of English as a Foreign Language (TOEFL) to a group of deaf adolescents with deaf parents and to a group of deaf adolescents with hearing parents. Subjects with deaf parents scored significantly higher than subjects with hearing parents on all but one sub-test. Of interest was the result that performance by normally hearing, foreign students on the TOEFL was more highly correlated with the performance of deaf subjects with deaf parents than with the performance of deaf subjects of hearing parents. This finding was interpreted as indication that English might be considered a second language for deaf children with deaf parents, with ASL the primary language.

In an examination of language performance of deaf children, Charrow (1976) observed that deaf children's English productions shared linguistic deviations, best termed as "deafisms," to support the presence of a dialectical variation of standard English used by deaf people, namely, Deaf English. Examination of deafisms indicated to Charrow that they were not a result of the interference of ASL, but rather should be viewed as simplifications common to deaf children trying to master spoken English. Of course it could also be argued that these simplifications are so systematic that they may be a result of teaching strategies rather than of a system developed spontaneously by deaf children themselves.

In the past few years, educators who have recognized the differences between ASL and English have suggested the introduction of manual systems that conform to the surface structure forms of spoken English. Signing Essential English (Anthony, 1971) and Signing Exact English (Gustason, Pfetzing, and Zawolkow, 1972) are examples of these suggestions, hereafter referred to as Signed English. Signed English systems are replications of spoken English with regard to word order, noun and verb inflection, auxiliary verb system, and so forth. An additional alternative has also evolved for instruction, designated Manual English. Manual English casts ASL forms into standard English word order while retaining the lexical realizations of ASL. There is a suggestion (Wilbur, 1976) that such systems are at best pidgin versions of both ASL and English, systems that delete the most important, rich, and unique features of both languages in order to generate socially acceptable, although not necessarily meaningful, surface structure forms. Despite this concern, Signed and Manual English have become important pedagogical forces in many classes for the hearing impaired.

Of late there has been some research directed toward the impact of Signed or Manual English on the acquisition of English language forms in hearing-impaired children. Among these efforts is a report by Brasel and Quigley (1977), who compared the language performance of Signed English instructed deaf children of deaf parents with Manual English or ASL instructed deaf children of deaf parents and two orally trained groups of hearing-impaired children. On the Test of Syntactic Ability, standardized reading tests, and analysis of spontaneously generated written compositions, a most interesting finding was that the Signed English group scored significantly better than the other three groups, which was thought to mean that exposure to clearly perceptible forms that closely approximated standard English leads to greater receptive and expressive fluency in English.

Costello (1972) studied the development of some linguistic rules in children exposed to either ASL, Signed English, or Manual English. Positive and negative declarative sentences and positive and negative question forms were found to develop in an order and with a frequency of appearance quite similar to that found with normally hearing children developing spoken English. The employment of manual systems did not have an adverse affect on the appearance of these forms. Three factors were felt to have a significant bearing on the variance among subjects that did appear: degree of hearing impairment (a factor repeatedly found to be important in language development); the number of deaf teachers and houseparents with whom the child has had linguistic contact; and the number of home visitations, but, in this case, a negative relationship. The possible conclusions one might reach from such results include the idea that if appropriate models are made available to hearing-impaired children, they can succeed in acquiring a language system, be it manual or otherwise. Second, if the decision is made to employ sign language with a deaf child whose parents do not sign, they should be assisted in acquiring manual skills so that they may be productively involved in the language environment.

One of the major criticisms leveled by opponents of ASL in educational settings has been that ASL does not have an inflection system like Standard English, and as a consequence, these features are not learned before encountering printed English materials. See Essential English was developed to overcome this situation. Raffin (1976) studied the acquisition of inflectional morphemes by deaf children instructed using See Essential English. The results of this study indicate that deaf children, who are consistently exposed to a morpheme-based sign code, are capable of recognizing the correct use of inflectional morphemes. They also exhibited an orderly acquisition of the inflectional morphemes tested: perfect present, superlative, comparative, third person present indicative, possessive, present progressive, past tense, and plurality, not unlike that of the normally hearing comparison group. It is not clear whether there was a developmental delay with the hearing-impaired sample, even though they demonstrated ability to use inflections. Given the chronological age of the deaf sample, as well as the fact that the sample did not achieve full control over all inflections, some degree of delay must be presumed.

Semantic Function in Sign Language Acquisition   Interest in the semantic development of children who use sign language systems of some sort has been a traditional concern of researchers. Several studies have attempted to evaluate the encoding strategies of ASL users engaged in traditional semantic assessment tasks such as serial learning or word associations. For example, Putnam, Iscoe, and Young (1962) evaluated the ability of normally hearing and hearing-impaired adolescents to remember lists of words. The lists were organized in four ways: (a) lists of real words that when signed were quite similar to one another, (b) lists of real words that were dissimilar when signed, (c) lists of nonsense words that were similar in form, and (d) lists of nonsense words that were dissimilar in form. Deaf subjects learned all the lists more quickly than the normally hearing subjects. The sign-similar real word list was more easily mastered by the deaf subjects; the reverse was true for the nonsense lists. These results could be interpreted to mean that signing accelerates word memorization in hearing-impaired subjects, but that notion does not necessarily explain why the sign-similar word list should be learned more easily than the sign-dissimilar list. The lack of vocabulary growth in deaf children may have worked to their advantage in this situation. A limited vocabulary could reduce potential interference from the knowledge or memory of too many words. In other words, limited semantic differentiation may have aided performance rather than deterred it in this special task. Another factor might have been that similar sign words could be filed into memory more easily because they share similar formational characteristics, but given what we know from learning theory, that dissimilar items are easier to remember than similar items, it would seem more reasonable to suggest that similarity should have been a more difficult condition than dissimilarity. The fáct that it was not suggests that the words thought to be similarly signed were only superficially alike, but were not closely related formationally to an ASL user.

Tweney and Hoemann (1973) were interested in whether the syntagmatic-paradigmatic shift—the shift from word order responses to same form class responses—occurred when hearing-impaired children were encouraged to store and respond to a word association task in sign language. Observation of such a shift would indicate that deaf children probably organize their semantic fields in ways that are similar to normally hearing children. Both deaf and normally hearing subjects in this study were shown to manifest a clear syntagmatic-paradigmatic shift, although the number of paradigmatic or form class responses was lower for deaf children, suggesting quantitative but not qualitative differences, in contrast to previous reports on testing deaf children using English lexical items.

Tweney, Hoemann, and Andrews (1975) reported on deaf and normally hearing children's ability to form hierarchal clusters in a noun-sorting task. In one study, performance differed for sorting a set of words referring to acoustic events for which deaf subjects would have little or no experience, but not on sets of common nouns. In a second study, sorting of matched sets of high- and low-imagery words was comparable between the two groups of subjects. It was concluded that deaf subjects manifested abstract hierarchal relations and were not strictly dependent upon visual mediators or hindered by the absence of acoustic mediators. Of course, it can be argued that although deaf children may group words or pictures in a way similar to that of normally hearing children, the basis upon which these constellations are built may or may not be similar, especially when considering the organizational differences between English and ASL.

Immediate and delayed recall abilities of deaf and normally hearing children were tested by Bonvillian (1974) by presenting words that varied on the dimension of imagery and signability. Deaf children's performance improved when words of high imagery and high signability were used, even though the normally hearing subjects completed all tasks better than the deaf subjects. Differences between deaf and hearing subjects on previous studies of memory or word recall might be attributed to failure to encourage or allow deaf subjects to use sign language to aid in problem solving. Bellugi, Klima, and Siple's (1974) study on the use of signs to aid memory in deaf adults confirms that notion.

The dearth of information on the developmental stages of sign language, in whatever form, is most unfortunate and should be remedied, so that sensible descriptions of manual language forms and functions can be related to the problem of improving the level of literacy in deaf children. Sign language can be regularized by addition of appropriate markers, so that it approximates English forms. Such modification may facilitate acquisition of surface structure forms by deaf children. The influences of sign systems on the acquisition of read, written, and spoken English must still be explored to determine whether simultaneous or sequential presentation of manual and non-manual systems is most appropriate for facilitating language growth in hearing-impaired children.

Communication Competence

Interest in communication competence or the events that surround and condition communication has increased in recent years both with normally hearing and deaf children. Communication patterns in classrooms have been the subject of several studies designed to evaluate the quality of linguistic input provided hearing-impaired children. In addition, there have been a few studies examining the types of communication interactions among older deaf children, studies that have begun examination of communication competence whether spoken or sign language was employed. The nature of communication competence development in children learning spoken English has only recently been brought into focus. It is hoped that with this impetus there will be serious effort to gain a fuller understanding of communication competence of hearing-impaired persons as well.

Using a modification of the Flanders' Interactive Scale (Flanders, 1965), Craig and Collins (1970) observed that classroom conversations tended to be dominated by the teacher, with few student-initiated communication attempts evident. No differences in teacher dominance were noted, regardless of the communication modality used or the grade level of the educational unit examined. Questioning and informing were the two most frequently observed categories of communication employed by teachers, whether the lessons were language-dependent or consisted of other special subject instruction. This degree of communication dominance by teachers raises the possibility that deaf students may not lack the ability to acquire mature communication competence, but simply do not get the chance to practice communication, or initiate interactions in the classrooms.

Lawson (1978) used an adaptation of the Craig and Collins (1970) procedures to observe five classes of intermediate-age deaf students. Student-directive and student-compliant communication behaviors were observed with equal frequency. Student-directive communication involved student initiated behaviors, and student-compliant communication resulted from teacher initiatives. The most prevalent student-directive communication was informing, which usually consisted of offering information, ideas, or comments about ongoing topics. Following directions was the most frequent student-compliant communication act. It was noted that development or indications of acceptance and use of another's ideas or thoughts in building the student's own ideas occurred infrequently. This was considered unfortunate, because it suggested that deaf children do not actively integrate information into their own thinking, a strategy that might be considered the ultimate outcome of education. Lawson's results are in partial contradiction to those of Craig and Collins (1970), because teacher dominated communication was not observed. Lawson suggests that the reason may be that Craig and Collins used, in addition to intermediate age subjects, both primary and high school classrooms, where didactic methods might be employed on a more routine basis. Better yet, perhaps communication involvement patterns are changing in classes for the deaf.

A specially constructed scale, the Cognitive Verbal/Non-verbal Observation Scale, was used by Wolff (1977) to investigate communication patterns in classes for the deaf, that employed different communication modes—fingerspelling, an oral method, and total communication. It should be noted at the onset that many of the teachers observed had participated in an inservice program that encouraged non-directive, language supportive instruction. In any event, teachers of younger children tended to dominate conversation, but in classrooms with older deaf youngsters, who were probably more sophisticated linguistically, student-initiated discourse was observed more frequently. There was a trend for total communication classes to show more open communication than the oral classes examined, with classes employing only fingerspelling the least open in communication. Whether this is a function of teacher style or of the methodology used is unclear. Of significance, however, is the content of the conversations observed among the deaf subjects and their teachers. Most centered around activities involving memory work and classifying, with little attention directed toward inference building. Therefore, although communication was more open with deaf students, these teachers tended not to encourage use of communication to enhance cognition, fluency in linguistic processing, or in verbal thinking.

The influence of teacher responses on communication or linguistic form usages of deaf students has been considered as well. For example

Erber and Greer (1973) observed teacher response styles in classes employing oral instruction of deaf children. Teachers adopted four basic response patterns to the oral communications of their students: (a) repetition of all or part of the utterance, (b) application of acoustic or oral/facial emphasis to all or part of the utterance, (c) manipulation of vocabulary or syntax to effect a structural change, and (d) provision of supplementary information in the form of additional cues or prompts. Restated in linguistic terms, the teachers seemed to employ expansion, repetition, and modeling techniques in response to children's utterances, with emphasis and repetition the most frequently observed patterns, although teachers tended to demonstrate idiosyncratic preferences for communication interactions. The effects of such widely varying strategies upon linguistic progress in children whose own styles may vary widely is uncertain. With young normally hearing children, style incongruence with the mother may temporarily stall, but not prevent, language acquisition. The question of how communication disyncrony may influence deaf children whose communication competence may be already seriously impaired by a lack of nonverbal experience or an impoverished linguistic environment cannot be clearly answered, but should not be ignored as a factor in language development.

Scroggs (1975) trained three teachers to use expansion techniques as described by Brown and Bellugi (1964). An expansion was defined as a complete adult version of a child's incomplete utterance. The teachers were requested to use expansions for at least 50% of the students' incomplete communications. In two of three classrooms studied, the rate of both non-oral and oral communications increased or decreased as a function of the number of expansions employed by the teacher. In the third classroom, no parallel movement between communication output and percentage of expansions used was apparent, although in this classroom there was a large increase in non-oral communications observed. These findings suggest that children's communication rates are sensitive to teacher manipulation; indeed, in early stages of use of such strategies, increases in children's communication rate depend on the quantity of teacher efforts. How quickly deaf children learn to communicate without teacher domination or support must be answered. In at least one instance (Craig and Collins, 1970), high school age deaf students were still teacher dependent, but Lawson (1978) observed a balance between student and teacher initiated communication.

The accuracy and quality of peer-to-peer communication in 8- and 11-year-old deaf children using manual language was compared with that of normally hearing children using spoken English by Hoemann (1972). All subject pairs were required to send and receive information about a variety of picture referents, referents from the receivers' perspective, and rules of a game. Significantly poorer communication performances by the deaf children were attributed to an experiential deficit that was thought to affect their acquisition of conventional language and to impair their development of communication skills. These findings are certainly suppportive of the deficits observed by others in classroom communication.

Pendergrass and Hodges (1976) observed deaf students' involved in group problem-solving situations to learn about their interactive communication patterns. Six groups of four to six children were brought together for the purpose of solving a predetermined problem presented to them by the examiner. Using Bales's Interaction Process Analysis procedures (Bales, 1950), the quantity and quality of communicative interactions among the subjects were evaluated. The results indicated a low percentage of interaction in the questioning categories, which was interpreted to mean that these deaf children were not proficient in questioning techniques. They generally lacked ability to ask for information, make suggestions, provide orientations, or clarify others' opinions. In the comparison of positive and negative social-emotional areas there was the trend for the older deaf subjects observed to be more positively supportive of the efforts from others in the group. In addition, there seemed to be more interactive attempts with age, although without a comparison group of normally hearing subjects it is not possible to state whether there were normal amounts of interaction among the deaf subjects. Gorrell's (1971) observations concerning the paucity of preschool interactive patterns for deaf children seems to be true for many deaf students, even in the early adolescent period. If normally hearing subjects had been evaluated, it might be possible to say whether communication through ASL provides an adequate base for interactive participation among older deaf youngsters.

The linguistic control of classrooms for deaf children tends to be in the mouths and hands of the teacher, regardless of communication modality or ages of the children. There are indications that teachers can be more sensitive to communication needs of deaf children to a degree that the students' communication output can be altered. Conspicuous by their absence are studies examining communication patterns among older deaf children and their parents, especially because there is evidence that parents of young deaf children have impaired communication with their children. All in all, there is reason to believe that deaf children lack well-developed communicatiom competence at all ages, the causes of which are not yet fully understood. This issue is clearly deserving of more attention by educators and researchers, however.

SUMMARY

Despite the length of this chapter, it should be clear to the reader that comparatively little is known about the language/communication abilities, or the developmental rates or stages of language acquisition in hearing-impaired children and youth, perhaps because research continues to focus on lack of achievement or on divergences from normalcy rather than on detailed documentation of the performance capabilities of children with varying degrees of hearing impairment. In light of the consensus among educators of the hearing impaired that communication development is a primary issue for deaf children, this is a disappointing state of affairs. Professional educators are continuing to develop programs for language instruction based on insufficient information about abilities of the deaf children themselves, or on incomplete documentation relative to the quality of success of such programs. Let us see if, in spite of these problems, there are any ideas or trends that could be used as a basis for initiating and encouraging English fluency in deaf persons.

It has been suggested that the linguistic capabilities of deaf children can be viewed as: (a) delayed in nature because of a lack of linguistic/cognitive experience but shown to progress with age, (b) as deviant in nature because of the effects of hearing impairment on cognitive development as well as influences from an alternative symbol system (ASL), (c) as dialectical in nature because English is a second language and ASL the primary language, or more probably (d) as showing language proficiency that is the result of some or all of the foregoing influences.

The results of data currently available would argue that deaf children cannot be viewed as monolithic in language capabilities, but instead deaf children are fragmented relative to the degree of their English fluency. It is appropriate to say that too many are still linguistically handicapped relative to the literacy standard in read, written, and spoken English in light of the high quality of linguistic and educational achievement attained by a minority of deaf persons.

If the hearing impairment of a child is diagnosed early, if he is capable of profiting from auditory input, and if the quality and quantity of his linguistic experience at home is normalized, his subsequent language performance, whether oral or manual, and his performance in reading and writing seems to parallel that of normally hearing children. On the other hand, children who are identified at older ages or who are subject to indifferent quality of linguistic experiences and stereotyped instruction, whether in sign language or not, develop performance in English that is significantly impoverished compared to normally hearing children, resulting in impaired educational progress. These children frequently come to school as non-English language users, or even without a symbol system that is understood by those around them.

In the initial stages of acquisition, manual and spoken language systems have much in common, as can be seen from recent accounts of language acquisition in both modalities. Acquisition of syntactic, or surface structure, fluency seems to be the least affected by auditory defects or by potential interference of the two language systems. Semantic and pragmatic development seems more affected by the presence of deafness and/or language interference.

The semantic/pragmatic bases of gesture and sign languages are determined in part by their spatial/visual orientation. Therefore, the cognitive/symbolic organization must differ in many respects from auditorily based languages such as spoken English. Regularizing surface structure forms, as suggested by Signed English advocates, does not guarantee that knowledge of the semantic/pragmatic bases of English will be acquired. Indeed, the usefulness of such systems needs to be systematically explored.

The potential for interference between visual and auditory systems raises questions about the introduction and use of visually based language. If an educator believes that auditorily based language learning should not be the predominate system for the majority of hearing-impaired children, which these authors are not willing to concede at this point, then the question of when and how to introduce visually based systems remains. If visually based systems are organized symbolically in a different way from auditorily based systems, then simultaneous presentation of divergent systems does not seem reasonable. An alternative is to present the visual system first to ensure the child's proficiency, and then piggyback standard English onto this symbol system either as spoken or read/written language. In effect, such a situation faces deaf children of manual deaf parents who enter many programs for the deaf. Their educational task involves second language learning, with manual/visual language as the primary system and standard English as the second language. As in all second language learning situations, potential areas of interference would have to be recognized, and teaching strategies would have to be developed to minimize interference, perhaps by drawing on available second language learning literature. A similar argument might also be made for introducing auditory experiences and spoken English first, because of the relative difficulty of acquiring oral language as a mode of expression.

These statements should not be viewed as value judgments about the use of auditory or visual systems with hearing-impaired children. They are offered in an effort to identify the range of problems confronting teachers of the hearing impaired who must make decisions about improving language performance and competence of deaf children.

Clearly, provision must be made for enhancing the general cognitive/linguistic experiences of all deaf children, because the single theme recurring in most of the research reviewed in this chapter is the seeming lack of control of any aspect of Standard English, not because of inability to symbolize, but because of a lack of practice in generating symbolic behavior.

CHAPTER 5

LANGUAGE ASSESSMENT

CONTENTS

Language assessment is an important but complicated process, complicated because of the difficulty in adequately evaluating many aspects of language performance, or determining whether the sample of behavior bears any relationship to a child's generally demonstrated capabilities. In spite of this problem, language evaluation is a necessary component in educational planning if language instruction goals are to be formulated, if duplication of teaching efforts is to be avoided, and if evidence is to be gathered about whether children are learning. Language assessment may be viewed by some as needed only at the beginning of instruction. To be truly effective, however, assessment must occur routinely in the instructional process.

The purpose of this chapter is to explore contemporary assessment of language performance with emphasis on procedures that are useful with hearing-impaired individuals.

Comprehensive assessment of linguistic functioning should involve examination of two sets of data. One set should be derived from formal test procedures using instruments specifically designed to evaluate linguistic or communicative behavior. The second set, based on observation of children's performance in spontaneous communication settings, should be used to confirm, clarify, or expand results obtained through formal testing. Needless to say, each set of results has its drawbacks relative to the validity of the language behaviors obtained. Unless formal tests are selected carefully, they may not tap the areas of linguistic or communicative performance intended. Considering only spontaneously-generated language, on the other hand, may lead to inappropriate conclusions about a child's knowledge of language.

In spite of the potential difficulties with formal and informal assessment, language communication abilities of hearing-impaired children and youth must be evaluated. In the following sections, formal and informal test or evaluation strategies that seem to have usefulness in describing the language performance of children who have significant auditory impairment are considered. This review is not exhaustive, but it is sufficiently comprehensive to provide information about and guidelines for the teacher or clinician engaged in evaluation of the language performance of hearing-impaired persons.

FORMAL TESTING PROCEDURES AND INSTRUMENTS

As with all formal tests, procedures for language evaluation must be able to satisfy certain criteria: (1) Does the test objectively measure what it purports to measure? (2) Are the normative data for the test adequate in variety and quantity and were the standardization samples representative of the children to whom the test will be administered? and (3) Is the test reliable?

Test Validity

Test validity can be defined in at least two ways—through content validity or through statistical validity. Statistical validity refers to the attempt by the test developer to prove that the results of his test parallel those obtained on other tests that are acknowledged to be useful. Unfortunately, in language or communication evaluation, efforts to compare tests or to derive statistical comparison are difficult because of a lack of well-established formal tests of language performance. Disagreement about the theoretical bases for particular tests has led to questions about whether those tests should be used as a standard in language evaluation. The Illinois Test of Psycholinguistic Abilities (ITPA) (Paraskevopoulos and Kirk, 1969) poses such a difficulty today, because the definitions of psycholinguistic abilities that form the bases for the ITPA are not compatible with either a developmental or generative-transformational linguistic approach as discussed in Chapters 2 and 3. As a consequence, concern about the relatively frequent and uncritical employment of the test to describe language performance or to establish statistical validation for other tests has been expressed (Newcomer and Hammill, 1976).

In lieu of, or in addition to, statistical validation, a test developer may focus on test content to affirm validity, which generally involves use of references to external research or theory, or even use of arguments about the internal logic of the test itself. In evaluating content validity, one might ask whether the test author provides a logical argument based on research findings to justify the existence of the test in its current form.

When considering content validity of a language test, the reader might try to answer questions such as:

1. What is the definition of language used in development of this test? On what aspects of language/communication performance does this particular test focus?
2. Is there evidence of knowledge of contemporary research in child language or linguistics to support the definitions and applications for the test?
3. Do the names and contents of subtests or test components articulate in a logical manner based on the theoretical orientation of the test?
4. Are the justifications for the definitions and selection of test items clear enough, so that a user could generate additional test items or exercises to fit the test model? If so, then the theoretical bases and the test items are consistent with one another. If it is not possible to generate new items, then the reader may not understand the purposes of the task well enough, the theoretical underpinnings of the test may be questionable, or the items in the test may not support the test model.

Standardization

The second area of concern about formal tests is the standardization procedure, with particular focus on the persons with whom the test is supposedly useful. Test normative scores are collective standards obtained by averaging the test performance of many individuals, usually expressed in terms of age or school grade, occasionally by sex or even speech community.

Test norms should allow some quantitative or qualitative statements to be made about individual subjects who take the test; an individual's score(s) should be understandable relative to average scores and to the expected performance variability for any test. Variability around the mean is expressed statistically as the standard deviation. One standard deviation above and below the mean on a test with normal or so-called bell-shaped score distribution is expected to encompass 68% of all the test scores for that test. Two standard deviations above and below the mean should encompass 96% of all test scores. In other words, if the mean score of a test is 100 and the standard deviation is 15, 68 out of 100 testees should obtain scores somewhere between 85 and 115. For test purposes, scores ranging from 85 to 115 would be considered equivalent or indistinguishable from one another. The assumption of average test performance for a particular child would mean that his score would fall within the 85 to 115 range from one testing to another, although his actual score would vary from test to test. Thus, considering test norms, one should examine not only average performance, but variability dimensions as well. The greater the variability among scores, the less precise the test seems to be in providing a clear description of performance from any sample of subjects. These considerations apply, of course, only if a particular test is thought to be based on a sample whose scores are normally distributed. Some formal language tests fail to meet this requirement, or are designed to do so. They may focus on reporting performance developmentally, such as percentages or numbers of items achieved by a particular age, as in 90% of normally developing children show mastery of the /p/ phoneme by age 3.

The composition of the test sample when developing normative data is another matter of concern, because test authors must decide on the sample to use in standardization. It is important to ascertain when test standards have been generalized from a variety of language users, or from only a small speech community. For tests of language/communication, standardization decisions may be difficult to make because English as a spoken form is hardly uniform. Stated differently, a variety of dialectical differences exist in American society that must be considered in test construction. In fact, dialectical differences are so pronounced that in some ways it may not be possible to establish a comprehensive test of spoken English that is equally responsive to all segments of the American linguistic community.

The size of the standardization sample should also be a concern, because some developmental aspects of language cannot be accurately described unless very large groups of children are evaluated. Indeed specific aspects of language performance may be so variable even in mature language users that enlarging sample size still will not generate an accurate account of normal performance.

Test Reliability

The last issue to be considered relative to formal test construction is test reliability. Reliability can be defined in at least three ways: temporal reliability, internal reliability, and examiner reliability. Temporal reliability refers to the liklihood that test-retest scores will be comparable for any child on a particular test. In some types of tests of language development, such reliability would be an indication of lack of language growth, because the expectation of improvement over time would be the foremost concern of the test procedure. However, even with these tests, some sort of consistency in test behavior for each child should be expected.

Internal reliability is primarily an issue for tests that have more than one form, or have many items that evaluate the same linguistic principle. In these cases the organization and relative ease or difficulty of such items should be comparable; any child's performance should be similar on so-called equivalent forms, or from the beginning to the end of a test of a limited number of language principles.

The last form of reliability concerns whether different examiners using the same test instrument can achieve comparable results. Administration of the test should be described in sufficient detail so that persons other than the test author can learn to administer it and obtain reliable results.

THE RELATION BETWEEN IMITATION, COMPREHENSION, AND PRODUCTION—THE ICP HYPOTHESIS

Before beginning an examination of specific test procedures, the relationship between the three areas of linguistic performance most often evaluated should be considered: imitative ability, comprehension ability, and production ability. Examining the research in these areas should assist in forming a perspective about where to place emphasis in evaluation or about how to judge the usefulness of tests designed to assess these areas of language performance.

In 1963, Fraser, Bellugi, and Brown reported on children's control or expression of linguistic knowledge under conditions of imitation (I), comprehension (C), and production (P). Comprehension was determined by evaluating subjects' ability to point to pictures felt to correspond to test sentences. Imitation tasks required subjects to reproduce exactly sentences spoken and cued by pictures. Production tasks required subjects to generate picture labels; the examiner asked each subject to generate one of two sentences that best described a particular picture. The results of this study were taken to mean that language facility shown in the imitative condition was greater than language facility shown in the comprehension condition, which in turn was greater than language facility shown in the production condition. The developmental pattern of imitation proficiency exceeding comprehension, which in turn exceeded production, became known as the ICP Hypothesis. This hypothesis states that developing linguistic principles tend to manifest themselves first in children's imitations, then in their comprehension of a principle, and finally in their production of that principle.

In a study using mentally retarded children, Lovell and Dixon (1967) found that the ICP Hypothesis generally held. Slobin and Welsh (1973) concurred in part after evaluating the performance of a single subject. They observed that this child did imitate forms that generally did not appear in her spontaneous language productions. However, there were also instances when she modified her imitations in accordance with forms already spontaneously produced.

In contrast, Nurss and Day (1971) observed that young children's comprehension behavior generally preceded their imitation of forms, which led them to conclude that, with their sample, the ICP Hypothesis should be revised to read CIP (Comprehension-Imitation-Production). Fernald (1972) revised Fraser, Bellugi, and Brown's (1963) scoring procedures to reduce the influence of guessing on test results. Among the modifications, subjects were credited with knowing a syntactic principle even if it was produced in a phrase that was not an imitation of the test sentence, which Fraser, Bellugi, and Brown did not allow. When a child failed to respond to a particular item, that item was repeated at the end of the test to reduce the influence of motivation variations. Credit was given only if the subject identified or comprehended the first item of a minimal contrastive pair. It was felt that the second item of the pair did not constitute an independent judgment by the child, because its solution was contingent upon the response generated for the first item. As in the Fraser, Bellugi, and Brown study, the child had to correctly generate or produce answers for both items in order for the productive task to receive credit. With these modifications in scoring, Fernald found that children's comprehension was better than their imitation of syntactic principles, but both exceeded production. Fernald concurred with Nurss and Day (1971) that CIP more accurately described developmental performance on language tests. Based on these observations, the authors of this book would tend to support CIP as the most likely developmental order.

Baird (1972) attributed the discrepancies among imitation, comprehension, and production scores to statistic inequality with respect to the chance of a correct response being generated. This inequality in chance for responses calls into question whether direct comparisons between the three conditions should be made. Despite Baird's contention, imitation, comprehension, and production are still used commonly in language evaluation procedures. A review of the development and structure of what is generally known about each process or test condition follows, with particular reference to the problems of using each in children's language assessment.

Imitation

Imitation is defined in the preceding studies as elicited imitation, which is distinct from delayed or spontaneous imitation (Rees, 1975). Elicited imitation results from requesting the subject to repeat immediately after the examiner, whereas delayed or spontaneous imitation refers to imitations produced after the fact, or without direct prompting from the examiner. An example of the latter occurs in an exchange in which the adult says, "I see a bird.", and the child replies *bird* without prompting. Elicited and spontaneous imitation are considered to be different events linguistically, with the latter form commonly identified as an important behavior in the child language development literature.

The expectation when elicited imitation is employed in testing is that a child will normally reduce his imitations in proportion to degree of linguistic knowledge he has about a particular principle (Brown and Bellugi, 1964; Slobin and Welsh, 1973). Partial imitations are felt to be reflective of the child's conscious level of linguistic knowledge. There is a fine, and not always discernible, line between such meaningful imitation and mimicry, with the latter being quite common among young hearing-impaired children. Mimicry, or more properly echolalia, is the imitation of language with no presumption of comprehension on the speaker's part.

Prutting (Prutting and Rees, 1977) and Johnston (Bates and Johnston, 1977) indicate that in some elicited imitation situations, children try to make sense of the task by treating the test sentences as part of a discourse exchange. As a consequence they produce utterances that are discourse related, not exact imitations of the examiner. For example, when asked to reproduce the sentence *The boy is walking up the stairs.*, the child might say *He is walking fast.*, or even *He is walking up the stairs.*, both of which are conversationally acceptable, but do not adhere to the rules of the imitation task.

Direct imitation, although not the primary process by which children learn language, does seem to have a role in language learning, and, as previously reported in Chapter 3, can be observed in the utterances of children. Recent studies by Bloom, Hood, and Lightbown (1974), Moerk (1977), and R. Clark (1977) have focused on the role of children's imitation in language performance. Bloom, Hood, and Lightbown (1974) observed that children's imitations tended to be employed for lexical acquisition or syntactic-semantic practice in individual children, but only with those principles that were already known and used in the child's spontaneous language, a finding supported by Whitehurst and Vasta (1975). Moerk (1977) argues that morpho-phonemic rule acquisition (local transformations) is a function of imitation, but concurs that the process occurs primarily with those forms already known to the child. R. Clark (1977), on the other hand, states that the appearance of some syntactic forms may be accounted for by a child's use of delayed imitation. For instance, children's productions such as *What he wants?* and *Why you can't open it?* could be accounted for by the fact that children are introduced to wh-words through indirect discourse from adults in such sentences as *Ask him what he wants.* or *He told you why you can't open it.* The adult forms are usually generated in answer to children's questions, so it is Clark's contention that children are highly motivated to pay attention to the adult response, which becomes transferred, through delayed imitations, into early question forms. In addition, Clark views some forms as memorized elements that serve as sentence frames upon which children's spontaneous productions are built. It should be emphasized that such behavior by children is not the result of imitation of random sentences, but must be related to information already known or required by the child.

Tests using elicited imitation can be valuable evaluation tools if the constraints on its use are understood. It is imperative however, not to equate behavior noted in elicited imitation conditions with behavior associated with delayed or spontaneous imitation conditions.

Comprehension

Language comprehension tasks are used frequently to evaluate or describe the linguistic abilities of children. Comprehension should be defined on two levels. One involves subject recognition of instances of a particular linguistic principle; the other presupposes that the child comprehends principles that he can use to make judgments about grammatical acceptability. Each level is important in developing an estimate of what children understand about language. If evaluation involves only recognition, it is often difficult to determine specifically just what aspect of test materials a subject actually comprehends.

When developing a comprehension task or evaluating the usefulness of comprehension tests, several variables should be considered. Non-verbal cuing may be an important contaminant, as could behavioral preferences of children at various ages. These two factors are discussed in greater detail later in this chapter. Logical constraints of the test material may also influence comprehension. For instance, in the passive sentence: *The cake was eaten by the man.*, only one interpretation is possible; cakes just do not eat men. This example could raise the question in comprehension testing of whether one is testing syntactic principles or children's awareness of logical behavior.

If comprehension is tested through use of sentences, too often multiple rather than single, linguistic cues are actually being tested (Waryas and Ruder, 1974). For example in testing for comprehension of plurality, sentence contrasts such as *The boy is running.* and *The boys are running.* might typically be used. Unfortunately, if correct comprehension is demonstrated, it is uncertain which aspect of this sentence cued the child—the /s/ marker on the noun, the verb change, or both. Unless the child can also make judgments about grammatical acceptability of sentences that are designed to check understanding of a specific linguistic principle, a full appreciation of the child's level of language comprehension cannot be gained. Unfortunately, unless a child has language, he can not talk about language, which makes the application of grammatical judgment evaluation to young children difficult, if not impossible.

The language structure used by the examiner has been of interest to those who evaluate young children's syntactic accuracy. Shipley, Smith, and Gleitman (1969) presented groups of young children in the "telegraphic" speech stage with test sentences that included telegraphic-like utterances, fully formed and anomalous sentences. Young telegraphic speakers seemed to comprehend telegraphic-like utterances more fully, whereas older subjects were more responsive to fully formed sentences. It was concluded that comprehension of sentences parallels production abilities in very young children. Unfortunately, the small sample size of this study has caused it to be criticized.

Petretic and Tweney (1977) completed a study modeled on Shipley, Smith, and Gleitman's work, with some modifications of sentence presentation and with an increased sample size. Their findings contradicted those of Shipley, Smith, and Gleitman, since all their subjects responded best to well-formed sentences. This finding was supported by Stanton (1976), who studied language-impaired children. Kramer (1977) concurs that the best performance is achieved when well-formed or nonanomalous sentences are used with young children. However, with 21- to 34-month-old subjects, she also noted substantial dependence on situational cues to succeed in linguistic tasks, suggesting that syntactic competence should not be inferred from apparent comprehension, especially at very young ages.

In spite of the many problems inherent in comprehension testing, both language recognition and ability to discriminate among levels of grammaticality should be evaluated, especially with deaf children, whenever possible.

Production

The third area of language performance that has received considerable attention is production. It is generally agreed that production abilities tend to lag behind comprehension and imitative abilities. Judgments about the degree of the comprehension-production gap tend to differ significantly among researchers. Some, such as Bloom (1973), suggest that it is small in the earliest stages of language development; others, such as Menyuk (1971), imply that there is a considerable gap between the two at all levels of language development, even during the earliest stages.

Production samples can be gathered from at least two environments: productions generated under controlled conditions or productions generated in spontaneous situations. Analysis of the latter samples is discussed in considerable detail in the last section of this chapter.

Production generation can be controlled by use of modeling, or by employing completion strategies. Modeling procedures in this context refers to the presentation of a set of test sentences followed by the requirement that the child generate one or more of those sentences under varying conditions, such as when cued by pictures (Fraser, Bellugi, and Brown, 1963). The difficulty with the modeling strategy is that the influence of delayed imitation on the child's response cannot be well controlled for. If R. Clark (1977) is correct about syntactic imitation, then it may be unclear whether a child, who has been provided with sentence models, is generating an original response from his own linguistic storehouse, or whether he is producing a delayed imitation.

One way to manage the imitation factor is by use of item completion tasks. The child is presented with an incomplete sentence, phrase, or word, and he is encouraged to generate the complete form. Berko's (1958) Test of Morphology is a prime example of this type of approach. Unfortunately, the usefulness of completion tasks has so far been limited to minute aspects of language production, because testing for knowledge of more complex forms such as relative or adverbial clauses can rarely be done in a way to guarantee the generation of these specific forms from all children.

The use of nonsense words as opposed to real lexical items has also frequently been employed in assessment of children's production knowledge. If the child can apply a linguistic operation to nonsense words, it is argued that he has mastered the underlying linguistic rule. Children who have tenuous command of English, such as those with impaired hearing, seemed to be confused by such a process. Perlman (1973), with hearing-impaired subjects, and Dever (1972), with mentally retarded subjects, found them able to generate many local transformations (morphophonemic endings) on real but unfamiliar words when they could not do as well with nonsense words.

Finally, although language completion tests yield valuable information about specific linguistic principles, they generally do not test children's comprehension of the requirements of discourse with regard to linguistic rules. For example, although children may demonstrate production of past tense in isolated sentences, they may show lack of understanding about how to maintain tense throughout a conversation, suggesting that they do not understand the function of past tense within discourse. Such knowledge is difficult to evaluate when test items are isolated from one another. Unfortunately, increasing test length to simulate discourse introduces the potential for variability of other sorts that could confound evaluation of discourse understanding. It may be reasonable to evaluate discourse knowledge in the context of spontaneous productions.

In summary, the three areas of linguistic performance most frequently evaluated are imitative abilities, comprehension abilities, and production abilities. Imitative abilities are usually assessed in elicited imitation situations. Comprehension involves both recognition of language and eliciting of grammatical judgments. Recognition can be assessed by subject responses of manipulation of objects or picture identification. Production is evaluated most frequently by encouraging generation of linguistic principles under controlled conditions, such as language completion tests.

TEST FORMATS

Tests of language/communication currently available could be classified based on the test response mode: tests that require imitation of the examiner's language behavior; tests that require object manipulation or demonstration in response to questions or directions; tests that require identification of an object or picture in response to questions or directions; tests that require judgments of grammaticality; and finally, tests that require completion of linguistic units provided the subject. Each of these test formats is discussed relative to the strengths and weaknesses of its use with deaf children. Current or proposed instruments that exemplify a category are reviewed when appropriate.

Elicited Imitation Format

Background Elicited imitation has been suggested repeatedly as a potentially valuable tool for language assessment. The meaning of children's performance is imitation tasks, as well as perceptual/memory influences or limitations, needs to be considered, however, when employing elicited imitation techniques (Prutting and Connolly, 1976).

Studies by Blasdell and Jensen (1970), Freedle, Keeney, and Smith (1970), Risley and Reynolds (1970), and Weener (1971) demonstrate, for example, that changing stress patterns on test sentences can produce differential results in imitation tasks. Slobin and Welsh (1973) found that changing the sentence stress or emphasis could yield imitation of function words previously omitted by their young subject. Differing results can be achieved by simply varying the linguistic cues provided the child in an imitation task. Consistent presentation of material to be imitated must be achieved if the task is to have any meaning across children tested or for a particular child in repeated test situations.

When sentences to be imitated exceed the memory capacity of children, they often rephrase such sentences to make them compatible with their memory span (Carrow and Mauldin, 1973; Miller, 1973; Miller and Chapman, 1975; Slobin and Welsh, 1973). A child may understand a particular principle, but because the test sentence to be imitated exceeds his memory abilities, he reduces the sentence to a simpler form compatible with his recall. If principles are phrased within acceptable length sentences, paraphrasing or partial imitation can be prevented.

Menyuk and Looney (1972), in evaluating language-disordered children, found that the length of test sentences produced differences in their performance as compared to normally speaking children. Within their test format, however, there were differences in the two groups' respective abilities to imitate varying syntactic conventions. Imperative and declarative sentence frames were the easiest forms for both groups of children.

If sentence length is critical to a sample of language handicapped children with normal hearing, what greater influences might be observed with hearing-impaired children? Memory restrictions alone may not be responsible for poor performance, however. Inability to imitate accurately may also be the result of lack of knowledge about a particular type of linguistic form(s). Often teachers of the hearing-impaired obtain elicited imitation of a sentence, and a short while later retest to find that it can not be reproduced. Such behavior is frequently attributed to a memory deficit, when more accurately it may be a problem of insufficient experience with or lack of mastery of the language principle under consideration. If the child does not understand a particular linguistic principle, the liklihood of his internalizing knowledge about it by imitation alone is slim. Normal children certainly do not do it.

The proclivity of children toward use of imitation as a learning strategy should also be considered when employing imitation tests. As previously reported, Bloom, Lightbown, and Hood (1975) identified some children who were highly imitative in spontaneous situations, and others who were not. In elicited imitation tasks, then, children who are not imitators may choose to paraphrase sentences to make them conform to discourse expectations or to fit their own linguistic knowledge. These children might demonstrate low scores imitatively, yet show knowledge of the forms in question in their spontaneous utterances. Indeed, Prutting, Gallagher, and Mulac (1975) found that many children who failed items on the expressive portion of the Northwestern Syntax Screening Test (NSST) showed expressive mastery of those items in spontaneous production.

Bohannan (1975) reported that children's imitative ability was closely tied to their knowledge about the conversation or discourse roles of speakers. Conversational/pragmatic understanding may be related to children's use of imitation and to knowledge about the functions of imitation in language. When utilizing imitation tasks, apparently even the pragmatic insights of subjects may have a bearing on the quality of their performance.

Tests Using Elicited Imitation Format   An elicited imitation format has been used in the development of various tests. Among the most well known is the expressive portion of the Northwestern Syntax Screening Test (Lee, 1969). The expressive portion of the NSST requires the child to repeat one of two test sentences spoken by the examiner and then cued by one of two pictures. The test elicits delayed imitation from each subject, a requirement that is subject to the problems already outlined. The expressive and receptive portions of the NSST were used with some success by Presnell (1973) to evaluate hearing-impaired children as previously discussed in Chapter 4. Some additional comments about the psychometric characteristics of the NSST appear in the section on picture identification that follows.

In an interesting application of sentence repetition behavior, Berry-Luterman and Bar (1971) assessed children's abilities to repeat syntactically incorrect sentences taken from the child's own productions, syntactically correct versions of the same sentences, and reversed word order of the syntactically correct versions. The reason for employing such diverse tasks was the notion that the degree to which a child can add syntactical targets missing from original spontaneous language samples could serve as a prognosis for therapeutic success, depending on the quality of the subject's responses. Subjects able to imitate or include a structure spontaneously when syntactically incorrect models were provided were felt to possess the linguistic competence to easily learn to use that structure in their own speech. Subjects able to repeat a structure when the correct version was presented were thought to have good prognosis, because it probably indicated that mature knowledge of syntax was aiding the child in producing a correctly formed sentence. A subject able to include previously omitted structures when the reversed model was given, especially when he could not imitate the structure in the two other conditions, was thought to show poor prognosis for therapy on that structure because sentence syntax did not seem to be aiding him in sentence production. Last, if a subject is unable to include a structure under any of these imitative conditions, the prognosis for linguistic growth for that particular structure was felt to be extremely poor. This use of imitative testing seems potentially useful and should be explored with hearing-impaired children.

Carrow (1974) described the Elicited Language Inventory test, the purpose of which is to measure a broad repertoire of syntactic structures. Reliability and external validity correlations reported were thought to be of sufficient strength to warrant statistical confidence in the test. In examining some of the linguistic principles to be evaluated, a question arises as to whether pragmatic issues were fully considered, since imitation of some single words or individual forms is suggested. Forms such as articles have been shown to be discourse-related constructions (Warden, 1976), and testing only single instances, especially with a lack of contextual support, might be sufficient to invalidate some of the tasks included in the test.

Elicited imitation tasks have been employed with hearing-impaired subjects by D. Holmes (1972), Sarachan-Deily and Love (1974), and Smith (1972), but these studies may be criticized for their lack of attention to issues such as the influence of discourse restraints, memory functioning, or preference for imitation by some children. There is continued need for investigation of hearing-impaired children's use of imitation, both elicited and delayed, particularly to determine whether nonproductive mimicry is as frequent a behavior as is supposed among deaf children in the early stages of language behavior, or whether hearing-impaired children engage in imitative behavior in a fashion similar to normally hearing youngsters.

Demonstration Format

Background   Several investigators (Bellugi, 1974; deVilliers and deVilliers, 1973a,b; Huttenlocher, 1974; Huttenlocher and Strauss, 1968; Sinclair, 1973) have argued that comprehension may often be best evaluated by utilizing subject demonstration of knowledge. Demonstration techniques consist of having a subject move objects or dramatize his understanding of the meaning of sentences, phrases, or words presented by the examiner. In some instances such testing is accomplished through the use of standard materials; in others, the examiner is free to use any objects available to him and familiar to the subject.

Bellugi-Klima (1974) has suggested some conditions that should be met when constructing a language test that uses demonstration responses. These suggestions include: (a) eliminating situational cues that might influence the generation of a response or comprehension of the test situation, (b) ensuring that each child knows the test vocabulary so that investigation of knowledge about a particular linguistic principle is not confounded by a lack of lexical understanding, (c) ensuring, as far as possible, that syntactic knowledge is being tested and not the child's ability to recognize test patterns.

Test strategies that allow the child to dramatize or act out his understanding of sentences require careful planning, as well as awareness of the possible reasons for a child's response, or lack of it, to requests by the examiner. The child who makes no response should not be assumed to lack knowledge. His behavior could be the result of any number of performance limitations, such as inattention, lack of motivation, unwillingness to interact with the examiner, or lack of comprehension of what his response should be. On the other hand, a seemingly appropriate response cannot always be taken as a clear indication of knowledge of a specific linguistic principle, because situation cuing can influence the comprehension process.

Situation cues that can contaminate test presentations include unintentionally reinforcing behavioral preferences in children, presenting materials in such a way that a subject's responses are shaped, or inadvertently increasing the probability of a particular response through test organization.

A small child who is presented with a set of items, one of which is unusually appealing, should not automatically be credited with knowledge of the object's name simply because he reaches for it. The examiner may ask for that most interesting object at once, which many testers are prone to do, thereby playing into the child's normal response or behavioral preference, which is to investigate an appealing toy when he sees one. Children at 1 1/2 to 2 years of age will often perform some actions in preference to others when confronted with the need to demonstrate understanding of a sentence (E. Clark, 1973a,b,c; 1974). For instance, in response to test sentences with *in* or *on,* young children will put objects in if there is a hole available. If there is no hole but there is a flat surface, children will place the object on it, regardless of which preposition the examiner is trying to test. In this case, external context and behavioral preference take precedence over the linguistic task presented to the child, a frequently overlooked factor in language testing involving demonstration responses.

Children's behavioral preferences should also be considered when constructing language tests with demonstration responses. Strohner and Nelson (1974), when investigating children's understanding of strategies for decoding of passive sentences, observed that at age 3, children demonstrate minimum use of syntactic information and maximum use of probable-event information in constructing their responses. That is, 3-year-olds seem to respond to sentences based on what the lexical items suggest probably happened rather than paying attention to what was actually expressed in the test sentence. Older children pay more attention to actual syntactic information, showing preference for the agent-action-patient sequence at first, particularly when the sentences presented are reversible—that is, when the action could be performed with equal probability by either the subject or object. These developmental aspects of processing have been confirmed in part by deVilliers and deVilliers (1973) and Sinclair (1973).

The way in which objects are made available in a test situation also seems to interact with the subjects' perception of whether the task is easy or difficult, what the purpose of the task seems to be, or even the strategies the subject chooses to employ in problem-solving (Hutten-locher, Eisenberg, and Strauss, 1968; Huttenlocher and Strauss, 1968). Huttenlocher and Weiner (1971) observed these influences when they asked subjects to demonstrate sentences such as *A is above B.* or *B is above A.* using blocks. When provided with identical trays containing a block and asked to demonstrate their responses, the subjects, presumably having a point of reference, had more success than when given only one empty tray in which they had to construct their answers. Environmental arrangement can support an easy solution to a problem, or it can provide obstacles that must be overcome in addition to those imposed by the test sentence itself.

Huttenlocher (1974) stressed that the nature of the verbal and conceptual context through which a child is expected to demonstrate language knowledge may bias test results. For instance if the child is asked to find a particular object, this biases the testing procedure in that the child may be able to determine the correct answer by systematic exclusion as each item is identified from the group. She also suggests that if the child is asked to demonstrate some aspect of an object, the examiner must be sure that the child is also asked to demonstrate things about the object that are not true. Can the child, for example, show what to do with an *orange* as well as what not to do with it?

Huttenlocher offers another sound suggestion for avoiding spurious test results in vocabulary comprehension testing: that the child not only be required to locate an object when it is present, but as importantly to find it when it is not present. For instance, testing for knowledge of the word *ball* would require that the child retrieve a ball from another room, or if given a collection of items, *ball* would be asked for even when it was not there, with the expectation that the child will recognize this fact and indicate its absence to the examiner.

At least one study has examined the influence of manipulation responses on normally hearing subjects' ability to simultaneously recall or generate sentences. McCabe, Levin, and Wolff (1974) required children to recall stimulus sentences presented to them under various conditions, including recalling those sentences with and without simultaneous manipulation of objects. Subjects were better at recall when not manipulating objects, which was interpreted as evidence of a potential for conflict between two motor acts performed simultaneously—speaking and manipulation. Such results suggest that combinations of motor acts should be employed cautiously to avoid interference with successful performance in both spoken and manipulative performance.

Tests Using Demonstration Format   There are few if any formal language tests that utilize demonstration response modes exclusively, although standardized intelligence tests such as the Stanford-Binet Intelligence Scale (Terman and Merrill, 1960) contain a few such items that could be used to test linguistic knowledge in deaf children. Solly (1975) discusses several tests developed for use with hearing-impaired children that employ some variation on the demonstration response format. The tests, adapted from the Reynell Language Developmental Tasks (Reynell, 1969), consisted of four separate tests: Sentence Comprehension I and II, and Directions I and II. Sentence Comprehension I and II require picture identification and are discussed later in this chapter. Of interest in this section are the Directions I and II tests. Directions Test I was developed for children aged 5 to 6 years and involves the manipulation of small objects and toys in response to 10 spoken instructions that increase in length and complexity as the test progresses. Three test items are included to illustrate the increasing complexity of test items: *Show me a car and a chair.*, *Put a blue button under the toy table.*, and *Choose a green button, put it in the box, put the lid on, and put the box on the toy table.* Directions Test II, for children 7 years and older, involves drawing figures in relation to printed geometric shapes when given directions by the examiner. Instructions are given orally for both tests, although adaptation to a reading mode was discussed.

Standardization of the test was achieved using two groups of 20 hearing-impaired children each, at the 5- and 7-year levels, as well as two normally hearing groups of comparable ages. Intertest correlations between the two groups of children indicated that both sections of the test were developmentally sensitive, and that they discriminated between normally hearing and hearing-impaired children. Unfortunately little information was presented on reliability. Solly concludes that Directions I and II are highly promising procedures for assessing oral-auditory comprehension in hearing-impaired children. All the test items were not presented, so that question of whether attention was paid to the conditions mentioned, such as behavioral preferences, event probability, nonverbal and logical constraints, or the influence of test material presentation cannot be resolved.

Picture Identification Format

Background Information A second prevalent category in comprehension testing consists of those language tests in which the subject is directed to select a picture(s) that best exemplifies sentences, phrases, or words presented by the examiner. Three issues should be considered in relation to the use of picture identification formats: guessing, rate of sentence presentation, and pragmatic competence.

In administrating the comprehension section of the ICP test procedures, Fraser, Bellugi, and Brown (1963) warned that guessing can confuse interpretation of the test results. Subjects who did not know an answer often pointed to the same picture twice, acting as if the responses to contrastive pairs were independent of one another, or they would point simultaneously to two pictures, or simply present unscorable results. It has been these authors' experience that unscorable results occasionally result from a child paying attention to only part of a picture rather than simply guessing. For example, when asked to identify a picture of an apple, a child might point to a foil picture of an apple tree. On the surface it seems that the child has confused *an apple* with *some apples,* but his point, which clearly is to one apple *on* the tree, is his way of complying with his understanding of the task.

A related issue to guessing is the situation in which forced choice responses are used; these reduce the probability of incorrect responses. When given a forced choice situation with four pictures, a child can often deduce the correct answer by systematically eliminating improbable answers. For instance if the stimulus sentence is *The boy is walking down the stairs.,* with pictures representing a girl walking down the stairs, a dog walking down the stairs, a boy walking down the stairs, and a boy walking up the stairs, the first two pictures can be eliminated because of the lack of the lexical item *boy,* thereby reducing the choice to an even chance of one of two pictures. The test has not really presented a four-choice problem, but rather a two-choice problem.

If this were a two-choice contrastive test, such as choosing between *up* and *down,* solution of the first problem automatically gives the subject the answer to the second problem. It is important in using picture identification formats that the correct pictures as well as the foils be constructed so that they offer viable choices for the linguistic principle under consideration.

Presentation rate has been investigated in relation to picture identification tasks. Labelle (1973) studied children's performance on a picture identification task as related to pause position within the presentation of the test sentences and to absence of pauses. Test sentences recorded with pauses as major syntactic boundaries within sentence frames, pauses within major phrases, and with no pauses were used. The results indicated that 3-year-old children made significantly fewer errors when pauses were placed at major phrase boundaries than when they were placed within major phrases or were not present at all. Pauses did not seem to be an important factor with older children. This may have been a function of linguistic sophistication rather than merely increase in chronological age. These results would call into question the practice of simply speaking test sentences to young or linguistically immature children, as opposed to use of tape recordings or language master presentations.

Berry and Erickson (1973) investigated the comprehension on the receptive section of the Northwestern Syntax Screening Test in children at various stages of language development as a function of the speed of presentation of the test sentences. Results indicated that comprehension was higher at the two slowest rates of speech compression as compared to the three fastest rates, again suggesting the need to control presentation rate in picture identification tasks.

The children identified by Bohannan (1975) as competent imitators and superior interpreters of conversational roles were also able to comprehend fully formed sentences in a picture identification task better than children who were less aware of certain pragmatic or communication dimensions. This observation could be taken to mean that children who have less information about pragmatic issues may have difficulty with expression of comprehension, such as picture identification.

Tests Using Picture Identification Formats   In spite of the limitations of picture identification formats, they have proved to be widely used in assessing language performance of children. Two popular tests that use picture identification are the Northwestern Syntax Screening Test (NSST) and the Carrow Auditory Test of Language Comprehension (ATLC).

The NSST (Lee, 1969) is a language screening test that was designed for use with children from standard English environments. The receptive portion of the NSST involves the presentation by the examiner of two sentences that contrast a particular linguistic principle. The child selects the correct answer for first one sentence and then the other by choosing one of four pictures. Normative data are presented for children from ages 3 to 7 years, although Lee stresses that data for children beyond 6 years are incomplete and tentative at best.

In a critique of the NSST, Arndt (1977) found the test lacking in many of the normal psychometric controls. Paramount questions concerned the nature of the normative population, test reliability, discriminative ability, and the likelihood of identifying children with genuine language problems as compared to children who have normal language but because of test anxiety fail to perform satisfactorily. Lee stipulates that the sample on which she standardized the test was drawn from a middle socioeconomic class, standard English speaking population, and was geographically confined to the midwest. Larson and Summers (1976) did report that application of the original test norms to samples of children from different geographic areas resulted in a high degree of failure, casting doubt on the NSST's applicability to all segments of the English-speaking community.

Reliability of the NSST scores is not addressed in the test manual itself. However, Ratusnik and Koenigsknecht (1975) have established that there is reasonable internal consistency, with the receptive portion being of lower reliability than the expressive portion. Test-retest expectations are still uncertain.

Although Prutting, Gallagher, and Mulac (1975) found that the expressive portion of the NSST did not discriminate well between children with language difficulties and those without difficulties, no such studies exist for the receptive portion of the test. Such an oversight should be corrected. In defense of the NSST, Lee (1977) does stress that it is only a screening device, and that perhaps only collective discriminatory power is necessary, rather than specific discriminatory power for any particular test item, which was the concern of Prutting, Gallagher, and Mulac in studying the expressive portion of the NSST. In other words, the power of the test should be in the identification of children with general language problems rather than children who might use a specific principle but could not complete an isolated item on a test. If, after in depth evaluation, children who fail the NSST prove to have language problems in areas not tested by the NSST, the discriminatory power of the test would be considered excellent for its intended purpose, to identify children at high risk for language difficulties.

The Auditory Test of Language Comprehension (Carrow, 1973), standardized in both English and Spanish, assesses linguistic comprehension with a picture identification format. A variety of language forms, emphasizing particularly lexical and morphological comprehension and in less detail syntactic knowledge, are included for evaluation. The test is considered by some to be a wide ranging test of linguistic comprehension, but more realistically it should be considered as a detailed screening device. Employing this test, Carrow and Lynch (Carrow, 1973) found a statistically significant difference between the performance of samples of deaf children and children with disorders of articulation and language. Statistically significant differences have also been found between the performances of children with clinically diagnosed language disorders and children without linguistic handicaps (Carrow, 1973; Weiner, 1972). Children with articulation disorders were also found to have more difficulty on the ATLC as compared to children with proficient articulation (Marquardt and Saxman, 1972). Trainable mentally retarded children's responses when compared to normally developing children were also poorer (Bartel, Bryen, and Keehn, 1973). The validity of the instrument seems well established, although comparison of spontaneous verbalizations with ATLC performance has not yet been completed. Such data would yield further information on validity if error patterns from the test paralleled atypical linguistic usage in children.

Internal and temporal reliability have also been well documented for the ATLC, which lends additional support to the notion that the test should be a useful in-depth screening instrument with hearing-impaired children.

As reported previously, a portion of the language test developed by Solly (1975) employs picture identification techniques. Sentence Comprehension I and II tasks consist of items selected from the comprehension section of the Primary A, Form I and Primary B, Form I Gates-MacGinitie Reading Tests (Gates and MacGinitie, 1965). Enlarged pictures and some modification of sentences to make them more compatible with a spoken English test format are the primary changes. Solly noted that these subtests were not as useful as the previously described Directions tests, which required object manipulation or drawing responses. The reasons for this lack of success with the Sentence Comprehension sections were not made clear because of the absence of specific information on the test materials in the research report.

Grammatical Judgment Format

Background Information Of all the techniques available for language assessment, the least used approach has been the one requiring judgment of acceptability or grammaticality of language events. This technique can be employed by presenting sentences to subjects for rating or judgment about adherence to standard English forms and functions, most frequently defined as syntactic and semantic sensibleness. Consideration of semantic aspects would be an important dimension, since most tests thus far reviewed focus almost exclusively on syntactic or lexical evaluation. Some grammatical judgment studies have forced subjects to choose between the presence or absence of accuracy. Evaluation of degrees of sensibleness such as the study designed by R. E. Kretschmer (1976) seems preferable, because it would permit relatively systematic investigation of the interaction of syntax and semantics in sentence comprehension.

Age and linguistic sophistication are factors in determining the appropriateness of grammatical judgment techniques, as shown by deVilliers and deVilliers (1972), who asked normally developing children ages 28 to 45 months to judge syntactic and semantic acceptability of test sentences. Children's success in this task was found to correlate highly with mean length of utterance and with comprehension of reversible active and passive sentences. Only the linguistically most advanced children were able to make a significant number of appropriate judgments and were able to correct reversed word order imperatives. Less mature children could judge and then correct semantically anomalous sentences, but they could not correct reversed word orders in sentences. The importance of semantic, as opposed to syntactic, factors in children's judgments of acceptability of sentences seems to be an important developmental factor. Children who lack syntactic sophistication probably will not be able to use language to make judgments about language. However, if semantic comprehension needs to be studied, this procedure might be tried, even for children with linguistic limitations.

Liles, Shulman, and Bartlett (1977), who presented sentences of varying degrees of grammaticality to normally speaking and language disordered children, ages 5 through 7, found that when violations of syntactic agreement and/or word order were presented, language disordered children had more judgment difficulty. The groups studied were similar in recognition of lexical restrictions, suggesting that at least word meaning intuitions can be evaluated in children with language performance limitations.

At least one instance is reported in which a talking toy panda bear was substituted for an adult examiner to induce very young children to converse more freely in a language evaluation setting (Lloyd and Donaldson, 1976). The nonverbal response mode of button pushing was used to overcome the subject's reluctance to talk audibly, thus increasing correct responses to a general language task. Coupling impartial presentation and response techniques with a grammaticality judgment test might be a productive approach for testing very young children, or nonspeaking but auditorily capable hearing-impaired children. Its use with severely hearing-impaired children is limited, however, unless additional visual cues could be employed.

Tests Using Grammatical Judgment Formats   The most comprehensive language battery developed specifically for evaluation of the language of hearing-impaired children employs grammatical judgment as its cornerstone—the Test of Syntactic Abilities (TSA) developed by Quigley and associates (Steinkamp and Quigley, 1976). The test is still in the research stages, but a formal version will be available for general use sometime in the near future.

Two primary formats are used in this test: completion tasks similar to those to be discussed in the next section, and sentence correction or grammatical judgment tasks. In the latter situation, the subject is presented with a sentence that he must declare to be fully formed or syntactically restricted. If violations are detected, the student must write a correct version. As reported in Chapter 4, the TSA has yielded information on a variety of syntactic constructions, ranging from verb structure to more complex forms such as complementation and relativization. Good reliability scores have been reported for hearing-impaired subjects, as well as very sizable samples for normative purposes (Quigley et al., 1976). One might argue that the scope of the deaf subjects sampled has focused primarily on students from self-contained programs for the hearing impaired. A more representative sample should include deaf children who are mainstreamed successfully. This issue, however, does not negate the potential usefulness of the TSA for programs in need of tests to evaluate aspects of the linguistic abilities of groups of hearing-impaired children.

The evaluation of children's grammatical sense seems to hold promise as a procedure for understanding linguistic knowledge. However, some caution must be exercised. DeVilliers and deVilliers (1974) noted that the production of language ontogenetically precedes judgments of the suitability of linguistic features, which in turn precedes the ability to correct the unsuitable features. Leonard, Bolders, and

Curtis (1977) also reported that order of language forms seems to reflect different processes. Ability to judge sentence acceptability may not reflect linguistic knowledge or performance mastery but merely the ability to identify instances of ungrammatical or restricted language forms. Therefore, it would seem necessary to have children generate reasons for their decisions in order to determine if they know why a sentence is incorrect rather than merely indicating a problem based on a sense of lack of grammaticality.

Language Completion Format

Background Information Language completion tasks require the subject to complete a sentence, phrase, or word presented by the examiner. The stimuli are usually constructed so that the subject's response could be said to reflect knowledge of a particular linguistic principle or construction. Two major issues should be considered when adopting this type of response format: the relation of subject test responses to their linguistic knowledge as shown in spontaneously generated language, and the influence of test or subject dialect on test performance.

Dever (1972) verified the reality of the first issue when he administered a morphological completion task using nonsence words to a group of mentally retarded children and then collected a spontaneous language sample for each subject to determine whether the test results reflected actual language usage. There was not a high correlation between test performance and actual language usage, suggesting that failure to generate inflectional endings for nonsense words may only be a test artifact rather than indication of lack of linguistic knowledge. If this is true of one sample of language delayed children, wouldn't it also potentially be true of another sample of English delayed children such as those with significant hearing impairment?

Studies utilizing the Grammatic Closure sub-test of the ITPA (Kirk, McCarthy, Kirk, 1968; Paraskevopoulos and Kirk, 1969) offer evidence that the second issue of dialectical influence is also a reality. The Grammatic Closure sub-test assesses morphologic knowledge with real lexical items; by virtue of this fact, it has a built-in dialectical bias (Grill and Bartel, 1977). Children who do not speak standard English tend to do poorly on this sub-test because the inflections tested are standard English derived. Test performance may be an important indicator of the degree of mastery of standard English forms, but caution should be exercised to ensure that test performance is not equated with lack of general language ability. Deaf children may also be different language or "deaf" dialect users, so perhaps a test similar to the James Test of Spanish Dominance (James, 1974) is required to determine whether deaf children are deaf English dominant, standard English dominant, or fluent in neither or in both dialects.

Tests Using Language Completion Formats   The best-known examples of the language completion approach are the Berko Morphology Test (Berko, 1958) and its derivative, the Grammatic Closure Sub-test from the ITPA (Kirk, McCarthy, and Kirk, 1968). In each case, sentences or phrases are presented with picture cues so that the last word of the test sentences must be filled in by the subject, using application of an appropriate morphophonemic (local transformational) rule. The tests use either nonsense words to be inflected (Berko, 1958) or real words (Kirk, McCarthy, and Kirk, 1968). Examples include: This is a dog. This is two ____. and This is a wug. Now there are two of them. There are two ____.

The Berko Morphology Test, which focuses on inflectional word endings for plurality, past tense, comparative adjective forms, etc. has been used with hearing-impaired children by R. Cooper (1967), Perlman (1973), and Raffin (1976). In each case the researchers employed visual modes such as reading and signed English for test instructions and writing for subject response to avoid the issue of misperception of test items or confounding of response intelligibility by poor articulation skills. This need to restructure for deaf subjects indicates a major problem of formal language completion tasks: they are primarily useful for those linguistic principles that are regular and stable with regard to morphological English rules. Unfortunately, the speech events most affected by hearing impairment and showing subsequent difficulty with speech performance are the aspects most frequently tested.

Natalicio and Natalicio (1969) indicate a few difficulties with the Berko standardization procedures that are not unique to this language assessment procedure, but that should be mentioned so that their influences may be avoided. First, subject selection for the Berko test was on a convenience rather than preplanned basis, which sets up the possibility for presence of sex or socioeconomic class bias because of the homogeneity of standardization samples.

Second, Berko's test was directed toward the evaluation of several linguistic principles, but test items were indiscriminately ordered. As a result, relation of a test item to those preceding or following it might affect a subject's response. For instance if a child produces a plural correctly, then follows by inflecting the noun for third person singular, is the incorrect behavior a result of lack of rule application or a carryover from one test item to the next? Such problems cannot be properly avoided unless test items evaluating the same linguistic principle are arranged to account for potential carryover influence.

Third, Natalicio and Natalicio suggest that the test word may be misperceived, resulting in an incorrect response for the test word, but correct inflection based on the child's perception. For instance if the nonsense word *heaf* is presented, but perceived by the child as *heas*, a response of *heases* would be incorrect to the examiner, but correct based on the child's perception of the original stimulus word. It is imperative in completion tasks that the child's role be clearly understood by him and that the test item be clearly presented as well, which is a good argument for use of real words rather than nonsense items.

Bliss, Allen, and Wrasse (1977) report use of the language completion format to evaluate children's performance with complex sentence structures. The procedure was a modification of Goodglass et al.'s (1972) Story Completion Task designed for use with adults with aphasia. The task involves presenting a story that ends with the question *What?* to stimulate a response appropriate to the context of the story. For example, *My friend comes in. I want him to sit down, so I say to him . . . What?* is such an item. The correct response would be *Sit down.* or a similar construction. Items examine the use of simple imperatives and declaratives, questions, passives, and adjectival noun phrases. The results of the study evidenced a developmental trend in ability to accurately complete less complex and then more complex structures. The major difficulties with this approach include a presupposition of knowledge of standard English discourse constraints, constraints that influence the production of sentences within context; scoring of test items on a pass-fail basis, which may overlook valuable information contained in the child's actual response; and the prompting devices used, which may bias toward production of specific lexical items rather than more general expressions of rule knowledge. This approach, nevertheless, is a most interesting one that warrants additional investigation of its usefulness, especially with hearing-impaired persons.

Other Language Assessment Formats

Additional procedures that can be or have been used to assess linguistic performance of hearing-impaired children include: (1) interview schedules and/or checklists of linguistic abilities, (2) referential communication analyses, (3) prelinguistic assessments, and (4) assessment of related cognitive abilities, such as play behavior.

Interview Schedule and/or Checklist Format   Instead of or in addition to evaluating the child's language performance directly, it is possible to obtain some appreciation of a child's linguistic performance by interviewing his parents or other caregivers. There are many inventories that group questions according to topic or according to age expectations (Doll, 1965; Gesell and Amatruda, 1962; Mecham, 1959; Watson and Pickles, 1957). In order to obtain valid information based on the parents' perceptions, it is suggested that the interview be based on indirect and overlapping questions. Direct questions often threaten parents, causing them to withhold or distort their answers. The value of such inventories or scales is only as great as the skill of the interviewer in understanding and ensuring the willingness of the parents to discuss the child's behavior. The interview results should assist the examiner in understanding home and communication styles. It is also useful to employ a schedule or scale to act as a cross-check on formal test results.

Referential Communication Analysis Formats Language performance should always be considered in the context of communication effectiveness, a child's ability to participate meaningfully in interpersonal communications. One method that has been pioneered by Glucksberg and Krauss (1967; Glucksberg, Krauss, and Weisberg, 1966) is referred to as referential communication. In this procedure, one individual communicates instructions, such as how to assemble a set of blocks or arrange a set of toys, to another while both are separated by a partition. The success of the speaker is evaluated by observing how well the listener's behavior is controlled, how long it takes for completion of the assigned task, and the efficiency of the speaker in accomplishing his communication tasks, defined as the number of exchanges required to effect changes in the listener's behavior.

Retarded children or very young children confronted with the referential communication task solve the problem by simply repeating one utterance or instruction again and again at increasingly louder levels (Glucksberg, Krauss, and Higgins, 1975). Hoemann (1972) found a similar pattern of results with deaf children communicating by sign, who employed repetition and excessive accentuation when communication broke down. Communication ability should be considered routinely to assist in developing a full understanding of every child's language/communication competence.

To make a communication evaluation useful, several issues need to be considered. First, any communication situation used in evaluation should be meaningful and should offer opportunity for success. This can usually be achieved by selecting a communication partner who is familiar to the child and with his communication system, and by providing a task that is comparatively easy. Second, the child should be placed in a communication situation that has potential breakdowns, which is most easily accomplished by adding a complex message to be transmitted to a partner by whatever manner he chooses. Valian and Wales (1976), Peterson, Danner, and Flavell (1972), and Corsaro (1977) indicate that adults and children resort to clarification techniques as listeners and to revision behaviors as speakers in order to facilitate communication. Clarification techniques involve strategies such as asking *What was that?*, whereas revision techniques are employed by rewording or rephrasing the original message to increase its clarity.

Third, the subject should be placed in both the speaker and the listener role for purposes of sending and receiving simple and complex communications. Hoemann's (1972) results suggest that deaf children, for example, have difficulty in both roles. Finally, to obtain a comprehensive understanding of any child's referential communication skills, he should experience a variety of communication situations with the most important of his communication partners, particularly his parents, teachers, and peers. Parents of language-impaired children were observed by Bondurant (1977) to use different referential communication strategies with their children than parents of a comparable group of normally speaking children used, offering some interesting implications for communication management of deaf children and their parents. The issue of evaluating communication competence is also especially important with hearing-impaired children who are being considered for educational mainstreaming.

Language Prerequisite Assessment Formats Some children, whether deaf or otherwise may not be able to learn language because they lack the behaviors thought to be prerequisite to language acquisition. Those prerequisites include ability to selectively attend to verbal stimuli and to ignore extraneous auditory (visual) stimuli; ability to participate in joint activities with an adult, at the least through eye contact; and ability to provide feedback to the adult through acts such as smiling that stimulate continued communication (Snyder and McLean, 1976). Without such behaviors, the child may not profit from linguistic stimulation and may lose contact with adults because of a lack of interactive response.

Assessment of these behavioral prerequisites is the basis of programs such as Horstmeier, MacDonald, and Gillette's Environmental Prelanguage Battery (EPB) (MacDonald, 1976). Besides such formal programs, observation of communication behavior or lack of it can be utilized, particularly for very young children, or children with multiple problems. Berger (1972) has utilized such an approach to aid in planning communication therapy for hearing-impaired youngsters with complicated learning problems.

Assessment of Related Cognitive Areas   There is, as suggested in Chapter 3, considerable evidence that linguistic behavior may be only one expression of cognitive development. Studies by Bates (1976b), Bloom (1973), and Morehead and Morehead (1974) seem to indicate that, in concert with the theorizing of Piaget, children proceed through various sensorimotor stages, developing both the cognitive substrates of language and the symbolic processes that are prerequisite to language. One might consider evaluation of cognitive function, from the Piagetian viewpoint, as one avenue for determining whether a child possesses prerequisite understanding to develop increasing sophisticated language usage.

Although still in the formative stages, several formal test procedures have been suggested for evaluating cognitive function in a Piagetian framework. In a procedure suggested by Mehrabian and Williams (1971), 27 items ranging from evaluation of representation, causality, and object constancy to imitation could be administered, presumably to provide insight into the conceptual organization of a child.

A second battery was developed by Uzgiris and Hunt (1975). They describe six scales to evaluate visual pursuit and permanence of objects: means for obtaining desired environmental events, vocal imitation, gestural imitation, operational causality, object relations in space, and schemes for relating to objects. A profile of results can be developed to identify the areas of strength or facility. This test was used by Bates et al. (1977) to investigate the correlation of each scale with various language measures. Their results were equivocal, with the sole exception of the scale evaluating means-to-ends relations. The major difficulty with the foregoing tests is the very complicated nature of their administration, which will deter many teachers and educational innovators from using them.

Bates (1976b) has suggested that once language begins to develop in children, there emerges symbolic play as well, and indeed much has been written concerning the relation between play and language symbolization. In a recent study, Williams (1977) observed that language-impaired children displayed greater difficulty in developing symbolic play than did normally speaking children. Consequently, it might be useful to explore play behavior in deaf children for whom specific language instruction is being considered, especially if a child is beyond the preschool years when entering school or has been classified as multihandicapped. Observation of symbolic play in such children would seem to offer positive evidence of their probable potential for linguistic acquisition if the appropriate instructional mode can be found.

Various systems have been suggested to investigate play behavior. Fenson and Kagan (1976), Goodson and Greenfield (1975), Gove (1976), Lovell, Hoyle, and Siddall (1968), Nicholich (1977), Teece (1976), and Williams (1977) all have suggested that the style of interaction with objects is the crucial variable to be examined in children's play. For instance, does a child merely handle a toy, or does he engage in some form of pretend behavior with it? It is the latter condition that is truly symbolic play, a behavior albeit primitive at early stages that should emerge at the same time as early symbolic language forms (Bates, 1976b).

In evaluating deaf children's play behavior, however, it is important to distinguish between the behavior during a warm-up or preplanning period and subsequent play behaviors. Kretschmer (1972a) found that when deaf preschool children ages 3 to 5 years were placed in a play environment, up to 15 minutes were required before the child actually engaged objects meaningfully. During this period, most deaf subjects engaged in visual and tactual scanning behaviors, which at best seem to have minimal symbolic implication. Young deaf children should not be evaluated on play behavior until it is clear that they have completed preplanning exploration of the play environment and of the objects available.

SPONTANEOUS LANGUAGE ANALYSIS PROCEDURES

Analysis of spontaneous utterances has two primary advantages over more formal testing procedures. First, research on normal language development has focused primarily on spontaneous speech productions, resulting in a sizable body of normative data. Second, formal testing situations are generally artifical estimates of performance, whereas a conversational format should yield more natural behavior from the child. Analysis of spontaneous utterances has limitations, of course. The size of the sample needed and the method by which it is obtained are both open to question. The standard sample suggested for use in clinical settings is 50 to 100 utterances. However, the most informed basic research on language development has been based on far larger samples, 300 to 800 utterances minimum, and in most cases even more. Such large language samples seem cumbersome for therapeutic use because with children who are language delayed, shy, or both, it may be very time consuming to obtain and analyze such samples. On the other hand, too small a speech sample is likely to be misleading with regard to a child's linguistic capabilities.

Cazden (1970) has shown that the influences of the environment on both the quantity and quality of children's spontaneous utterances is substantial. Variations in amount and detail of spoken language can occur depending on the topic of conversation, the task a child is engaged in, the age of the listener, and his familiarity with the speaker. Questions such as *What do you see?* or *What are you doing?* usually result, for instance, in limited language samples consisting primarily of single words or short phrases. If children are presented with topics that they have had some part in generating, such as taking photographs, the level of spontaneous productions increases significantly as compared to discussion of objects or pictures chosen by an adult.

An adult's interview technique can enhance linguistic productions or retard them. The nature of the questions asked of the child can shape the types of productions. As has been suggested, *who, what,* or *where* questions will limit the child's output. Turnure, Buium, and Thurlow (1976) found that young children would elaborate answers if certain interrogatives were used for prompting, with the most effective question forms being *why, how,* and *how come.* Longhurst and File (1977) examined the results of the Developmental Sentence Procedure (Lee, 1974), discussed in greater detail later in the chapter, elicited by four conditions: use of single-object pictures, use of toys, use of multiple-object pictures, and use of adult-child conversations. Less structured conditions (adult-child conversations) produced the highest output scores. After a review of the pertinent literature, Hubbell (1977) also concluded that interpersonal aspects must be stressed in interviews to increase children's spontaneity.

Unfortunately, informal or conversational interviews lend themselves to criticism as well. How is such an interview approach to be recorded or preserved for analysis? Does such an approach yield comparability from one sample to another? Involving several persons in taking samples may also contaminate the procedure because adults unskilled in exact recording may fill in language forms they suppose were intended but did not actually occur.

R. Clark (1976) presented the technical outline of a recording arrangement that could be used for collecting the language samples of young normally hearing children, but that could also be adapted to record utterances of hearing-impaired children, particularly those with clear speech. Unfortunately, mechanical and monetary requirements of the strategy would prevent most public school programs for the hearing-impaired from utilizing it. Friedlander et al. (1972) suggested an audio-recording technique designed for home use. Although less cumbersome than Clark's suggestion, it might be logically and electromechanically expensive for home training use. A variation on this recording technique might be helpful for classroom situations, however, to evaluate natural communication between teachers and children that could be listened to at leisure for analysis purposes.

Wasserman (1976) found that when judges were asked to analyze utterances of deaf children under conditions of: (1) auditory tapes alone, (2) auditory tapes plus indication of topics, and (3) auditory tapes, conversation topics, and pictures discussed, that there was no difference in their ability to identify, segment, and analyze language samples. Under any condition there were many instances of spoken language that were not intelligible. Juenke (1971) and Hess (1972) employed videotapes for analysis, and raters had little difficulty in identifying communication intents of deaf children or of transcribing their spoken utterances. Combination of visual and auditory cues obtained through videotape seems a reasonable way to record language samples so that they may be examined several times, or stored for baseline comparisons.

After the strategies for eliciting and recording a reasonable sized sample have been decided, one must still be concerned about establishing some comparability from child to child or test situation to test situation relative to the type of variety of linguistic forms elicited. Development of a list of topics or tasks that any adult, whether teacher or parent, could use along with practice in interviewing would be helpful. For instance, Snow et al. (1976) chose reading to each child as the common test situation, but Bondurant (1977) chose to have each mother talk to her child about the same items. With constant topics from child to child, the potential for comparability might be enchanced.

Up to this point, interpersonal communication situations have been discussed. In some instances evaluation of spontaneous written language is of concern. With this mode it is still imperative that the issues outlined be considered. Comparability between test situations is easier to obtain, because the same topics can be assigned to be written about. Sample size, however, becomes more of an issue. Because writing is a laborious task for most children, hearing-impaired or not, obtaining a sufficient sized composition(s) to allow for meaningful analysis becomes a problem. On the other hand, because writing is a permanent record, there is little chance that productions will be lost as a result of their being misunderstood. A permanent record of writing, however, does not mean that it can be analyzed more easily than spoken samples.

Techniques for Spontaneous Production Analysis

Developing a complete grammar for every hearing-impaired child would be an ideal approach to assessment and planning, but such an extensive task is hardly practical and certainly exhausting for the teacher or therapist responsible for developing language learning experiences.

A variety of analysis procedures are reviewed in this section. These procedures differ in the aspects of language on which they choose to focus and in their techniques of description. Some procedures, such as the final one developed by the senior author and his colleagues, will seem complicated because language itself consists of more than words arranged in a string. The reader is cautioned that the full understanding of language usage or of language restrictions cannot be gained from a single textbook however detailed. The study of contemporary linguistics, psycholinguistics, and child language must be pursued in formal and informal settings with assistance from persons knowledgeable in language description. Anyone seriously interested in teaching deaf children or learning to productively analyze their language difficulties should follow this course.

Mean Length of Utterance (MLU)   Mean length of utterance has been used repeatedly as a descriptor of language development. Although it is crude in some ways, MLU still seems to be the best single indicator of language growth in children with MLUs of five morphemes or less. Its validity has been demonstrated in several studies. Shriner (1969) found MLU to be highly correlated with psychological judgements of language development. Sharf (1972) compared measurements of verbal output (MLU and number of different words) with measurements of structural analysis, Length-Complexity Index (Miner, 1969), and Developmental Sentence Types (Lee, 1966). He found that variability in the rate of growth of test scores made age an unstable basis for determining normality, although there was considerable agreement among the measures employed in describing the fact of language growth. Sharf felt that of all the evaluation techniques, MLU was the most easily derived and could serve as a screening device to detect children with potential language problems. Last, Brown (1973) has shown that many specific aspects of syntactic development are correlated with MLU.

Total reliance on MLU, of course, is not reasonable because it is only a gross measure of output, not a description of linguistic complexity. Dale (1976) indicates that the most serious objection to the use of MLU is its dependence upon language elicited in situations that may not be carefully controlled. As the situation varies, so may the language sample on which the MLU is computed. Any evaluation of spontaneous utterances may suffer from this problem. The MLU may be less affected than other procedures, however, because it is based on the entire sample, whereas many analysis techniques are applied to describing only specific constructions, or part of the sample (Mylkebust, 1965).

The computation of MLU has been completely described by Brown (1973) in his book *A First Language: The Early Stages*. The interested reader who is unfamiliar with the procedure is directed to this source.

Developmental Sentence Types (DST)   In 1966, Lee reported one of the first contemporary assessment procedures with a linguistic orientation, Developmental Sentence Types. The DST was intended as a system for studying and evaluating grammatical development in children at the pre-sentence level. It employed traditional grammar terms to make the information meaningful to teachers and clinicians, who might need the information to plan remedial procedures for young language-impaired children. Based on the developmental psycholinguistic literature available, Lee constructed a four-level chart that detailed probable targets of acquisition in six areas of linguistic functioning: two-word noun phrases; two-word designative sentences containing demonstrative pronouns such as *this, it, here,* or *that*; two-word predicative sentences, declarative sentences that contain attribute or locative modifications such as *car broken* or *truck here*; two-word verbal or verb phrase constructions; two-word fragments, usually prepositional phrases, negation, or question forms; and two-word stereotypical phrases. The four developmental levels into which these six categories are cast consist of two-word combinations, noun phrases, constructions, and kernel or simple active declarative sentences. For instance, with noun phrases at the two-word combination stage, possible constructions could involve article + noun, possessive + noun, quantifier + noun, or adjective + noun. Examples for each of these would be *a car, Daddy('s) car, more car,* and *big car,* respectively. Emphasis was on describing the development of declarative sentence frames and associated noun and verb phrases. The task of the teacher or therapist was to identify from the language sample generated by a child those pre-sentence components that were developing, and to place them in the chart to obtain some estimate of language development. The basic assumption of the DST was that early constructions on the chart were developmentally essential to the complete evolvement of later constructions on the chart. Unfortunately, no normative data were published with the original article to verify this assumption.

As indicated by Bloom (1967), four major shortcomings could be seen in the DST approach. First, the underlying assumption that children learn kernel sentences and then transformations was disputed, especially the notion that children develop noun phrases and verb phrases before they develop constructions and that they develop constructions before learning functional kernel sentences. Bloom argued that children apparently learn these components in a simultaneous fashion, preferring to establish grammatical frames for various constructions and then work out specific details, rather than the other way around, as implied by the DST procedure. Second, children use successive utterances, which was not treated in DST procedure. In a later publication, Lee (1974) argued that such consideration might be sacrificed because language-impaired children were characteristically lacking in "strings" of words. That notion is not supported by research on hearing-impaired children (Hess, 1972). Third, the DST made no allowance for sociolinguistic context or the influence of others on the child's behavior, or at least there was no indication of such in the original report. Fourth, there was no indication of how one might ensure what category an utterance would fit into, because situational cues are often the only way to determine whether a child's utterance was intended to be a designative or a predicative construction. This last classification problem must be considered an important oversight in the DST procedure in the application to pre-sentence utterances of young children.

As part of her 1974 publication, Lee presented revisions of her Developmental Sentence Types. She acknowledged that sociolinguistic constraints and contextual cues should be considered in classifying children's utterances. The revised DST categories included: noun elaboration, designative elaboration, predicative elaboration, verbal elaboration, and fragments. The developmental levels were changed to two-word combinations and constructions only. The revised DST is considered to be useful for descriptive purposes and for organization of therapeutic goals, but not as a set of teaching or training targets. The problems already mentioned relative to semantic aspects and to successive utterances are still not addressed, but the system itself may prove to be valuable for description of spoken output of some children with limited auditory abilities.

Linguistic Analysis of Speech Samples (LASS)   Engler, Hannah, and Longhurst, (1973) detailed a procedure for analyzing patterns of language, identifying constructions that are inappropriate, and ascertaining which constructions are conspicuous by their absence. They postulate five sentence types by which any sentence may be described: copulative verb constructions, intransitive verb constructions, transitive or object-taking verb constructions, sense and infinitive-taking verbal constructions, and passive verb constructions. Besides assigning a sentence type, the examiner determines the slots for each sentence that the child fills appropriately, as well as those he does not fill. Tabulations are made of each of the sentence types and of the filled and unfilled slots, followed by a qualitative analysis of each slot within a sentence. The subject slot, for example, may contain a noun, or any of a number of words that can replace or function as a noun, ranging from a single pronoun, a marked infinitive, or a gerund to a phrase with a noun head and modifiers containing whole clauses. The task of the examiner is to identify and tabulate each of these slot fillers, as well as to identify the errors that might occur within a particular slot.

The verbal slot is generally considered after the noun slot. Engler, Hannah, and Longhurst posit at least 14 verb slot fillers, including copulative-be, copulative-get, copulative-become, complement-copulative, copulative-sense-intransitive, and so forth. It is also deemed important to analyze the verb slot for possible expansions such as compound verb constructions with auxiliaries and main verbs.

A post-verbal slot that may contain a complement such as nominal, adverbial, or adjectival constructions as well as four optional slots for adverbial constructions (primarily prepositional phrases and single-word adverbials of manner, time, and location) would be considered next.

The last operation is identification of all instances of coordination with primary focus on juxtaposition, coordination, subordination, and embedding of constructions such as relative clauses. The incidence and quality of conjoining practiced by the child is identified and tabulated, along with the arrangements and types of linkages employed.

From a detailed examination of sentence types, construction slots, and types of coordination, an examiner should be able to describe performance abilities as well as providing specific statements about deviations observed from expected patterns of linguistic use. In this way, specific strategies can be generated to correct deviations, or to expand language expression. One of the positive aspects of this system is that it permits descriptions of deviations from expected language performance. Without reference to normal language development literature, however, it is not clear how one determines whether a particular child's performance reflects normal development patterns achieved at later than expected ages, or significant deviations from normal acquisition patterns.

Developmental Sentence Scoring (DSS)   Lee (1974) reported on a second system, called Developmental Sentence Analysis, a procedure to describe both non-sentence and sentence constructions. The former section is a further elaboration of the Developmental Sentence Types, and the latter developed out of the Developmental Sentence Scoring procedure originally reported by Lee and Canter (1971). The latter scale is of immediate interest in its focus on eight aspects of English: indefinite pronouns and noun modifiers, personal pronouns, main verbs, secondary verbs, negatives, conjunctions, interrogative reversals, and wh-questions. For each construction, data on normal language development were used to establish a weighting scale (1 to 8 points). For example within the personal pronoun category, instances of first and second person pronouns receive a score of 1; use of third person pronouns recieve a score of 2; plural personal pronouns, a score of 2, and so on, with pronouns such as *one, oneself,* or *whichever* receiving the highest point value of 7. Each sentence is scored according to eight categories, and a total complexity score is computed for the sentence. The mean score of a 50-utterance sample constitutes the developmental sentence score for that child. Lee reports normative data on 20 boys and 20 girls in each of five age groups from 2 to 6 years. All were middle-class children geographically distributed over several midwestern and eastern states. Extensive validity and reliability studies have been reported to establish the DSS's utility for clinical use.

Although a useful procedure, the DSS has a limitation—there is no provision for specifying deviations from normal linguistic usage. This omission seems important if the DSS is to be used with hearing-impaired children who routinely have problems in both syntactic and semantic usage. A second shortcoming, which can be compensated for by the use of other tests, is the DSS's emphasis on syntactic description to the exclusion of pragmatic and semantic aspects. Use of the DSS, with its focus on syntactic categories that are important to function in classroom settings, does seem potentially useful for hearing-impaired children being considered for mainstream placement, at least up to 6 years of age.

Trantham and Pederson (1976) employed a modified DSS approach to describe the language of eight normally developing children passing through the five stages of language development described by Brown (1973). Language samples were obtained from the subjects at 3-week intervals beginning at ages 15 to 18 months, or at the appearance of two-word combinations, through age 3 years. Initial description was completed using Developmental Sentence Types analysis, but when at least 50% of a sample consisted of sentence constructions, the DSS was employed. In addition, five other procedures were used. Mean sentence length and the percentage of correct sentences were computed and compared with the DSS results. The types of sentences were noted and each sentence was classified according to the following categories: simple declarative, negative declarative, imperative, negative imperative, interrogative, and negative interrogative. Sentences were also classified as being either successful or attempted simple, compound, or complex sentences. Each sentence was classified according to the traditional tenses of past, present, and future. Last, because the authors were concerned about noting the age of emergence and eventual mastery of various syntactic forms, each of the DSS categories was recorded as being emergent, inconsistent in usage, or mastered in all contextual situations. Lee's construction category from the DST was felt to play a minor role in describing the development of sentences. In addition, few isolated noun or verb phrases were noted in the normally developing subjects, contrary to the expectations of the DST model. Trantham and Pederson do note that isolated unit production was characteristic of language-impaired children with whom they had worked. This has not been substantiated for preschool hearing-impaired children, however, because they seem to follow the normal child's preference for combining nouns and verbs into mini-sentences.

DSS scores and sentence length over time showed an interesting relationship. In the earliest samples, sentence length was greater than DSS scores, but by the end of the study the relationship was reversed. The age at which sentence complexity (DSS scores) began to exceed length varied among children, but was most frequently between 27 to 30 months. The percentages of correct sentences were high by 3 years of age, ranging from 58 to 88%. In all the language samples, the predominate sentence form was declarative. Imperative and negative forms were also apparent, although no discernible patterns of acquisition were discovered. The majority of sentences used by all children were simple, with compound sentences emerging in the language of all subjects between the ages of 23 and 29 months, and complex sentences emerging between the ages of 22 and 36 months. In general the patterns noted in the study approximated the levels and orders proposed for the DSS, which was felt to be a validation of the DSS procedure.

Although the Tratham and Pederson approach is useful in documenting language growth in normally developing children and in at least a single instance of a language-delayed subject, its primary emphasis is on syntax, with little attention to semantic aspects of language development. This is an important oversight, because research on hearing-impaired children suggests that semantic/pragmatic divergence may be a key issue in their language development. If a formal and relatively simple quantitative procedure for description of spoken syntactic forms is desired for use with hearing-impaired children, however, this modified DSS procedure may be an appropriate choice.

Longhurst and Schrandt (1973) compared four procedures for language description: Developmental Sentence Type (Lee, 1966), Developmental Sentence Scoring (Lee and Canter, 1971), their own Linguistic Analysis of Speech Samples (Engler, Hannah, and Longhurst, 1973), and the Indiana Scale of Clausal Development. The last procedure is similar to the Linguistic Analysis of Speech Samples because it identifies slots to be analyzed in detail in terms of both correct and incorrect usage. The slot analysis approaches were found to be more discriminative of linguistic differences between a linguistically advanced child and a linguistically delayed child used as subjects in this study. The effectiveness of the Engler, Hannah, and Longhurst system rested in its provisions for descriptions of feature violations for every slot category. The DSS seemed to have two limitations. First, it did not account for utterances that expressed syntactic understanding, but did not contain any of the categories included in the system, such as adverbial constructions. Second, the DSS was described as lacking the fine feature discriminations necessary to detect subtle differences among children's knowledge of language. Developmental Sentence Types analysis discriminated between the two subjects, but the usefulness of the information was considered to be limited, because areas of developmental difficulty were not specified. A difficulty with the LASS system and the DSS in contrast to the DST and the Indiana Scale was the low interjudge reliability when applying the procedures, although this aspect of reliability was still considered acceptable for all tests.

Tyack and Gottsleben's Language Analysis System Tyack and Gottsleben (1974) described an analysis system based on normative results reported by Morehead and Ingram (1973). Each child's utterance is compared to an adult model or gloss, first with regard to the communication intent, as determined by the environmental and conversational contexts in which the utterance was produced. Each utterance is also scored by description of the major syntactic units in terms of appropriate word class designations, such as _me going home_, designated as a Noun + Verb + Noun syntactic string. The presence of all function words and morphological inflections are noted. Obligatory forms, major constituents, function words, or morphological inflections that have been omitted are also noted. Next, the total number of words produced is divided by the total number of morphemes to compute a word-morpheme index, which is used to place the child at a developmental level similar to those developed by Morehead and Ingram. For instance, Level I is for those children with a word morpheme index of 2.00; Level V is for children with a word-morpheme index of 4.63 or greater. Finally, all forms and constructions are examined for percentage of use, with 90% correct use in obligatory contexts defined as mastery. Because no minimum number of utterances or contexts is indicated as necessary to compute this level of correct use, the number of sentences needed to declare 90% mastery will show sizable variation from tester to tester, calling into question the validity of using this type of statistical procedure.

This system is unique from previously described systems in that it is developmentally organized. Therapeutic goals can be based on forms and constructions that are not mastered, but that are expected at levels below the child's index level. However, it shares the same shortcomings—little provision for describing semantically/pragmatically based difficulties, or systematic deviations from expected behavior. As with many of the previous systems, if the goal of evaluation is to provide systematic description of syntactic development, this system may prove to be useful, particularly in conjuction with other systems such as that of Engler, Hannah, and Longhurst.

Grammatical Analysis of Language Disability Another recent spontaneous utterance analysis system was proposed by Crystal, Fletcher, and Garman (1976), who suggested a multilevel scanning procedure. Each language sample is examined for eight levels of information explicitly noted as syntactic, not semantic or pragmatic, analysis. This restriction limits its usefulness with hearing-impaired children much in the same way that previously discussed systems are limited.

The language sample, which is elicited in a manner similar to that described by Tyack and Gottsleben (1974) or Lee and Canter (1971), is scanned first to determine which sentences cannot be analyzed. Sentences that are excluded from further analysis include: (a) sentences that are completely unintelligible, (b) symbolic noises such as *moo*, (c) deviant sentences—sentences that fall out of the normal expectations of language use, (d) incomplete sentences that may be used later for clarification of other sentences that can be analyzed, (e) ambiguous sentences, sentences whose meanings even with context are not clear.

The second scan is used to establish the proportion of self-generated utterances to utterances that are merely responses to the examiner. Responses are classified into normal response types, whether elliptical and full sentences; repetitions of what was said by the adult; and atypical, inappropriate or absence of response to examiner inquiries.

Scans Three and Four attempt to identify and tabulate connective devices such as initial adverbials, instances of coordination, and subordination. Scans Five through Seven involve detailed examination of clauses, sentence phrase structure, and word structure patterns such as noun-verb-noun. Scan Eight, the last, is for scrutinizing difficulties or problems previously identified.

The focus of this technique is on simultaneously determining correct syntactic performance and instances of deviations from normal patterns. Unfortunately it lacks statistical evidence of its reliability at this time. In addition, many of the decisions that need to be made in the analysis requires a relatively sophisticated knowledge of linguistic terminology, which probably cannot be avoided today, since such knowledge is imperative. The system has promise for use with language-impaired children because it provides for systematic identification of response behavior or lack of it, which can be translated into meaningful teaching goals.

Case Relation Analysis Scroggs (1977) suggested a method for describing the language performance of hearing-impaired children who have progressed to the two-word stage but may be well behind the children of their chronological age. In a sample of eight children, she found that Brown's (1973) eight semantic relationships, along with his two three-word utterance categories of embedding and conjoining, successfully described the linguistic status of the subjects. She developed profiles on the eight children that revealed definite patterns of performance and lack of performance. For example, one subject used a restricted range of only two relationships, entity-attribute and action-object, whereas others in the group exhibited the full range of relationships. The primary question about this approach is whether the 10 categories of eight basic semantic relationships and two three-word utterances are sufficient to describe the full range of utterances produced by hearing-impaired children. It should be noted that in the authors' employment of similiar techniques with samples from young hearing-impaired children these categories can account for approximately 92% of all utterances produced.

Bloom and Lahey's Language Sample Analysis Still another spontaneous utterance analysis procedure was reported by Bloom and Lahey (1978). Their system distinguishes between several stages of language development: (1) single-word usage, (2) early emerging semantic-syntactic relationships (two-word combinations), (3) further emerging semantic-syntactic relationships (three-word combinations), (4) embedded relations and grammatical morphemes, (5) successive related utterances (the origin of conversation competence), (6) complex sentences, (7) syntactic connectives and modal verbs, and (8) relative clauses. This system is distinct from other systems discussed because of its use of semantic categories to classify utterances. An examiner is expected to locate all those sentences that exemplify the same semantic category, such as existence, non-existence, recurrence, or action, and group these sentences together to permit a tally of the expected and of the actually occurring constituents within each category. Information on the appearance of grammatial morphemes is also noted as part of the establishment of therapeutic goals. Instances of more complex forms such as connectives, relative clauses, and subordination are also noted.

The focus of the system is clearly on semantic identification and then on syntactic description, not vice-versa. Provision for describing development of language functions such as conversational awareness and knowledge of speech acts has been made, but these aspects of the system are not as clearly spelled out as other portions of the system. With reference to the system's use with hearing-impaired children, strategies for description of atypical linguistic rule performance are lacking, which would seem to limit its total usefulness in the present form.

KRETSCHMER SPONTANEOUS LANGUAGE ANALYSIS PROCEDURE

Most of the analysis techniques described in the previous section seem promising, to varying degrees, for analyzing the utterances or writings of hearing-impaired children and youth. Often, however, these language productions present unique analysis problems because of the discrepancy between the speakers' or writers' cognitive capabilities and their knowledge of standard English forms. Many deaf children perform syntactically, semantically, or pragmatically at levels significantly below that of their cognitive awareness or processing abilities. Language description techniques for hearing-impaired children should be able to account for the unusual language performance of some children, and also be able to analyze samples in which performance is not so atypical, as in English proficient older students or preschool children. The system that follows has been proposed to account for language differences as well as delays. It has been employed with some success in a university training program for the past five years, in description of more than 2500 compositions in deaf and normally hearing children, and in local classroom settings.

The analysis system consists of the following steps: (a) identification of the underlying propositions of each utterance or written unit produced by a child, (b) description of the semantic content of each proposition, (c) description of the syntactic devices employed by the child to realize the semantic content of each proposition in the surface structure of the sentence, (d) description of the degree of communication competence with which the child accomplishes this task, and finally, (e) description, in contemporary terms, of the deviations or restricted forms that the child makes through identifying the restricted form as semantically, syntactically, and/or pragmatically motivated, The analysis proceeds on a sentence-by-sentence basis. The situation and communication context as well as the entire sample are employed to guide the description of communicative intents and to clarify the probable reasons for the restricted forms.

The analysis process should be pursued in the following manner to gather maximum information. The first task is to identify the syntactic devices used in the sentence. As each device is identified, the examiner can then break the sentence down into the propositions that underlie it. When each proposition is identified, assignment of case relations can be made. As restricted forms are encountered, their identification and description should occur in as much detail as possible. This procedure is amply demonstrated in Tables 8 and 9 (see p. 194 and p. 205).

The analysis protocol to be used in this process is presented in Table 7. It is divided into six sections. The first is devoted to descriptive categories on the preverbal level, that level where children's utterances or communication efforts contain no propositional content. Sections Two through Four provide descriptors of the semantic categories and syntactic devices that can be used by children. Section Five provides for description of communication competence, concentrating on such issues as speech acts, conversational devices, and procedures for conducting dialogue exchanges.

The final section provides a general description of the most commonly encountered categories of restricted forms. It is still incumbent upon the examiner to specify in detail the production difficulties of each child, identifying and articulating the conditions surrounding the execution of particular restricted forms. These conditions include discussion of frequency of occurrence, motivation for production, and specific feature violations.

English restricted forms produced by deaf persons can be of several general varieties:

1. Node omission with sentence frames. The child consistently omits basic nodes in sentence frames, whether subject, verb, object, or object of preposition. Where more complex sentence frames are attempted, node omission may include absence of modalities or some aspect of an elaborated node. Examples of node omissions made by deaf subjects include the following:

> subject node omission: *All days fix the toys.*
> verb node omission: *Boy big now.*
> adverbial node omission: *The boy put the ball on.*
> conjunction node omission: *The cat dog run across the*
> *street,* or *It is raining, we go outside.*

2. Violation of subcategorization restrictions. When a child uses a word in the incorrect sentence node, he has violated a subcategorization restriction. In the example *John girled the toy.*, *girl* is a noun being used in the verb node. *Girl* does not normally carry a verb feature in English, and thus cannot be used in the verb node. Some

Table 7. Kretschmer Spontaneous Language Analysis System

I. Preverbal behaviors:
    Exhibits ability to attend to joint activities
    Exhibits ability to attend to communication
    Exhibits ability to provide meaningful feedback
    A. For speech:
        1. exhibits voluntary phonation
        2. exhibits open and close contrasts
        3. exhibits oral and nasal contrasts
        4. exhibits loudness contrasts
        5. exhibits pitch contrasts
        6. exhibits reduplicative babbling
        7. exhibits sustained jargoning
    B. For sign language:[a]
        1. exhibits awareness of the following hand configurations:

a	f	v
o	g	5
b	x	claw-5
c	h	open-8
3	y	7
L	other (please specify):	

        2. exhibits awareness of the following places of articulation:

forehead	chin	chest
face	mount	shoulder
nose	cheek	arm
eyes	neck	other (please specify):

        3. exhibits awareness of the following movements:

contact	horizontal-depth
alteration	verticle
horizontal-width	other (please specify):

    C. For communication competence:[b]
        1. exhibits ability to attend to pointing
        2. exhibits use of proto-declarative point
        3. exhibits use of proto-imperative point
        4. exhibits use of word-like unit (sign) with proto-declarative point
        5. exhibits use of word-like unit (sign) with proto-imperative point
        6. exhibits use of referential word (sign) with proto-declarative point
        7. exhibits use of referential word (sign) with proto-imperative point
II. Single-word and two-word combination productions:
    A. Syntactic description
        1. Number of single-word productions
        2. Number of successive utterance productions
        3. Number of two-word combination productions
        4. Number of instances of the following pre-syntactic devices:
            a. referential word plus phonetically unstable speech unit
            b. referential word plus phonetically stable speech unit

Table 7—*continued*

      c. reduplicative two-word combination production
      d. rote two-word production
      e. two-word combination plus phonetically unstable speech unit inserted between the words
      f. two-word combination plus phonetically stable speech unit inserted between the words

B. Semantic description

   1. Instances of the following noun cases:
      a. agent: me (*I hit Jimmy.*)
      b. mover: cow (*The cow ran away.*)
      c. patient: picture (*I tore up the picture.*) Mary (*I thought about Mary.*)
      d. experiencer: Eric (*Eric loved Miriam.*)
      e. complement: picture (*I painted a picture.*) idea (*I thought up the idea.*)
      f. recipient: mommy (*I gave the ball to mommy.*)
      g. possessor: Jimmy (*Jimmy has a ball.; Jimmy's ball*)
      h. entity: ball (*There is the ball.*)
      i. content: Cinderella (*The story is about Cinderella.*)
      j. phenomenon: footstep (*The boy heard the footsteps.*)
      k. vocative: mommy (*Mommy, look here.*)

   2. Instances of the following verb cases:
      a. action-causative: hit (*Jack hit Robert.*)
      b. action-affective: cry (*Connie cried.*)
      c. process-causative: think (*Dominic thought about school.*)
      d. process-affective: sleep (*David slept.*)
      e. ambient-action: rain (*It is raining.*)

   3. Instances of the following modifier cases:
      a. existence: that (*I see that ball.*)
      b. non-existence: no (*There are no bananas.*)
      c. recurrence: more (*I want more milk.*)
      d. disappearance: all gone ((*The milk is all gone.*)
      e. size: little (*I see a little boy.*)
      f. condition: torn (*I have a torn shirt.*) happy (*Jerry is happy.*)
      g. shape: round (*The moon is round.*)
      h. quality: rough (*The cloth is rough.*)
      i. age: (*John is an old man.*)
      j. color: red (*Eleanor has a red dress.*)
      k. cardinal: ten (*I see ten boys.*)
      l. ordinal: fifth (*I want the fifth apple.*)

   4. Instances of the following adverbial cases:
      a. instrument: knife (*I cut myself with a knife.*)
      b. reason: party (*I made some cookies for the party.*)
      c. locative-action: school (*I hit Mary at school.*)
      d. locative-stative: table (*The book is on the table.*)
      e. locative-goal: hospital (*Jim walked to the hospital.*)
      f. locative-source: school (*Ted walked from school.*)

continued

Table 7—*continued*

g.　time-action: Tuesday (*The class went on Tuesday.*)
h.　time-duration: all week (*Milt worked all week.*)
i.　time-beginning: one o'clock (*He began at one o'clock.*)
j.　time-end: two o'clock (*He finished at two o'clock.*)
k.　time-beginning, end: one o'clock, two o'clock (*He worked from one o'clock to two o'clock.*)
l.　time-frequency: Sunday (*He goes to church every Sunday.*)
m.　manner: quick (*The rabbit runs quickly.*)
n.　other cases (please specify):

5.　Instances of the following question forms:

yes-no question: Mommy? (*Is mommy here?*)

who	when
what	where
how	why

III.　Single proposition productions
　　A.　Syntactic description
　　　　1.　Instances of the following modulations:[c]
　　　　　　a.　progressive
　　　　　　b.　irregular past
　　　　　　c.　regular past
　　　　　　d.　possessive
　　　　　　e.　irregular plurality
　　　　　　f.　regular plurality
　　　　　　g.　regular third person
　　　　　　h.　irregular third person
　　　　　　i.　articles
　　　　　　j.　case markers (prepositions)
　　　　　　k.　uncontractible copula
　　　　　　l.　contractible copula
　　　　　　m.　uncontractible auxiliary
　　　　　　n.　contractible auxiliary
　　　　　　o.　modals
　　　　　　p.　other (please specify):
　　　　2.　Instances of the following elaborated nodes:
　　　　　　a.　adjective embedding
　　　　　　b.　noun adjunct embedding
　　　　　　c.　genitive (possessive) embedding
　　B.　semantic description
　　　　1.　Instances of the following noun case:
　　　　　　a.　entity-equivalent: me, boy (*I am a boy.*)
　　　　2.　Instances of the following verb cases:
　　　　　　a.　stative-static: apple red (*The apple* is red.*)
　　　　　　b.　stative-dynamic: fire hot (*The fire is hot.; The fire became hot.*)
　　　　　　c.　ambient-stative: that nice (*That's nice.*)
　　　　3.　Instances of the following adverbial cases:
　　　　　　a.　intensifier: so good, too good, very good

Table 7—*continued*

        b.   inclusion: me too (*I want to go too.*)
        c.   comparison: like rabbit (*He runs like a rabbit*).

IV. Complex sentence productions:
    A.   Instances of the following syntactic occurrences:
        1.   Modalities
            a.   negation
            b.   indirect discourse
            c.   direct discourse
            d.   embedded question
            e.   imperative
            f.   yes-no question
            g.   wh-question
        2.   Conjoining
            a.   subordinate conjunction
            b.   coordinating conjunction
        3.   Elaborated Nodes
            a.   relative clause
            b.   nominalization: possessive + verb + ing
            c.   nominalization: infinitive
            d.   nominalization: participle
            e.   factive clause
        4.   Transformations
            a.   do-support
            b.   contraction
            c.   adverbial preposing
            d.   indirect object preposing
            e.   auxiliary preposing
            f.   pronominalization
            g.   passive
            h.   deletion
            i.   there
            j.   other (please specify):

V. Communication competence:
    A.   Instances of the following speech acts:

declaring	requesting
soliciting information	commanding
confirming	promising
other (please specify)	

    B.   Number of times child initiates conversation
    C.   Number of times child changes topics
    D.   Number of times child pursues topics
    E.   Number of times child formally ends conversation
    F.   Instances of the following conversation acts:
        1.   Child-initiated contingency inquiries
        2.   Adult-initiated contingency inquiries
        3.   Spontaneous utterances
        4.   Full imitations

continued

Table 7—*continued*

---

     5. Partial imitations
     6. Other (please specify):
  G. Instances of the following conversation devices:
     1. Use of determiners to cue given/new information
     2. Use of pronominalization to encode given/new information
     3. Use of relative clauses to topicalize
     4. Use of adjective embedding to topicalize
     5. Use of subordinate conjunction to tie one sentence to another
     6. Use of coordinating conjunction to tie one sentence to another
     7. Use of verb tense to tie one sentence to another
     8. Use of adverbial connectors to tie one sentence to another
     9. Use of adverbial constructions to signal topic change
     10. Other (please specify):
VI. Restricted form types:
  A. Node omissions in sentence frames
  B. Subcategorization restriction violations
  C. Selectional restriction violations
  D. Local transformation omissions
  E. General transformation restriction violations
  F. Transformation selectional restriction violations
  G. Case restriction violations
  H. Componential feature violations
  I. General semantic restriction violations
  J. Communication breakdowns
  K. Pragmatic restriction violations

---

[a] Taken from Friedman, L. 1977. On the Other Hand. Academic Press, New York.

[b] Taken from Bates, E. 1976. Language and Context: The Acquisition of Pragmatics. Academic Press, New York.

[c] Taken from Brown, R. 1973. A First Language: The Early Stages. Harvard University Press, Cambridge.

deaf children have considerable difficulty with subcategorization restrictions, for example:

> using verbs as nouns: *The petted is nice.*
> using adjectives as nouns: *The red is big.*
> using adjectives as verbs: *The boy large the box.*
> using prepositions as verbs: *The boy up the stairs.*

3. Violation of selectional restrictions. Inappropriate use of function words or word endings constitutes a selectional restriction violation. Some examples produced by deaf children would be:

> using past tense as a plurality marker on nouns: *two pocketed.*
> using an ordinal determiner in place of a cardinal determiner: *I saw tenth boys.*

4. Local transformation omission. In many cases, the hearing-impaired child executes a local transformation omission by omitting a function word or word ending entirely, rather than inappro-

priate application of a selectional restriction. For instance, deaf children often:

> omit plurality markers: *Two chicken.*
> omit tense: *He run.*
> omit determiners: *I see ball.*

5. Violation of general transformation restrictions. Errors of constituent arrangement or word order are included in this category. Children who possess all the sentence frame nodes but assemble them incorrectly have failed to observe the restrictions imposed by a general transformation. The most classic example from deaf children's language would be inappropriate placement of the adjective, as in *the ball red.*

6. Violation of transformational selection restrictions. Certain lexical items dictate the use of congruent constituent or sentence frames. Failure to adhere to these expectations would be termed a transformational selectional restriction violation. For example, enjoy precedes participles, never infinitives, so that the sentence *He enjoys to play.* contains an example of a failure to observe a transformational selectional restriction. Some transformational selectional restriction violations result from a lack of information about contextual/discourse constraints, such as when to use pronouns. For instance new topics are not introduced, or topics are introduced through the use of nouns. After their introduction, the noun becomes old information and can then be pronominalized. This is an excellent example of the interface between pragmatic and syntactic constraints within language.

7. Case restrictions violation. These violations result from the use of words that do not fit the underlying case relationship intended in a sentence, or the omission of cases or case markers in the surface structure of the sentence. Thus, case restriction violations can involve misuse of content words, or misuse of case markers such as prepositions. For instance *make* is a complement-taking verb, but deaf children often use it as a patient-taking verb, thus confusing it with either *fix* or *arrange.* Another common case restriction violation is the omission of prepositions, so that the correct case is not cued in the sentence frame. In other situations, the child may code a relationship, but he selects a preposition that is inappropriate to the relationship he intended. For instance, deaf children frequently encode locative relationships as if they were stative, not realizing that a variety of relationships other than stative, such as goal and source, may be expressed using other prepositions.

8. Componential feature violation. Deaf children may properly fill and arrange sentence constituents, select case relationships and realize

them in surface structures, and yet produce a sentence with atypical meaning. Sentence meaning may be confused by the use of a word that fails to share all the correct features with the appropriate lexical item that should have been used. For instance the child might say *He took the ball in the bag.*; the context shows unquestioningly that *put* is the appropriate choice. In this case, *put* and *took* share features such as action, requiring hands, and movement, but differ on direction; *put* carries the feature of moving toward, but *took* suggests moving away.

9. General semantic violation. This category is a catch-all, concerned with semantic restrictions such as confusions in the use of modals, adverbials, and conjunctions, especially in sentences where the constituents have been filled, all grammatical restrictions have been observed, but an inappropriate semantic relationship still results. In the sentences *John and Mary ate the ice cream. All the children got sick.,* *all* is syntactically appropriate, but its use does not observe the semantic restriction that John and Mary are only two in number, so that *both* or even *they* would have been better choices. Misuse of modals and of verb tense could also be considered a type of semantic restriction violation.

10. Communication difficulties. This category includes those instances where the child has not observed the conventions tied to initiating, maintaining, and closing conversations. Failure to use connectors to indicate maintenance or change of topics would fall into this category.

11. Pragmatic violations. This last category refers to those instances when the child has failed to use a particular syntactic/semantic form in the way it should be used for communicative purposes. For instance, using relative clauses without attempting to establish topics would be an example of a pragmatic violation.

These restricted form categories are not mutually exclusive. Instead, a particular restricted form production may result from one or many of the above reasons. The task of the examiner is to detect consistent patterns of restricted form production and to determine the reason or reasons for their generation.

This protocol (Table 6) has been developed with the practicing teacher or therapist in education of the hearing-impaired in mind. Spoken, gestured, pidgin signed, fingerspelled, and/or written English can be evaluated with this procedure, although categories for describing writing at the preverbal stage have not been included. This procedure does not offer guidelines for evaluation of American Sign Language, except for the preverbal level. Rather, the focus is on the degree of congruence between manual or signed English expression and standard English forms, which may include spoken and written forms as well.

To demonstrate the analysis procedure and the use of the test protocol, two samples are analyzed with a summary of results provided. Table 8 contains a language sample generated by a normally hearing adolescent (Kevin), and Table 9 shows a sample by a hearing-impaired adolescent (Justin). In both instances, the sample is an abbreviated one and is from the written modality. It is important that the reader realize that the authors do not suggest that definitive results can be completed upon such a limited sample. However, these examples show something of the steps necessary to derive a meaningful description of language performance. It is also important, of course, not to confine analysis to one modality, but to sample across modalities before firm conclusions about performance levels are made. Writing was selected in this instance only to demonstrate the system, not to provide conclusive evidence of English mastery.

In each of the examples provided, only a semantic/syntactic analysis is shown. No communication analysis was attempted because of the abbreviated nature of the sample, and because communication analysis of a written sample is generally meaningless since it does not constitute a dialogue situation. Attention has been paid, however, to the use of conversational devices such as articles or verb tense whenever they are felt to contribute to a clarification of the analysis process.

In Table 8, it can be seen that Kevin, the normally hearing subject, generated sentences containing one to six propositions, whereas Justin produced a maximum of four propositions per sentence. It should be remembered that propositions are shown in sentence form throughout both analyses for sake of clarity, but it should not be concluded that any writer constructs propositions in this form or even in this order when forming a sentence. The analysis sentences represent a convention for describing propositional content, the same convention adhered to throughout this book.

Kevin produced a number of elaborated nodes within his sentence frames, but Justin did not. The range of Kevin's elaborated nodes was varied, including nominalizations, subordinate conjunctions, and coordinating conjunctions. Justin, on the other hand, confined his elaborated nodes to embedded adjectives and genitive forms, usually of the pronominalized variety.

Kevin demonstrated some sense of dialogue cohesiveness, as demonstrated by his use of connectors such as *of course* and his adherence to conventions concerning verb tense and article usage. In spite of this, his story was choppy in that each paragraph did not flow logically into the next. Justin, on the other hand, had great difficulty with

Table 8. Analysis of a language sample elicited from a normally hearing adolescent

Name: Kevin   Age: 12:9

Context: Sample elicited in response to the Myklebust Picture Story stimulus picture. Subject was asked to produce a story about the picture.

Sample:

The little boy is learning how to be a good husband. He is playing with some toy people. He is pretending to be the husband of the girl he has just picked up from the table. He asked his new wife, "Do you love me?" The wife said, "Oh honey, how can you ask that? Of course, I love you." He was very happy about that.

Being a new husband is very hard. He tries to make himself useful by doing things around the home. Every time he does something, he has an accident that makes his wife very angry. Finally, she can't stand it anymore, so she tells him to please leave everything alone because she will take care of it.

Some people may think it's stupid for little boys to play with dolls, but as you can see, it's really not. Playing with dolls can be very educational. Little boys can learn lessons that will be very useful in the future.

Analysis:

Sentence 1: *The little boy is learning how to be a good husband.*

Embedded question	The little boy is learning ( ).[a]	
	The boy is a good husband ( ).[b]	
Adjective embedding	The boy is learning ( ).	Experiencer, process-causative, complement
	The boy is little.	Entity, stative-static, size.
Adjective embedding	The boy is a husband ( ).	Entity, stative-static, entity-equivalent, manner
	The boy is good.	Entity, stative-static, condition

Sentence 2: *He is playing with some toy people.*

Pronominalization: personal	The boy is playing with some toy people.	
	The boy is playing with some people.	Agent, action-causative, patient
Noun adjunct embedding	The people are toys.	Entity, stative-static, entity-equivalent

Sentence 3: *He is pretending to be the husband of the girl he has just picked up.*

Relative clause: deletion[c]	He is pretending to be the husband of the girl.	
	He is pretending to be the husband of the girl.	
	He has just picked up the girl.	
Nominalization: infinitive	He is pretending ( ).	
	The boy is the husband of the girl.	
Pronominalization: personal	He is pretending ( ).	Experiencer, process-causative, complement
Possessive: of + NP	The boy is pretending ( ).	Entity, stative-static, entity-equivalent
		Possessor, process, patient
	The boy is the husband.	
Pronominalization: personal	The girl has a husband.	
	The boy has just picked up the girl.	
Obligatory adverbial preposing	The boy has just picked up the girl.	Agent, action-causative, patient, time-action

Sentence 4: *He asked his new wife, "Do you love me?"*

Direct discourse: question	He asked his new wife ( ).	
	Do you love me?	
Pronominalization: personal	The boy/husband[d] asked his new wife ( ).	
Pronominalization: genitive	The boy/husband asked the boy's/husband's new wife ( ).	
Adjective embedding	The boy/husband asked the boy's/husband's wife ( ).	
	The wife is new.	Entity, stative-static, condition

---

[a] The parenthesis represents an elaborated node. Because the node has been filled by an entire proposition, it was felt that this fact could best be represented by employing a null or empty position represented by a set of parentheses.

[b] In this case, the parenthesis represents the question node, which is adverbial here.

[c] Subordinate clauses and relative clauses can be reduced within sentences, particularly when the context can support such deletion of information.

[d] In this context, the boy has assumed the role of the husband. Thus he is at one time both the boy and the husband.

continued

Table 8—continued

Possessive	The boy/husband asked the wife ( ).	Agent, action-causative, recipient, complement
	The boy/husband has a wife.	Possessor, process, patient
Yes-no question	You do love me.	
Pronominalization: personal	The listener does love me.	
Pronominalization: personal	The listener does love the speaker.	
Do-support	The listener loves the speaker.	Experiencer, process-causative, patient

Sentence 5: *She said, "Oh honey, how can you say that? Of course, I love you."*

Direct discourse:	She said ( ).	
question	Oh honey, how can you say that?	
statement	Of course, I love you.	
Pronominalization: personal	The wife said ( ).	Agent, action-causative, complement
Auxiliary preposing	Oh honey, how you can say that?	
Wh-question	Oh honey, you can say that ( ).	
Pronominalization: personal	Oh honey, the listener can say that ( ).	
Deletion	Oh honey, the listener can say that (question) ( ).	Vocative, agent, action-causative, complement, manner
Pronominalization: personal	Of course, the speaker loves you.	
Pronominalization: personal	Of course, the speaker loves the listener.	Connector[e], experiencer, process-causative, patient

Sentence 6: *He was very very happy about that.*

Transformation	Sentence	Features
Pronominalization: personal	The boy/husband was very happy about that.	
Obligatory adverbial preposing	The boy/husband was happy very about that.	
Deletion	The boy/husband was happy very about that (statement).	Entity, stative-dynamic, condition, intensifier, reason

Sentence 7 (new paragraph): *Being a new husband is very hard.*

Transformation	Sentence	Features
Nominalization: participle	( ) is very hard. The boy/husband is being a new husband.	
Obligatory adverbial preposing	( ) is hard very.	Entity, stative-dynamic, condition, intensifier
Adjective embedding	The boy/husband is being a husband. The husband is new.	Entity, stative-dynamic, entity-equivalent Entity, stative-dynamic, condition

Sentence 8: *He tries to make himself useful by doing things around the home.*

Transformation	Sentence	Features
Nominalization: participle	He tries to make himself useful by ( ). The boy/husband is doing things around the home.	
Nominalization: infinitive	He tries ( ). The boy/husband makes himself useful by ( ).	Experiencer, process-causative, complement
Pronominalization: personal	The boy/husband tries ( ).	

[e] *Of course* is interpreted here as an adverbial construction that links one sentence to another.

continued

Table 8—continued

Nominalization: infinitive	The boy/husband makes ( ). Himself is useful by ( ).	Agent, action-causative, complement
Pronominalization: reflexive	The boy/husband is useful by ( ).	Entity, stative-dynamic, condition, manner
Pronominalization: indefinite	The boy/husband is doing (some activities) around the home.	Agent, action-causative, complement, locative-action

Sentence 9: *He has a problem.*

| Pronominalization: personal | The boy/husband has a problem. | Possessor (experiencer), process (process-causative) complement[f] |

Sentence 10: *Every time he does something, he has an accident that makes his wife very angry.*

Relative clause: deletion[e]	Every time he has an accident that makes his wife very angry.	
	He does something every time.	
Relative clause	Every time he has an accident.	
	The accident makes his wife very angry.	
Pronominalization: personal	Every time the boy/husband has an accident.	
Optional adverbial preposing	The boy/husband has an accident every time.	Experiencer, process-causative, complement, time-frequency
Nominalization: infinitive	The accident makes ( ).	Instrument, process-causative, complement
	His wife is very angry.	
Pronominalization: genitive	The boy's/husband's wife is very angry.	
Possessive	The wife is very angry.	
	The boy/husband has a wife.	Possessor, process, patient

Obligatory adverbial preposing	The wife is angry very.	Entity, stative-dynamic, condition, intensifier
Pronominalization: personal	The boy/husband does something every time.	Agent, action-causative, complement, time-frequency
Pronominalization: indefinite	The boy/husband does (some activities) every time.	

Sentence 11: *Finally, she can't stand it anymore, so she tells him to please leave everything alone because she will take care of it.*

Subordinate conjunction	Finally, she can't stand it anymore. She tells him to please leave everything alone because she will take care of it.	
Pronominalization: personal	Finally, the wife can't stand it anymore.	
Pronominalization: indefinite	Finally, the wife can't stand (the situation) anymore.	
Contraction	Finally, the wife cannot stand (the situation) anymore.	
Negation	Finally, the wife can stand (the situation) anymore.	
Optional adverbial preposing	The wife can stand (the situation) anymore finally.	Experiencer, process-causative, complement, time-frequency, time-end
Indirect discourse: imperative	She tells ( ). Please, (listener) leave everything alone because she will take care of it.	
Deletion	She tells (the boy/husband) ( ).	
Pronominalization: personal	The wife tells (the boy/husband) ( ).	Agent, action-causative, recipient, complement

' When faced with a problem, one can possess it, but simultaneously undergo an internal experience labeled "having a problem." Thus both notions must be considered.

continued

Table 8—*continued*

Subordinate conjunction	Please, (listener) leave everything alone. She will take care of it.
Pronominalization: indefinite	Please, (listener) leave (the objects/situation) alone.	Explicative[g], agent, action-causative, patient/complement, manner
Pronominalization: personal	The wife will take care of it.	
Pronominalization: indefinite	The wife will take care of (the objects/situation).[h]	Agent, action-causative, patient/complement

Sentence 12 (new paragraph): *Some people may think that it's stupid for little boys to play with dolls, but as you can see, it's really not.*

Coordinating conjunction	Some people may think that it's stupid for little boys to play with dolls. As you can see, it's really not.	
Indirect discourse[i] statement	Some people may think ( ).	Experiencer, process-causative, complement
	It's stupid for little boys to play with dolls.	
Nominalization: infinitive	It's stupid for ( ).	Ambient-stative, condition, reason
	Little boys play with dolls.	
Adjective embedding	Boys play with dolls.	Agent, action-causative, patient
	Boys are little.	Entity, stative-static, size
Subordinate conjunction	You can see. It's really not.	
Deletion	You can see (the fact).	
Pronominalization: personal	The listener can see (the fact).	Experiencer, process-causative, complement

Deletion	It's really not (stupid).	
Negation	It's really (stupid).	
Contraction	It is really (stupid).	
Obligatory adverbial preposing	It is (stupid) really.	Ambient-stative, condition, intensifier

Sentence 13: *Playing with dolls can be very educational.*

Nominalization: participle	( ) can be very educational. The boys are playing with toys.	Agent, action-causative, patient
Obligatory adverbial preposing	( ) can be educational very.	Entity, stative-dynamic, condition, intensifier

Sentence 14: *Little boys can learn lessons that will be very useful in the future.*

Relative clause	Little boys can learn lessons. The lessons will be very useful in the future.	
Adjective embedding	Boys can learn lessons.	Experiencer, process-causative, complement[j]
	Boys are little.	Entity, stative-static, size
Obligatory adverbial preposing	The lessons will be useful very in the future.	Entity, stative-dynamic, condition, intensifier, time-stative

[g] Some words are used as emotional releases or social conventions. In either case they can be referred to as explicatives.

[h] *Will take care of* is the complete verb in this sentence.

[i] In this context, *think* can be viewed as a verb signifying an internal discussion with one's self.

[j] *Lessons* is an ambiguous word. It could represent materials designated as lessons, which would then make it a patient. However, it could also represent knowledge to be mastered as a result of dealing with the materials, which would make it a complement. Given the context of the story, the authors have made the decision to call it a complement, but a patient interpretation is defensible.

continued

Table 8—*continued*

Summary

Number of propositions—46
Number of sentences—14
Number of propositions per sentence—3.3
Range: 1-6

Syntactic Summary

Modality:

Negation—2
Imperative—1
Yes-no questions—1
Wh-question—1
Direct discourse—2
Nominalization: participle—3

Conjunction:

Subordinate—3
Coordinating—1

Elaborated Nodes:

Indirect discourse—2
Adjective embedding—6
Relative clause—3
Nominalization: Infinitive—5
Possession—3
Noun Adjunct Embedding—1
Embedded Question—1

Transformations:

Pronominalization—27
Deletion—7
Do-support—1
Contraction—2
Preposing—10

Semantic Summary

Noun Categories:

Experiencer—10
Complement—17
Entity—16
Entity-equivalent—4
Agent—13
Patient—11
Recipient—2
Vocative—1
Possessor—4

Verb Categories:

Process-causative—11
Stative-static—8
Action-causative—13
Process—4
Stative-dynamic—8
Ambient-stative—2

Adverbial Categories:

Manner—4
Location—1
Time—6
Reason—2
Intensifier—6
Instrument—1

Modifier Categories:

Size—3
Condition—11

Table 9. Analysis of a language sample elicited from a hearing-impaired adolescent

Name: Justin   Age: 12:11
Context: Sample elicited in response to the Myklebust Picture Story stimulus picture. Subject was asked to produce a story about the picture.
Sample:
  One little boy love playing with his toys. His name is Tommy Rickett.
He did not have to do play with something. His parents looked at him. He was not glad. His parents feel sorry for him. His parents went to shop toys. They bought toy for him. He was so glad. Now he have to do.
  He really love playing with his toys. His house is very nice.

Analysis:
Sentence 1: *One little boy love playing with his toys.*

Nominalization: participle	One little boy love ( ).	
	The boy is playing with his toys.	
Adjective embedding	One boy love ( ).	Experiencer, process-causative, complement
	One boy is little.	Entity, stative-static, size
Pronominalization: genitive	The boy is playing with the boy's toys.	
Possession	The boy is playing with the toys.	Agent, action-causative, patient
	The boy has toys.	Possessor, process, patient

Comment: In attempting this sentence, two problems seem to emerge. First, even though Justin is writing a story, his choice of determiner to begin the composition seems unrelated to discourse. *One* implies that there is more than one young man in the stimulus picture, which is not the case. A more appropriate choice would have been to select an article that encoded the given-new contract, such as *the*. Given that Justin is looking at the picture while writing, *boy* would be given information, making *the* the most appropriate choice. Examination of the remainder of the sample reveals a conspicuous absence of *a* and *the*, suggesting that they may not be functional in his language.
  A second problem is the absence of the local tense transformation on the verb *love*.

continued

Table 9—*continued*

Sentence 2: *His name is Tommy Rickett.*

Pronominalization: genitive	The boy's name is Tommy Rickett.
Possession	The name is Tommy Rickett. Entity, stative-static, entity-equivalent
	The name belongs to the boy. Patient, process, possessor

Comment: On the surface this is a perfectly acceptable sentence. Taken in the context of his entire effort, however, a question arises about his use of the present tense on the verb *is*. Most of the remainder of his story is in past tense, which would dictate that the tense for this verb should probably be past tense. Many hearing-impaired children seem prone to introduce names into stories in the present tense. Perhaps this is related to names being shown in classrooms in the present tense, which the child takes to mean that within discourse, names are presented in the present tense rather than the past. In other words, previously learned discourse requirements take precedence over immediate discourse requirements—to keep the tense consistent within a given paragraph.

Sentence 3 (new paragraph): *He did not have to do play with something.*

Pronominalization: personal	The boy did not have to play with something.
Negation	The boy did have to do play with something.
Do-support	The boy have to do play with something.
Pronominalization: indefinite	The boy have to do play with (some object).

Comment: At this point, some analysis decision about the infinitive has to be made, because it seems clear that there are two underlying propositions. Some cue as to processes at work is present in Sentence 10. *Now he have to do.* It seems likely that *have to do* is a memorized form of some sort that he uses by stringing on other propositions. Such a notion is similar in principle to some of the examples provided by R. Clark (1977) in her article on delayed imitation. There are three examples of infinitives present in the sample; in all three instances, difficulty with the infinitive form was noted. Therefore, it is reasonable to explore his knowledge for details about this syntactic form.

| Nominalization: infinitive | The boy have to do (   ). | Agent, action-causative, complement |
| | The boy play with (some object). | Agent, action-causative, patient |

Comment: As in Sentence 11, Justin has pronominalized the first use of boy in the paragraph. Within spoken discourse this is an appropriate use of pronominalization. However, within written discourse, each noun should be used in its full form with its appropriate information-based article (*a* or *the*) for each new paragraph. This is one of the most significant differences between discourse requirements for spoken and written language, which demonstrates that spoken and written language may have the same base, and yet be distinct from one another.

Sentence 4: *His parents looked at him.*

Pronominalization: genitive	The boy's parents looked at him.	Possessor, process, patient
Possession	The parents looked at him.	
	The boy has parents.	

| Pronominalization: personal | The parents looked at the boy. | Agent, action-causative, patient |

Comment: The major problem with this sentence is the choice of the unit *looked at. Looked at* would suggest that his parents are only doing this once, whereas the drift of the composition is toward the notion of *watching*, or looking at over a period of time. This presents a good example of how deaf children often master the general notions of words, but not the specific dimensions that surround lexical items to differentiate them from other words. It could be argued that *kept an eye on* was the actual idea the child wished to communicate, but he did not have the lexical items to do so. If this is the case, then the teaching task is to provide him with the necessary vocabulary. If, on the other hand, the problem is one of being unaware of the subtle difference, then practice in vocabulary contrasting might be useful—that is, taking constellations of words like *look at, watch,* and *kept an eye on* and discussing the differences between them, not their similarities.

In contrast to Sentences 1 and 3, this sentence demonstrates mastery of the local transformation for tense; unlike Sentence 2, it is in the past tense instead of the present tense. It is a regular form, but *love* (Sentence 1) can also be inflected using the regular form.

Sentence 5: *He was not glad.*

| Pronominalization: personal | The boy was not glad. | Entity, stative-dynamic, condition |
| Negation | The boy was glad. | |

continued

Table 9—continued

Comment: The choice of the word *glad* represents a problem similar to that of *look at* in Sentence 4. Given the context of the sentence in the story, a better choice in the story, a better choice would probably have been *happy. Glad* implies that something has happened, whereas *happy* implies a condition that occurs independently of given events. Again, Justin has the general notion about feeling, but not the subtle difference between *glad* and *happy.*

Sentence 6: *His parents feel sorry for him.*

Pronominalization: genitive	The boy's parents feel sorry for him.
Pronominalization: personal	The boy's parents feel sorry for the boy.
Possession	The parents feel sorry for the boy.
	Experiencer, process-causative, complement, recipient
	The boy has parents.
	Possessor, process, patient

Comment: Justin has failed to apply the local transformation past tense marker on the verb. One might argue that he has not mastered irregular past tense, but in Sentence 7 he correctly marked *go* for past tense. Perhaps *feel* has not been mastered even though he has some concept of marking past tense on irregular verbs.

Sentence 7: *His parents went to shop toys.*

Pronominalization: genitive	The boy's parents went to shop toys.
Possession	The parents went to shop toys.
	The boy has parents.
	Possessor, process, patient
Nominalization: infinitive	The parents went ( ).
	Mover, action-affective, location-goal
	The parents shopped toys.
	Agent, action-causative, patient

Comment: Within the context of the story, the use of the infinitive form in this sentence is semantically/communicatively inappropriate. The infinitive is inserted in the locative position, resulting in emphasis on the activity, not the act of *shopping.* Given this interpretation, a participle form would have been more appropriate. This lack of use casts doubt on the knowledge of participle forms in Sentences 1 and 11. Further investigation of the semantic intent of those types of sentences is needed. Because this is the only legitimate use of infinitive in the composition and given the difficulties in Sentence 3 and 10, it may be that infinitives are just coming into Justin's language. If Slobin (1973) is correct that new forms are used to express old functions, perhaps his use of an infinitive in this sentence is an attempt at this use. Such an idea would have to be verified through additional testing, however. This line of thinking is provided to show how one can generate hypotheses about linguistic functioning in hearing-impaired children.

A second problem in this sentence is the absence of the particle from the two-part verb *shop for*. Because Justin includes other two-part verbs, such as *play with*, it is highly likely that this is a lexical problem, which is common for hearing-impaired children. The source of this problem may be related to the way they are presented in language teaching. Many teachers would argue that *shop* is the verb in this sentence, but actually the verb is *shop for*, with the following noun being the recipient of the action, or the patient.

Sentence 8: *They bought toy for him.*

Pronominalization: personal   The parents bought toy for him.

Pronominalization: personal   The parents bought toy for the boy.   Agent, action-causative, patient, recipient

Comment: Within the context of the story, there is an obligatory need to insert an information-related article before toy. This reinforces the statement made previously about Sentence 1.

In some ways this sentence is ambiguous, because it is unclear whether his parents bought a single toy or several toys. The previous sentence would seem to suggest that there was only one toy. However, even Sentence 12 would seem to suggest the possibility that there was only one toy. However, even Sentence 12 is ambiguous because it is not clear whether he was talking about a toy house or a real house. This is a good example of the need for adjectives to discriminate between two possibilities. It is interesting that his only use of an adjective was in Sentence 1, where an adjective was not really needed from a discourse point of view. This would suggest that Justin may not really understand the discourse contributions made by adjectives.

Finally, this sentence has another example of a correct application of a local past tense transformation to an irregular verb. This reinforces the observation that the failure to inflect *feel* in Sentence 6 was a lexical problem.

Sentence 9: *He was so glad.*

Pronominalization: personal   They boy was so glad.

Obligatory adverbial preposing   The boy was glad so.   Entity, stative-dynamic, condition, intensifier

Comment: On the surface this sentence seems appropriate, but because it is not clear what he is glad about, the comments for Sentence 5 hold here. To justify the use of *glad*, there is a need to tie Sentences 8 and 9 together somehow. This lack of coordination reflects a lack of discourse knowledge, that is, how Sentence 9 proceeds from Sentence 8, and so forth. He lacks internal language organization to make logical conclusions. Use of subordinate conjunctions or adverbial connectors often serve this discourse function within connected language.

continued

Table 9—continued

Note that in this stative sentence the child has correctly maintained past tense. This is in contrast to Sentences 2 and 12, both of which are general descriptive sentences.

Sentence 10: *Now he have to do.*

Pronominalization: personal — Now the boy have to do.

Optional adverbial preposing — The boy have to do now.

Comment: Analysis of this sentence is very difficult because it is unclear what the function of *have to do* is. If the interpretation of Sentence 3 is correct, then this sentence could be considered a single proposition sentence: Agent, action-causative, complement (deleted), time-action.

Sentence 11 (new paragraph): *He really love playing with his toys.*

Nominalization: participle — He really love ( ).

The boy is playing with his toys.

Pronominalization: personal — The boy really love ( ).

Obligatory adverb preposing — The boy love ( ) really.

Experiencer, process-causative, complement, intensifier

Pronominalization: genitive — The boy is playing with the boy's toys.

Possession — The boy is playing with the toys.

The boy has toys.

Agent, action-causative, patient

Possessor, process, patient

Comment: Again Justin has failed to apply a local past tense transformational marker on a regular verb. Given the inconsistency with this sample, he seems to have limited or partial control over verb tense marking.

As in Sentence 3, he has pronominalized the first use of boy in the new paragraph. This is a failure to observe written language discourse requirements concerning the introduction of new paragraphs.

Sentence 12: *His house is very nice.*

Pronominalization: genitive — The boy's house is very nice.

Possession — The house is very nice.

The boy has a house.

Possessor, process, patient

Obligatory adverb preposing   The house is nice very.   Entity, stative-static, quality, intensifier

Comment: As indicated, this sentence is ambiguous because it is unclear which house the child is referring to. Immediate clarification from the child needs to be made to interpret this sentence meaningfully. It is still obvious that he has little understanding about the role of adjectives in discourse.

Justin has written this sentence in present tense. Picture description is generally written in present tense in the classroom. Descriptive statements within context should adhere to the tense restrictions for that discourse/story.

Summary

Number of propositions—23
Number of sentences—12
Number of propositions per sentence—2.1
Range: 1–4

Syntactic Summary

Modality:
Negation—2

Elaborated Nodes:
Nominalization: Participle—2
Possession—7

Transformations:
Pronominalization—16
Do-support—1
Nominalization: Infinitive—1
Adjective embedding—1
Preposing—3

Semantic Summary

Noun Categories:
Experiencer—3
Complement—4
Entity—5
Agent—7
Patient—13
Possessor—7
Entity-equivalent—1
Recipient—2
Mover—1

Verb Categories:
Process-causative—3
Stative-static—3
Action-causative—7
Process—7
Stative-dynamic—2
Action-affective—1

Adverbial Categories:
Location—1
Intensifier—3

Modifier Categories:
Size—1
Condition—2
Quality—1

discourse constraints in his writing. It seemed as if each sentence had been generated without regard to either previous or following sentences. The relation from sentence to sentence was shown in content, but not through conversational/syntactic conventions. This is exemplified by the lack of determiners *a* and *the* or of adverbial connectors in their normal communication roles.

Vocabulary usage by Kevin is varied. Justin, in contrast, shows areas of vocabulary confusion. He seems to use words appropriately, but often they do not quite fit. There is a sense of generally correct meanings, but not of mature understanding of the subtle features that dictate a word's appropriate use in propositions or with other lexical items.

As can be seen from Tables 8 and 9, this analysis protocol can aid significantly in the description process. The strength of the present system over other, more established ones is in its potential to analyze English language samples generated in a variety of modalities and by both younger and older hearing-impaired youngsters.

Statistical validity for the entire system is still awaited, as is the question of reliability of examiner classifications or descriptions for language samples. The basic syntactic/semantic and restricted form categories have been refined, however, over some period of time, having been reported first in 1972 in application with spontaneous compositions of deaf and normally hearing adolescents (Kretschmer, 1972b).

Application of this or any system of spontaneous language analysis should lead first to the development of hypotheses about a child's linguistic functioning. Once hypotheses have been made, it is incumbent on the examiner to employ other procedures that confirm or supplement the findings from the spontaneous language sample. To guarantee a suitable base for generating therapeutic hypotheses, it is recommended that each educational or diagnostic unit agree on the conditions and materials through which language samples are to be gathered. Consideration should be given to sampling over time and in several communication situations rather than relying on a single set of 50 to 100 consecutive productions, generated in a single communication setting. The sampling strategy should be maintained both from child to child and from test period to test period to permit normative comparisons.

Use of this or any system for description of language production should be only the first step in the development of a language intervention program. To the extent that a child's language performance is delayed or deviant when compared to what is expected for his age and cognitive abilities, language intervention may be required. Chapter 6 addresses the issue of language learning and teaching for hearing-impaired children in an educational setting.

CHAPTER 6

EDUCATIONAL PROCEDURES

CONTENTS

Education of the hearing impaired has a long tradition of concern about improving linguistic performance of children with severe hearing loss. Professional writing or educational strategies that appeared before the current explosion of information in developmental psycholinguistics have tended to focus on the development of surface structure forms. The mergence of knowledge in linguistics, child development, and developmental psycholinguistics has suggested the need for a shift away from a sole concern with surface structure matters toward consideration of deep structure issues to include semantic and communicative performance. The need for departure from more traditional concerns to focus on development of understanding of the meaning of linguistic principles is clear. Rather than being concerned solely with word order, word choice, and application of surface structure forms such as word endings, practice in understanding and generating language rules should be stressed.

This difference in instructional approach can best be exemplified by comparing traditional and contemporary literature on the issue of how each treats the verb *have* and *be*. J. Bennett (1933) suggested that children must understand the difference between *is, have,* and *has on,* which she thought could best be achieved through the use of the Fitzgerald Key and *be, have,* and *has on* charts. Children were provided with drills in which they were encouraged to formulate *be, have,* and *has on* sentences by referring to the charts they had previously developed. The emphasis in such an approach is on "artificial" or externally generated communication, on the development of surface structures. Attention was not paid to the underlying deep structures implicit for each of the three verbs under consideration.

In contrast, Hargis and Lamm (1974) suggested instructional strategies for the verbs *have* and *be* from the point of view of contemporary linguistic theory. They identified 31 individual meaningful uses to which the verbs *have* and *be* can be applied. For instance, *have* can be used to indicate an entity to part relationship (*The spider has legs.*), immediate ownership (*I have a pencil.*), temporary possession (*I have Robert's book.*), and remote ownership (*I have some money in the bank.*). Hargis and Lamm contend that the deaf child's confusion of *have* and *be* in sentences such as *John is flu.* or *Jonathan have a boy.* occurs because of the surface structure similarity of such sentences. Both *have* and *be* can appear within the same type of sentence frame, so that the deaf child supposes that the two forms have identical meanings in English. It is suggested that instead of focusing on surface structure patterning, the teacher needs to focus on the variety of meanings that can be encoded by surface structure. This should add immeasurably to the deaf child's mastery of these two forms. One can conclude from the article that the entire range of possible meanings of *have* and *be* should be explored. Deaf children need to learn that the same surface structure can convey varied deep structures.

These two summaries serve to point out the contrast between a surface structure orientation and deep structure approaches. The study of meaning is less well explored because focus on deep structure is an enormous task. Focus on surface structure is easier because forms may be constant from construction to construction, but meaning can shift subtly from sentence to sentence. Without an understanding of deep structure, of course, language forms are essentially meaningless for deaf children—or for any child, for that matter.

Instructional focus in this book with regard to hearing-impaired children is on mastery of standard English forms. Although intervention issues are approached as first language learning tasks, it has been emphasized repeatedly that for children who have been exposed to and are using American Sign Language, school English is probably a second language. American Sign Language is organized along lines that emphasize different semantic deep structures and syntactic ordering than those in many, if not all, spoken languages, especially English (Friedman, 1977). If the deaf child is ASL dominant, then standard English will have to be approached in a second language context insofar as reading and writing are concerned. If manual or total communication instruction is utilized in the school setting, then efforts at creating a system congruent with English forms and function would be necessary.

Although emphasis in this chapter is on educational procedures for hearing-impaired students, considerable information exists in other disciplines such as special education, applied linguistics, communication disorders, and developmental psycholinguistics concerning language development programs. Accordingly, contributions may be drawn from these areas in suggesting instructional strategies for deaf children.

TEACHING PROCEDURES WITH HEARING-IMPAIRED CHILDREN

Over the years many language teaching methods have been suggested for use with hearing-impaired children. The more prominent systems that apparently have some grass-roots support in United States programs for the hearing-impaired are considered in the next sections: the Wing symbols, the Barry Five Slates, the Fitzgerald Key, the Natural Approach, the Patterning Approach, the Programmed Language Instructional Approach, and Behavior Modification and Linguistically Based Approaches.

The Wing Symbols

Developed in 1833 by George Wing (1887), the Wing Symbols system uses letters and numbers to represent the functions of different parts of speech in a sentence. The symbols are placed over a word, phrase, or clause to cue the syntactic form, function, and position of the various parts of the sentence. The symbols are grouped into four basic categories: (1) the essentials such as subject (S), verb (V), or intransitive verb (V_I); (2) modifiers such as noun or pronoun in apposition or possessive; (3) connectives such as coordinating conjunction or subordinate conjunction; and (4) special symbols to include auxiliary verbs and tense.

As soon as the child produced a simple sentence, the symbols were to be used. Within a particular lesson, after a number of sentences had been produced, each aspect of each sentence was coded to teach the child the reference of the symbols. Sentences were treated whenever possible in the context of paragraphs with Wing Symbols used to cue syntactic organization. Unfortunately, as indicated in the introduction to this chapter, the Wing Symbol procedure emphasizes syntactic performance rather than sentence meaning or communicative competence. For instance, the subject symbol was used only to cue the syntactic subject. Linguistic theory provides considerable evidence that there must be a differentiation between the syntactical subject and the actual or logical subject in English (Fillmore, 1968; Katz, 1972). An example can be seen in the sentence *Mary received a ball from John.* In this sentence, *Mary* is the syntactic subject as in the Wing system, while by logic the subject of the sentence is actually *John*, the actor. Another example of difficulty with the Wing Symbol system can be seen with use of symbols for coordinating or subordinating conjunctions. There is no cue within either category to the underlying differences among the conjunctions because there are only two symbols for the whole category. In addition, the position of the subordinate conjunction within the sentence is related to its informational status. If the information contained within a subordinate clause is old information, the clause generally is placed at the beginning of the sentence. If the clause represents new information, it is normally placed at the end of the sentence. Thus, simply identifying the single conjunction does not provide a cue to aspects such as informational coding.

The Barry Five Slates

The Barry Five Slates developed by Katharine Barry (1899) was a method to teach deaf children an understanding of classes of words and their interrelations within sentences. It was contended that the relations of words must be made visible in order to teach language to deaf children. The slates were thought to provide sight rules on which a child could rely in the same way that a hearing child relies on sound rules in language acquisition.

In the Barry system, five large slates were placed on the walls of the schoolroom to provide structure for language explanations. The first slate was for the subject of the sentence, the second for the verb, the third for the direct object, the fourth for the preposition, and the fifth for the object of the preposition. The slates were first used when the children were able to recognize their names and knew how to produce the names of a few objects. Initial emphasis was placed on the development of action-intransitive verb sentences that the teacher associated with a heading from each slate: *who* and *what* for the subject, *what doing* for the verb, *whom* and *what* for the direct object, *where* for the preposition, and *whom* and *what* for the object of the preposition. Once knowledge of the appropriate headings was axiomatic for the child, numbers were substituted for slate writing so that the sentence *John was hitting the ball in the park.* would be analyzed as 1 above *John,* 2 above *was hitting,* 3 above *ball,* 4 above *in,* and 5 above *park.*

McAloney (1931) demonstrated that the Barry system could be used to analyze complex syntactic patterns. For instance, embedded sentences could be seen as a recurrence of a pattern within a pattern. The sentence *Gabrielle kissed Martin while they were in the kitchen.* could be analyzed using the following pattern: 1,2,3,1,2,4,5, with no number placed above the word *while.* Even with this coding of so-called complex sentences, it is obvious that the Barry system was designed for describing syntactic organization rather than providing insight into meaning and pragmatic use of constructions.

The Fitzgerald Key

Edith Fitzgerald (1949) described a sentence pattern guide in her book *Straight Language for the Deaf*. The Fitzgerald Key consists of six columns headed by interrogative words and some symbols indicating parts of speech and sentence functions, similar to Barry's categories. The headings were: (1) subject (who, what), (2) verb and predicate words (=, =, and ⌐ for verb, infinitive, and adjective, respectively), (3) indirect and direct objects (what, whom), (4) phrases and words telling where, (5) other phrases and word modifiers of the main verb (for, from, how, how often, how much, etc.), and (6) words and phrases telling when. The use of connective symbols allowed for compound sentences to be classified. Young deaf children were to begin language learning by classifying words according to the more basic headings, such as subject and verb. The child's first few years in school were to be spent "building the Key." New language patterns and principles were explained in terms of the Key, which served as a reference and self-correction device for language work.

Fitzgerald (1943) herself emphasized two aspects of her system that made it different from systems developed previously. First, she stressed that it was to be used to assist children in visualizing language from a syntactic viewpoint. Second, she stressed that the Key should be used in a language learning atmosphere, allowing for constant exposure to language experiences like those encountered by normally hearing children who were learning language. She urged that language instruction be tied to reality and experience, which would help to establish notions of the underlying relationships within language. It is unfortunate that in practice the deep association with experience that Fitzgerald thought so important has too frequently not occurred. Too often the Key is used as the primary language input system for deaf children, a function for which it was never intended.

Thomas (1958) presented an updated version of the Fitzgerald Key that emphasized phrase understanding. Eight different patterns, considered to be ones that children frequently encounter in reading, were outlined. The patterns included: intransitive verb, transitive verb, predicate adjective, predicate adverbial, transitive verb plus adverbial construction, indirect object, intransitive verb plus adverbial construction, and predicate adjective plus adverbial construction sentences. The eight patterns were introduced first to establish a basic understanding of language. Later, instruction focused on subtle variations and deviations from these basic sentence patterns. These later variations are generally semantically derived, of course, which would not be learned through purely syntactic emphasis.

Walter (1959) presented another variation on the Key that involved a rotating Key chart the students could use at their desks rather than headings from the blackboard. This adaptation demonstrates the range of modifications that have been made to ensure maximum use of the Key in the classroom.

The Natural Approach

In 1958, Mildred Groht wrote of an approach to language instruction that emphasized a more naturalistic view of language development as opposed to simply employing syntactic ordering devices such as the Fitzgerald Key, predetermined word lists such as the Central Institute for the Deaf Language Outline (1950), or workbooks as exemplified by the Croker-Jones-Pratt language drill workbooks (1920, 1922, 1928). The primary tenet of the Natural Approach is that concepts are to be developed through language. Language is seen as a means to an end rather than an end of instruction itself. From this position, Groht evolved certain operating principles: (1) language and vocabulary must be supplied according to the child's needs rather than according to rigid word and language principle lists; (2) natural language is acquired by repetition in meaningful communication settings rather than by drill or textbook exercises apart from meaning; (3) language usage is best taught through conversation and discussion, written compositions of all kinds, and through academic and skill areas of the curriculum; (4) when language principles need to be taught, they should be introduced incidentally in natural language learning situations, then explained by the teacher in real situations, then practiced by the children through the use of games, questions, stories, pictures, and conversations. Upper grade language requires exactness in planning, organization, and self-criticism on the part of the pupils.

Accordingly, the deaf child is seen as having the same need for a naturalistic language learning environment as normally hearing children do. Groht clearly expected teachers to have understanding of the linguistic principles they were striving to have the child learn, rather than presenting language in a haphazard fashion. This latter point is critical, because many proponents of the so-called Natural Method have interpreted the natural part to mean talk, talk, talk, but in an incidental fashion, depending on what comes up. Groht did not intend this to be the case. She stressed that the teacher should be preparing natural experiences for each of the linguistic principles she feels the child should be acquiring in light of his conversational, intellectual, and cognitive status. Thus, unlike other language instruction systems, the emphasis of the Natural Approach is on development of deep structure and communication competence at a rate commensurate with the child's ability to assimilate information. The only weakness of the system was that Groht provided no clearly outlined developmental stages by which to judge children's linguistic and/or cognitive needs, which linguistic principles would best be learned before others. This is a particularly important issue for older deaf children who may lack even the rudiments of English. In addition, Groht makes no provision for developmental responses by children. Children do not begin with mature language productions or even approximations of these productions. Instead, as per Chapter 3, children proceed through stages of learning the adult model before finally achieving mature expression. With guidelines relative to developmental needs of children and indications of child language behavior, the Natural Approach offers a framework for development of linguistic and communication competence rather than strict concern with surface structure patterns.

The Patterning Approach

Sr. Jeanne d'Arc (1958) presented the view that there was instructional need for linguistic patterning to aid many deaf children in learning language. She suggested that systematic exposure to a limited variety of linguistic units in order to facilitate linguistic understanding and usage was a necessary requirement to any language instructional program. The focal point of the procedure is employment of command forms that vary according to the constructions that follow the core command verb. The first pattern to be emphasized is the verb-what relationship, which is followed by verb-where, verb-what-where, verb-adjective, verb-whom, and verb-whom-what. Language exposure is achieved in natural situations that emphasize a conversational format between teacher and the deaf child.

In a subsequent report on patterning, Buckler (1968) indicated that the seven basic sentence patterns outlined by d'Arc should continue to serve as the basis for any further patterning efforts. To increase linguistic sophistication, it was suggested that these seven sentence patterns also be used in conjunction with stems that cued more complex sentences. For instance, it would be possible to cue or pattern with sentence stems such as *I know how to . . .* or *It's fun to . . .* , which would allow use of the seven patterns already developed through command training. Buckler contended that question forms and indirect discourse forms particularly difficult for hearing-impaired children can easily be handled through patterning as well, using stems such as *When will . . .* or *Mary told me to. . . .* This approach draws upon the strength of structured language approaches; it argues for structure in language learning in linguistically sound terms, while encouraging natural experiences by keeping the content of patterns in line with the developmental needs of the child. The problem of an apparent lack of stress on deep structure understanding or overt consideration of communication competence could leave one uncertain as to how to achieve fluent language performance at all levels. It should be noted, however, that the functional realization of a patterning approach has been impressively demonstrated by the students of St. Joseph's School for the Deaf in St. Louis.

The Programmed Language Instructional Approach

In the 1960s, as part of the general trend in education to employ teaching machines and computer technology, programmed language instruction was developed for hearing-impaired children. Falconer (1962), Stuckless and Birch (1962), Fehr (1962), and Rush (1964) developed programs to teach specific linguistic knowledge such as noun vocabulary, articles, or following written directions. Initial results from these approaches seemed to be promising. However, later there were indications that English drill programs such as those developed by Stanford University had not proved to be entirely successful (Fletcher and Suppes, 1973).

In a recent report by Bochner (1976) on a verb drill program designed for deaf young adults, it was concluded that programmed approaches lacked instructional power. An effective drill and practice program should elicit and reinforce acceptable responses from the student on a consistent basis. Bochner's subjects' responses deviated so substantially from expected behavior that the program was unable to shape or reinforce responses. In many instances the responses that the students produced were grammatically appropriate, but the computer program was forced to reject them as unacceptable because they did not conform to the predicted response.

These difficulties are not particularly surprising for many reasons. Children who truly generate language show preference for paraphrasing rather than for direct imitation. It has also been shown that language drills are only meaningful if placed into experiential context which is not possible with most computer-based programs. Studies by Ruder, Hermann, and Schiefelbusch (1977) indicate that drill activities do not result in generative language behavior. Comprehension work coupled with imitative or drill responses was found to produce changes in expressive language, however, strengthening the arguments for experiential learning.

This should not be taken to mean that teaching machines and computerized instruction have no educational role. However, such approaches should not be expected to lead to the establishment of deep structure understanding if they merely provide surface structure monitoring or practice.

Behavior Modification

Learning theory from the psychological point of view has been and continues to be concerned with stimulus-response relationships and operant learning as related to language acquisition. Although external motivation and manipulation are not seen by developmental psycholinguists as primarily responsible for language acquisition in normal children, the application of learning theory to establishing speech and/or language in children who demonstrate severe language disability has been promising. Children who fall under the rubric of severely retarded, autistic-like, or multihandicapped have been the focus of operant conditioning paradigms, and in recent years there have been attempts to apply these principles to the instruction of multihandicapped, hearing-impaired children as well.

The reports on hard-to-teach children generally report results in four areas (Snyder, Lovitt, and Smith, 1975; Yule, Berger, and Howlin, 1975): (1) identification of target behaviors, (2) establishment of baseline behaviors, (3) implementation of therapeutic procedures, and (4) evaluation of the results by comparing the final results with the baseline data.

Identification of target behaviors requires description of how behavior change will be quantified, as well as decisions about what terminal behaviors will be sought. When behavior targets, or reduction in particular behaviors, have been decided on, charting or description of the naturally occurring rate or duration of the desirable, or undesirable, behavior is done. This charting establishes a pre-intervention baseline for evaluating the effects of treatment. Because children's behavior can vary considerably over time even in a structured situation, it is often necessary to continue observations until a representative sample of behavior is thought to have been obtained, which may involve a number of observations in the child's environment.

Having obtained baseline observations of the relationship between target behaviors and the environment, the treatment manipulations are introduced. Most techniques employ some reinforcement procedure, either of a social (secondary) or consumable-token (primary) nature. Modeling, shaping/fading, or other imitative variations are the specific types of procedures employed. Modeling consists of providing the subject with examples of the target behavior with the expectation that the child will approximate through direct imitation the established model. Shaping/fading techniques require differential reinforcement of stimulated productions by the child. Differential reinforcement leads the child to produce behaviors that come closer and closer to a predetermined standard established by the examiner.

Regardless of the choice of procedures to change behavior, the observations started during the baseline periods are continued. This ongoing monitoring of behavior should provide indications of the efficacy of the modification techniques selected. If the strategy is working, there should be a decrease of those behaviors one wishes to eliminate, or an increase in behaviors that are desirable. It is not always possible, of course, to establish this cause and effect relationship, because teaching a preliminary behavior may simply trigger or facilitate expression of the behavior or linguistic principle that is actually already known to the child (Yule, Berger, and Howlin, 1975).

In language acquisition, application of behavior modification has emphasized the establishment of expressive skills by and large, although development of receptive abilities using picture identification techniques has also been reported in the literature. Specific areas of expressive behavior focused on have included establishing noun vocabulary items (Sailor et al., 1973; Salzinger et al., 1965); use of plurality (Baer and Guess, 1973; Garcia, Guess, and Byrnes, 1973; Guess et al., 1968; Sailor, 1971); use of articles and auxiliary verbs (Wheeler and Sulzer, 1970); use of verb inflections (Schumaker and Sherman, 1970); decreasing verbal behaviors (Barton, 1970); use of prepositions (Sailor and Taman, 1972); use of question forms (Twardosz and Baer, 1973); encouraging two-word combination production (Jeffree, Wheldall, and Mittler, 1973); and use of noun and verb phrases (McReynolds and Engmann, 1974; Whitehurst and Novak, 1973). Lawrence (1971) described techniques for establishing prelinguistic behaviors in children such as attending to speech or learning to provide feedback to caregivers. These factors have been identified as crucial to the development of spontaneous language forms (Snyder and McLean, 1976). Fygetakis and Ingram (1973), on the other hand, emphasize the use of reinforcement principles to increase mean length of utterance and syntactic complexity in children.

Although receptive development has been studied, as suggested, the range of behavior explored is more limited. Bricker (1972) and Bricker, Vincent-Smith, and Bricker (1973) have reported on attempts to develop receptive comprehension of a simple noun category in severely retarded older children and in language-delayed toddlers, respectively. Baer and Guess (1971) focused on the development of adjectival inflections and superlative and comparative forms in mentally retarded children. Guess (1969) also investigated the understanding of plurality in retarded children. In a subsequent study, Guess and Baer (1973) attempted to develop plurality both receptively and expressively. They found that it was possible to teach comprehension and production of plurality, but there proved to be little or no generalization from one modality to the other.

Hartung (1972) outlined a tentative series of targets that should be achieved in order to guarantee minimal linguistic functioning in autistic-like children, including: (1) elimination of disruptive behaviors before initiating actual communication/linguistic programming efforts, (2) conditioning attention and eye contact, (3) establishing motor imitative behavior, (4) establishing a transition from motor imitative behavior to verbal imitative behavior, (5) establishing control over predetermined spoken vocabulary usually beginning with nouns, (6) establishing transition from imitation to naming, (7) establishing ability to answer questions, (8) establishing spoken phrases, (9) conditioning functional speech, and (10) generalizing imitative speech appropriately to new situations.

The cornerstones of this approach are the notions that imitation serves as the basis for establishing linguistic behavior; that there is a transition from motor imitative behavior to verbal imitative behavior; that vocal targets should be selected so that they can be easily produced with manipulative help from the teacher, contain sounds visually apparent to the child, and contain sounds already within the production repertoire of the child; and finally, that targets should proceed from single-word responses to phrases to functional sentences such as *open the door* or *get your shoes*.

Employment of similar types of linguistic developmental outlines have been described by Bricker and Bricker (1974), Guess, Sailor, and Baer (1974), Kent et al. (1972), and Risely, Hart, and Doke (1972). All presented programs emphasized the importance of imitation, early motor imitative training, and a progression from single words to complete sentences. If Snyder and McLean's (1976) contention that certain prelinguistic behaviors are important for children to possess before they are able to process linguistic information is correct, it would seem that the goal of eliminating disruptive behaviors and establishing eye contact would be worthwhile. The need to establish appropriate feedback mechanisms in children, such as smiling or selectively attending to speech, should be added. Joint activities are important to the establishment of a common topic of conversation between normally developing child and mother (Bruner, 1977). Establishment of motor imitative behavior also seems reasonable for children who do not spontaneously develop ability to imitate or process the communication of others.

Application of behavior modification procedures to teaching hearing-impaired children has been reported (Bennett and Ling, 1972; Berger,

1972). In Bennett and Ling's study, a 3-year-old hearing-impaired girl who used neither the article *the* nor the auxiliary verb *is* was taught to use these words in describing a picture, initially through imitation and then in response to the command *Tell me about this*. She was also able to use the present progressive form to describe a number of pictures on which she had received no training. To test its generative status, the newly acquired behavior was subsequently extinguished and then reinstated.

The question one might ask about this study is whether the *is—the* knowledge is generalized to situations other than picture description. The semantic role of the auxiliary verb *be* in English is limited, and could be generalized to other present progressive environments without a need for knowledge of its meaning. *The,* on the other hand, serves as an important cue to the listener about information in conversational noun phrases, a form that would not be expected to be learned by imitation alone.

Berger (1972) used a program similar to Hartung's to teach severely retarded deaf children. Manual communication was substituted for vocal behavior. The report lacks specific details about procedures employed and success rate with specific target behaviors.

The role of imitation in language learning has been shown to be a rather specific one, as discussed in Chapter 3. Behavior modification programs depend heavily upon imitation to shape behavior, but that dependence presents a problem when the question of language learning is considered.

Rees (1975), for one, examined the clinical use of imitation in the enhancement of linguistic performance in language-disordered children. She concluded that although imitation may have only a limited role in the development of linguistic competence in the normal child, or in increasing or modifying the language-disordered child's linguistic competence, clinical procedures involving imitation may be important in the development of the communicative process. In the case of nonverbal children, the establishment of a tendency to imitate and an initial vocal or verbal repertoire might be the first step in production of communication, if not symbolic behavior. In fact, the attempt to establish language performance in the child who has no notion of communicative behavior is likely to be unsuccessful. Imitation could be used to establish communication between the language disordered child and his mother, and different techniques could be employed to develop his linguistic competence.

The usefulness of imitation in developing verbal behavior in children with language-learning problems was also discussed by Ruder, Hermann, and Schiefelbusch (1977). Their study was designed to determine whether imitation or comprehension training alone, or some combination of imitation and comprehension training, would facilitate verbal production in children with language disorders. Comprehension training alone resulted in some verbal production, but imitation training alone did not. A marked improvement in verbal production was observed when comprehension training was followed by imitative training. When initial imitative training was followed by comprehension training, verbal production increased, but not to the degree or with the consistency that marked the comprehension-imitation training sequence. Furthermore, children in comprehension training required more trials to reach a similar level of proficiency after imitation than they did when comprehension work preceded imitation. Beginning with imitative training apparently interferes with acquisition of subsequent comprehension and production skills.

Courtright and Courtright (1976) compared the effectiveness of a modeling procedure and direct imitation in teaching certain syntactic patterns. Modeling in this context involved repeating the test sentence several times in the presence of a picture cue. In direct imitation, the subject was required to produce the examiner's sentence immediately and exactly. The results were thought to support the conclusion that modeling was more effective than imitation in teaching a syntactic pattern, initially lacking in the subject. Greater retention of the pattern and a more successful generalization to novel contexts were noted with modeling more than with direct imitation.

These findings are not too startling if Bloom, Hood, and Lightbown's (1975) observation that children imitate only language that they have some knowledge about is accurate. One could argue that comprehension training establishes tentative knowledge about a language form, which would encourage imitation of that form in subsequent instruction.

Another problem with behavior modification has been the criticism that violations of developmental patterns in working with children are made regularly. Teaching targets are established with no regard to the cognitive and/or developmental trends expected in children, even developmentally delayed ones. Lynch and Bricker (1972), to counteract such a charge, suggested that developmental psycholinguistic data could be used as the content for behavior modification programs, while conditioning or operant procedures could become the mechanisms by which these developmental expectations are realized. Stremel (1972), Stark et al. (1973), Jeffree, Wheldall, and Mittler (1973), and Garber and David (1975) have reported on applications of this suggestion. Each has appealed to various aspects of linguistic theorizing and/or language developmental knowledge to establish meaningful language targets in children. Stremel (1972) stressed agent-action-patient (subject-verb-object) relationships; Stark et al. (1973) used Bloom's functional and grammatical categories to teach behavior; Jeffree, Wheldall, and Mittler (1973) studied the pivot-open class relationship; and Garber and David (1975) used the semantic demands of questioning to eliminate echolalia in children. These programs were successful to varying degrees, so the strategies of combining developmental targets with behavior modification techniques shows promise, particularly with children demonstrating difficulties in language learning.

Linguistically Based Approaches

Increased interest in linguistic theory and descriptions of children's language has resulted in efforts to apply such theories to helping communicatively handicapped children acquire language. Programs based primarily on linguistic theory and programs based on developmental findings have become the most popular. Linguistic theory approaches use information gained by appealing to the adult model. Difficulty and complexity of language is defined by what the adult finds difficult and complex. Approaches classified as developmental use information derived from observations of normally speaking children. Difficulty and complexity level are defined from the point of view of the child, not the adult. The former type of program may be referred to as clinician oriented, whereas the latter would be considered child oriented. In either case, as indicated by Leonard (1973), developing rule-governed behavior should be the goal of the therapeutic or educational program, building in the child some sense of the rules governing the understanding and production of English sentences.

Detailed examples of each category of instructional program are considered in the next two sections. The first emphasizes linguistic approaches, and the second emphasizes developmentally based approaches.

Instructional Programs Based on Linguistic Theory   Blackwell and Engen (1976) presented an entire curriculum (Rhode Island School for the Deaf Language Curriculum) geared to the development of linguistic rule knowledge in hearing-impaired children. Although much of the curriculum is geared to syntactic mastery, attention is also paid to semantic development and to consideration of the relation of language and cognitive growth. The basic premises of the curriculum are twofold:

1. Language is not taught to children using vocabulary as its base of operation. Instead, the immediate goal of the educational process

must be the development of underlying linguistic knowledge for sentence generation.

2. Language cannot be taught in isolation. It must be an integral part of the school curriculum, which in turn is geared toward the child's needs and intellectual/emotional interests.

As stated previously, there is intense focus on the syntactic component of language. Initial work begins with what Streng (1972) and others have called the basic sentences of English: the transitive sentence (*John hit the dog.*), the intransitive sentence (*John ran.*), the predicate nominative sentence (*John is his son.*), the predicate adjective sentence (*John is big.*), and the predicate adverbial sentence (*John is in the park.*).

Control of linguistic input is advocated by using events, stories, personal identification, or social relationships that the child has already experienced. These concepts are expressed consistently in the five simple sentence patterns that must be mastered before the introduction of more complex forms. Complex sentences are seen as the interface of two or more simple sentence relationships. Thus, complexity is introduced through consideration of those changes that operate to change the simple sentence pattern, but not its semantic complexity such as negation, question forms, and imperative operations. Later, complex forms that change the semantic organization of the sentence are introduced, such as nominalization, relativization, coordination, and complementation.

The five basic sentence types are described to the children and then contrasted over a period of time by emphasizing the distinction between transitive and intransitive sentences, and the difference between these two types and the remaining three. This description process is unhurried and is applied only to those sentences that have some meaning for the children. The goal is not the memorization of the syntax of simple sentences, but the internalization of simple relationships through which the child will be able to produce and comprehend an infinite number of sentences. Thus, opportunities for spontaneous generation of sentences are emphasized as an integral part of the instructional process from the earliest stages of exposure to the system.

At the point of spontaneous generation of language, Blackwell and his colleagues advocate the initiation of formal analysis techniques, using generative-transformational diagrams. It is argued that such diagramming assists the child in identifying the major sentence components and the major groupings of those components. It is also thought to aid the child in constituent development, a significant aid to reading, in opposition to word-by-word decoding techniques, which are highly damaging to reading comprehension. Diagramming is further defended as a way of helping children to develop a grasp of the underlying relationships that exist for more complex sentence patterns. For instance, by combining visual diagramming skills and intonational practice, it seems possible to prevent the deaf child from assuming that the end of a medially embedded relative clause is the end of the main sentence; thus sentences such as *John who is my friend* are avoided.

Blackwell and his colleagues made a monumental contribution in demonstrating how linguistic theory could be applied to educational instruction with hearing-impaired children. Still, two shortcomings must be pointed out. First, because of their predominant reliance upon adult models from linguistic theory, it is the authors' feeling that some of their decisions are contradictory to the developmental literature. For example, mastery of basic sentences is advocated before consideration of the syntactic forms that change the semantic organization of the sentence, such as coordination and complementation. The child language literature shows that *and* forms and early infinitives appear quite early in children's utterances (Limber, 1973). Therefore, not encouraging their growth would work against the natural developmental processes of children.

Second, the use of diagramming with young children is thought to aid in their conceptualization of language. This technique may be helpful for those children who have substantial language mastery, but the authors have serious reservations concerning its use with children in the initial stages of learning language. Employment of diagrams could encourage children in the early language learning stage to focus on external surface structure manifestations of language rather than encouraging internal semantic manipulation of language. It has been demonstrated repeatedly that the focus of children's earliest attempts to master language are semantically, not syntactically, motivated. It is only after the child has mastered the basic components of the underlying semantic relationships that he pays attention to syntactic matters such as word order and constituent grouping. Consequently, a more natural approach in which basic sentences are controlled semantically, not syntactically, and patterned so that the child has an opportunity to induce the underlying meaning relationships of language is advocated. In this process, children will produce utterances that are developmentally approximations of the adult model. Only when a child has a clear understanding of word order constraints and constituent groupings would introduction of sentence diagramming be reasonable.

In summary, the curriculum outlined by Blackwell and Engen is unique in the effort to develop an entire language program based on contemporary linguistic theory, an effort that must be applauded in its innovation. The design of the curriculum is a dynamic one that is continuing to undergo revision and modification; changes in the Rhode Island curriculum will be awaited with interest. It is hoped that it will steer toward a developmental model rather than being confined to a purely linguistic one.

Another example of a linguistically based program for deaf children was outlined by Peck (1972). The Patterned Language system is organized into three units. Unit 1 is geared toward the development of single-word productions from hearing-impaired children who, regardless of age, have not achieved this stage. The basic premise is that deaf children should start in the stage of production in the normal developmental process that they have not mastered. Success in each stage, even in the single-word stage, should be assured even for older children through the use of socially appropriate but linguistically controlled experience. Items in the one-word stage include introduction of negation, confirmation (yes), names of people and pets, names of objects, *where* concepts, and *time* concepts. Use of these items should be practiced in two sociolinguistic contexts—asking (requesting) and telling. Interestingly, although presented in 1972, Peck's concepts are sound, but they failed to go far enough. Basic semantic categorization such as agent, action, or patient is lacking.

Unit 2 involves productions of word strings from two to five words. It is suggested that expansion techniques be used to help children achieve this level of proficiency. Unfortunately, Peck provides few guidelines concerning the focus of these expansions other than to work on basic sentence patterns or syntax. Unit 3 involves verbal descriptions that utilize a slot organization similar to the Fitzgerald Key. Eight slots are listed, including sentence transforms, subject + modifiers, verb + direct object, object + modifiers, where, when, conjunction, and end of sentence punctuation. Children are provided with these categories in slot form to assist them in generating sentences. This suggestion suffers from the same criticisms leveled against the Key earlier in this chapter.

Muma (1974) outlined 10 instructional procedures derived from linguistic theory that he recommended for use in developing rule understanding in language disordered individuals. He suggested for example that the teacher or clinician point out the child's error to him and then provide the appropriate form. For instance, if the child utters *I is going.*, the teacher can reply, "No, it's not *I is going*; it's *I am going.* Say *I am.* Mellon (1967) and Cazden (1965) indicate, however, that this correction technique is not an efficient way to help children learn basic language rules. The correction technique is not a positive one for language learning and may even be destructive from the standpoint of language usage, particularly when it is used too frequently.

The second, or expansion, technique, as outlined in studies of the parental input to normal children (Brown and Bellugi, 1964), has also been suggested for use with hearing-impaired children (Scroggs, 1975). Linguistic expansion occurs when a child's utterance is expanded into an adult version of the forms he produced. For instance if the child says *me go*, the adult might say *Yes, you are going.* As reported previously, Scroggs (1975) found that teachers' systematic application of expansion techniques increased oral and non-oral communication attempts by hearing-impaired children significantly.

In the third, or simple expatiation, technique, the teacher makes comments about children's utterances. The comments are confined to a single propositional sentence, keeping the syntactic and semantic demands at a low level. For instance, if the child says *Birdie fly.*, the teacher might say *Yes, the birdie is pretty too.* Expansion with simple expatiation might result in a response such as *Yes, the birdie is flying*, with the comment *The birdie is pretty.* Cazden (1965) found this particular technique effective in stimulating language growth in disadvantaged nursery school children because it broadened the communication context for the child, but allowed his utterances to serve as the focus of the communication exchange.

The fourth, or complex expatiation, technique is merely a syntactic variation of simple expatiation. The semantic aspects are featured and extended, but only in more complicated syntactic structures. It was suggested that complex expatiation be reserved for children in more advanced stages of language development, such as children who demonstrate knowledge of various transformational operations but need to learn fluent use of these transformations.

The fifth technique, designated the alternative model, was thought by Blank and Solomon (1968) to be effective for developing abstract thinking. Operationally, a teacher inquires either directly or indirectly about the underlying logic of a particular utterance. Such probes should serve to make the speaker aware of the logical power of language and to consider alternative ways in which a given thought can be expressed. For instance, the child might say *Daddy go.*, to which the teacher replies *Yes, is daddy going? Why is daddy going?* Because the critical characteristic of this technique is the use of a question format, there are additional studies that comment on its effectiveness. Turnure, Buium, and Thurlow (1976) tested educable mentally retarded children to determine whether interrogatives would induce verbal elaboration. The results indicated that children in question conditions elaborated more than children in nonquestion conditions. The question conditions also induced greater semantic analysis by children than the nonquestion conditions, which can be taken as an affirmation of the alternative technique's basic purpose.

The questions of young children themselves in educational settings may be most informative about the child's point of view. Examples of children's questions from Chukovsky (1968) include: *Do chickens go without rubbers?* or *Mothers give birth to boys, too. Then what are fathers for?* Adults could employ these types of child questions in order to assist children to develop understanding of the world through the use of language. Guidelines for the production of child-like questions include pairing unrelated categories, such as *rubbers* and *chicken*; posing incorrect hypotheses, such as *What is a knife, a fork's husband?*; and postulating discrepancies that need to be resolved, such as *Why don't we see two things with two eyes?* Presentation of these types of alternatives is a novel way to assist the child in understanding the underlying cognitive relations between objects and events. Chukovsky points to two important constraints on the use of such questions. First, they should not be used to initiate conversations with children, but should proceed out of prior discussions with the child. A second constraint is the assurance that questions are asked in the presence of relevant materials or in proper context. Unless children are presented with the tools necessary to solve the problems posed by the question, learning will not occur.

Muma's sixth technique is completion, a procedure in which children are encouraged to complete items presented to them. The child may be provided with a word to be used in a new sentence, or the adult may provide the child with a stem for completion. The patterning methods already described (Buckler, 1968; d'Arc, 1958) represent a sort of elaborated completion strategy. If properly used, the completion technique can provide a child with syntactic experience, such as constituent analysis and observation of word order constraints, as well as semantic interaction, such as concept or lexical boundaries and selectional restrictions. It should also be recalled from Chapter 3 that mothers often employ completion strategies to encourage linguistic productions in normally developing children.

Muma's three remaining techniques are applicable only for those children or adolescents who possess linguistic sophistication. In the replacement technique, the teacher presents a sentence and instructs the child to replace one element once, or several times, or to delete an element. A replacement exchange might be:

> Teacher: The chair is big.
> Child: The chair is old.
> Teacher: The chair is rocking.
> Child: The old lady is rocking.

The advantage of the replacement strategy is that each child can be helped to practice on constructions that pose particular problems for him. Replacement encourages syntactic and semantic flexibility, which is of benefit to any child with language performance problems. Replacement is a common strategy of young children who are learning to engage adults in conversations (Bloom, Rocissano, and Hood, 1976). The child under this condition will replace an expanded element or another construction for an aspect of the adult's utterance.

The alternative replacement strategy involves the principle that exemplars of one form class or construction are available for alternative replacement with exemplars from another form class or construction. For instance the teacher could ask for *I, he, we, they read.*, to which the child replies *He reads, I read, we read, they read.* In some instances the exemplars were anachronisms, which will provide the student with an opportunity to decide about the semantic accuracy of syntactic patterns.

The final technique is termed "revision," which consists of presenting sentences that must be combined into new units. For instance the teacher might say *Put these sentences together: I have some oranges., I have some apples., I have some bananas.* The child might respond with *I have some oranges, apples, and bananas.* The reverse of this option would be to ask the child to derive the underlying propositions when given instances of complex sentences.

McCarr (1972) details application of Muma's 10 techniques to the teaching of complex language forms to high school age hearing-impaired students. In teaching relative clauses it was suggested that children be presented with two sentences. The teacher demonstrates how the insert sentence is changed by modifying the concurrent noun phrase with a wh-word and shifting it to the beginning of the clause before inserting it into the main sentence following the noun phrase it modifies. This would be an example of the revision technique. Explanations for teaching hearing-impaired children yes-no questions, do-support, wh-question forms, relative clauses, participle phrases, indirect discourse, and passive are provided. Plainly, the emphasis is on the manipulation of surface structure forms, not semantic or conversational understanding.

The implication of techniques such as those suggested by Muma (1974) is that the primary language of all deaf children is some form of standard English. This assumption has been repeatedly challenged, particularly for children with ASL environments. Goldberg and Bordman (1975) have suggested that English-as-a-second language (ESL) techniques might be used in language improvement programs for manually oriented hearing-impaired children. In regular ESL classrooms students who cannot yet express themselves adequately in English do not attempt to study grammar, learn rules for effective writing, or gain knowledge of subject matter in English. Instead they spend time comprehending and producing language in the context of reliable models provided by the teacher. Adults learning a second language in a total immersion program proceed through many of the same developmental patterns shown by normally hearing children who are acquiring a first language (Larsen-Freeman, 1976). Contextual cuing is a crucial variable in second language learning just as in first language learning. Interference between languages in the syntactic area is known to be less than interference in the semantic/communicative aspects. If this is so, then it would seem reasonable to suspect that the ESL method would be most effective with those hearing-impaired children familiar with standard English forms, a prerequisite not often met with many deaf children enrolled in formal school programs.

Developmentally Based Language Instruction Programs   Programs for children with language development difficulties can also be based on principles derived from descriptions of child language. Leonard (1975a,b,c) exemplifies such an approach. He argues, for example, that if children normally acquire information about semantic aspects of language first, then this must represent some important perception about language that should be considered in planning language remediation programs. These authors would argue that if this is true for normally developing children, it should also be true for hearing-impaired children, whose language learning capacities at preschool ages have been found to be normalized if appropriate educational experiences are provided (Collins-Ahlgren, 1974, 1975; Hess, 1972).

A comprehensive effort to incorporate semantic considerations into language development programming for children with limited linguistic performance was reported by MacDonald and Blott (1974). Their approach, identified as the Environmental Language Intervention Strategy (ELIS), places the semantic findings of Bloom (1970), Schlesinger (1971), and Brown (1973) in a therapeutic framework by selecting as the content for diagnosis and training those eight rules underlying the early semantic functions of two-word utterances. Rule knowledge is evaluated and described in terms of all the linguistic and nonlinguistic cues available as context for children's utterances. The ELIS also samples a child's language abilities in imitation, conversation, and play from the beginning of training experiences to aid in generalization of newly learned language to spontaneous situations.

In subsequent articles, MacDonald and his associates (MacDonald, 1976; MacDonald et al., 1974) presented additional ideas about the role of parents in diagnosing and implementing many of the training procedures with their own children. The home is viewed as providing maximum context for mastery of language, a concept that has found considerable support in education of the hearing-impaired by such educators as Horton (1974), Northcutt (1977), and Simmons-Martin (1976).

Miller and Yoder (1972; 1974) outlined language development programs that emphasize the development of 13 semantic categories at the single-word level. The categories derived from research on normally developing children include: recurrence, non-existence, disappearance, rejection, cessation, existence, comments, greetings, vocatives, agent, object, action, and possession. As can be recalled from Chapter 3, these constitute the relational and substantive functions that have been identified at the single-word stage. With these categories, the child can be aided in developing two-word combinations, primarily; functional relations (existence, recurrence, non-existence, rejection, and denial); and grammatical relations (agent-action, action-object, agent-object, possessive, locative, attributive, experiencer-stative, dative, commitatives, and instrumentals). The three-word combinations and expansions as described by Brown (1973) in Chapter 3 serve as the focus for the next stage of the program.

In use of these categories with severely developmentally disabled children, Miller and Yoder suggest the following principles:

1. Semantic concepts should be ordered for teaching on the basis of frequency of occurrence of those concepts and expression by normal children, and selection of the utterance form for expression should be determined by the sequence of forms acquired by normal children as well.
2. A single frequently occurring experience demonstrating a particular semantic function should be selected and paired with appropriate lexical items. After the child demonstrates mastery of the item one might move to multiple experiences expressing the same function. For instance, one can demonstrate disappearance by removal of objects from a table. Once the child has mastered this concept, other instances of disappearance could be used.
3. Once a child begins to produce single words consistently, these first expressions should be tied to relational functions about which the child has already demonstrated knowledge.

Miller and Yoder stress that this technique should be employed only with low functioning (severely retarded) children. However, it could also be considered for use with multihandicapped hearing-impaired children who are of elementary or junior high school age, but have not been in a formal educational program, or have had limited success in more traditionally oriented programs.

Lee, Koenigsknecht, and Mulhern (1975) presented a technique based on the DSS scoring procedure that they called Interactive Language Development Teaching. This procedure should be used primarily with children having a sufficient amount of language that it could be analyzed using the DSS procedure, such as those hearing-impaired children being considered for mainstreaming. The system involves writing stories that contain a target language principle. Each story concludes with a probe to initiate appropriate responses from each child. The techniques that can be used as probes are completion, reduction, expansion, repetition, repetition of error, self-correction, or rephrased questions.

Each of the programs outlined above are developmentally based, but have only been employed with normally hearing children. Most seem to hold some promise for use with some hearing-impaired children, but further research as to their range of usefulness is required.

Alternative Expression Systems

The discussion to this point has assumed employment of traditional communication modes with normally hearing or hearing-impaired children: spoken language and manual communication. For some hearing-impaired children even these traditional systems for expression are unrealistic, as for example children who lack all but minimum motor control.

Vicker (1974) suggested communication board formats that could be used effectively with developmental psycholinguistic information as the basis for organization. Such a communication mode coupled with appropriate suggestions on communication/language development might be beneficial for hearing- and motorically-impaired children.

Vanderheiden et al. (1975) suggested that even written symbols may be inappropriate with communication boards. They outlined the use of another symbolic system less dependent upon phonemic constraints—the Bliss symbol system. The Bliss symbols represent basic vocabulary, with sentences constructed by arranging these symbols appropriately.

Premack and Premack (1974) suggested that instead of conventional symbol personal communication systems, other nonverbal symbols could be used to convey the basic operations underlying language use. Use of such symbols have been reported by Carrier (1976), Hughes (1974), and McLean and McLean (1974) with reasonable success for nonverbal, autistic, and severely retarded children. Application of these procedures with hearing-impaired, severely behaviorally disturbed children might also be considered. Such procedures do not lend themselves to presentation from a developmental or sociolinguistic point of view, but given the lack of communication abilities of most of the children with whom these systems are used, such a violation of instructional principles is clearly permissible.

It is important not to think exclusively in terms of conventional communication systems when working with severely multihandicapped hearing-impaired children. Teachers should be flexible in their consideration of modes for performance in order to establish communication with every hearing-impaired child who is capable of meaningful interaction.

The final sections of this chapter are devoted to a discussion of a developmentally oriented language intervention program that could be implemented with hearing-impaired children and youth.

GUIDELINES FOR DEVELOPING
LANGUAGE LEARNING PROGRAMS

The final section of this chapter summarizes the authors' contentions about developmental language learning programs for hearing-impaired children, including an outline of possible instructional emphasis for some language forms.

Before proceeding, a few remarks about instructional modalities are offered. Without question, the preferred modality for language learning is the auditory one, and insofar as possible, this should be considered the goal for any child with hearing impairment. The content of auditory training programs for young hearing-impaired children should be predominately linguistic in character to assure that the acquisition of spoken language is achieved through the sense best designed for this mastery. A detailed argument for the role of audition can be found in R. R. Kretschmer (1974).

It would be a mistake for the reader to conclude that this strategy is reasonable or possible for every child with significant hearing loss. On the other hand, however, it may be an alternative for many more children than in previous years because of improvements in early identification procedures, infant management programs, and the consistent application of personal amplification. Such advances should ensure that English is mastered by every child who is capable of learning language. Unfortunately, the milennium has not been realized; despite the evidence that children with hearing loss can be fluent language users, too many continue to be described as having language learning disorders. Impoverished experience and lack of attention to developmentally oriented intervention strategies account for the majority of performance problems with English forms and functions exhibited by deaf children.

The suggestions that follow are offered as one approach to utilizing results of language assessment techniques to encourage language learning.

Through analysis of language performance as outlined in Chapter 5, several levels of information about a child's linguistic knowledge should be derived. First, as detailed a description as possible of current performance capabilities should be gathered. Second, any differences or deviations from standard English usage should be identified. Third, these apparent differences should be classified as probably developmentally based or deviant in nature.

Once these determinations have been achieved, decisions on the order that language performance aspects are to be emphasized should be based on the following considerations:

1. Forms that deviate from English usage should take precedence over developmentally restricted forms because unmodified deviant forms will probably lead to greater deviation from normal communication if left unchecked.

2. Experience with or instruction about semantically powerful language forms should take precedence over less powerful forms, or those that are more restricted in meaning. When given two forms that are needed by the child, instructional preference should be given to the form that carries the most meaning and will facilitate acquisition of other aspects of meaning. If the child happens to be in the modulation stage and lacks mature use of determiners and of the copula *be,* emphasis should probably be given to the determiner system rather than the copula system. As indicated by Brown (1973), articles potentially carry meanings such as number and given/new information distinction; surface structure absence of the copula does not seriously interfere with meaning. The only purpose of the copula *be* in English is to mark tense, which can be easily shown through the addition of an appropriate time adverbial. When deciding whether to work on an early occurring form that carries little meaning or on a more complicated form that has considerable communication importance, the choice should always be in favor of the more difficult but more meaningful unit. For instance, if the child has equivalent difficulty with the copula sentence frame and with infinitive forms, it is more reasonable to work on the latter construction because its mastery facilitates communication by allowing the child to embed one proposition in another.

3. Problems of a developmental nature should not take preference over the development of semantic flexibility. An older child who has some

developmental delays, such as absence of a variety of modulations, but simultaneously shows a lack of flexibility in his use of transitive sentence frames, such as exclusive use of agent, action-causative, patient relationships, should have stress on the latter problem.

4.   When confronted with two possible teaching targets of equal communication and semantic value, the less complex form should take precedence. For instance if a child lacks complementation, infinitives should be practiced as the first complement, because it would be relatively easy to incorporate infinitives into existing sentence frames. Infinitives tend to be among the earliest forms of complementation to emerge in normal children's language (Limber, 1973).

Table 10 is a developmental outline of English structures to guide teachers or clinicians in planning for language experiences to be emphasized with children who are not fluent linguistically. The chart is organized so that the columns represent general syntactic categories specified important in linguistics, and the rows represent the six stages into which the developmental data for each syntactic category have been grouped. Whenever necessary, examples either adult-like or child-like are included.

The data have been derived from a variety of contemporary research reports on children's language performance. It was felt that because this information exists in so many different sources, it would be useful to compile it into a single chart. To avoid further bulk in the narrative, the specific sources, most of which are referenced elsewhere in this book, are not listed separately.

It is important that the teacher or clinician locate the child on the chart for each type of linguistic rule, which will vary considerably over the six stages for a particular child. It must also be remembered that this guide is merely that—a guide to the teacher or clinician in organizing his teaching efforts. If a particular child evidences linguistic sophistication beyond the entries for the next stage, it is hoped that the teacher or clinician will go with the child, not with the guide, in formulating language experiences. Taken as a whole, Table 10 represents the forms and functions considered most important for a basic language program.

Communication categories per se are not included, although it must be understood that communication constitutes the framework into which semantic/syntactic development has to be placed. When considering the experiences necessary to illustrate any category from Table 10, the teacher or clinician must also consider the pragmatic and communicative purposes of each principle and the conversational contexts in which each should be presented. Emphasis must also be placed on helping the child learn how to initiate, maintain, and conclude conversations with others, areas not covered within Table 10.

The issue of how a child's expressive use of a particular structure develops is important. Complete mastery of surface structure expression of any principle is not likely to occur at first in normal language development, nor should such mature performance be expected from deaf children, even older students who come to the language learning experience late. Examination of contemporary literature on the development of a particular linguistic principle is useful in understanding both the teaching and the learning process. For instance, with infinitive constructions, Limber (1973) suggests a possible developmental sequence. The child will probably be observed to use the construction initially with a limited set of verbs such as *like, want,* or other primitive process-causative verbs, resulting in sentences such as *I want go home.,* in which the two subject nodes are the same, and *I want he go home.,* in which the two subject nodes are different. From this effort, the child expands his use of infinitives to other verbs while maintaining the surface structure already suggested. After this extension the child generally begins to refine his constructions by inserting the local transformation (to) in front of the embedded verb, and adjusting the second subject node pronominalizations so that they are consistently in the objective case.

Without consideration of developmental data, a teacher or clinician might expect perfect infinitive performance from the beginning, which would work against the natural processes that the child might generate if given an opportunity to deduce the rules. By knowing the possible developmental sequence, the teacher can also be alert to deviations that might emerge, as with utterances such as *I want to home.* when *I want go home.* is meant. If deviations are noted, the teacher must plan special lessons to prevent the restricted pattern from emerging further while helping the child to produce developmentally congruent utterances.

Lesson planning for targets derived in the foregoing manner requires some consideration of the factors associated with remediational/developmental lessons for practice of specific linguistic principles. Libergott and Swope (1976) suggest five important principles to consider when planning language learning experiences.

First, cognitive development is felt to structure language learning, so it could be said that children profit most from new information when they are ready to assimilate the information. This means that children begin to acquire linguistic principles only when they are ready to deal with the underlying semantic representations. Thus, before deciding whether to work on a particular linguistic structure or principle, it is important to try to determine whether a child has the necessary cognitive

Table 10. Outline of developmental language teaching sequences

	Stage I	Stage II
Basic sentence frames		
Transitive verb frames	Agent, action-causative, patient (irreversible relationship): *The boy ate the cake.* Agent, action-causative, patient (reversible relationship): *Mary hit Carolyn.* Recipient, action-causative, patient: *Connie got a present.* Experiencer, process-causative, patient/phenomenon (using no-verbs like *hear, look at,* and *see*): *I saw a ball. Ken heard the bell.*	Agent, action-causative, complement: *The boy painted a picture.* Experiencer, process-causative, patient: *John thought about Mary.* Possessor, Process, Patient *Diana has a hat.*
Intransitive verb frame	Mover, action-affective: *Dominic ran.* Patient, action-affective: *The glass broke.* Experiencer, process-affective: *Jerry slept.*	Mover, action-affective, locative-source: *Peter came from school.* Mover, action-affective, locative-goal: *Peter went to school.*
Copula verb frame	Entity, stative-static, locative-stative: *The ball is on the table.* Entity, stative-static, entity-equivalent: *John is a boy.*	Entity, stative-static, attribute (adjective): *The apple is red.* Entity, stative-dynamic, attribute (adjective): *The fire is hot. The boy became sick.*
Indirect object frame		Agent, action-causative, patient, to + recipient: *Milt gave a present to Betty.*
Passive frame		
Optional adverb nodes	Locative-action: *The boy put the cake in the box.*	Instrument: *John cut the tree with an axe.* Manner: *John ran rapidly.*

	Time-action (present): *The boy is eating the cake now.*	
	Time-action (immediate past): *I ran already.*	
Modulations		
Prepositions	In, on	At, from, into, onto, to, up, with
Plurality		Regular plurality: *Two boys.* Irregular plurality: *Two children.*
Tense/Auxiliary	Present progressive: *I going.* Regular past (immediate past): *I painted a picture* (just now). Irregular past (immediate past): *I ran* (just now).	Uncontractible copula: *This is a ball.* Regular past (remote past): *I painted a picture* (yesterday). Irregular past (remote past): *I ran* (yesterday). Future (immediate future): *I have to go* (in a few minutes). *I will go* (in a few minutes), *I am going* (in a few minutes).
Modals		Modals indicating wish or intention: gonna, hafta (have to), lemme (let me), wanna
Determiners	Uh, (a): *See uh ball.* That (indicating nomination): *Want that ball.* This (indicating nomination): *Want this ball.* Ordinal numbers: *Want two ball.* More (indicating recurrence or addition to a set): *More swing. More apples.*	These (indicating nomination): *See these balls.* Those (indicating nomination): *See those balls.* Some, another, other (indicating the same kind of object) Lots (indicating more than one or an unspecified quantity): *Lots of apples. Lots of fun.*

continued

Table 10—*continued*

Modalities	Stage I	Stage II
Negation	Use of negation as an affirmation of following sentence: *No, Mary fix it* (meaning Mary can fix it, not someone else). Early usage of the semantic notions of non-existence, disappearance, non-occurrence, rejection, prohibition, and denial: *No bananas* (There are no bananas in the bowl.) *No girl* (The girl is gone.) *No swing* (He is not swinging.) *No play* (I don't want to play.) *No play* (You can't play.) *No truck* (That's not a car.)	Not, don't, can't (indicating non-existence, disappearance, nonoccurrence) Negative determiner, no (indicating non-existence or disappearance)
Imperative (request or directive)	Vocative requests: *Mommy!* Desire statement requests: *Sally want dolly.* Goal object or location requests: *Up.* Requests indicating possession: *That mine* (give it to me). Direct imperatives: *Read the book.*	Interrogative requests: *Open it?* Problem statement requests: *Mimi hungry.* Use of "please" with requests and directives.
Question forms	Yes-no question with copula. Verb frame sentence and sentence with auxiliary, cued intonationally: *That a boy? Jimmy running?* *What is* question: *What dat?*	*Who is* question: *Who is dat?* *What* as a subject question: *What is jumping?* Yes-no question with copula preposing in copula verb frame sentence: *Is this a ball?*

Coordinating conjunction

What as an object question: *What is the boy riding?*

What do question: *What is Mary doing?*

Where question: *Where is Tad going?*

And (indication enumeration or addition): *Gene eat apple and pear.*

Forward and backward verb + object sentential conjoining: *Drink water and drink orange juice. Fold paper and cut paper.*

Backward subject + verb sentential conjoining: *Doggy jump and kitty-cat jump.*

Forward verb + object conjunction reduction: *Drink water and orange juice.*

And (indicating temporal sequence): *Me go town and then eat.*

And, but (indicating opposition): *This truck go and this truck no go. This girl big but this girl not big.*

Forward subject + verb sentential conjoining: *Mommy clean and Mommy cook.*

Backward verb + object conjunction reduction: *Feed and kiss the dolly.*

Forward and backward subject + verb conjunction reduction: *The dolly talk and sing. The girl and the boy cry.*

Forward and backward subject + verb + object sentential conjoining: *Mommy cook dinner and Mommy set the table. Baby want bottle and baby want toys. Mommy gave toys and baby play toys. The cow jump fence and the dog jump fence.*

Forward and backward subject + verb + object conjunction reduction (deletion of two nodes): *Harry ate the apples and the pie. Mommy and the baby played a game.*

Subordinate conjunctions

continued

Table 10—continued

	Stage I	Stage II
Elaborated Nodes		
Possession	Use of the semantic notion of possessor, object of possession: *Mary('s) dress*	Possessive markers /'s/ and of + N: *Mary's dress. Window of the house*
Embedded adjective		Expanded noun phrases to include size, color, condition, material, or quantity modifiers (they are used to identify a specific item, not to distinguish it from other similar items). *Big, little* (indicating amount): *Diana has the big bag of candy.*
Relative clause		Attaching basic sentence frame onto an indefinite form such as thing, one, or kind: *Thing I got. One Mother made. Kind I need.*
Nominalization: infinitive		Using early forms such as *wanna, gonna,* and *hafta.*
Nominalizations: Participle		
Embedded questions		Attaching early wh-question forms onto an indefinite form, such as place, way, thing, one, or kind: *Nancy want the thing what is eating.*
Direct/Indirect discourse		
Factive clause		

Transformations

	Stage III	Stage IV
Pronominalization	Personal pronouns: *I*, *it* as object, *it* as subject, *them*, *my*, and *your*	Personal pronouns: *you* as subject, she, we, they, mine, me, and *you* an object Indefinite pronouns: there, here
Do-support		
Transitive verb frame		Experiencer, process-causative, complement: *Barry thought up the idea. Lesli had a dream.*
Intransitive verb frame	Ambient-action: *It is raining.*	
Copula verb frame	Entity, stative-static, time-static: *The party is on Tuesday. The race was yesterday.* Entity, stative-static, reason: *The cupcakes were for the party.* Entity, stative-static, recipient: *The dress is for Barbara.* Ambient-static: *It was fun.*	
Indirect object frame		Agent, action-causative, recipient, patient (the patient consists of D + N): *Marty gave the girl some dolls.*
Passive frame		
Optional adverb nodes	Time-action (remote past): *I ran yesterday.* Time-action (future): *I am running tomorrow.*	Time-duration: *I cried all week.* Inclusion: *I am going too.*

continued

Table 10—continued

	Stage III	Stage IV
	Reason: *Andy made the cupcakes* for the party.	
	Comparison: *He ran like a rabbit*.	
Prepositions	Above, across, at (time)[a], away from, below, by, down, in (time), like, near, of, off, off of, on (time), out, over, over to, through, under, for	During, within, without
Plurality		
Tense/Auxiliary	Future (remote future): *I will run* (tomorrow). *I have to run* (tomorrow). *I am running* (tomorrow).	First person singular copula: *I am happy*.
	Contractible copula: *He's nice*.	
	Second and third person plural and singular copulas: *You are, he is, she is, it is, they are*.	
	First person plural copula: *We are*.	
	Uncontractible auxiliary: *The children are running*.	
	Contractible auxiliary: *They're running*.	
	Regular third person singular: *He runs all the time*.	
	Irregular third person singular: *He has no money. He does nothing*.	

Modals	Modals indicating certainty and possibility: can, will, could, shall, lets	Modals indicating necessity and obligation: gotta (got to), would, might, should, better, ought to
Determiners	A and the (indicating a member of a class of objects)	A and the (indicating the difference between specific and non-specific objects)
	Pronominals: somebody, something	Any, both, each, every, few, last, many, most, much, next, several, cardinal numbers: *I saw the first one.*
		That/those (indicating position with the child as the reference point)
		This/these (indicating position with the child as the reference point)
Negation	Can't, don't, won't, not gonna to (indicating rejection and prohibition)	Couldn't, wouldn't
	That's not (indicating denial)	Never
	Why not question	
Imperative (request or directive)	Yes-no questions as request forms, usually to indicate permission to perform a task: *Can I go to the movie?*	Declarative sentence frames containing modals as request forms: *You could give . . . You can give . . . .*
		Questions used as a request for clarification of previous statements or questions: Mother says: Did you go to the store? Child says: *What?*
Question forms	Yes-no question with auxiliary or modal preposing in transitive or intransitive Sentence frames: *Are the children running? Will Don run?*	Who as an object question: *Who is Mary hitting?*
		When question.

continued

Table 10—*continued*

	Stage III	Stage IV
	Yes-no question with do-support preposing: *Do girls sleep?* *Who* as a subject question: *Who is running?* Why question: *Why he sick?* How come question: *How come he sick?* What for question: *What for he sick?* How question: *How he go?* How about question: *How about me going?*	Backward adjective + subject + verb sentential conjoining: *The happy boys danced and the brown bears danced.* Forward adjective + subject + verb conjunction reduction: *The big boy jumped and ran.* There transformation sentential conjoining and conjunction reduction using verb + subject sentences: *There is a ball and there is a bat. There is a ball and a bat.*
Coordinating conjunction	And (indicating causality): *I stay at home and I sick.* But (indicating exception): *I put it in box, but it don't go there.* Or (indicating choice): *I want an apple or a peach.* Forward and backward subject + verb + object conjunction reduction (deletion of one node): *Jane made the cookies and cooked some water. Mom petted and Daddy feed the Kitty-cat.* Forward adjective + subject + verb sentential conjoining: *Big boys jump and big boys run.*	
Subordinate conjunctions	Because, so (indicating causality)	

Possession		
Embedded adjective	Expanded noun phrases to include size, color, condition, material, or quantity modifiers (they are used to contrast one item from other possible items that it could be confused with). **Big, little** (indicating size): *I have a big house.* Expanded noun phrases that contain more than one modifier	**Big, little** (indicating tallness): *The big man is a giant.* The following unmarked-marked pairs: tall-short, long-short, high-low: *The marked form different.*
Relative clause	Attaching a relative clause to the end of a sentence, where both the wh-word and the definite for it modifies are objects in their respective propositions: *I like the ball that I got.*	Inserting a relative clause medially into a sentence where both the wh-word and the definite form it modifies are subjects in their respective propositions: *The boy who is running helped me.*
Nominalization: infinitive	Using infinitive forms where the subject is the same for the two propositions: *I want to go. I need to pee-pee.*	Using infinitive forms where the subject is different for the two propositions: *I want Bill to go. I watch Bill run.*
Nominalization: participle		Use of periphrastic causative verb relationships: *I dyed the egg red.* Use of simple causative verb relationships: *I made the door open.* Participle forms as part of expanded noun phrases: *Washing machine. Fighting men.*
Embedded questions	Attaching wh-question forms onto definite forms (indicating certainty or uncertainty about a particular state of affairs, object specification, and	

continued

Table 10—*continued*

	Stage III	Stage IV
	notice): *I know how to cook dinner now. I see the room where Norman sleep. See what I'm doing.*	
Direct/Indirect discourse		
Factive clause		
Pronominalization	Personal pronouns: *its, her, he, his, him, us, our, their* Anaphoric *it*: *There is a box with six balls. Give it to me.*	Indefinite pronouns: *everything, everyone, everybody, anything, anyone, anybody*
	Indefinite pronouns: *something, someone, somebody*	Reflexive pronoun
		Use of intrasentential pronominalization (indicating old information): *Tom slapped Sarah and she cried.*
		Use of pronominal co-reference in sentence when the pronoun refers to the object of the first proposition: *Marvin kicked Max, and Louise slapped him* (Max).
		Use of pronominalization in contingent pairs to signal old information: Mother: *What did Jane do?* Child: *She went home.*
Do-support	Emphatic *do*: *He does work.*	Support *do*: *He didn't go.*

	Stage V	Stage VI
Transitive verb frame		
Intransitive verb frame		
Copula verb frame	Entity, stative-dynamic, entity-equivalent: *The boy became a man.*	Entity, stative-static, content: *The story is about Bambi.*
Indirect object frame	Agent, action-causative, recipient, patient (the patient consists of ∅ + NP): *Marty gave the girl dolls.*	
Passive frame	Truncated passive (irreversible relationship): *The cake was eaten.* Truncated passive (reversible relationship): *Mary was hit. Mary got hit.* Full passive (irreversible relationship): *The cake was eaten by the dog.*	Full passive (reversible relationship): *Mary was hit by Jane. Mary got hit by Jane.*
Optional adverb nodes	Time-frequency: *Larry goes home every Friday.*	Time-beginning: *Al began the game at one o'clock.* Time-end: *They boy stopped at two o'clock.* Time-beginning, end: *John worked from one o'clock to two o'clock.* Intensifier: *Laura was very good.*
Prepositions	After, around, back of, before, behind, beside, between, beyond, except, except for, from (time), front of, to (time)	About, after (time), along, among, before (time), over (time), until
Plurality		

continued

Table 10—*continued*

	Stage V	Stage VI
Tense/Auxiliary	First, second, and third person singular and plural auxiliary forms	Perfect tense: *I have eaten my breakfast.* Attracted tense in multipropositional sentences
Modals	Must (indicating obligation)	
Determiners	Some, another, other (indicating the same object)	*A* and *the* (indicating new and old information) That/those (indicating position with others as the reference point) This/these (indicating position with others as the reference point)
Negation		Negative passive Negative tag questions: *We went to the movie, didn't we?*
Imperative (request or directive)	Hints without explicit imperatives: *That's where the dolly goes. Put it over there.* Pretend directives: *Pretend that is my doll.* Obligation (has to) directives: *You have to go.* Conditional directives: *If we are good, we will go outside.*	Directives indicating ability to perform task: *Johnny, can you hold the money?* Directives indicating willingness to perform: *Do you wanna sit here?* Directives indicating need to adjust performance: *Will you move over, please?* Directives indicating reason for performance: *Why don't you eat supper?* Directives indicating don't forget something: *Don't forget to pick up the books.*

Question forms	Which question: *Which cow is eating?*	*What did* (subject) (verb) question: *What did the girl hit?*
	Auxiliary preposing in all non-subject wh-questions: *What is Penny hitting?*	*Who did* (subject) (verb) question: *Who did the boy hit?*
		Which (object) *did* (subject) (verb) question: *Which boy did the girl hit?*
		Where did (subject) (verb) (object) question: *Where did the girl hit the boy?*
		What if question: *What if we go home?*
		Tag questions: *We didn't go to the movie, did we?*
Coordinating conjunction	Or (indicating inclusion): *You can take one or all of them.*	But first (indicating condition): *You can go, but first tie your shoe.*
	Backward adjective + subject + verb conjunction reduction: *The big boys and the little girls are playing.*	Either-or, neither, nor
	There Transformation sentential conjoining and conjunction reduction using verb + adjective + subject sentences: *There are little dishes and pretty napkins. There is chocolate cake and cold pop.*	
Subordinate conjunction	Before, after (indicating a logical relationship): *Mary fills the bottle before she feeds the baby. Before Mary cried, she peeled the onions.*	Before, after (indicating an arbitrary relationship): *Mary fills the bottle before she washes her face. Before Mary cried, she went outside.*
		As, as long as, as soon as, although, even though, however, if, if not, if only then, since, therefore, though, unless, unless not, when, while

continued

	Stage V	Stage VI
Possession		With: *The man with the hat is nice.*
Embedded adjective	The following unmarked-marked pairs: thick-thin, deep-shallow, wide-narrow.	The following unmarked-marked pair: old-young.
	Comparative and superlative forms with absolute adjectives: *This apple is redder than that apple. This apple is the reddest.*	Adult adjective ordering rules in expanded noun phrases *more than, less than* with discrete and mass substances: *He has more apples than John. He has more water than John.*
		More, less in question forms (indicating amount): *Which box has more?*
		Most in question forms (indicating amount): *Which boy has the most?*
		Double comparative forms: *Which box is wider than it is deep?*
		Comparative and superlative forms with relative adjectives: *John is bigger than Tom. Benjamin is the biggest.*
		Comparative and superlative forms with contrastive adjectives: *Joan is sadder than Norma. Marion is the saddest.*
Relative clause	Attaching a relative clause to the end of a sentence, where the wh-word is the object of its proposition and the definite form it modifies is the subject of its proposition: *I like the cow that is eating.*	Inserting a relative clause medially into a sentence, where the wh-word is the object of its proposition and the definite form it modifies is the subject of its proposition: *The horse that the boy is riding is a mustang.*

	Double embedded relative clauses: *The boy that kissed the girl that petted the dog is my brother.*
	Relative clause with deletion: *The boy playing in the park hit Joe. The boy behind the door is a scaredy-cat.*
	Apposition: *Mr. Barker, my teacher, gave me a present.*
Nominalization: infinitive	Use of event-causing causative verb relationships: *She tied the ribbon on Barbie's pigtail.*
	Use of infinitive of purpose: *We went in order to get some apples. We went to get some apples.*
	Use of infinitive with adjective: *He was clever to go.*
	Use of minimal distance principle with respect to infinitive with adjective constructions: *John is easy to see. John is eager to see.*
	Iteration: *I asked him to go to get some apples. I asked him to go and get some apples.*
	Infinitive as a subject in a proposition: *To be a good boy is hard.*
Nominalization: participle	Use of negative causative verb relationships: *John kept him from falling off the ledge.*
	Participle forms as objects in propositions: *He likes playing with toys.*
	Participle forms as subjects in propositions: *Playing with toys is not fun.*

continued

	Stage V	Stage VI
		Participle froms embedding transitive and intransitive sentence frames into other propositions: *John's destruction of the painting was very sad. Mark's running in the race upset his mother.*
Embedded questions		
Direct/Indirect discourse	Use of factive verbs to encode imperative messages: *He told him to go.*	Use of factive verbs and negation to encode imperative messages: *He didn't tell him to go.*
	Use of factive verbs to encode declarative messages: *I know that he will go.*	Use of factive verbs and negation to encode declarative messages: *I didn't know that he would go.*
		Use of non-factive verbs to encode declarative message: *He said that Bill was sick.*
		Use of non-factive verbs and negation to encode declarative messages: *He didn't say that Bill was sick.*
		Use of counter-factive verbs to encode declarative messages: *He pretended that it was hard.*
		Use of counter-factive verbs and negation to encode declarative messages: *He didn't pretend that it was hard.*
		Use of *ask* plus infinitive to encode yes-no question messages: *He asked to go.*

		Use of *ask* plus *if* subordinate clauses to encode yes-no question messages: *He asked if he could go.*
		Use of *ask* plus embedded questions to encode wh-question messages: *He asked who could go.*
		Use of minimal distance principle with respect to *ask* and *tell: Ask Bill about the story. Tell Bill about the story.*
		Direct quotes
Factive clause		Factive clause: *The fact that he is sick didn't stop him. That he was sick didn't stop him.*
Pronominalization	Use of pronominal co-reference in sentences when the pronoun refers to the subject of the first proposition: *Marvin kicked Max, and Sarah slapped him* (Marvin).	Appropriate use of number and case features with personal pronouns
		Use of intersentential pronominalization (indicating old information): *Jason went to the store. He liked going very much.*
		Conjoining of nominal personal pronouns: *He and I wanted to go.*
Do-support		

---

[a] Some prepositions can be used as locative or temporal indicators.

underpinnings to profit from exposure to that particular structure or principle. When watching a child play, for instance, it might be appropriate to introduce infinitive constructions if he shows notions about emotions and about social interaction. Infinitive constructions usually occur in connection with process-causative verbs, verbs that express a feeling, with the infinitive being the reason for the occurrence of the process-causative verb. Communicatively the child tends to use the infinitive form to prompt the caregiver to allow him to perform some action. For example in the sentence *I want go.*, the internal emotion is *wanting* and the social interaction desired is *going.* The child who indicates to his teddy bear to take a drink and then makes teddy bear drink is nonverbally encoding the notions of emotional desire for a social interaction and fulfillment of that desire by completion of the action, thus demonstrating the prerequisite cognitive abilities for performance of the infinitive construction.

Second, the development of representation occurs as a result of the differentiation of meaning from symbol and symbol from content. The child must evidence distancing behavior, ability to separate objects from speakers and listeners and meaning from context. As indicated by Bates (1976b), distancing knowledge usually develops when the child enters Piaget's sensorimotor Sub-stage 5. The child begins to learn how different means can be used to achieve the same end. According to Bates, children who pass through this stage begin to use language representationally and also begin to demonstrate symbolic play. One way of determining whether the hearing-impaired child is ready for language work may be to examine his play behavior. If he does not show a capacity to play symbolically, then play experience might be a reasonable preparation for development of linguistic principles. Libergott and Swope have suggested that instruction in play might be highly useful in developing the notion of representation. In some instances, however, lack of play behavior may be caused by more pervasive learning problems such as a lack of interest in social interaction, a lack of attention, or a lack of adequate feedback systems. Following the lead of Synder and McLean (1976), Miller and Yoder (1972, 1974), and Bricker and Bricker (1974), establishment of the above behaviors must occur before language teaching is attempted.

Third, an important foundation for language is symbolizing through the use of actions, which suggests that action should serve as the basis for language instruction. The environment for language teaching or instruction must be a natural one. Children need to be taught how to interact with objects and people that are being talked about. Language, to be meaningful, also needs to be dealt with in a form that the child can comprehend. Sedentary activities or activities that involve static materials such as pictures or drawings may not be sufficient in the beginning stages to illustrate the dynamic aspects of language learning to deaf children, particularly those with an impoverished symbolist experience or intellectual limitations. Once the child is generating enough language to be able to talk about language, use of static forms such as pictures and other visual representations can be employed when appropriate. Nonlinguistic cues and activities are clearly as vital to the acquisition of language forms as many kinds of linguistic/communicative cues. Language learning apart from language context, whether sandbox, bathroom, breakfast table, or family gathering may yield some surface structure performance in children, but its usefulness may carry no farther than the classroom door.

Fourth, new content should first be expressed through old forms, and new forms should first encode old content. When working with hearing-impaired children, one should not confuse issues by trying to convey the frame of new linguistic forms with new content. The definition of content is important; it is meant to refer to the specific vocabulary employed in a sentence, the underlying semantic relationships implied by the linguistic forms, and the information to be conveyed. When considering how to practice forms such as infinitives, one should make sure that the child already knows the vocabulary items to be used, as well as something about the semantic relationships contained within the sentence propositions. In the sentence *John wanted to go.*, the child must know who *John* is and the meaning of *want* and *go*, but he must also know about *process* verbs, and action-affective verbs that take mover nouns. This does not mean that the child must be able to define process verbs or write definitions for *want* and *go*, but he should have had previous experience with the underlying propositions, and he should have had opportunity to generate such notions himself. Experience in this context does not mean sitting passively while certain language principles are read, spoken, or signed to him. It does not mean filling in blanks on a comprehension test for that language principle. It *does* mean that the child has had an opportunity to deal cognitively, perceptually, and linguistically with mover nouns and action-affective verbs, that he has been encouraged to generate such expression himself, and that he has observed some positive consequences of his communicative efforts. Without these experiences, mastery of English infinitive forms may be quite difficult. Information that is new must also be articulated in some fashion with old or known information. For the child with no verbal language, old information may be the context. If the child has played at rolling balls before, then when the mother says or signs *The ball is rolling.* as it rolls across the floor, the sight of the moving ball is old information and the sentence *The ball is rolling* is new information.

Fifth, social interaction plays an important role in structuring cognitive and linguistic growth. The discussion on child language emphasized that language experience occurs predominately within the context of mother-child communication exchanges almost from the moment of birth. Formal language instruction cannot occur in isolation either, but must be clothed in the social context of communication exchange, especially in the early stages. With the trend toward individualization and mechanized instruction, it is important to realize that social interaction is a vital component of language intervention programs. It is certainly possible to have individual goals for children in the context of group activities. For instance if James needs experience with infinitive constructions and Linda needs work on pronominals, it is possible to say to James during a story period *Goldilocks wants to go in the house,* and to Linda say *She went into their house.*

The use of social context is important for at least two reasons. Through dyad or small group experience the context of formal conversation will emerge. Conversations or experiences with more than one sentence at a time can encourage mastery of conversationally related linguistic principles such as articles, particularly *a* and *the,* and pronouns. The frequency of determiner and pronoun problems in deaf children may be related to the teacher's tendency to work on language one sentence at a time.

The uses of social context also have meaning for the growing practice of mainstreaming. Hamilton and Stewart (1977) have indicated the importance of peer models on the acquisition of linguistic principles, particularly new lexical items. It has been shown that nonhandicapped children's communication does adjust toward the linguistic requirements of handicapped children who are integrated into a regular classroom (Guralnick and Paul-Brown, 1977). Therefore, social context can have an influence on language performance, but such context is best used when the hearing-impaired child is able to use fairly sophisticated language, at least three- to four-word utterances. Even for the mainstreamed child, however, instruction in isolation is not profitable.

These comments about use of experience, action, cognition, preparation, and context should not be interpreted as confined to teaching younger children. The older deaf child who lacks language facility also needs the support of action-related experience. Too often with the older, linguistically limited child teachers decide to use language to teach language. This strategy is a complication for hearing-impaired children with low verbal skills. Sometimes in lieu of action media are employed because pictures, filmstrips, and even movies are seen as more mature experience. Action as a phenomenon is not completely captured by pictures, even those that move. The notion of *hit* is not an isolated event, as portrayed in so-called action pictures. It involves a sequence that has a beginning and perhaps a painful end—it has cause and consequences. Without direct experience the notion of continuous action may not be understood by the child.

It is often argued that direct experience approaches are socially demeaning to older children, because experiential techniques are viewed strictly in the context of making Jello with a preschool child. Nonetheless, the direct experience of vocational training, a common component of every school program, is not considered demeaning. Prevocational and vocational programs operated on guided learning (another name for direct experience) could easily be used as the basis for meaningful language experience. For instance, *Millie threaded the needle.* and *Leroy painted the trim.* are sentences that could be generated about experiences in vocational settings that satisfy the basic requirements for structured language input to promote rule induction.

In teaching older, low verbal children, language context is often confused with language sophistication. Control over vocabulary does not necessarily require reduced sentence complexity. The capabilities and needs of the older student can be considered in both choice of lexicon and syntactic emphasis. Lexicon can be chosen to satisfy the academic or intellectual needs of the older child, and sentence structure can be selected that will match his knowledge of language form and function.

Once single proposition sentence frames have been established in older students, further language goals can still be guided by the developmental outline shown in Table 10. The communicative needs of students are not met simply by having experience with vocabulary that is job or life related, but as should be recognized by now, use of that vocabulary in sentence frames is necessary for communication to occur.

As indicated in Chapter 1, language is a means to facilitate communication. Language may be inseparable from communication. For the verbally limited student, language learning should be experienced in a communication context. Otherwise its role and function are not clear to the learner. The learner comes to think of English as a classroom exercise totally unrelated to real events or people in his life. Regardless of the student's age, meaningful dialogue is the key to development of communication/linguistic competence. Meaningful dialogue refers to the process of not saying what is obvious to everyone when that behavior is appropriate, or saying what is obvious if that would be done normally. In dialogue with low verbal children, the teacher seems to view her task as requiring children first to identify and then discuss the characteristics of the object or topic under discussion. If a child makes a comment rather than a topic remark, teachers frequently dismiss those comments as irrelevent while busily pursuing the task of topicalization. In many cases the child's comments about situations that he and the teacher are sharing together are very productive. His behavior is similar to the reports on early mother-child interactions, with the primary difference, perhaps, being the remote reference of the comment compared to those made by very young children who talk about the here and now.

To illustrate the point, imagine that the teacher presents a picture of a Christmas tree in order to encourage the child to say *Christmas tree.* The child might respond by saying *home* with an appropriate gesture. The teacher who responds as if this comment was a ploy to divert attention from the task of naming says, *Oh, you have a tree at home. That's nice, but what is this?* It might have been more meaningful to try and continue the child's comment with a dialogue to have the child practice the language that he desired to say in the first place.

In normal child-mother interactions, dialogue is coupled with modeling and expansion techniques that could easily be used in exchanges with low verbal children. If the child fails to respond to expansion and comment, then one might encourage further dialogue by asking questions conducive to conversation. Communication exchanges provide opportunity for rule induction, as well as for spontaneous or delayed imitation, which may play a role in language acquisition for some children.

Such an approach may seem time consuming and initially unrewarding. Unless the deaf child sees language within the context of dialogue, however, it is uncertain whether he will ever learn it for functional use outside the classroom. It has been the authors' experience that many students with an apparent lack of meaningful knowledge about English sentences will respond favorably to experience-dialogue techniques. Depending upon the age of the student when the program is initiated, however, the upper limit of success remains uncertain. Although completely normal English function may not be a reasonable goal, strides in language fluency should be obtainable. Progress with very young hearing-impaired children will seem slow as well in the beginning stages. Given a motivated and emotionally secure caregiver who can achieve the level of communication necessary to encourage language acquisition, good results are possible.

As part of the decision about educational or therapeutic goals, control of the lexicon that will become old information in the teaching process is necessary. Holland (1975) suggested a core lexicon of 35 words that could be learned and used in combination to aid in the acquisition of sentence frames. This list includes items such as *me, you,* the child's name, the names of "significant others," *kiss, hate, gimme* or *wanna, more, no, yes, gone, up, down, there, that, hi, my, your, big, little, car,* and the clinician/teacher's name, among others. This list was chosen to include all these categories: names for significant persons, things, and objects in the child's environment, words that allow for expression of emotional states, words that allow for expression of the state of objects, and finally words that allow for the initiation of social exchanges. These items were selected based on pragmatic concerns, without attention to developmental data other than Bloom's (1970) report on functional and substantative relationships.

Lahey and Bloom (1977) also offer suggestions on the selection of the lexicon for language intervention programs. They suggest selection of words that are easily portrayed, either through demonstration for children who can handle that type of instruction or through pictorial representation for those who cannot. Words should be selected on the basis of the number of contexts in which they can appear, as for instance, many objects can be *dirty,* but fewer objects are *round.* Words selected should also relate to ideas that are commonly coded in early language according to child language researchers. With respect to the last suggestion, it was proposed that words for encoding—rejection, non-existence, cessation of action, prohibition of action, recurrence of objects and actions on objects, noting the existence of or identifying objects, actions involved in locating objects or self, attribution or description of objects, and persons associated with objects—be selected. Application of these categories would yield words such as *no, all gone, stop, more, this, give, make, get, put, up, down, sit, big, hot, dirty,* and person names. They also recommend the exclusion of some classes of words from consideration: expression of internal states such as *hate* or *scared*; affirmation by *yes* because yes expresses existence, which is better handled by *this*; pronouns, because many young children do not use pronouns, especially pronouns such as *you*; colors and opposites, because colors do not seem to be particularly interesting to children, and because opposites suppose an understanding of polar adjectives that some researchers (Clark, 1973a,b,c) have demonstrated does not occur at very young ages. By selecting and helping children to learn a lexicon, the teacher has built a store of old information that can be used in turn for content, and around this new linguistic principles or constructions can be woven.

Vocabulary development, aside from establishment of a basic lexicon, has traditionally had high priority in educational programs for the hearing-impaired. It is important when considering vocabulary teaching to distinguish between substantive words and syntactic-related words.

The latter are really meaningful only in the context of sentences (prepositions, articles, subordinating and coordinating conjunctions, or pronouns), and are not discussed in this section. Words of content or meaning, substantive words—traditionally labeled nouns, verbs, and adjectives—are considered.

Substantive words have traditionally been taught either through dictionary work, through analogy, or through identification procedures. Identification procedures usually consist of labeling or pointing to the existence of an object. For instance, naming a particular object a chair, another a table, or using existence or nomination statements such as *That's a table.* are common identification procedures. For low verbal or linguistically immature children, such procedures may not be sufficient to master language. Knowledge about words involves knowing not only what is subsumed by a particular word, but how it can be used with other words. Therefore, it is imperative that new vocabulary be introduced to children in discourse/sentence conditions using a variety of experiences to clarify new items.

Dictionary work has many of the same disadvantages of identification procedures. Simply reading the meaning of a word is not enough to guarantee its entry into a child's lexicon. Instead, new words need to be used in sentences in meaningful contexts.

Words are most frequently used because they identify differences among objects, attributes, location, or actions. No two words mean exactly the same thing; if they did, one of the words would die out in the society's lexicon. Word meanings are based as much on differences as on similarities. Teaching vocabulary through analogy may be a great disservice to hearing-impaired children, because they too frequently arrive at the idea that pairs of words mean the same thing, and as a consequence, misuse vocabulary items.

A child who has gained reasonable language fluency through contextually cued experiences and continues to demonstrate subtle lexical problems may be in need of vocabulary training and discussion of word differences, not similarities. For instance, when it is useful to discuss the difference between *steer* and *cow,* it might also be important to consider the difference between *stampeded, trampled,* or *loped.* Concept formation is not built on the establishment of similarities alone; a concept includes some instances and excludes others. Items in the lexicon should be learned by the process of inclusion and exclusion in the language.

Although the use of experience sentence strips and charts have been encouraged in the past, there has been no discussion of such techniques in this chapter. The restraint is not because of their lack of usefulness; their role is clearly reinforced in Chapter 7 on reading. Rather, language learning through conversational or interpersonal exchange has been emphasized because the authors are firmly committed to the notion that only when children internalize symbols as well as the way of organizing those symbols will they truly have a self-generated command of English. The child who constantly depends on patterns written on the blackboard or across the top of his paper will not know language, although he may have some knowledge of language surface structure.

Experience charts or other printed materials may serve as reminders of past experiences just as the family photo album calls up memories, but such charts must never be substituted for the child's own communication efforts, because without exception it is the child with the hearing loss who needs communication practice, not the teacher.

Application of Guidelines

Having considered the instructional prerequisites for a language program based on developmental experiences, examples of the application of linguistic analyses suggested in Chapter 5 are considered in the context of the remediation needs of hearing-impaired children. Although an adequate analysis of linguistic performance cannot be made with the limited samples provided in this section, the problems shown should be considered representative of the regular recurring language expression problems of hearing-impaired children. Each set of problems is discussed and then followed by some suggestions on how to organize lessons to aid a child in rectifying difficulties such as those exhibited. Because the types of language performance problems presented by hearing-impaired children are as varied as the children themselves, it will be possible to discuss only a few types of expressive difficulties. Indeed, only those most commonly encountered in language analysis of the type described in Table 7 are presented.

Tables 11 through 14 are organized in three columns; the left-hand column represents the contextual cues for interpreting the utterance or written forms shown in the middle column. The right-hand column contains an analysis summary of the problems exhibited in the middle column. The topics covered are relative clauses, articles, verbs, and non-meaningful language performance.

Table 11 presents problems often encountered with relative clauses. The problems demonstrated by these five children can be broken down into three categories: problems in communication/pragmatic intent, problems with structural organization, and problems in application of selection restrictions. Of the five children in Table 11, Bridget's sample demonstrates communicative/pragmatic problems; Claire's, David's, and Mary Ellen's demonstrate structural organization problems; and Chuck's sentences show selectional restriction difficulties.

Table 11. Examples of relative clause restricted forms

Student	Context	Utterance/Writing	Comments
Bridget	While looking at a picture of a boy eating an apple, she says:	The boy, who is white, is eating the apple.	Bridget's use of relative clauses is structurally complete and accurately executed. However, in each case she is providing information that is unnecessary in the communication situation. Relative clauses are used to establish topics that are potentially unclear to the audience. In each case the topic is clear, negating the need for the relative clause.
	After seeing an experiment completed by her teacher, she says to her classmates:	Mr. Hinton, who is my teacher, finished the experiment.	
	While looking at a picture of a boy standing near a tree, she writes:	The boy, who has brown pants, is standing near the tree.	
Claire	While writing about her new friend in California, she writes:	Jimmy, who lives in San Pedro, California. He wrote me a letter.	Claire's use of relative clauses is communicatively accurate in that she is using relative clauses for normal English purposes. Unfortunately she does not know their structural organization, that topics are included in sentences along with their comments.
	While looking at a picture of a boy deciding between different kinds of apples, she writes:	The boy is choosing his apple. The apple, which is red. He picked up the apple and took it home with him	
David	While writing about a picture that contains several cows, he writes:	The cow that it it is standing by the tree, looks sad.	In this case, the relative clause is communicatively correct; it is also structurally inserted as an elaborated node within the sentence. The problem is that the relative clause introducer is apparently not viewed as a pronoun, with a resulting redundancy. This is similar to what Quigley et al. (1977) call reduplication.
	While describing an accident to his mother, he says:	The man who he hit the car did not get hurt.	

Mary Ellen	While talking about a picture with two boys in it, she says: The boy is typing looks very sad. While describing a zoo scene to her classmates, she says: The zebra is walking has a baby.	In this case, the relative clause is communicatively accurate; she has not filled the wh-word node in the relative clause, a structural organization problem.
Chuck	After seeing an accident along with David, he tells his mother: The man which hit the car was not hurt. While describing a picture that has several trees in it, he writes: The tree who has a bird in it is very tall.	Chuck has fulfilled all the requirements of relative clause use communicatively and structurally. His problem seems to be that he has not worked out the selectional restrictions germaine to the wh-words selected for the sentence.

Bridget apparently does not know when to use relative clauses; she misunderstands the pragmatic purpose of this construction. This is not an uncommon problem for many hearing-impaired children because relative clauses are often taught in a structural framework, not a communicative one. To remediate this problem, Bridget could be given communication experiences in which relative clause use is needed and in which it is not. For instance, giving instructions to another person about which objects to use or not to use with objects of equal value except for placement or position might be tried. When presented with three balls in a row, the child can be asked to direct another child to retrieve one of the balls, e.g., *the ball that is on the right* or *the ball that is in the middle*. In this instance the relative clause is serving an important communicative function that is pragmatically appropriate for relative clauses: the establishment of topics for listeners. Children who have this type of problem with relative clauses probably also have difficulty knowing when to use adjectives and genitive pronouns/possessives. Each of these forms is used much in the same way as relative clauses to distinguish between objects that may be confused with one another.

Claire, David, and Mary Ellen from Table 11 all seem to be demonstrating structural organization problems. Each seems to understand when to use relative clauses, but not how to correctly use the surface structure. A possible solution to Claire's and Mary Ellen's problem would be to employ a patterning technique similar to that suggested by d'Arc (1958) and Buckler (1968). Each of these children could be engaged in communication situations in which they had to generate relative clauses that could be cued with a sentence strip such as _____ who _____. By generating sentences with and without a structural cue, flexibility in use of surface structure forms might be enhanced.

David, on the other hand, presents a problem in understanding the semantic/syntactic role of wh-words in relative clauses—the notion that wh-words semantically are pronouns, not introducers. It is possible, of course, that David understands this feature, which might be clarified by asking him who is represented by the various pronouns. If the problem is double entry into the wh-word node, then a patterning method as suggested above would be profitable. If, on the other hand, David does not understand that the wh-word is a pronominal form, then it is likely that he would have a reduplication problem with wh-question forms as well. This possibility should be investigated, and if a common problem is detected, then it might be more reasonable to work with the wh-question form problem first. This could be done by structuring communication situations where exchange of information is important. A twenty-question game could be played with David, perhaps with another child acting as a monitor to help him use the pronominal wh-word without reduplication. The effects of reduplication would be reduced in this situation, because the wh-question referent would be unknown to the child. Thus, he would have no knowledge about the referent and could avoid generating a reduplication in the clause. Once David had sorted out wh-word questions without reduplication, relative clauses could be tackled again, this time employing a patterning method in meaningful communication. Through analogy, knowledge of wh-question forms would transfer to relative clause structures.

Chuck's problem, from Table 11, is one of determining which wh-word to employ with each type of relative clause, a problem of understanding the selectional restrictions of relative clause wh-words. This problem might be approached by setting up meaningful communication situations to contrast uses of wh-words. For instance the child can be presented with pictures of two similar objects and of two people performing the same act. The child could ask the teacher to generate a descriptive statement about one of the objects and one of the people to be written on the blackboard. It could be pointed out that *who* refers to humans, and *that* refers to inanimate objects. Given another set of contrasting objects and persons, the child could be asked to generate descriptive statements using the teacher's productions as a model. By providing contrasting examples, the child will come to understand the contrastive difference. It is important to stress contrastive difference. It is important to stress contrasts rather than exemplars of principles in order that the child learn what the form encodes and what it does *not* encode.

This discussion on relative clauses is offered to show how communication, language functions, and forms are interwoven in language performance. In reality, many deaf children display problems in all three areas simultaneously. In this case, communication and function requirements must take precedence over form issues in teaching. Once these former problems have been resolved, the teacher should focus on surface structure practice.

One of the major problems facing hearing-impaired children is mastery of the English verb system (Heider and Heider, 1941; R. R. Kretschmer, 1972). Table 12 presents examples of deaf children's difficulties with this type of construction. The problems presented in Table 12 represent "pure" forms in that only one problem is exhibited in each sample. In reality, most deaf children exhibit a myriad of problems simultaneously, which makes development of fluent use of the verb system difficult.

Jason and Nathaniel exhibit communication/semantic difficulties in

Table 12. Examples of verb structure restricted forms

Student	Context	Utterance/Writing	Comments
Jason	When asked to describe a movie he has just seen in class, he says:	The boy see the girl. He like her very much. He want to kiss her, but she tell him no. He feel bad, so she say okay. He kiss her, and say he love her.	Jason has omitted tense from all verbs within this sample. His choice of verbs seems semantically varied and communicatively appropriate.
Alice	When describing a story she has just read, she writes:	Long time ago, king live in a palace. He have a daughter. A man come to the palace. He want to marry the king's daughter. The king tell the man he can marry daughter after he kill dragon. So the man go and kill dragon. Now he happy because he marry king's daughter.	Although Alice also omits tense throughout the sample, she does cue changes in time by using time adverbials such as *long time ago* and *now*. This is a common practice by many hearing-impaired children who display tense problems.
Michael	In response to the questions "What was Alice doing?" "What did Jason do yesterday?" "What is Annette doing?" and "What does Monica do in the morning?" he replied:	Alice ran around the room. Jason was hitting the door. Annette sits on the chair near the door. Monica is brushing her teeth.	From these responses, it is clear that Michael has some semantic misunderstandings about simple past and past progressive and simple present and present progressive. Simple past usually represents completed action; past progressive represents completed action in the recent past. Simple present represents action repeated at regular intervals; present progressive represents action that is going on at the present time.

Monica

When asked what she would like to do for summer vacation, she replied:

I want go to Colorado. I want see some Indians. I like ride with my parents very much.

Monica seems to have a surface structure problem in that she consistently omits the infinitive marker in her sentences.

Valerie

When asked about her favorite pastimes, she replied:

I enjoy to play with toys. I enjoy to see movies. I like to play with dolls. I like to eat pizza.

When asked what she wanted to do for the class trip, she told her teacher:

I want to go to the zoo. I want to see some toys.

Valerie demonstrates a tranformational selectional restriction problem. She has not differentiated between when to use participle nominalization forms and when to use infinitive nominalization forms. When the emphasis is on the event, the participle form is used; when the emphasis is on the action itself, the infinitive form is used.

Nathaniel

In response to the questions, "What will Mary do now?" and "What must Jerry do at home?" he writes:

Mary go home now. Jerry do his chores.

When reporting on a story he has just read, he writes:

Mary wanted to go to the beach with John. She not have any money, so she tried to get a job. She went to a store and asked for a job. The owner asked her, "You can run a cash register?" She said, "Yes." The owner gave her a job, but she work every day. Now she has no time to go to the beach.

Nathaniel seems to have an understanding of the main verb system, but lacks any understanding of the modal system. He has consistently failed to insert a lexical item into the auxiliary node of the sentence frame.

continued

Table 12—*continued*

Student	Context	Utterance/Writing	Comments
Rhoda	When asked what chores she has at home, she replied:	I can make the beds. I will watch my brother. I may clean up my room.	Based on Rhoda's answers, it would seem that she has some misunderstanding of the semantic meanings underlying the modal system. She may have surface structure understanding in that she has filled the auxiliary node in each sentence frame, but she lacks specific knowledge about when to use which modal.
	In response to the question "Do you clean up your room without your mother asking you?" she replied:	Yes, I may clean my room because mother told me to clean up my room. That is one of my chores.	

that both children lack any evidence of knowledge of certain aspects of the verb system—in Jason's case tense, and in Nathaniel's case modals. In contrast, Michael and Rhoda demonstrate more semantically related problems. They are communicatively aware of verb system components, but lack precise understanding of all the semantic intentions conveyed by various aspects of verbs. Valerie also exhibits semantically related problems. They revolve around an expanded node rather than local transformations or modulations off the verb.

Monica and Alice, in contrast, both seem to have surface structure breakdowns. Monica's problem is related to the encoding of the infinitive verb. By virtue of Alice's cuing of time through the use of adverbials, it could be argued that her lack of inflectional endings is probably a surface structure difficulty.

In working with Jason, Alice, and Michael, the problem is one of sorting out the various aspects of tense in English. This is best achieved through contrastive procedures that point out the differences between two tenses. It would be necessary for Michael to understand the expression of time with reference to the confusions he exhibits. Jason should be given more adverbial constructions so that he might learn to use them as Alice does, to cue tense or time. Once he achieved this variety of expression, he could be shown how tense relates to each of the adverbials he has mastered. There is danger inherent in this approach, however; too often teachers describe relationships as rigid when in fact they are not so inflexible. For instance, it is frequently said that future tense is indicated by the use of *will,* as in *They will go to town.* However, there are many other concepts conveyed by *will,* such as capability or determination. Likewise, present progressive can indicate future time when coupled with an appropriate adverbial, as in *I am going to the movie tomorrow.* When working on tense, therefore, it is important to couple tense training with adverbial and modal experience.

Nathaniel's and Rhoda's utterances represent difficulties with modals. In both instances it would seem reasonable to use contrastive techniques to emphasize the variety of meanings that modals convey. This can be done both by contrasting modal and non-modal sentences, as well as contrasting several sets of modal sentences. Such contrasting is best done in the context of conversation. For instance children could be given a hypothetical situation to talk about that would require use of various modals. After they have generated these sentences, they should discuss what the repercussions might be if different modals were used. Practice in modal use might also be pursued by asking the student to generate a sentence employing a sentence strip cue. For instance, the student might practice asking mother permission to go on a date. A sentence strip with the modal position omitted could be used: _____ I go on a date with (name)? The next step is to decide by role playing what mother's response might be, depending upon the modal used.

Monica's problem seems to be purely a surface structure insertion issue and could be handled through patterning, perhaps using a sentence strip such as _____ want to _____. Valerie's problem is more serious, however. It might be possible to assist her in understanding the communicative/semantic function of infinitives vs. participles through communication experiences. The next step might involve grouping verbs that take either form together: those that take participles are grouped separately from verbs that take only infinitives, which are separated from verbs that take both forms. Grouping of verbs should not be done, however, until it is clear that the child understands the underlying semantic properties of both forms. Otherwise, the child would simply be attending to surface structure concerns of making word groups rather than acting on underlying meaning.

As can be seen, the English verb system is highly complex. Accordingly, working with children who have verb problems is complicated. It is easy, for instance, to emphasize surface structure slot filling techniques that will still not guarantee the child's comprehension of meaning. As a consequence, it is sometimes better to sacrifice certain forms in favor of others that convey meaning more clearly, that is, using adverbials in lieu of morphological endings for tense coding.

Table 13 presents problems demonstrated by five children's use of the determiner system. These problems can be broken down into three areas: problems in expression of communicative intent, semantic confusions regarding items such as selectional restrictions, and surface structure breakdowns.

Of the five children, Jonathan and Mark demonstrate communicative/pragmatic misconceptions, Pamela demonstrates semantic breakdowns, and Tony demonstrates surface structure problems. Anne presents a somewhat confusing problem because it is not clear whether her problem is semantically based or a surface structure breakdown. Until she begins to use determiners, the details of her determiner knowledge will be unknown. In most children who demonstrate an absence of articles, the problem stems from semantic/communication misunderstandings rather than from failure to insert surface structure nodes.

Jonathan and Mark demonstrate problems that reflect two points on the same continuum. Both have difficulty with the pragmatic requirements that surround the use of the definite and indefinite determiners, specifically, *a, an, the,* and *some.* Because both demonstrate some understanding of the more semantically or meaning related determiners such as *one, each, few,* or *many,* the emphasis of their language program should be on developing pragmatic, not necessarily semantic, understandings. To accomplish this task, more than one sentence at a time should be worked on. Emphasis must be on several sentences in which new topics are first introduced and then converted to old information in subsequent conversation. This can be easily achieved by using activities in which the child must use more than one sentence. Children might be instructed to write directions for other students about doing something, for instance, instructions on how to sew on a button, as: *Pick up a button. Then, figure out where you want to put the button on the blouse. . . .* In this example, *a button* stipulates new information and *the button* indicates old information. With Jonathan the task may be easy because he apparently does not have operational knowledge of informationally related determiners. Mark does have such knowledge, albeit a confused one. Clearly, it is important that the informational status of determiners should be emphasized, rather than issues such as plurality or indefiniteness.

Given that Tony understands the actual communication and semantic functions of determiners, his problem is one of learning to insert determiners in noun phrases other than subject position. One strategy that could be used would be to have him generate a sentence with a properly formed noun phrase in the subject position. Next he could be asked to shift that noun phrase to the object position. For instance, when asked to caption a series of pictures perhaps for younger children, he could be helped to write *The nut was big.* and then, *The boy picked up the big nut.* In writing these sentences, it could be pointed out to Tony that articles are to be employed in all positions. Work on extending articles to prepositional phrases could be attempted next.

If Tony's problem was more serious, such as a lack of communicative mastery of the determiner system, then he might be included with Jonathan and Mark in practice sessions to help him to understand that articles are not merely surface structure markers, but that they play an important role in facilitating communication between individuals.

Anne's problem could be either semantically or surface structure related. When uncertainty occurs, it is always best to presume the deeper level problem until proven otherwise; it would be better to work with Anne from a semantic framework first. As previously stated, determiners can serve a meaning function or a communicative function. In order to insert articles into determiner nodes it might be easier to work on the semantic aspect, first by providing meaningful situations that exemplify concepts such as *many, few, each, every,* cardinal numbers, or ordinal

Table 13. Example of determiner usage restricted forms

Student	Context	Utterance/Writing	Comments
Anne	When describing a picture of a man removing his pencil from a box, she wrote: When telling her best friend about how she dressed her Barbie doll, she said:	Man pick up pencil and then he put pencil on desk. I picked up ribbon and tied ribbon around right ponytail. I picked up ribbon and tied it around left ponytail.	Anne obviously is having problems filling the article node with any portion of the determiner system.
Jonathan	When describing the picture Anne saw, he wrote: When telling his mother about the egg-dying project at school, he said.	Man picked up one pencil and then put pencil on desk. I take each egg and put it in right cup. I leave egg in cup. Few minutes go by, and I take egg out of cup. Egg turn different color. I like red. I have many red eggs.	Jonathan has some appreciation of the determiner system. He has some understanding of how the determiner position can convey semantic information such as *each* and *many*. However, *a* and *the* are nonfunctional, perhaps because he does not understand how determiners encode the given-new informational notion. He has some understanding of this concept, as witnessed by his use of pronominalization.
Mark	When describing the picture Anne saw, he wrote: When describing an accident that he has just witnessed, he said:	A man picked up the pencil and then put a pencil on the desk. The car hit the man. A man got hurt. The man hit his head on a street. A head got broke and there was the blood on a street.	Mark's samples demonstrate that he knows that the determiner node needs to be filled, but it is obvious that he lacks understanding of the given-new distinction with reference to the use of *a* and *the*.

Pamela	When describing a TV program she saw to her teacher, she wrote:	There was a man in the movie. He was very thirsty. He wanted a water. He looked for the water, but he couldn't find any water. He saw a Indians and asked them for the water. They said, "Okay," and gave him a water. He drank the water, and he was not thirsty any more.	Pamela seems to have good semantic and communicative control over the determiner system. What she lacks is complete control over the selectional restrictions that govern determiner use in sentences, particularly plurality and mass/count agreement.
Tony	When describing the picture that Anne saw, he wrote:	The man picked up pencil and then he put pencil on desk.	Tony obviously has command over the communication aspects of the determiner system by virtue of the fact that when he employs determiners he uses them correctly. For some reason, he has learned to use them only in subject position. In some cases, children who do this do not know the communication purpose of determiners, as witnessed by their use of a single form, usually *the*, in the article node of the subject.
	When confirming Mark's report of the accident they saw, he said:	A car hit man. The man got hurt. The man hit his head on street. His head got broke and there was blood on street. A policeman come and he helped man go to hospital.	

numbers. This can easily be accomplished by setting up situations for communication in which it is important to have mastery over determiners such as making a cake or discussing events that involve several objects that differ on only one key dimension. Once Anne achieves more skill with use of semantically based determiners, she should be in a position comparable to Jonathan, in which case communicatively important determiners could be introduced.

If it should be the case that Anne's problem is one of surface structure confusion, then it might be useful to group her with someone like Tony. In her case work on sentences that contain only one noun phrase such as intransitive sentences should be first, extending her knowledge next to other noun phrase constructions, such as direct and indirect objects and prepositional phrases.

Pamela's problem seems to be related to insufficient knowledge of selectional restrictions, particularly with reference to communicatively related determiners. It is probable that if she has problems with these forms, she will also have difficulty with semantically based determiners, which should be explored. With regard to the selectional restrictional problem, a contrastive technique might be useful as well. Communication situations that emphasize single items and plural items in new and old information settings could be arranged so that Pamela learns that certain determiners cue certain concepts. In addition to single-plural contrasts, mass-count differences might be stressed. Writing stories for younger children, involving one person meeting another or groups of people, consuming mass nouns such as water, and count nouns such as sandwiches or apples could be used for this purpose.

As is true with complex forms such as relative clauses, use of basic forms such as determiners reflect the interaction of knowledge about communication, semantic, and syntactic demands. Most hearing-impaired children will have difficulties in all three areas, not just one.

The level of performance demonstrated by April, Kenneth, and Robert in Table 14 is prevalent among many hearing-impaired children, especially in written English. The teaching problems faced with late identified children, for example, are similar to those faced by preschool/ nursery school teachers with linguistically limited young deaf children. Older linguistically limited deaf children unfortunately are often contaminated with some poorly defined knowledge of English, requiring that unlearning precede learning in some cases.

It is best to assume that these children have little or no understanding of English rather than a poor grasp, suggesting a need to start "at the beginning." It is important that the child not be expected to master surface structures in preference to the establishment of underlying

Table 14. Examples of non-meaningful productions

Student	Context	Utterance/Writing	Comments
April	In response to the Myklebust Picture Story Test stimulus, she wrote:	boy, toy, chair, play, table, book, car	These three children must be considered equivalent in language facility. Each does not demonstrate much understanding of English sentence frames. It would seem that each child has an understanding of some English lexical items, but no sense of arrangement into sentence frames.
	While describing a movie that she had seen the previous day, she wrote:	man and woman, cat, die, knife, away	
Kenneth	In response to the Myklebust Picture Story Test stimulus, he wrote:	I see a ball. I see a boy. I see a play. I see a big. I see a chair.	Kenneth and Robert have one advantage over April. They have some sense of sentenceness, whereas April apparently lacks even this appreciation.
Robert	In response to the Myklebust Picture Story Test stimulus, he wrote:	Is boys the good. Girl a play floor car. Boy walk word see book red.	

semantic/communicative meanings. The language instruction of children such as April, Kenneth, and Robert must emphasize acquisition of meaning, not mastery of surface structure forms.

What goals should be the first for children devoid of linguistic performance? Research from normal child language can serve as a guide. If children learning a first language tend to focus on development of action verbs within the agent-action-patient-location sequence, then it seems logical to start at this point with older deaf children who are also learning language for the first time. Lahey and Bloom (1977) have suggested that the earliest lexicon taught to language-delayed children should reflect categories established by young children, including agents, actions, patients, and locatives, as well as non-existence, existence, and recurrence. This means that early lexicon usage should focus on action-causative, action-affective, and function words such as *no, that,* and *more.*

The earliest linguistic task for such children should be to establish basic sentence frames, usually of the single propositional type. To accomplish this task, emphasis should be placed on the action-transitive and action-intransitive sentences, such as *April hit Robert.* or *April cried.* The issue of what to expect the child to produce becomes a crucial one. Too often teachers insist that every node in the sentence be filled when a sentence is produced. This level of performance is usually achieved by elicited imitation and drill. If language is cognitively related and if it develops in gradual stages in children, it is reasonable to expect that even older children will progress developmentally in the acquisition of basic sentence frames. Therefore, the initial goal should be toward self-generated insertion of basic lexical items into sentence frames. Once this is achieved by the child, more detailed work on inflectional and article nodes could be considered.

In normal language acquisition, language is facilitated by the efforts of mothers who engage their children in communication activities. Language learning involves an interactive process, which raises two questions: what is the extent of the experiential base needed for language learning to occur and what is the role of dialogue in the language learning process?

Both experience and dialogue are paramount to the normalization of language learning in children with significant hearing loss. The authors challenge each reader to ensure that these factors become a routine part of educational programs, so that every child may have an opportunity to enter the communication mainstream.

CHAPTER 7

READING AND LANGUAGE

Roberta R. Truax

CONTENTS

A human society is characterized as having an oral mode of communication; a literature society is further characterized as having a written mode, which permits an even wider range of communication forms. It is possible for members of a literate society to complement the traditional oral mode, which emphasizes conversation, story telling, and poetry with a mode that is better adapted to communicating statements, arguments, directions, essays, and chronicles (Olson, 1977). In a literate society, reading is viewed as a vital means for vicariously acquiring information and concepts, and for gaining access to a wide variety of attitudes, insights, understandings, and values (Lefevre, 1973).

In American society, learning to read has been deemed one of the important tasks of childhood. For this reason it is important for anyone who is responsible for helping children learn to read to consider some of the critical factors and issues related to the reading process. The factors and issues discussed in this chapter have been grouped into four general categories: (1) the uses of printed language, (2) the processing of printed language forms, (3) the role of a reader in constructing meaning from print, and (4) the scope and sequence of a reading program.

THE USES OF PRINTED LANGUAGE

Reading as a means of communication serves many different purposes. What a person selects to read is guided by a purpose (Hart, 1963). If he wants to know someone's phone number, he consults a telephone directory; if he wants to know what is happening politically in the Middle East, he may look for an article in a newspaper or weekly news magazine; if he wants to relax, he may pick up a mystery; of if he wants mental stimulation, he may select an anthology of essays.

Not only do reading materials serve a variety of purposes, but they also have different formats (Allen, 1972). Newspapers utilize headlines and columns of print that may or may not run consecutively. Novels utilize chapters and full pages of print without advertisements or other incidental materials. Television schedules utilize charts that carry time and channel listings for programs and need to be read both horizontally and vertically.

Just as formats vary from one type of written material to another, so do the discourse structures. Novels follow discourse structure rules that specify what is to be presented in opening chapters, how a plot may develop, and how and when resolutions occur. Fairy tales and detective stories follow discourse structure rules that are similar to those of novels, yet there are subtle differences.

As an individual reads different types of materials, he learns to set expectations about the information that will be provided. A reader depends upon the predictability of printed material to help him interpret incoming information meaningfully and to integrate it into an overall schema. News articles, recipes, editorials, science texts, and poems all seem to follow predictable discourse structure guidelines.

A reader relies on his knowledge of the content contained in a piece of printed material and his purposes for reading it as well as his understanding of the types of discourse structure to set some expectations about the literary style he will encounter (Allen, 1972). As discussed in Chapter 2, speech registers change according to the communication circumstances. In printed language there are a variety of literary styles that are appropriate for different purposes and different types of printed materials. For example the use of dialogue might be an effective and appropriate means for conveying a message in some circumstances, but might be inappropriate in others. An experienced reader can anticipate the use of literal or figurative language for a particular piece of material based upon his past experiences with printed language. Similes and metaphors occur frequently in stories, but not in math texts. Personification is a popular convention in folk tales, but would be unusual if found in a news article.

From an early age a child's experiences with printed material begin to prepare him to learn about the uses of printed language. Awareness is developed through experiences with print as it is used in the general environment—on cereal boxes, on television, on road signs, and in books and magazines. Opportunities to observe adults and older children using printed language provide a child with the understanding that reading may afford enjoyment and relaxation, provide important information, or provide the means for learning how to do things.

A young child seems to progress though developmental stages in his handling and use of books (Monroe and Rogers, 1964). Learning initially centers on how to take care of books, on how to hold books right side up so they open at the front, and on how to turn pages. Learning about the handling of books and their visual presentations is frequently complemented by language and social learning as the child and adult engage in conversations about the pictures in a book. The size and color of individual pictures usually maintain attention until the child is ready to focus on a story line. As adults and older children read to him from books he is led to an understanding that each book tells a different story. Throughout these developmental stages, the child becomes increasingly more interested in the story line, the characters, and the ideas contained in printed materials. Eventually the pictures begin to complement the language, instead of the language complementing the pictures. The child's attention begins to focus on the print and its potential for meaning. A child may even begin to ask direct questions about the meaning of particular printed forms.

In environments that foster reading there should be adults to model reading, social activities associated with reading, and reading materials of all kinds available for use by a child. As the child is exposed over and over again to his favorite books and to new books, he gains an awareness of discourse structure and the literary styles used to tell stories. The reading of nursery rhymes, poems, or advertisements with a child helps him to understand that printed language appears in different formats and is used in a variety of ways for a variety of purposes and effects.

For a child who grows up in an environment where he is read to, where adults and older children read, and where he has access to books, going to school to learn how to read has personal significance. The child anticipates learning how to supplement what he already knows and values about the world of print with what the teacher knows. Throughout his school career, he will continue to need appropriate reading experiences that will increase his abilities to use printed language more effectively in a wider variety of circumstances. With meaningful practice he will become a skillful reader who will be able to put the world of print to work for his own purposes.

For a child who grows up in an environment where there are few readers to model and where experiences with printed materials are limited, going to school to learn how to read may not be a goal that the child sets for himself. He may question the emphasis on learning to read, and based on the attitudes and activities of the adults in his environment, he may see no outstanding reasons to value reading or to work at learning how. The teacher of this child will initially need to provide enjoyable and rich experiences with printed language so that the child will come to see the role that reading can play in the life of an individual. Without a rich background of experience with printed materials, their uses, and the special language forms of printed language, a child will not be adequately prepared to focus on the reading strategies stressed in most reading programs. Emphasizing the mastery of specific skills and strategies may be a waste of valuable time unless the child is able to view reading as serving some meaningful functions in his life.

A hearing-impaired child has the same basic need for meaningful exposure to the wide world of print as does a normally hearing child. He needs direct experiences with handling books and magazines; he needs to see others use printed materials; and he needs to have others read him the stories, poems, and nursery rhymes that are the literary heritage of his culture. It is common for experience charts and other written materials to be used with a young hearing-impaired child when parents and teachers are working to establish language and communication. Even though a child becomes aware through such techniques that important information can be written down, his needs for rich and varied experiences with books and magazines and exposure to printed language, as it is used normally in the everyday environment, are still great.

THE PROCESSING OF PRINTED LANGUAGE FORMS

Reading is a dynamic psycholinguistic process (K. Goodman, 1972). As such, it relies upon the common bases of linguistic competence and performance constraints that also support and control other language processes, namely, listening, speaking, and writing. Although all of the language functions share a common base, each mode uses linguistic competence somewhat differently (Ryan and Semmel, 1969; Strickland, 1962; Tatham, 1970).

Both a reader and a listener are faced with the task of developing perceptual strategies that will lead to efficient, meaningful interpretation of verbal messages. Indeed the language processing model discussed in Chapter 2 fits nicely as a framework for the description of reading as a language process, with some few alterations for differences in printed and spoken language. As a listener attempts to interpret an auditory message, he can usually verify his interpretations by using nonlinguistic contextual cues and, if necessary, by checking directly with the speaker. A reader, on the other hand, needs to interpret printed language without ready access to the author and with fewer nonlinguistic contextual cues for reference. However, a reader can review the printed message any number of times as he endeavors to construct the author's message (Allen, 1972). As a reader samples printed language he must actively employ his linguistic competence, his past experiences, and his conceptual attainments, as well as proficiency with the strategies needed to process the language encoded in graphic symbols (Allen, 1972; K. Goodman, 1973b).

Smith and Holmes (1973) developed a feature analysis model for visual perception of print that describes the conditions under which a reader identifies individual letters, individual words, or comprehends meaning directly from larger units of printed language. The active role of the reader is central in this model, because his expectations and purposes direct him to select cues that will lead to the identification of individual letters, to select cue relationships that will lead to the identification of whole words, and to select cue relationships that will lead to the identification of larger language units. The identification of meaningful units, such as words and phrases, is of prime importance to a reader who needs to construct a message (Carroll, 1972; Miller, 1973).

As a beginning reader becomes accustomed to seeing meaning coded in printed form, he also develops knowledge of the transitional probabilities of the cues or distinctive features within words that permit their identification without prior identification of individual letters. When a reader applies his knowledge of syntactic and semantic redundancies and constraints to the selection of cues presented by a sequence of words, he is able to comprehend the meaning of a sentence without needing to identify each and every word. This can be demonstrated by asking a reader to tell what he has read after he has completed a long sentence. He usually cannot repeat the sentence word for word but rather offers a paraphrase based upon his interpretation of the meaning of the sentence (Smith, 1975).

Wolf (1977) has described a full scale model called analysis-by-synthesis that was proposed by Neisser (1967) to explain how an individual uses knowledge stored in long-term memory to aid in the interpretation of perceptual information. In the analysis-by-synthesis model, perception is not characterized as a passive process that allows a flow of unlimited, unorganized, and undifferentiated information to be forwarded from the short-term memory to the brain. Instead perception is viewed as an active process in which a listener or reader begins to organize information into significantly related units as soon as information is presented.

When a reader first perceives printed language, he attempts to match the new visual experience with similar past experience. The matching process may include both: (1) general experiences, such as those related to the format or to the discourse structure, and (2) specific experiences, such as those related to particular words or linguistic constructions. The matching process is viewed as a rapid search that takes only a fraction of a second. As soon as the search is completed the reader uses the results to construct a hypothesis about the nature of the new information. Whenever a hypothesis proves to be inaccurate, the original hypothesis needs to be replaced or modified by generating a new match as additional information becomes available.

A reader, as characterized in Neisser's model, cannot be limited to perceptual strategies that set a high premium on taking in every item of information for equal attention. The reader must instead use sampling strategies that select relevant cues to aid a search of the long-term memory for what is needed to develop a hypothesis about the rest of the sample. Whether for spoken or printed language, a few sounds or a few letters might be enough for the recognition of a word; a few words in turn might allow the reader to guess a phrase or whole sentence.

As a reader processes a message, each bit of new information allows him to feed back and confirm, modify, or discard hypotheses, and to feed forward predictions of what is to come (Ruddell and Bacon, 1972). The procedures involved in confirming, modifying, discarding, and predicting can be applied to the hypothesized meanings of words, phrases, sentences, paragraphs, long stretches of dialogue, or even whole discourse structures.

Neisser (1967) has drawn a connection between the reading process and thought itself:

> Where rapid reading is concerned . . . the end product of cognitive activity is not a bit of verbal behavior but a deep cognitive structure; not a verbalized name but a continuing analysis-by-synthesis, a construction which builds a non-sensory structure just as "lower levels" of cognition synthesize visual figures or spoken words. Reading is externally guided thinking (p. 136).

Using reading strategies can thus be viewed as a process of sampling cues to use in establishing appropriate perceptual units to relate to previous experience. It is important to remember that the eye is only a tool of the brain in any perceptual activity (Smith and Holmes, 1973). In any reading task the eye can only take in a limited amount of information (Miller, 1956). It is the brain that must make use of the available cues to construct a meaningful message by supplying essential and relevant knowledge about the world, knowledge about language in general, and knowledge about the reading mode in particular (Kolers, 1973a,b; Kolers and Katzman, 1966; Smith, 1977).

The task of the beginning reader is to develop strategies to locate and use cues that will enable him to make appropriate hypotheses about the meaning of a message (Barr, 1972; Biemiller, 1970; Miller, 1973). At first he will need time to attend to the broad spectrum of cues that are available in a printed display (Jones, 1973). One of the biggest discoveries that a reader has to make is that, in reading, not all of the visual information on the page is significant for meaning, and not all of the meaning is presented in print (Goodman, 1972; Miller, 1973; Ryan and Semmel, 1969). The reader may already know this as a general perceptual principal and apply it to other perceptual activities. However, if a program of reading instruction does not help a reader organize his perception according to what is or is not significant to him in terms of his own individual linguistic competence, the reader may be forced to attend primarily to surface structure forms and not to the reconstruction of underlying meaning. A skillful teacher is able to serve as a guide and encourages a reader to make maximum use of all facets of his linguistic and conceptual knowledge, experience, and curiosity in each reading task (Burke, 1972).

As a reader gains proficiency in selecting and organizing cues, he can turn more and more of the reading process over to the brain. However, even the most proficient reader will encounter situations where reading can be difficult, if not impossible. This can occur when a reader is presented with printed language that uses unfamiliar linguistic constructions and lexical items, or when he is presented with printed language that codes content that is outside his experience or beyond his conceptual abilities to interpret. It is the responsibility of the teacher to anticipate difficulties at each and every stage so that the reader may be assisted before problems arise to interfere with the child's continued development as a reader.

THE ROLE OF THE READER
IN CONSTRUCTING MEANING FROM PRINT

As a reader processes printed language he makes use of: (1) cues within words, (2) cues related to the prosodic, syntactic, and semantic relationships among word units, and (3) cues related to discourse structure and other contextual references, including information provided by a teacher (K. Goodman, 1973b).

Cues Within Words

Strategies that make use of cues within words enable a reader to recode printed words into their spoken forms. These strategies are based upon cues that specify the relationship of: (a) individual grapheme-to-phoneme or graphemic to phonemic patterns in English, (b) spelling patterns to morphemic meanings, and (c) whole word configurations to whole word pronunciations. A reader can employ these strategies independently or interdependently as he reads.

The use of grapheme cues within words relies on rules that a reader develops specifying how sound is represented in printed language. In English the rules would include those that regulate pronunciation, such as: (1) a *c* before *i, e,* or *y* represents the phoneme category *s* and not *k,* as in *city*; or (2) the patterns *a—e* and *ay,* as in *make, mate, tame* and *today, may, say* are spellings to cue the vowel long *a.* In attempting to pronounce printed words, a reader might also look for small words within bigger words to help unlock the pronunciation, such as *sand* as part of the pronunciation pattern in both *sandwich* and *sandle.* He might also try to pronounce the words that compose a compound word such as cow and boy and use those independent pronunciations to recode the printed compound word *cowboy* into its spoken form.

All of the strategies that make use of cues within words help a reader translate printed language forms into spoken language forms and as such are recoding strategies. The decoding for meaning is thus presumed to be carried out indirectly via the auditory channel. When the reader "hears" the word he will attach the appropriate meaning to it based upon its use and function within the sentence or phrase (K. Goodman, 1973a,b,c).

Words that are recognized by their total configuration or internal cue relationships are often called sight words or sight vocabulary. These vocabulary items are usually not analyzed grapheme by grapheme but are learned by associating a printed word form with its spoken counterpart. Learning whole word pronunciation strategies is another way for a reader to make use of the auditory channel as the primary decoding channel. It is assumed that the reader will know how to synthesize the words he can sight read into meaningful phrases and sentences.

The use of underlying spelling patterns or structural analysis may or may not lead to recoding printed forms into vocal forms (Allen, 1972). A reader who uses this strategy uses the morphemic components to discern meaning. For example in the sentence *The doctor gave her new medication for the infection,* a reader who has never seen the word *medication* but knows *medicine* would probably be able to hypothesize an appropriate meaning for the new vocabulary item. Although this strategy assists a reader in his search for meaning, it may not assist him in pronouncing the word, because knowing how to pronounce "medicine" does not necessarily mean one knows how to pronounce another related word, such as *medicinal.*

When a reader utilizes the underlying representations to recode words such as *national/nation*; *anxious/anxiety* and *medicine/medicinal*, he probably determines the pronunciation by recognizing the basic morpheme and applying what he knows of the pronunciation of that word as it is used in the context, rather than by applying specific phonemic rules (Allen, 1972; Chomsky and Halle, 1968; Weir and Venezky, 1973). In oral reading, words such as *minute, present, wind,* and *permit* are pronounced differently depending upon how they are used in a linguistic structure. A reader's knowledge of the multiple meanings and uses of lexical items allows him to select the appropriate meaning based on use. Meaning, therefore, cannot be viewed as relying totally upon pronunciation rules and recoding strategies. In fact, meaning can be used to determine pronunciation, and often is (Smith, 1973b).

Cues Related to Linguistic Organization

Another group of strategies enable a reader to select cues that relate to the prosodic, syntactic, and semantic relationships among word units. As a result of having used his linguistic competency in other communication situations, a beginning reader, even in the early stages of learning to read, relies on his own normal use of language to facilitate the decoding of units larger than syllables and words (Weber, 1969). This usually happens regardless of the instructional program. The roles of sentence structure and discourse structure have already been established, and the use of this knowledge can facilitate visual perception and help the reader construct a message.

Research indicates that the eyes do not progress across a page letter by letter or word by word when a person reads (Buswell, 1970; Pillsbury, 1897). Instead they fixate at widely spread points along the printed line to sample what is to be processed for meaning by the brain. In oral reading the eyes are usually well ahead of the voice. In searching ahead with the eyes an oral reader may be employing strategies that use cues that indicate stress patterns, pitch change, and juncture. These cues are supplied by syntactic structures, word order, and semantic intents. These strategies help a reader bridge the gap between printed language and spoken language, which do not treat the relationships between words and sentences in the same way in their surface structures (Barr, 1972). In spoken language, sounds and words flow together and usually cannot be identified as discrete units (Jones, 1973). Very young children often cannot identify individual word units in spoken phrases and sentences (Huttenlocher, 1964). In printed language, conventions specify that equal spaces must exist between word units in sentences. If, as Lefevre (1973) maintains, intonational patterns are the basic determiners of perceptual units in both written and spoken language, strategies that lead to appropriate grouping of words for processing are of prime importance. In order to read with expression a reader seems to sample ahead to combine syntactic and semantic cues with knowledge about prosody so that he can blend words into recognizable auditory forms. These kinds of strategies allow a reader to render graphic forms such as *What is the matter?* and *I want a cup of cocoa.* into the more familiar and, therefore, more easily decoded *Wutsa madder?* and *I wanna kupuv koko.*

In order to know what kind of sentence intonation pattern to use, a reader need not wait to see the punctuation. In English, periods, question marks, and exclamation points appear at the ends of sentences, not at the beginnings, and serve as confirmations for decisions already made based on word order cues and syntactic constructions. For example if a sentence begins with a wh-word, it seems reasonable to hypothesize that a question intonation pattern would be most appropriate.

Syntactic and semantic strategies make use of information provided by function words and affixes, which serve as markers for semantic functions and structural signals for noun phrases, verb phrases, and so on (Burke and Goodman, 1970). Even in nonsense sentences some hypotheses about relationships can be made by using function words, affixes, and basic word order conventions. After reading the sentence *The gligs mimmeled a wup.* a reader can tentatively hypothesize that "more than one glig did something to a single wup at some time in the past." After reading *A hypett was geeked by the nad.* the reader cannot be sure if *the nad* refers to a location or to an agent. However, the reader does know that the particular bit of information probably has been made available in an earlier sentence because *the* indicates old or known information. In a sentence such as *The soldiers ambushed the mitter.*, the semantic constraints associated with the verb *ambush* specify an object noun that is mobile. The *er* affix indicates that the mobile noun is also most probably human. Therefore, any notion of *the mitter* being a stationary object or location is probably discarded by the reader. The semantic constraints imposed by individual vocabulary items, affixes, and syntactic constructions help a reader make educated guesses about the general meaning of unknown words, even though only limited meaning may be available from syntactic cues. A reader can learn to make use of surface structure cues to provide an appropriate answer for a wh-question even if he does not know the meaning of the content words or understand the question (Burke, 1972). For example *What did the gligs mimmel?* can be answered by the response *a wup* by selecting the appropriate syntactic component from the surface structure of the original sentence.

Cues Related to Discourse Structure

A reader can also learn to use cues based upon the discourse structure. Such phrases as *Once upon a time* and *The End* are usually learned early because of the consistent discourse functions they serve.

Sometimes a reader needs to make use of pictures or charts to determine meaning. In the case of reading signs, situational cues related to where the sign is placed in the environment often provide enough cues to facilitate decoding. The incorporation of situational information into the thinking process used for reading is important.

At times a reader may need to consult others or may resort to looking up a critical word on a reference chart or in the dictionary. Of course the reader must be sophisticated enough linguistically to read a dictionary and must be able to select the appropriate definition if he is expected to use one independently.

A proficient reader is not restricted to a single strategy or a single set of strategies for getting meaning from print, but instead can use a variety of strategies interdependently. In fact, relying on a single strategy at any stage of reading may interfere with learning to read (Ruddell, 1973). For a hearing-impaired individual the importance of becoming a proficient reader cannot be under estimated. Reading can be a vital communication mode and a strong means for both learning and enjoyment. Teachers must prepare themselves as fully as they can to provide the best instruction and environment to support a hearing-impaired reader as he learns to use printed language.

SCOPE AND SEQUENCE OF THE READING PROGRAM

Strategies Emphasized in Instructional Programs

Becoming a proficient reader takes a long time. In societies that use an alphabetic system of writing there has traditionally been debate over where to begin and what to emphasize in reading instruction (Huey, 1970, originally published in 1908). The reading programs that have evolved in these societies can be arranged along a continuum that has at one end programs of instruction that teach reading by emphasizing meaning bearing units such as sentences, phrases, and words in early instruction (Hodges and Rudorf, 1972; Huey, 1970; Smith,

1973a,b,c,d,e); and at the other end programs that teach reading by emphasizing units that represent individual sound to print relationships (Bloomfield, 1933; Fries, 1963). A teacher who is responsible for helping a child learn to read or to develop further as a reader needs to be aware of the strengths and assumptions of the various reading approaches so that she can use them in designing an appropriate program for each student. In this section two general program approaches are reviewed briefly: (a) a developmental language approach that relies on sentence units, and (b) a recoding skills approach that relies on phoneme-to-grapheme and sight word units.

A Developmental Language-Based Reading Program   A reading program that approaches learning to read as a developmental language activity makes decisions about where, when, and how to begin reading instruction by evaluating a child's cognitive development, his linguistic development, his communication understandings and his experiences with print. Therefore, a developmental reading program ought to use observational techniques and evaluation procedures that help set objectives to reflect an acceptance of the developmental behaviors a child exhibits as he learns to read (Y. Goodman, 1972).

An advocate of the approach to reading instruction that reflects developmental learning would hold the belief that perceptual learning is enhanced by, and indeed depends upon, contextual cues from the start (Smith and Goodman, 1973). Language used in any modality, including print, should be used in relation to experiences, and words should be learned in the context of sentences and appropriate discourse structure (Allen, 1972; Lefevre, 1973). Learning to read is seen as proceeding from general and often telegraphic understanding of meaning to the ability to understand details and presuppositions. Therefore, approaches that emphasize exact oral reproductions of printed language, at the expense of comprehension, would be regarded as developmentally inappropriate (Smith, 1973e).

The sentences first used in a developmental program are frequently dictated by the child or are written by the teacher after discussion about an experience (Allen, 1972). In the beginning stages the reader does not have to construct an unknown message, but rather has to discover how known information has been coded in print (Jones, 1972). The teacher needs to play an active and supportive role during all stages of reading development, just as adults are supportive and actively involved in spoken language acquisition and development (Smith, 1971). As more is learned about language acquisition in general and about learning to comprehend and use language in the various modes, reading instruction may need to be modified to fit an expanded developmental model.

Developmental reading programs depend upon research evidence that describes developmental stages in learning to use print. The following summary of a research study by Read (1975) is presented as an illustration of the type of study that needs to be considered and executed to help define strategies employed by young children as they attempt to learn to use printed language.

Read's (1975) findings indicate that children may not organize phonemes in the same way adults do. Unlike adults, they may be inclined to categorize speech sounds in "slowed-down speech" (speech produced sound by sound) through tactile-kinesthetic, not auditory, cues.

In reviewing the spelling patterns developed by a number of preschool age children who taught themselves how to write, Read found that they consistently wrote vowel symbols /a/, /e/, /i/, /o/, and /y/ to represent vowel sounds as they are pronounced in *bait, beet, bite, bone,* and *beauty.* Furthermore, in writing, the children did not rely upon the acoustic qualities of the vowels in the words they wrote but seemed to depend instead upon tongue placement within the mouth to make spelling decisions. Read argued that because the tongue is in the long *e* position in the production of both *sheep* and *ship,* they were both spelled *sep.* Both vowels can be felt in the same place if the words are slowed down to a phoneme-by-phoneme production. The tongue position for both the /s/ and the /sh/ are also the same or very similar. The similarities of place of articulation for *sheep* and *sip* can be felt by slowing down pronounciation and saying each of the sounds very slowly without voicing them.

Such an explanation offers very reasonable support for Read's notion about why the children he studied developed a general spelling system that spelled *pen* as *pan, fell* as *fal,* and *left* as *lafft.* The children also developed a category that classified fricative sounds by both place and manner of articulation. This category included the feeling and position that occurs initially in words such as *CHair* and *CHicken.* Children's attempts to capture the feelings of friction and point of contact, which also occurs in words such as *TRain* and *TRy,* resulted in the similar spelling of the TR and CH words. *TRain* was spelled as *CHran* and *TRy* as *CHRie.* The TR combination feels very much like CH when a word is slowed down and produced phoneme by phoneme. In fact, the initial sounds produced in *CHair* and *TRain* feel much more alike that do the initial /t/ phonemes in *tame* and *train.*

More research is needed to describe children's strategies in the early stages of learning to read and write. Too often research focus has been on instructional methods and not on the developmental strategies of children. Many traditional notions about the acquisition and development of oral language have had to be re-evaluated in recent years because of the extensive study of emerging language in young children. Teachers who are committed to developmental reading approaches should look forward to and encourage new studies that will help them better understand how a child goes about learning to read and write.

A Skill-Oriented Reading Program   A reading program centered on skills assumes that the reader will ultimately be able to integrate narrowly defined "reading" skills and use them to read. The progression of activities emphasizes part to whole learning, from the mastery of isolated skills to the application of those skills in meaningful activities.

Many skill-centered programs begin reading instruction by focusing on individual graphemes and grapheme patterns and by maintaining that the best way to foster perceptual learning for reading is to begin with strategies that facilitate recoding, sound by sound, of what is seen in print. The emphasis in these programs is on learning letter details and producing exact translations from visual forms into vocal forms.

Bloomfield (1933), a linguist, initiated the application of formal findings from his study of phonemes to reading instruction and reading materials designed for children. Fries (1963) furthered this application by describing in detail the graphic arrangements used to spell the phonemic patterns of English and the presumed relationship of this information to the teaching of reading skills. Both of these authors have had a strong influence on modern reading programs that are characterized as using a linguistic approach.

The textbooks and materials published as linguistic readers in the 1960s (Bloomfield and Barnhart, 1961; Buchanan, 1963; McCracken and Walcott, 1963) pioneered a movement that used reading materials with controlled vocabulary to assure that the graphic symbols utilized have a constant phonemic value. These linguistic readers, which are still used, propose that by repeating grapheme-phoneme associations coded in word forms over and over, a child's general code cracking skills will be facilitated. These skills presumably enable a reader to independently crack the symbol-sound relationship code of any printed language (Olsen, 1973).

Thus the initial focus of skill-oriented reading programs is on learning the pronunciation rules governing printed forms rather than on interpretation of meaning from language (Smith, 1973a,b). However, the need for a strategy other than one of establishing grapheme-phoneme relationships becomes necessary because too many basic words do not adhere to phonic rules. The use of sight vocabulary is usually the first additional strategy to be added to a reader's repertoire to meet the need for additional skills.

It is not realistic to expect a young reader to rely on pronunciation rules for too long, because in order to have a sufficient amount of information to pronounce most English words spontaneously, a reader would need to engage in an extensive rule learning program to master the hundred or so major and minor rules needed to fully explain the pronunciation of English words (Smith, 1973c,d). In a purely phonemic language system it is not necessary to learn an extensive number of pronunciation rules. English, however, is not a purely phonemic language (C. Chomsky, 1973).

In an analysis of the grapheme to phoneme correspondence of the 20000 most common words in English, Weir and Venezky (1973) found that English spelling was a composite of graphic, morphemic and phonemic patterns. The most regularity was not in the phonemic system but rather in the underlying morphophonemic system, upon which most lexical spelling is based; that is, words that look somewhat alike do not necessarily sound alike, such as sign/signal, signature/signify, hymn/hymnal, and vehicle/vehicular. These findings seem to support Chomsky and Halle's (1968) and C. Chomsky's (1973) contention that English spelling is the result of rules that represent lexical meanings more efficiently in visual forms than auditory ones. For instance English words that sound alike but are not related in meaning have clear visual differences in printed form: to/too/two, pair/pear/pare, lead/led, and nun/none.

It would appear that English orthography has sought to group the letters of many words of the language in meaning-relevant rather than sound-relevant ways. One advantage of this type of system is that a reader can form expectations as to where to look for maximum meaning. It has another advantage of helping a reader acquire new words composed of familiar morphemes, which he may or may not know how to pronounce, but will still be able to use effectively in reading. A system such as printed English also lessens the impact of dialect differences that arise from phonological rule variations. English orthography can be used in Britain, Australia, and the United States, regardless of how each set of readers pronounces the phonemes of English (C. Chomsky, 1973).

Reading programs that focus on skills resulting in the recoding of surface structures seem to assume that meaning will automatically be triggered via the auditory channel. Unfortunately, children with hearing losses or language deficiencies of any kind may not be able to supply the necessary prerequisites to succeed in a program that does not start with meaning.

Components of a Reading Program for Hearing-Impaired Children

A teacher who is responsible for helping a hearing-impaired child learn to read needs to examine his own definitions of reading and the reading process. He needs to judge his expectations in light of what he knows about language acquisition and development in general, as well as what he knows about reading as a psycholinguistic process. He needs to determine whether his priorities place meaning and purpose or the mastery of isolated skills and strategies at the center of learning to read. He needs to define meaning and purpose as related to reading skills and strategies (Olsen, 1973).

If a teacher believes that printed language is merely speech or signed English written down then he may initially provide a program that fosters the learning of strategies needed to recode surface structure forms from one mode to another with little or minimal regard for the interpretation of meaning. If, on the other hand, he believes that printed language is an independent comprehension mode, then he will provide assistance in learning strategies for decoding surface structure printed language forms into meaning. If he believes that learning to read will be influenced by developmental factors that are predictable he will strive to learn more about what the developmental stages of reading might be and how they might be manifested.

A teacher not only needs to decide on the instructional emphasis he will use, but he must also determine the types of reading activities and materials he will consider for each child's program.

For a child with a language deficiency of any kind it would seem appropriate to provide an integrated communication curriculum. Within the framework of such a curriculum a child's development would be charted in all areas. His individualized program would reflect his needs in all modes of communication. Activities designed to foster aural-oral language development and usage could be related to activities emphasizing reading development and usage. Learning to express ideas in drama or through creative and expository writing could grow out of reading experiences. If a child's language program in communication areas such as writing and spelling, reading, and speech and auditory training is not coordinated and not based on an overall language acquisition and development plan, then the child may spend much valuable time in fragmented learning experiences, which in some instances might be counterproductive to educational progress.

As a teacher plans a sequential program he should consider the scope of the program. Three major categories of reading materials with their associated general purposes can be identified as fundamental components in a program that aims to develop reading abilities. They are: (1) recreational reading, (2) functional reading, and (3) informational reading. Each of these areas is important and all of the developmental reading activities can be accomplished within these three components of a reading program. It is the teacher's responsibility to provide the appropriate materials and teaching strategies so that the young child will learn to read proficiently in all areas.

While the teacher and reader are engaged in recreational, functional, or informational reading, the teacher can utilize a variety of instructional strategies. He may initiate an oral discussion of the material to encourage the types of thinking he hopes to develop. He may lead a reader to examine the pictures, maps, or charts that accompany a sample of printed language. He may pose questions that stimulate thinking and lead to guessing possible story outcomes. He may encourage the child to make judgments or to focus attention on important details. At times he may need to encourage the reader to read without stopping in order to promote reading in thought units. He may help him learn to skim to get a general overview of the topic. Sometimes he will ask the reader to read orally instead of silently (Hart, 1963).

As a reader progresses through a reading program he will probably use teacher-prepared materials, adapted materials, basal readers, trade books, workbooks, magazines, newspapers, textbooks, and various other resources, not to mention practical reading materials such as signs, candy wrappers, games, menus, schedules, and coupons. The developmental sequence should influence the types of materials selected by reflecting the reader's increasing ability to: (1) use more complex and varied language, (2) deal with a broader range of content, (3) use print in a wider range of experiences, and (4) deal with increasingly more abstract interpretations of printed language (Hart, 1963).

Recreational Reading   The preparation to read for pleasure ought to be a planned part of every reader's program. The teacher needs to create in the young child an awareness of the use of prose and poetry for pleasure. This awareness needs to be transformed during a reader's school career into a later life appreciation for a good story or poem. If the school program is to foster a love of literature and the use of reading as a leisure time activity, then time needs to be provided for learning how to enjoy reading.

From an early age, some time should be set aside when the child may read what he wants without having to report or answer questions. Adults who read for pleasure do not want to be quizzed about what they read. If they thoroughly enjoy a novel, a short story, or an article they may seek out someone of similar tastes or interests to share it with. A child needs to have some of the same types of opportunities; times when he does not need to justify a selection or feel responsible for identifying details, remembering the sequence of events, or summarizing the main ideas.

Another basic activity in the recreational component involves teachers, parents, other adults, and older children reading to the child. The childhood classics, adult classics, contemporary literature, and poetry of all kinds should be introduced. Some will be read over and over again. During these sessions a child is exposed to the rich use of language supplemented by the reader's dramatic interpretations, the pictures, and timely explanations. Such activities acquaint the child or adolescent with the stories and characters that have become part of our culture, such as "The Three Bears," *The Adventures of Tom Sawyer,* and "The Ransom of Red Chief."

The role of the teacher or parent as a narrator or story teller cannot be underestimated. Before reading can become productive for the child, he needs to have experiences with language and books, language and magazines, language and comic strips, and so on. Too often a child is expected to undertake the task of learning how to read without enough input or active support from adults. Just as learning the enjoyment of talking to others requires active support from adults and older children, so does learning the enjoyment of reading.

Through artful storytelling sessions a child can learn about character roles, the use of dialogue, the sequencing of events, and the development of plots. A teacher may complement these sessions by showing movie or filmstrip versions of a story or relying on a television presentation. The young reader can bring a story to life himself by putting on a show with puppets or dolls. The use of drama may be a useful means for a reader to learn that the printed language and pictures on a page do not supply all of the information. The actors in a reader's production can be used to fill in what is not explicitly printed by inferring what lies between and beyond the lines of print.

Because of the English language limitations that many hearing-impaired children bring to the task of learning to read, commercial materials for recreational reading should be gradually introduced. In the beginning the teacher may need to prepare and adapt most, if not all, of the materials that are used by the child. Many of the stories in the basal reader can be used as recreational reading materials, but the teacher still needs to evaluate each story to determine what needs to be taught before the reader begins a story. This preliminary teaching may involve using the basal reader vocabulary and linguistic structures in experience charts or other contexts so that the items become familiar and the meaning of their use is understood. The teacher may also need to plan activities that will provide the child with experiences necessary to understand the concepts in a story.

If, for example, a teacher wants a child to read fairy tales in a basal reader, he must first supply basic information about fairy tales by reading some to the potential reader. In this way the teacher can introduce the child to the types of characters, plot development, settings, and vocabulary to be expected.

After the basic input stage the teacher can provide reading experiences, in which he will play an active role with the child, by preparing some stories that use language the child is capable of processing, or by controlling syntax and vocabulary to foster prediction. Props or pictures may serve as supportive references for use with tailor-made fairy tale booklets that could be presented through an experience chart format.

Next the teacher might prepare some familiar make-believe stories written in more complex language. A new story could be introduced, but written in language that the child can handle easily. In any instance where a child's reading abilities do not permit him to read the stories he wants to he should not be denied the opportunity of listening to someone else read that story to him.

At the input stage of a program for hearing-impaired children the teacher must always control the complexity of language forms, complementing stories with dramatic interpretations, pictures, or personal summaries and comments.

If the reader is at a level where he is able to decode primary level English and its discourse structures with ease, the teacher may provide more independent reading. The language in that independent reading should be congruent with the type of language a reader can best interpret using his own linguistic resources.

If a rich recreational reading component is not available at school or at home, then it is not to be expected that a reader will become an adult who enjoys reading for pleasure. The use of books for pleasure must be nurtured throughout the school years. The teacher must always find time to provide input and help so that the reader can learn to peruse stories and poems for himself. Listening to the teacher read a chapter a day or a special short story every week should be standard fare in all schools and classes.

Functional Reading   Each reading program must also provide opportunities for the hearing-impaired reader to learn how to read and use functional reading materials. Hart (1963) has defined functional reading as reading that takes place in order to foster some other activity. Many of the activities fostered by functional reading are non-reading activities. For example recipes are read to help us cook; advertisements and coupons are read to help us shop more economically; directions and instructions are read to help us use appliances, play games, or repair items; a sign may help us to avoid danger or to make a right turn.

The appropriate use of functional reading materials is as important as being able to read them. When planning the functional reading component of a program the teacher needs to consider such things as the circumstances under which the materials will be used, the format of the materials, and the experiential understandings that must support interpretation of the language forms. Each type of functional reading material has a unique format and language use. Tickets and theater programs, maps, catalogues, and job applications all serve different purposes, present information in different formats, and use different language forms.

If a teacher wants a teenager to learn how to read and fill out job applications, it would be wise to do more than rote drilling of responses for items such as *D.O.B.* and *Marital Status.* It might be useful for the teacher to start by simulating job interviews. From the interview experiences the reader and teacher could draw up a list of topics that employers think are important. The types of items that appear on actual job application forms could then be compared to the topics discussed. For example, *where you were born* and *when you were born* could be related to *Place of Birth* or *Birth Place* and *D.O.B.* or *Date of Birth.*

By approaching the functional reading task as something more than rote learning the student is afforded a better opportunity to make use of his general understandings about a piece of reading material. His expectations about what might appear on application forms may help him to read them better or at least ask the most appropriate questions in an interview situation. For some groups of students it might be worthwhile to compile a reference book of functional reading materials for post-school use.

Even at the preschool level the teacher can employ functional reading materials to carry out daily activities. Job charts, picture schedules, attendance charts, and picture recipes can all be used to foster reliance on printed material.

For the student who needs a curriculum that emphasizes the knowledge and strategies to cope with persisting life problems, the major component of the reading program may be learning to read and to use functional reading materials.

Informational Reading   Informational or subject matter reading is needed for many school, occupational, and social activities. It may be necessary to systematically prepare a reader to make use of printed materials in each of the subject matter areas, because each area has its own technical vocabulary, special syntactic styles, text formats, and reference skills (K. Goodman, 1972). Learning to use the daily newspaper and weekly magazines would be a form of social information reading that should receive special attention.

The teacher may begin this type of reading program by the use of experience charts or teacher-made reports that grow out of meaningful experiences such as a science experiment. The teacher can control for style, format, discourse structure, as well as for semantic relationships, syntactic structure, and vocabulary. The charts could then be used for listening exercises, oral reading, silent reading, or could even be transformed into a textbook or newspaper article format.

Sometimes charts are written about familiar topics so that confusion about content does not deter the child from reading. When this approach is planned the teacher should use the chart presentation to introduce new linguistic forms or functions, to introduce new technical lexical items, or to have the reader interpret the content in a new way. Care should always be taken to avoid the introduction of new forms, content, or lexicon all at the same time.

Special preparation may be needed to help a reader interpret math problems with understanding. The teacher may need to study the language forms and the concepts in math and then devise experiences to help the reader understand the meaning of linguistic constructions peculiar to math operations. If the teacher expects to help a reader learn to use reading strategies of different types then she must remember to control the forms and content of materials so that the reader can use what he knows to learn what he does not know.

A reader also needs to learn that in some informational reading situations he need only skim materials to get a general idea of the topic or topics covered, whereas in another instance, he will need to search for important details. A skillful teacher plans exercises to foster flexible approaches to reading materials based on the purpose of the assignment. In the initial stages the teacher has to actively support a reader as he learns new strategies to cope with the new kinds of materials, new language forms, new content, and new purposes for reading. Sending a reader in the developmental stage off to tackle independent reading too soon may lead to failure. The teacher must have enough information to recognize potential for failure by observing each reader for a time before letting him try a task on his own so that he will have a clear notion of the causes of the child's difficulty with particular materials. A child does not learn to read by having a teacher put red XXs or question marks on his papers. The teacher must observe and collect information to determine why an error or incorrect decision was made and then seek ways to help the reader learn what he must know to appropriately complete assignments. The reading teacher's primary responsibility is to find ways to help children learn to read, not to determine how many wrong answers they have made.

There will be times when a teacher will incorporate recreational, functional, and informational reading materials into a single unit of study. For example a science unit on birds would require use of science texts or other references to find the answers to questions posed at the beginning of the unit. Stories and poems could be selected from the basal reader series and library books could be considered. Directions could be used to build a bird feeder so that birds could be observed from the school room window. Learning to read and using reading go hand in hand, just as learning to talk and talking happen simultaneously.

Planning a Reading Program For Hearing-Impaired Children

If a reader is expected to become a wise user of printed language, reading should not be viewed as an isolated subject or be restricted to a sterile activity that occurs at a set time each day with the same types of materials and routines for checking comprehension (Burke, 1972). A reading program cannot be limited to the mastery of a single set of skills, nor can experience be limited to a single reading series or set of textbooks. The reading program for a hearing-impaired reader has to include a whole array of reading materials and activities (Hart, 1963). The reader deserves an individually designed reading program in the areas of recreational, functional, and informational reading that will take into account: (a) his personal interests and preferences, (b) his personal experiences and concept development, (c) his linguistic development and modes of communication, and (d) his cognitive development. The reading program should use the composite of this information to plan and execute an appropriate reading program.

Teachers should always keep in mind that they must do more than teach a child how to read; they must inspire him to want to read. The reader himself will then learn what, why, and where to read (Hart, 1963).

Personal Interests and Preferences A teacher who is aware of the personal interests and preferences of a child can often use them as powerful means for helping him learn to read. A skillful teacher identifies interests and preferences early and finds ways to incorporate them into the reading program, using them to motivate the child to become actively involved in learning to read.

For a child who loves baseball, learning to read the names of ball players and the positions they play may be easier than learning to read the vocabulary for a basal reader of low interest. Reading materials for a child who wants to read about baseball might be developed to reflect what happened during a game or a particular player. Real or teacher made-up events could be acted out with cardboard players, discussed, and written up by the teacher for the child to read. In the case of reporting actual events the teacher might try to emulate the discourse structure and style of a newspaper account. If the topic is to revolve around the accomplishments of a single player, then a story structure might more appropriately be employed. Each episode could become a chapter, with the introduction written later along with the conclusion, so that all materials could be compiled into a booklet.

To give a child the opportunity to broaden his knowledge in an area of interest the teacher can expose him to a wide variety of printed materials, such as library books, newspapers, and magazines, depending upon the age and abilities of the reader. The child might be encouraged to begin a scrapbook or a collection of baseball cards or to set up a bulletin board display. The teacher might read "Casey at the Bat" to him or teach him "Take Me Out to the Ball Game"; or read him the biography of a famous ball player, a chapter at a time. The possibilities are limitless.

A reader's personal interests should be taken into consideration, regardless of the instructional area or level of instruction, because of the powerful role interest can play in facilitating mental processes. A skillful teacher should be able to teach all of the different reading strategies and to use all types of reading experiences regardless of the topic or materials. It may take more planning and preparation to approach reading instruction in this way, but it may accomplish more than the mechanical reading of a series of stories that are of little or not interest to the reader or to the teacher; or that are beyond the sphere of experience or linguistic performance level of the reader.

Personal Experiences and Concepts   Even if a hearing-impaired reader has a high level of interest in a topic, has had a variety of experiences relevant to a topic, and has developed elaborate concepts from his experiences, he may not have the facility to handle his knowledge in any verbal modality.

A hearing-impaired child has experiences, but what he does, sees, hears, feels, and thinks about during or after the experience may not be coded verbally; or, if what he experiences is coded verbally, the coding may be generic, not specific. A vocabulary item such as *happy* might be used generically to code a range of feelings from joy, ecstasy, or surprise to satisfaction. With no convenient verbal representation of a word or idea stored in long-term memory, that word or idea in its printed, spoken, or signed form will not initiate a responsive match for the child.

Often a teacher needs to begin exploration of what a child knows about a topic with verbal inquiries or probes, supplementing these with pictures or other nonverbal probes. Pictures can elicit acting out or illustration of an experience. The dramatization or illustrations may or may not need or have verbal accompaniment, and may or may not be communicatively adequate, depending upon the child's capabilities.

It is imperative that a teacher remember that a nonverbal experience cannot be easily tapped and incorporated into the reading process. Too often a teacher and child carry on elaborate discussions that involve little substantive linguistic information that can subsequently be used in the reading process. The teacher needs to determine the parameters of a child's nonverbal and verbal understandings as objectively as possible in order to plan how to relate nonverbal experiences to similar, verbal experiences so that an appropriate language base can be developed. Often appropriate language will need to be developed before using the printed version of the language with a child. In a program that is comprehension centered, reading instruction must start where the reader is, both linguistically and experientially (K. Goodman, 1972). The teacher needs to provide activities and materials that will help the child make the most effective use of his linguistic competence by relating that competance to his verbal conceptual development.

For example a teacher may be working with a little girl who loves to play with dolls, but has not necessarily coded her play experiences verbally. The task of the teacher will be to provide the child with language she needs to use as she plays, and the language she needs to talk with others about what she does with her doll. The teacher, by interacting with the child, will be able to supply the language input and to note the child's apparent concepts, interests, and spontaneously used language as well.

The teacher might set up a story situation by putting red dots on the doll so that the child could act out what she would do with her "sick baby." The teacher might need to encourage the child to supplement her drama with verbalization. Then the teacher and child could talk about what had happened and go through the drama again. Next a chart story might be prepared with sentences and pictures that reflect the child's ideas, incorporating as much of her language as possible. A series of doll adventures and stories could be planned to ensure the use of familiar vocabulary items in all of the experiences.

The doll episodes might be based on stories that occur in a basal reading series that is planned for future use. These play and experience chart activities would constitute the preliminary teaching of experiences, vocabulary, and linguistic constructions that will occur later in the reading series.

Language Abilities   Too often a hearing-impaired child is said to have a reading problem, when in fact the problem is really language based (Smith, 1975). The role of a child's linguistic competence in learning to read cannot be underestimated. His ability to learn to read and to progess in reading depends upon his use of linguistic abilities to organize visual perceptions into meaningful units such as words, phrases, and larger units (K. Goodman, 1973c). The teacher who assumes the responsibility of helping a hearing-impaired child learn to read must not only be aware of the relationship of language to experiences and concepts but also of the role that linguistic structures play in perceiving meaning from printed language (Biemiller, 1970).

No one can assume that helping a child with a hearing loss learn to read can be done without understanding language—how it functions, how it develops, how the various modes interrelate, and how language relates to the reading process. The basic assumptions upon which most reading programs for normally hearing children are based may not be appropriate assumptions to use in designing a program for a hearing-impaired reader. It is true that a hearing-impaired reader can learn to recognize individual words by using contextual cues, picture cues, configuration cues, phonetic analysis, structural analysis, and the cues of special word features; however, recognition cannot be equated with the facility to know what the word means in a given context (Hart, 1963).

A reading program that begins with skill acquisition, whether it is a phonic-phonemic or sight word approach, supposes that the reader will recognize words and synthesize them into sentences once they are spoken. This assumes the reader will have had enough experience with those words to know their various functions and meanings. A first grader with normal language realized that *ball* may mean *a toy, a dance,* or *a good time,* depending upon the context. On the other hand, a hearing-impaired child may or may not even know that some of the round objects he plays with are not *balls,* but are called *marbles.* The probability that he would know the other uses and meanings of the word *ball* without special preparation is very unlikely.

The teacher must determine which reading strategies to develop at any given time with any given piece of material so that the child's use of a particular strategy will lead to meaningful interpretation of a message. Being able to say words from a printed page does not demonstrate anything except pronunciation abilities (Lefevre, 1973). Being able to match printed words to picture referents does not ensure that the child will be able to understand the different semantic roles a word might assume or the different syntactic structures in which it might appear. For example, the word *car* can function semantically in a variety of roles: *The car rolled over the cliff. John won a car. Mary wrecked her car. Tommy made a model car. My car is red. That car won the 500 at Indy. My sweater is in the car. His car is his castle. The car's engine overheated.*

The teacher of a hearing-impaired reader and the reader himself need to be aware from the beginning that learning to read is much more than learning to respond to individual printed words with speech or drawings. All language uses are predicated on meaning and purpose, which implies the use of words in appropriate discourse structures. A teacher must be able to justify the skills he is teaching in terms of how they facilitate the retrieval of meaning. The strategies that facilitate only the recoding of print to another mode will often not facilitate the retrieval or reconstruction of meaning for a hearing-impaired reader.

In order to plan a program for any reader the teacher needs to have a detailed understanding of a child's linguistic abilities (Y. Goodman, 1972). The evaluation strategy suggested in Table 7 in Chapter 5 of this book should provide such information. The teacher must have performance information to be able to select or prepare materials that will allow the reader to practice on materials that are written so that he potentially would be able to understand the message (Barr, 1972). The teacher must capitalize on what a reader knows linguistically to help him learn to hypothesize appropriately about meaning of new vocabulary items, new linguistic structures, or to gain new content information (Miller, 1973). In cases where a teacher wants to introduce new linguistic forms that the reader is acquiring but has not yet developed control over, he will want to use content and vocabulary items that are well known to the reader so that his ability to interpret the new linguistic structures will be enhanced.

Teachers should rely on a variety of methods for checking on comprehension. They should be aware that a reader may at times comprehend what he has read but not comprehend a question that has been asked about the reading. To avoid this problem, teachers can use any or all of the following (1) dramatization, (2) oral questions and discussion, (3) drawing pictures to illustrate parts of the story or a whole sequence of events, (4) paraphrasing, (5) workbook assignments, (6) teacher-made exercises and tests, and (7) formal tests (Hart, 1963).

The *Reading Miscue Inventory* (Y. Goodman and Burke, 1972; Goodman and Goodman, 1977) is an excellent method of collecting information relevant to the strategies a child uses as he reads. The child is given a passage to read and is told that he will have to read it out loud without any assistance. The teacher then notes: (a) the types of substitutions the reader makes and whether or not he goes back to correct them; (b) whether or not the substitutions are syntactically appropriate, (whether the reader substitutes a noun for a noun or a verb for a verb); (c) whether or not the substitutions are semantically appropriate, such as *woman* for *lady,* not *woman* for *wooden.* The miscues are also checked to see whether the reader is substituting words that look alike, such as *start* for *stay,* or words that sound alike. The teacher also notes omissions and intrusions made by the reader, which are evaluated relative to their semantic and syntactic appropriateness.

At the conclusion of the passage the reader is asked to tell in his own words what the passage was about. This summary coupled with the oral reading information can help a teacher formulate a description of the strategies a reader uses as he reads and the ability he has to comprehend what he has read. A reader who substitutes words that are appropriate and do not change meaning substantially, such as reading aloud *the woods* for *the forest,* is processing printed language differently from a child who substitutes words that look somewhat alike but are semantically inappropriate. The first child seems to be reading for meaning, whereas the second child may be calling out words one at a time rather than seeking the meaning relationships among words.

It is important for a teacher to observe a reader in as many ways as possible so that the teacher can better understand how he goes about reading. If a teacher is going to help a child learn to read, then he needs to know as much as possible about what the child already knows and about how he puts his knowledge into action.

Cognitive Development A teacher also needs to observe a reader and to form notions about his verbal and nonverbal problem solving abilities. These findings will be important to him as he plans reading activities.

Reading is thinking (Neisser, 1967). It is the interpretation of material that involves the integration of meaning by using analytical, integrative, and evaluative thinking (Ruddell and Bacon, 1972). The interpretation of meaning is constantly being monitored and modified as new information is obtained and incorporated. As a child develops, his ability to use the thinking process in different ways should be encouraged.

During the early years of reading development the reader is often limited to literal comprehension. At this stage he will be intent on getting the primary, direct, common sense meaning of a sentence, phrase, word,

Table 15.   Planning guide for reading programming

I.   Summarize general information on reading activities a reader normally engages in outside of school, including homework. (This information may be obtained by parent interview or survey, child interview or survey.)
   A.   Recreational reading
      1.   Note the types of reading activities: independent guided activities (by whom), input activities (provided by whom)
      2.   Note the major topics of interest
      3.   Note types of materials used: story books, comic books, etc., that are unaltered, adapted, or especially developed
      4.   Note the types or sources of materials
      5.   Note the types of formats, discourse structure, and style represented
      6.   Other recreational reading
   B.   Functional reading
      1.   Note the types of reading activities: independent, guided activities (by whom), input activities (provided by whom)
      2.   Note the major uses of functional reading
      3.   Note the types of materials used: directions, recipes, maps, schedules, etc., that are unaltered, adapted, or especially developed
      4.   Note the sources of materials
      5.   Other functional reading
   C.   Informational reading
      1.   Note the types of reading activities: independent, guided activities (by whom), input activities (provided by whom)
      2.   Note the most common topics and purposes for informational reading
      3.   Note the types of materials used: texts, newspapers, magazine articles, etc., that are unaltered, adapted, or especially developed
      4.   Note the sources of materials
      5.   Other informational reading
   D.   Describe how the foregoing information was obtained
II. Summarize general information on reading activities normally engaged in during the school day, including all class and non-class activities. (This information may be obtained by observing a child for a day or two and noting all uses of printed language, by surveying or interviewing a group of teachers who teach a child, or by asking the child directly.
   A.   Recreational reading
      1.   Note the types of reading activities: independent, guided activities (by whom and how), input activities (provided by whom)
      2.   Note the major topics of interest
      3.   Note the types of materials selected by the child or provided for him: straight commercial, adapted, especially developed
      4.   Note the types of and preference for different formats, discourse structures, and style.
      5.   Other in-school recreational reading

Table 15—continued

    B. Functional reading
- 1. Note the types of reading activities: independent, guided activities (by whom and how), input activities (provided by whom)
- 2. Note the major uses of functional reading
- 3. Note the types of materials used: staight commercial, adapted, especially developed
- 4. Note the types of formats, discourse structures, and styles represented
- 5. Other in-school functional reading

    C. Informational reading
- 1. Note the types of reading activities: independent, guided activities (by whom and how), input activities (provided by whom)
- 2. Note the most common topics and purposes
- 3. Note the types of materials: straight commercial, adapted, especially developed
- 4. Note the types of formats, discourse structures, and styles
- 5. Other in-school informational reading

    D. Describe how the foregoing information was obtained

III. Identify specific information about both the child and the course of study. (This information may be obtained by using formal instruments, teacher-made materials, teacher observation, teacher and child surveys, interviews and discussions, cumulative records, etc. The teachers manual for textbook and reading series is an excellent source of ideas for evaluating and planning in this area.)

    A. Note the interests and preferences in the areas of recreational, functional, and informational reading. Note the curricular interests and preferences of a reader. (Formal interest inventories are available.)

    B. Note the general attitudes toward reading. Note the specific attitudes toward recreational reading, functional reading, and informational reading.

    C. Note the concepts needed for comprehension and use of reading materials or curricular areas. Assess the child's conceptual development to ensure that appropriate experiences are introduced, developed, reviewed, or expanded in relation to concepts encountered in reading.

    D. Note the experiences needed to comprehend the content in selected reading materials. Assess the child's verbal and nonverbal understandings so that appropriate experiential activities can be introduced, developed, reviewed, or expanded in relation to concepts and language necessary for comprehension of reading.

IV. Describe the child's language performance to determine the language that needs to be introduced, developed, reviewed, or expanded in order to select commercially printed materials, adapt materials, or specially develop materials. (Chapter 5 of this text suggests evaluation strategies for this purpose.) Determine Abilities to Comprehend:

continued

Table 15—continued

    A. Paragraph level:
        1. Discourse structure rules
    B. Sentence level:
        1. Semantic relationships
        2. Syntactic rules
           a. phrase structure rules
           b. simple transformational rules
           c. complex transformational rules
    A. Lexical Level Expressions and Idioms and Vocabulary Items:
        1. Denotation
           a. primary definition
           b. secondary definition (s)
           c. synonyms and antonyms

V.

    A. Note the level and quality of comprehension abilities of a reader. (This information can be obtained by interacting with a reader as he reads, and by evaluating his summaries, dramatizations, illustrations, and explanations.) Identify literal comprehension abilities. Identify interpretive or inferential comprehension abilities. Identify critical and evaluative comprehension abilities.

    B. Determine familiar types of discourse structures, formats, and styles and those that need to be introduced, developed, reviewed, or expanded. (This information can be obtained by reviewing materials used previously, teacher interview, surveys, or by interacting with or observing a reader using a variety of materials.)

    C. Identify reading strategies needed for the course of study and evaluate the reader's ability to use the various strategies. (The *Reading Miscue Inventory* by Goodman and Burke, 1972, is one formal instrument that can be used to identify reading strategies.) Use of appropriate speed for purpose and material. Use of cues (appropriateness of application):
        1. Situational and environmental cues
        2. Discourse structure cues
        3. Format cues
        4. Sentence level cues
           a. syntactic cues
           b. semantic cues
           c. prosodic cues
        5. Word cues
           a. sight words
           b. phonemic cues

---

or idea. His ability to synthesize, generalize, and sequence materials will depend primarily upon information that is directly available in print and closely related to his own direct experiences.

As a child matures, his general linguistic and reading abilities develop, as well as his cognitive abilities. He begins to demonstrate more interpretative comprehension. He is able to supply, anticipate, or infer meanings that have not been directly presented in print. A skillful teacher can use printed materials to foster ability to use language to generalize and to reason cause and effect. A child can be helped to speculate about what happens between stated events and predict what will occur next, to identify the main ideas and the significant details. He will begin to be able to compare and contrast stories, characters, and authors' styles. At an even more advanced level a reader will begin to recognize an author's purpose, subtle humor, and the motives of different characters. Eventually he will be able to integrate more of his own personal experiences with what he reads, which should permit him to empathize, form sensory images, and experience emotional reactions.

Some students will not progress much beyond the basic literal interpretation stage; others will progress to the point of being able to engage in critical reading of materials, of being able to make personal judgments and evaluations of what they read. Each child's program must make provisions for a reader to realize his maximum potential. A program that sets goals too high, thus promoting failure, is as harmful as a program that sets goals too low.

Guide to Planning Reading Program

A teacher of reading or a teaching team needs to gather a wide range of information to use in establishing general yearly and quarterly objectives. All of the information on the child, the curriculum, and the materials can then be used by the teacher to make out monthly, weekly, and daily plans for reading. The topics listed in Table 15 are particularly critical to consider if information essential to planning programs for individual readers is to be collected. Periodically during the year this information would need to be updated, and a year-end summary ought to be written for each of the major topics.

SUMMARY

Learning to read is a complex and dynamic process. It should never be viewed as a daily period where students read a story and answer questions. Teachers and parents can play critical roles during the development of a reader's proficiency. They can actively participate with the reader by introducing him to new strategies and new materials and by coaching him as he attempts to incorporate these strategies in his approach to printed language.

To date no single reading series or kit has packaged all that a hearing-impaired reader needs to experience in order to learn to read, which means that the teacher or parent who wants a rich, appropriate program will have to continue to adapt and develop materials. At every step of the way, a teacher of reading must seek ways to incorporate what a child knows about the world and about language into every type of reading experience as he helps him learn to read.

REFERENCES

Abrahamson, A. 1977. Child Language: Interdisciplinary Guide to Theory and Research. University Park Press, Baltimore.

Akmajian, A., and F. Henry. 1975. An Introduction to the Principles of Transformational Syntax. MIT Press, Cambridge, Ma.

Allen, P. 1972. What teachers of reading should know about the writing system. In R. Hodges and E. Rudorf (eds.), Language and Learning to Read, pp. 87–99. Houghton and Mifflin Co., New York.

Anderson, J. 1971. The Grammar of Case. Cambridge University Press, Cambridge, England.

Anglin, J. 1977. Words, Object, and Conceptual Development. Norton, New York.

Anthony, D. 1971. Signing Essential English, Vols. 1 and 2. Educational Division, Anaheim Union School District, Anaheim. Ca.

Arndt, W. 1977. A psychometric evaluation of the Northwestern Syntax Screening Test. J. Speech Hear. Disord. 42: 315–319.

Asher, J., and R. Garcia. 1969. The optimal age to learn a foreign language. Mod. Lang. J. 53: 334–341.

Austin, J. 1962. How to Do Things with Words. Harvard University Press, Cambridge, Ma.

Bach, E. 1968. Nouns and noun phrases. In E. Bach and R. Harms (eds.), Universals in Linguistic Theory, pp. 90–122. Holt, Rinehart, and Winston, New York.

Bach, E. 1974. Syntactic Theory. Holt, Rinehart, and Winston, New York.

Baer, D., and D. Guess. 1971. Receptive training of adjectival inflections in mental retardation. J. Appl. Behav. Anal. 4: 129–139.

Baer, D., and D. Guess. 1973. Teaching productive noun suffixes to severely retarded children. Am. J. Ment. Defic. 77: 498–505.

Baird, R. 1972. On the role of change in imitation-comprehension-production test results. J. Verb. Learn. Verb. Behav. 11: 474–477.

Bales, R. 1950. Interaction Process Analysis: A Method for the Study of Small Groups. Addison-Wesley, Cambridge, Ma.

Balow, I., and R. Brill. 1975. An evaluation of reading and academic achievement levels of 19 graduating classes of the California School for the Deaf, Riverside. Volta Rev. 77: 255–266.

Barr, R. 1972. Perceptual development in the reading process. In R. Hodges and E. Rudorf (eds.), Language and Learning to Read, pp. 131–139. Houghton and Mifflin Co., New York.

Barry, K. 1899. The Five-Slate System: A System of Objective Language Teaching. Sherman and Co., Philadelphia.

Bartel, N., D. Bryen, and S. Keehn. 1973. Language comprehension in the moderately retarded child. Except. Child 40: 375–382.

Barton, E. 1970. Inappropriate speech in a severely retarded child: A case study in language conditioning and generalization. J. Appl. Behav. Anal. 3: 299–307.

Bates, E. 1976a. Pragmatics and sociolinguistics in child language. In D. Morehead and A. Morehead (eds.), Normal and Deficient Child Language, pp. 411–463. University Park Press, Baltimore.

Bates, E. 1976b. Language and Context: The Acquisition of Pragmatics. Academic Press, New York.

Bates, E., L. Benigni, I. Bretherton, L. Camioni, and V. Volterra. 1977. From gesture to the first word: On cognitive and social prerequisites. In M. Lewis and L. Rosenblum (eds.), Interaction, Conversation, and the Development of Language, pp. 247–307. John Wiley and Sons, New York.

Bates, E., and J. Johnston. 1977. Pragmatics in normal and deficient child language. Paper presented at the ASHA annual convention, Chicago.

Bellugi, U. 1974. Some language comprehension tests. In C. Lavetelli (ed.), Language Training in Early Childhood Education, pp. 157–169. University of Illinois Press, Urbana.

Bellugi, U., and S. Fischer. 1972. A comparison of sign language and spoken language. Cognition 1: 173–200.

Bellugi, U., and E. Klima. 1975. Aspects of sign language and its structure. In J. Kavanagh and J. Cutting (eds.), The Role of Speech in Language, pp. 171–203. MIT Press, Cambridge, Ma.

Bellugi, U., E. Klima, and P. Siple. 1974. Remembering in signs. Cognition 3: 93–125.

Bennett, C., 1973. A four-and-a-half year old as a teacher of her hearing-impaired sister: A case study. J. Commun. Disord. 6: 67–75.

Bennett, C., and D. Ling. 1972. Teaching a complex verbal response to a hearing-impaired child. J. Appl. Behav. Anal. 5: 321–327.

Bennett, J. 1933. 'To have' and 'to be' in the primary grades. Volta Rev. 35: 254–258.

Berger, S. 1972. A clinical program for developing multimodal language responses with atypical deaf children. In J. McLean, D. Yoder, and R. Schiefelbusch (eds.), Language Intervention with the Retarded: Developing Strategies, pp. 212–235. University Park Press, Baltimore.

Berko, J. 1958. The child's learning of English morphology. Word 14: 150–177.

Berko Gleason, J. 1967. Do children imitate? In Proceedings of International Conference on Oral Education of the Deaf, pp. 1441–1448. Alexander Graham Bell Assoc., Washington, D.C.

Berko Gleason, J. 1973. Code switching in children's language. In T. Moore (ed.), Cognitive Development and the Acquisition of Language, pp. 159–168. Academic Press, New York.

Berko Gleason, J. 1975. Fathers and other strangers: Men's speech to young children. In D. Dato (ed.), Developmental Psycholinguistics: Theory and Applications, pp. 289–297. Georgetown University Press, Washington, D.C.

Berry, M., and R. Erickson. 1973. Speaking rate: Effects on children's comprehension of normal speech. J. Speech Hear. Res. 16: 367–374.

Berry-Luterman, L., and A. Bar. 1971. The diagnostic significance of sentence repetition for language-impaired children. J. Speech Hear. Disord. 36: 29–39.

Bever, T. 1970. The cognitive basis for linguistic structures. In J. Hayes (ed.), Cognition and the Development of Language, pp. 279–352. John Wiley and Sons, New York.

Bever, T. 1972. Perceptions, thought, and language. In R. Freedle and J. Carroll (eds.), Language Comprehension and the Acquisition of Knowledge, pp. 99–112. V. H. Winston and Sons, Washington, D.C.

Biemiller, A. 1970. The development of the use of graphic and contextual information as children learn to read. Read. Res. Quart. 6: 75–96.

Bierwisch, M. 1970. Semantics. In J. Lyons (ed.), New Horizons in Linguistics, pp. 161–185. Penguin, Baltimore.

Blackwell, P., and E. Engen. 1976. A language curriculum for handicapped learners. In F. Withrow and C. Nygren (eds.), Language, Materials, and Curriculum Management for the Handicapped Learner, pp. 34–51. Charles E. Merrill Publishing Co., Columbus, Oh.

Blank, M., and F. Solomon. 1968. A tutorial language program to develop abstract thinking in socially disadvantaged preschool children. Child Dev. 39: 379–390.

Blasdell, R., and P. Jensen. 1970. Stress and word position as determinants of imitation in first-language learners. J. Speech Hear. Disord. 13: 193–202.

Bliss, L., D. Allen, and K. Wrasse. 1977. A story completion approach as a measure of language development in children. J. Speech Hear. Res. 20: 358–372.

Bloom, L. 1967. A comment on Lee's Developmental sentence types: A method for comparing normal and deviant syntactic development. J. Speech Hear. Disord. 32: 294–296.

Bloom, L. 1970. Language Development: Form and Function in Emerging Grammars. MIT Press, Cambridge, Ma.

Bloom, L. 1973. One Word at a Time. Mouton, The Hague.

Bloom, L., L. Hood, and P. Lightbown. 1974. Imitation in language development: If, when and why. Cog. Psychol. 6: 380–420.

Bloom, L., and M. Lahey. 1978. Language Development and Language Disorders. John Wiley and Sons, New York.

Bloom, L., P. Lightbown, and L. Hood. 1975. Structure and variation in child language. Monogr. Soc. Res. Child Dev. 38: No. 2.

Bloom, L., P. Miller, and L. Hood. 1975. Variation and reduction as aspects of competence in language. In A. Pick (ed.), Minnesota Symposium on Child Psychology, Vol. 9, pp. 3–55. University of Minnesota Press, Minneapolis.

Bloom, L., L. Rocissano, and L. Hood. 1976. Adult-child discourse: Developmental interaction between information processing and linguistic knowledge. Cog. Psychol. 8: 521–552.

Bloomfield, L. 1933. Language. Holt, Rinehart, and Winston, New York.

Bloomfield, L., and C. Barnhart. 1961. Let's Read: A Linguistic Approach. Wayne State University Press, Detroit.

Bochner, J. 1976. An evaluation of a computerized verb drill program designed for deaf young adults. Teach. Engl. Deaf 3: 19–28.

Bohannan, J. 1975. The relationship between syntax and discrimination and sentence imitation in children. Child Dev. 46: 444–451.

Bondurant, J. 1977. An analysis of mothers' speech provided to children with normal language as compared to mothers' speech provided to children with delayed language. Unpublished doctoral dissertation, University of Cincinnati, Cincinnati, Oh.

Bonvillian, J. 1974. Word coding and recall in deaf and hearing students. Unpublished doctoral dissertation, Stanford University, Stanford, Ca.

Boutte, J. 1975. A syntactical analysis of the oral language of ten black hearing impaired and ten black normal hearing adolescents. Unpublished master's thesis, University of Cincinnati, Cincinnati, Oh.

Bower, T. 1974. Development in Infancy. W. H. Freeman and Co., San Francisco.

Bowerman, M. 1975. Commentary on L. Bloom, P. Lightbown, and L. Hood,

Structure and variation in child language, pp. 80–90. Monogr. Soc. Res. Child Dev. 38: No. 2.

Bowerman, M. 1976. Semantic factors in the acquisition of rules for word use and sentence construction. In D. Morehead and A. Morehead (eds.), Normal and Deficient Child Language, pp. 99–179. University Park Press, Baltimore.

Bown, J., and M. Mecham. 1961. The assessment of verbal language development in deaf children. Volta Rev. 63: 228–230.

Braine, M. 1976. Children's first word combinations. Monogr. Soc. Res. Child Dev. 41: No. 1.

Brannon, J. 1968. Linguistic word classes in the spoken language of normal, hard-of-hearing, and deaf children. J. Speech Hear. Res. 11: 279–287.

Brannon, J., and T. Murry. 1966. The spoken syntax of normal, hard-of-hearing, and deaf children. J. Speech Hear. Res. 9: 604–610.

Brasel, K., and S. Quigley. 1977. Influence of certain language and communication environments in early childhood on the development of language in deaf individuals. J. Speech Hear. Res. 20: 95–107.

Bricker, D. 1972. Imitative sign training as a facilitator of word-object association with low-functioning children. Am. J. Ment. Def. 76: 509–516.

Bricker, D., L. Vincent-Smith, and W. Bricker. 1973. Receptive vocabulary: Performances and selected strategies of delayed and nondelayed toddlers. Am. J. Mental Def. 77: 579–584.

Bricker, W., and D. Bricker. 1974. An early language training strategy. In R. Schiefelbusch and L. Lloyd (eds.), Language Perspectives—Acquisiton, Retardation, and Intervention, pp. 431–468. University Park Press, Baltimore.

Broen, P. 1972. The verbal environment of the language-learning child. Monogr. ASHA 17: December.

Brown, H. 1971. Children's comprehension of relativized English sentences. Child Dev. 42: 1923–1936.

Brown, R. 1973. A First Language: The Early Stages. Harvard University Press, Cambridge, Ma.

Brown, R., and U. Bellugi. 1964. Three processes in the children's acquisition of syntax. Harvard Educ. Rev. 34: 133–151.

Brown, R., and M. Ford. 1961. Address in American English. J. Abnorm. Soc. Psychol. 62: 375–385.

Brown, R., and C. Fraser. 1963. The acquisition of syntax. In C. Cofer and B. Musgrave (eds.), Verbal Behavior and Learning, pp. 158–201. McGraw-Hill Book Co., New York.

Brown, R., and A. Gilman. 1960. The pronouns of power and solidarity. In T. Sebeok (ed.), Style in Language, pp. 252–276. MIT Press, Cambridge, Ma.

Bruner, J. 1974. From communication to language; A psychological perspective. Cognition 3: 255–287.

Bruner, J. 1975. The ontogenesis of speech acts. J. Child Lang. 2: 1–19.

Bruner, J. 1977. Early social interaction and language acquisition. In H. Schaffer (ed.), Studies in Mother-Infant Interaction, pp. 271–290. Academic Press, London.

Buchanan, C. 1963. Programmed Reading Series. Sullivan Associates, New York.

Buckler, Sr. M. 1968. Expanding language through patterning. Volta Rev. 70: 89–96.

Buium, N., J. Rynders, and J. Turnure. 1974. Early maternal linguistic environment of normal and Down's syndrome language-learning children. Am. J. Ment. Def. 29: 52–58.

Burke, C. 1972. The language process: Systems or systemic? In R. Hodges and E. Rudorf (eds.), Language and Learning to Read. Houghton Mifflin Co., New York.

Burke, C., and K. Goodman. 1970. When a child reads: A psycholinguistic analysis. Elem. Eng. 47: 121–129.

Burroughs, J. 1969. A study of sentence comprehension in hearing and deaf children. Unpublished doctoral dissertation, Vanderbilt University, Nashville, Tn.

Buswell, G. 1970. Reading sentences. In A. Blumenthal (ed.), Language and Psychology. John Wiley and Sons, New York.

Carr, M. 1971. Communicative behavior of three and four year old deaf children. Unpublished doctoral dissertation, Teachers College, Columbia University, New York.

Carrier, J. 1976. Application of a nonspeech language system with the severely language handicapped. In L. Lloyd (ed.), Communication Assessment and Intervention Strategies, pp. 523–548. University Park Press, Baltimore.

Carroll, J. 1972. Defining language comprehension: Some speculations. In R. Freedle and J. Carroll (eds.), Language Comprehension and the Acquisition of Knowledge, pp. 1–29. V. H. Winston and Sons, Washington, D.C.

Carrow, E. 1973. Test of Auditory Comprehension of Language. Learning Concepts, Austin, Texas.

Carrow, E. 1974. A test using elicited imitation in assessing grammatical structure in children. J. Speech Hear. Disord. 39: 437–444.

Carrow, E., and M. Mauldin. 1973. Children's recall of approximations to English. J. Speech Hear. Disord. 16: 201–212.

Carterette, E., and M. Jones. 1973. Phoneme and letter patterns in children's language. In K. Goodman (ed.), The Psycholinguistic Nature of the Reading Process, pp. 103–165. Wayne State University Press, Detroit.

Cartwright, R. 1962. Propositions. In R. Buller (ed.), Analytic Philosophy. Basil Blackwell and Mott, Oxford, England.

Cazden, C. 1965. Environmental assistance to the child's acquisition of syntax. Unpublished doctoral dissertation, Harvard University, Cambridge, Ma.

Cazden, C. 1968. The acquisition of noun and verb inflections. Child Dev. 39: 433–448.

Cazden, C. 1970. The situation: A neglected source of social class differences in language use. J. Soc. Issues 26: 35–60.

Central Institute for the Deaf. 1950. Language outline. Am. Ann. Deaf 95: 353–378.

Chafe, W. 1970. Meaning and the Structure of Language. University of Chicago Press, Chicago.

Chafe, W. 1972. Discourse structure and human knowledge. In R. Freedle and J. Carroll (eds.), Language Comprehension and the Acquisition of Knowledge, pp. 41–69. V. H. Winston and Sons, Washington, D.C.

Chafe, W. 1976. Givenness, contrastiveness, definiteness, subjects, topics, and point of view. In C. Li (ed.), Subject and Topic, pp. 25–55. Academic Press, New York.

Charrow, V. 1976. A psycholinguistic analysis of 'deaf English.' Sign Lang. Stud. 7: 139–150.

Charrow, V., and D. Fletcher. 1974. English as the second language of deaf children. Dev. Psychol. 10: 463–470.

Chomsky, C. 1969. The Acquisition of Syntax in Children from 5 to 10. MIT Press, Cambridge, Ma.

Chomsky, C. 1971. Write first, read later. Childhood Educ. 47: 296–299.

Chomsky, C. 1973. Reading, writing, and phonology. In F. Smith (ed.), Psycholinguistics and Reading, pp. 91–104. Holt, Rinehart, and Winston, New York.

Chomsky, N. 1957. Syntactic Structures. Mouton, The Hague.

Chomsky, N. 1965. Aspects of the Theory of Syntax. MIT Press, Cambridge, Ma.

Chomsky, N. 1966. Topics in the theory of generative grammar. In T. Sebeok (ed.), Current Trends in Linguistics, Vol. 3, pp. 1–60. Mouton, The Hague.

Chomsky, N. 1971. Deep structure, surface structure, and semantic representation. In D. Steinberg and L. Jakobovits (eds.), Semantics: An Interdisciplinary Reader in Philosophy, Linguistics, and Psychology, pp. 183–216. Cambridge University Press, Cambridge, England.

Chomsky, N. 1972. Language and Mind. 2nd ed. Harcourt Brace Jovanovich, New York.

Chomsky, N., and M. Halle. 1968. The Sound Pattern of English. Harper and Row Publishers, New York.

Chukovsky, K. 1968. From Two to Five. Translated by M. Morton. University of California Press, Berkeley.

Clark, E. 1970. How young children describe events in time. In G. Flores d'Arcais and W. Levelt (eds.), Advances in Psycholinguistics, pp. 275–284. North-Holland Publishing, Amsterdam.

Clark, E. 1971. On the acquisition of the meaning of *before* and *after*. J. Verb. Verb. Learn. Behav. 10: 266–275.

Clark, E. 1973a. How children describe time and order. In C. Ferguson and D. Slobin (eds.), Studies of Child Language Development, pp. 585–606. Holt, Rinehart, and Winston, New York.

Clark, E. 1973b. Non-linguistic strategies and the acquisition of word meanings. Cognition 2: 161–182.

Clark, E. 1973c. What's in a word? On the child's acquisition of semantics in his first language. In T. Moore (ed.), Cognitive Development and the Acquisition of Language, pp. 65–110. Academic Press, New York.

Clark, E. 1974. Some aspects of the conceptual basis for first language acquisition. R. Schiefelbusch and L. Lloyd (eds.), Language Perspectives—Acquisition, Retardation, and Intervention, pp. 105–128. University Park Press, Baltimore.

Clark, H., and E. Clark. 1977. Psychology and Language. Harcourt Brace Jovanovich, New York.

Clark, H., and S. Haviland. 1974. Psychological processes as linguistic explanation. In D. Cohen (ed.), Explaining Linguistic Phenomena, pp. 91–124. Hemisphere Publishing, Washington, D.C.

Clark, H., and P. Lucy. 1975. Understanding what is meant from what is said: A study in conversationally conveyed requests. J. Verb. Learn. Verb. Behav. 14: 56–72.

Clark, R. 1976. A report on methods of longitudinal data collections. J. Child Lang. 3: 437–459.

Clark, R. 1977. What's the use of imitation. J. Child Lang. 4: 341–358.

Cohen, L. 1974. Speech acts. In T. Sebeok (ed.), Current Trends in Linguistics, Vol. 12, pp. 173–208. Mouton, The Hague.

Cohen, S. 1967. Predictability of deaf and hearing story paraphrasing. J. Verb. Learn. Verb. Behav. 6: 916–921.

Collins, J. 1969. Communication between deaf children of preschool age and their mothers. Unpublished doctoral dissertation, University of Pittsburgh, Pittsburgh, Pa.

Collins-Ahlgren, M. 1974. Teaching English as a second language to young deaf children: A case study. J. Speech Hear. Disord. 39: 486–500.

Collins-Ahlgren, M. 1975. Language development of two deaf children. Am. Ann. Deaf 120: 524–539.

Collis, G. 1977. Visual co-orientation and maternal speech. In H. Schaffer (ed.), Studies in Mother-Infant Interaction, pp. 355–375. Academic Press, London.

Collis, G., and Schaffer, H. 1975. Synchronization of visual attention in mother-infant pairs. J. Child Psychol. Psychiatry 16: 315–320.

Conrad, R. 1964. Acoustic confusions in immediate memory. Br. J. Psychol. 55: 75–84.

Conrad, R. 1965. Order error in immediate recall of sequences. J. Verb. Learn. Verb. Behav. 4: 161–169.

Cooper, R. 1967. The ability of deaf and hearing children to apply morphological rules. J. Speech Hear. Res. 10: 77–86.

Cooper, R., and J. Rosenstein. 1966. Language acquisition of deaf children. Volta Rev. 68: 58–67.

Cooper, W. 1975. Selective adaptation to speech. In F. Restle, R. Shiffrin, N. Castellan, H. Lindman, and D. Pisoni (eds.), Cognitive Theory, Vol. 1, pp. 23–54. Lawrence Erlbaum Assoc., Hillsdale, N.J.

Corsaro, W. 1977. The clarification request as a feature of adult interactive styles with young children. Lang. Soc. 6: 183–207.

Corson, H. 1973. Comparing deaf children of oral deaf parents and deaf parents using manual communication with deaf children of hearing parents on academic, social, and communication functioning. Unpublished doctoral dissertation, University of Cincinnati, Cincinnati, Oh.

Costello, E. 1972. Appraising certain linguistic structures in the receptive sign language competence of deaf children. Unpublished doctoral dissertation, Syracuse University, Syracuse, N.Y.

Courtright, J., and I. Courtright. 1976. Imitative modeling as a theoretical base for instructing language-disordered children. J. Speech Hear. Disord. 19: 655–677.

Craig, W., and J. Collins. 1970. Analysis of communicative interaction in classes for deaf children. Am. Ann. Deaf 115: 79–85.

Critchley, E. 1967. Language development of hearing children in a deaf environment. Dev. Med. Child Neurol. 9: 274–280.

Croker, G., M. Jones, and M. Pratt. 1920, 1922, 1928. Language Stories and Drills, Books II, III, and IV. Vermont Printing Co., Brattleboro.

Cross, T. 1977. Mothers' speech adjustments: The contributions of selected child listener variables. In C. Snow and C. Ferguson (eds.), Talking to Children, pp. 151–188. Cambridge University Press, Cambridge, England.

Cruttenden, A. 1974. An experiment involving comprehension of intonation in children from 7 to 10. J. Child Lang. 1: 221–231.

Crystal, D., P. Fletcher, and M. Garman. 1976. The Grammatical Analysis of Language Disability: A Procedure for Assessment and Remediation. Elsevier-North Holland Publishing Co., New York.

Curtiss, S. 1977. Genie: A Psycholinguistic Study of a Modern-Day 'Wild Child.' Academic Press, New York.

Dale, P. 1976. Language Development: Structure and Function. Holt, Rinehart, and Winston, New York.

d'Arc, Sr. J. 1958. The development of connected language skills with emphasis on a particular methodology. Volta Rev. 60: 58–65.

Dato, D. 1972. The development of the Spanish verb phrase in children's second language learning. In P. Pimsleur and T. Quinn (eds.), The Psychology of Second Language Learning, pp. 35–44. Cambridge University Press, Cambridge, England.

Dato, D. 1975. On psycholinguistic universals in children's learning of Spanish. In D. Dato (ed.), Developmental Psycholinguistics: Theory and Applications, pp. 235–254. Georgetown University Press, Washington, D.C.

Davidson, A. 1975. Indirect speech acts and what to do with them. In M. Cole and J. Morgan (eds.), Syntax and Semantics, Vol. 3, pp. 143–185. Academic Press, New York.

Denton, D. 1966. A study in the educational achievement of deaf children. In Reports of the Proceedings of the 42nd Meeting of the Convention of American Instructors of the Deaf, pp. 428–433. U.S. Government Printing Office, Washington, D.C.

Dever, R. 1972. A comparison of the results of a revised version of Berko's test of morphology with the free speech of mentally retarded children. J. Speech Hear. Disord. 15: 169–178.

deVilliers, J., and P. deVilliers. 1973a. A cross sectional study of the acquisition of grammatical morphemes in child speech. J. Psycholinguist. Res. 2: 267–277.

deVilliers, J., and P. deVilliers. 1973b. Development of the use of word order in comprehension. J. Psycholinguist. Res. 2: 331–341.

deVilliers, J., and P. deVilliers. 1974. Competence and performance in child language: Are children really competent to judge? J. Child Lang. 1: 11–22.

deVilliers, P., and J. deVilliers. 1972. Early judgments of semantic and syntactic acceptability by children. J. Psycholinguist. Res. 1: 299–310.

Doll, E. 1965. Vineland Social Maturity Scale: Manual of Directions. American Guidance Service.

Dore, J. 1974. A pragmatic description of early language development. J. Psycholinguist. Res. 31: 343–350.

Dore, J., M. Franklin, R. Miller, and A. Ramer. 1976. Transitional phenomena in early language acquisition. J. Child Lang. 3: 13–28.

Drach, K. 1969. The language of the parent: A pilot study. Working Paper No. 14, Language Behavior Research Laboratory, University of California, Berkeley.

Dulay, H., and M. Burt. 1972. Goofing: An indication of children's second language learning strategies. Lang. Learn. 22: 235–251.

Dulay, J., and M. Burt. 1974a. Errors and strategies in child second language acquisition. TESOL Quart. 8: 129–136.

Dulay, H., and M. Burt. 1974b. Natural sequences in child second language acquisition. Lang. Learn. 24: 37–53.

Dulay, H., and M. Burt. 1975. A new approach to discovering universal strategies of child second language acquisition. In D. Dato (ed.), Developmental Psycholinguistics: Theory and Applications, pp. 209–233. Georgetown University Press, Washington, D.C.

Edwards, D. 1973. Sensory-motor intelligence and semantic relations in early child grammar. Cognition 2: 395–434.

Edwards, M. 1974. Perception and production in child phonology: The testing of four hypotheses. J. Child Lang. 1: 205–219.

Eimas, P. 1974. Linguistic processing of speech by young infants. In R. Schiefelbusch and L. Lloyd (eds.), Language Perspectives—Acquisition, Retardation, and Intervention, pp. 55–73. University Park Press, Baltimore.

Eimas, P. 1975. Speech perception in early infancy. In L. Cohen and P. Salapatek (eds.), Infant Perception: From Sensation to Cognition, Vol. 2, pp. 193–231. Academic Press, New York.

Eimas, P., E. Siqueland, P. Jusczyk, and J. Vigorito. 1971. Speech perception in infants. Science 171: 303–306.

Eisenberg, R. 1976. Auditory Competence in Early Life. University Park Press, Baltimore.

Elliott, L., I. Hirsh, and A. Simmons. 1967. Language of young hearing impaired children. Lang. Speech 10: 141–158.

Engler, L., E. Hannah, and T. Longhurst. 1973. Linguistic analysis of speech samples: A practical guide for clinicians. J. Speech Hear. Disord. 38: 192–204.

Erber, N., and C. Greer. 1973. Communication strategies used by teachers at an oral school for the deaf. Volta Rev. 75: 480–485.

Ervin-Tripp, S. 1964. Imitation and structural change in children's language. In E. Lenneberg (ed.), New Directions in the Study of Language, pp. 163–189. MIT Press, Cambridge, Ma.

Ervin-Tripp, S. 1970. Discourse agreement: How children answer questions. In J. Hayes (ed.), Cognition and the Development of Language, pp. 79–107. John Wiley and Sons, New York.

Ervin-Tripp, S. 1976. In Sybil there? The structure of some American English directives. Lang. Soc. 5: 25–66.

Falconer, G. 1962. Teaching machines for teaching reading. Volta Rev. 64: 389–392.

Farwell, C. 1975. The language spoken to children. Hum. Dev. 18: 288–309.

Fehr, J. 1962. Programming language for deaf children. Volta Rev. 64: 14–21.

Feldman, H. 1975. The development of a lexicon by deaf children of hearing parents or, there's more to language than meets the ear. Unpublished doctoral dissertation, University of Pennsylvania, College Park, Pa.

Fenson, L., and J. Kagan. 1976. The developmental progression of manipulative play in the first two years. Child Dev. 47: 232–236.

Ferguson, C. 1964. Baby talk in six languages. Am. Anthropol. 66: 103–114.

Ferguson, C. 1977. Baby talk as a simplified register. In C. Snow and C. Ferguson (eds.), Talking to Children, pp. 209–235. Cambridge University Press, Cambridge, England.

Fernald, C. 1972. Control of grammar in imitation, comprehension, and production: Problems of replication. J. Verb. Learn. Verb. Behav. 11: 606–613.

Fillmore, C. 1968. The case for case. In E. Bach and R. Harms (eds.), Universals in Linguistic Theory, pp. 1–88. Holt, Rinehart, and Winston, New York.

Fillmore, C. 1971a. Some problems for case grammar. In R. O'Brien (ed.), Linguistics: Development of the Sixties—Viewpoints for the Seventies, pp. 35–56. Georgetown Univ. Monogr. Ser. Lang. Linguist. No. 24.

Fillmore, C. 1971b. Types of lexical information. In D. Steinberg and L. Jakobovits (eds.), Semantics: An Interdisciplinary Reader in Philosophy, Linguistics, and Psychology, pp. 370–392. Cambridge University Press, Cambridge, England.

Fischer, S. 1973. Two processes of reduplication in American Sign Language. Found. Lang. 9: 469–480.

Fischer, S. 1975. Influences on word order change in American Sign Language. In C. Li (ed.), Word Order and Word Order Change, pp. 3–25. University of Texas Press, Austin.

Fishman, J. 1973. The sociology of language. In G. Miller (ed.), Communication, Language, and Meaning, pp. 268–279. Basic Books, New York.

Fitzgerald, E. 1943. As the deaf child travels the 'straight language' road. Except. Child 10: 108–115.

Fitzgerald, E. 1949. Straight Language for the Deaf. Alexander Graham Bell Assoc., Washington, D.C.

Flanders, N. 1965. Analyzing Teacher Behavior. Addison-Wesley Publishing Co., Reading, Ma.

Fletcher, J., and P. Suppes 1973. Computer-Assisted Instruction in Mathematics and Language Arts for the Deaf. U.S. Department of Health, Education, and Welfare, Washington, D.C.

Fodor, J., and T. Bever. 1965. The psychological reality of linguistic segments. J. Verb. Learn. Verb. Behav. 4: 414–420.

Fodor, J., and M. Garrett. 1967. Some syntactic determinants of sentential complexity. Percept. Psychophys. 2: 289–296.

Fouts, R. 1972. Use of guidance in teaching sign language to a chimpanzee. J. Comp. Physiol. Psychol. 80: 515–522.

Francis, W. 1973. Approaches to grammar. In T. Sebeok (ed.), Current Trends in Linguistics, Vol. 10, pp. 122–144. Mouton, The Hague.

Frase, L. 1972. Maintenance and control in the acquisition of knowledge from written materials. In R. Freedle and J. Carroll. (eds.), Language Comprehension and the Acquisition of Knowledge, pp. 337–357. V. H. Winston and Sons, Washington, D.C.

Fraser, C., U. Bellugi, and R. Brown. 1963. Control of grammar in imitation, comprehension, and production. J. Verb. Learn. Verb. Behav. 2: 121–135.

Freedle, R., and J. Carroll (eds.). 1972a. Language Comprehension and the Acquisition of Knowledge. V. H. Winston and Sons, Washington, D.C.

Freedle, R., and J. Carroll. 1972b. Language comprehension and the acquisition of knowledge: Reflections. In R. Freedle and J. Carroll (eds.), Language Comprehension and the Acquisition of Knowledge, pp. 359–368. V. H. Winston and Sons, Washington, D.C.

Freedle, R., T. Keeney, and N. Smith. 1970. Effects of mean depth and grammaticality on children's imitations of sentences. J. Verb. Learn. Verb. Behav. 9: 149–154.

Freedle, R., and M. Lewis. 1977. Prelinguistic conversations. In M. Lewis and L.

Rosenblum (eds.), Interaction, Conversation, and the Development of Language, pp. 157–186. John Wiley and Sons, New York.

Fremer, J. 1971. Recognition memory for approximations to English in deaf and hearing subjects at three age levels. Unpublished doctoral dissertation, Columbia University, New York City.

Friedlander, B., A. Jacobs, B. Davis, and H. Wetstone. 1972. Time-sampling analysis of infants' natural language environments in the home. Child Dev. 43: 730–740.

Friedman, J., and T. Bredt. 1968. Lexical insertion in transformational grammar. Stanford University Computer Science Department, Computational Linguistic Project, Stanford, Ca.

Friedman, L. 1975. Space, time, and person reference in American Sign Language. Language 51: 940–961.

Friedman, L. 1976. The manifestation of subject, object, and topic in the American Sign Language. In C. Li (ed.), Subject and Topic, pp. 125–148. Academic Press, New York.

Friedman, L. 1977. On the Other Hand. Academic Press, New York.

Fries, C. 1952. The Structure of English. Harcourt Brace Jovanovich, New York.

Fries, C. 1963. Linguistics and Reading. Holt, Rinehart, and Winston, New York.

Fromkin, V. (ed.). 1973. Speech Errors as Linguistic Evidence. Mouton, The Hague.

Furth, H. 1964. Research with the deaf: Implications for language and cognition. Psychol. Bull. 62: 145–164.

Furth, H. 1966. Thinking Without Language. Free Press, New York.

Furth, H. 1971. Linguistic deficiency and thinking: Research with deaf subjects 1964–1969. Psychol. Bull. 76: 58–72.

Furth, H., and J. Youniss. 1971. Formal operations and language: A comparison of deaf and hearing adolescents. Int. J. Psychol. 6: 49–64.

Fygetakis, L., and D. Ingram. 1973. Language rehabilitation and programmed conditioning: A case study. J. Learn. Disabil. 6: 60–64.

Ganschow, L. 1974. A transformational linguistic analysis of syntactical structures in the written language of selected preschool, kindergarten, and first grade children: Fifteen case studies. Unpublished master's thesis, University of Cincinnati, Cincinnati, Oh.

Garber, C. 1967. An analysis of English morphological abilities of deaf and hearing children. Unpublished doctoral dissertation, Ohio State University, Columbus, Oh.

Garber, N., and L. David. 1975. Semantic considerations in the treatment of echolalia. Ment. Retard. 15: 9–11.

Garcia, E., D. Guess, and J. Byrnes. 1973. Development of syntax in a retarded girl using procedures of imitation, reinforcement, and modelling. J. Appl. Behav. Anal. 6: 299–310.

Gardner, B., and R. Gardner. 1971. Two-way communication with an infant chimpanzee. In A. Schrier and F. Stollnitz (eds.), Behavior of Nonhuman Primates, pp. 117–184. Academic Press, New York.

Gardner, B., and R. Gardner. 1974. Comparing the early utterances of child and chimpanzee. In A. Pick (ed.), Minnesota Symposium on Child Psychology, Vol. 8, pp. 3–23. University of Minnesota Press, Minneapolis.

Gardner, B., and R. Gardner. 1975a. Evidence for sentence constituents in the early utterances of child and chimpanzee. J. Exp. Psychol. 104: 244–267.

Gardner, R., and B. Gardner. 1975b. Early signs of language in child and chimpanzee. Science 187: 752–753.

Garnica, O. 1973. The development of phonemic speech perception. In T. Moore (ed.), Cognitive Development and the Acquisition of Language, pp. 215–222. Academic Press, New York.

Garnica, O. 1977. Some prosodic and paralinguistic features of speech to young children. In C. Snow and C. Ferguson (eds.), Talking to Children, pp. 63–88. Cambridge University Press, Cambridge, England.

Garrett, M., T. Bever, and J. Fodor. 1966. The active use of grammar in speech perception. Percept. Psychophys. 1: 30–32.

Gates, A., and W. MacGinitie. 1965. Gates MacGinitie Reading Test, Teachers' Manual. Teachers' College Press, Columbia University, New York City.

Gelman, R., and M. Shatz. 1977. Appropriate speech adjustments: The operation of conversational constraints on talk to two-year olds. In M. Lewis and L. Rosenblum (eds.), Interaction, Conversation, and the Development of Language, pp. 27–61. John Wiley and Sons, New York.

Gesell, A., and C. Amatruda. 1962. Developmental Diagnosis: Normal and Abnormal Child Development, Clinical Methods, and Practical Applications. 3rd ed. Harper and Row Publishers, New York.

Giattino, J., and J. Hogan. 1975. Analysis of a father's speech to his language-learning child. J. Speech Hear. Disord. 40: 524–537.

Gibson, E., and H. Levin. 1975. The Psychology of Reading. MIT Press, Cambridge, Ma.

Gill, T., and D. Rumbaugh. 1974. Mastery of naming skills by a chimpanzee. J. Hum. Evol. 3: 483–492.

Gleitman, L., and H. Gleitman. 1970. Phrase and Paraphrase: Some Innovative Uses of Language. W. W. Norton and Co., New York.

Glucksberg, S., and R. Krauss. 1967. What do people say after they have learned how to talk? Studies of the development of referential communication. Merrill-Palmer Quart. 13: 309–316.

Glucksberg, S., R. Krauss, and E. Higgins. 1975. The development of referential communication skills. In F. Horowitz (ed.), Review of Child Development Research, Vol. 4. University of Chicago Press, Chicago.

Glucksberg, S., R. Krauss, and R. Weisberg. 1966. Referential communication in nursery school children: Method and some preliminary findings. J. Exp. Child Psychol. 3: 333–342.

Goda, S. 1959. Language skills of profoundly deaf adolescent children. J. Speech Hear. Res. 2: 369–374.

Goda, S. 1964. Spoken syntax of normal, deaf, retarded adolescents. J. Verb. Learn. Verb. Behav. 3: 401–405.

Goetzinger, C. 1962. Effects of small perceptive losses on language and on speech discrimination. Volta Rev. 64: 408–414.

Goldberg, J., and M. Bordman. 1975. The ESL approach to teaching English to hearing-impaired students. Am. Ann. Deaf 120: 22–27.

Goldin-Meadow, S. 1975. The representation of semantic relations in a manual language created by deaf children of hearing parents: A language you can't dismiss out of hand. Unpublished doctoral dissertation, University of Pennsylvania, College Park, Pa.

Goodglass, H., J. Berko, N. Bernholtz, and M. Hyde. 1972. Some linguistic structures in the speech of a Broca's aphasic. Cortex 8: 191–212.

Goodman, K. 1972. The reading process: Theory and Practice. In R. Hodges and E. Rudorf (eds.), Language and Learning to Read, pp. 143–159. Houghton and Mifflin Co., New York.

Goodman, K. (ed.). 1973a. The Psycholinguistic Nature of the Reading Process. Wayne State University Press, Detroit.

Goodman, K. 1973b. The psycholinguistic nature of the reading process. In K. Goodman (ed.), The Psycholinguistic Nature of the Reading Process, pp. 13–26. Wayne State University Press, Detroit.

Goodman, K. 1973c. Analysis of oral reading miscues: Applied psycholinguistics. In F. Smith (ed.), Psycholinguistics and Reading, pp. 158–176. Holt, Rinehart, and Winston, New York.

Goodman, Y., and C. Burke, 1972. Reading Miscue Inventory. Macmillan, New York.

Goodman, K., and Y. Goodman. 1977. Learning about psycholinguistic process by analyzing oral reading. Harvard Educ. Rev. 47: 317–333.

Goodman, Y. 1972. Qualitative reading miscue for teacher training. In R. Hodges and E. Rudorf (eds.), Language and Learning to Read, pp. 160–168. Houghton and Mifflin Co., New York.

Goodson, B., and P. Greenfield. 1975. The search for structural principles in children's manipulative play: A parallel with linguistic development. Child. Dev. 46: 734–746.

Gordon, D., and G. Lakoff. 1971. Conversational postulates. In Proceedings from the 7th Regional Meeting of the Chicago Linguistic Society, pp. 63–84. University of Chicago, Chicago.

Gorrell, S. 1971. An investigation of the social interactions occurring among comparable groups of normal hearing and hearing impaired children using an interaction scale. Unpublished master's thesis, University of Cincinnati, Cincinnati, Oh.

Gottsleben, R., G. Buschini, and D. Tyack. 1974. Linguistically based training programs. J. Learn. Disabil. 7: 197–203.

Gove, A. 1976. Symbolization and sequencing in the development of interaction skills in a one-year old child. Word 27: 170–178.

Granowsky, S., and W. Krossner. 1970. Kindergarten teachers as models for children's speech. J. Exp. Educ. 38: 23–28.

Gray, C. 1923. The anticipation of meaning as a factor in reading ability. Elem. School J. 23: 614–626.

Greenfield, P., and J. Smith. 1976. The Structure of Communication in Early Language Development. Academic Press, New York.

Greenstein, J., B. Greenstein, K. McConville, and L. Stellini. 1975. Mother-Infant Communication and Language Acquisition in Deaf Infants. Lexington School for the Deaf, New York.

Grewel, F. 1963. Remarks upon the acquisition of language in deaf children. Lang. Speech 6: 37–45.

Grice, H. 1975. Logic and conversation. In M. Cole and J. Morgan (eds.), Syntax and Semantics, Vol. 3, pp. 41–58. Academic Press, New York.

Grill, J., and N. Bartel. 1977. Language bias in tests: ITPA Grammatical Closure. J. Learn. Disabil. 10: 229–235.

Groht, M. 1958. Natural Language for Deaf Children. Alexander Graham Bell Assoc., Washington, D.C.

Grosjean, F., and H. Lane. 1975. Pauses and syntax in American Sign Language. Cognition 5: 101–117.

Gross, R. 1970. Language used by mothers of deaf children and mothers of hearing children. Am. Ann. Deaf 115: 93–96.

Guess, D. 1969. A functional analysis of receptive language and productive speech: The acquisition of the plural morpheme. J. Appl. Behav. Anal. 2: 55–64.

Guess, D., and D. Baer. 1973. An analysis of individual differences in generalization between receptive and productive language in retarded children. J. Appl. Behav. Anal. 6: 311–329.

Guess, D., W. Sailor, and D. Baer. 1974. To teach language to retarded children. In R. Schiefelbusch and L. Lloyd (eds.), Language Perspectives—Acquisition, Retardation, and Intervention, pp. 529–564. University Park Press, Baltimore.

Guess, D., W. Sailor, G. Rutherford, and D. Baer. 1968. An experimental analysis of linguistic development: The productive use of the plural morpheme. J. Appl. Behav. Anal. 1: 297–306.

Guralnick, M., and D. Paul-Brown. 1977. The nature of verbal interactions among handicapped and nonhandicapped preschool children. Child Dev. 48: 255–260.

Gustason, G., D. Pfetzing, and E. Zawolkow. 1972. Signing Exact English. Modern Signs Press, Rossmoor, Ca.

Hakuta, D. 1974. Prefabricated patterns and the emergence of structure in second language acquisition. Lang. Learn. 24: 287–297.

Hakuta, K. 1975. Learning to speak a second language: What exactly does the child learn? In D. Dato (ed.), Developmental Psycholinguistics: Theory and Applications, pp. 193–207. Georgetown University Press, Washington, D.C.

Halliday, M. 1967. Notes on transivity and theme in English: II. J. Linguist. 3: 199–244.

Hamilton, M., and D. Stewart. 1977. Peer models and language acquisition. Merrill-Palmer Quart. 23: 45–55.

Hammill, D., and N. Bartel. 1975. Teaching Children with Learning and Behavior Problems. Allyn and Bacon, Boston.

Hargis, C., C. Evans, and C. Masters. 1973. A criticism of the direct discourse form in primary level basal readers. Volta Rev. 75: 557–563.

Hargis, C., and C. Lamm. 1974. Have and be: A lexicon of verb forms. Volta Rev. 76: 420–424.

Hart, B. 1963. Teaching Reading to the Deaf. Alexander Graham Bell Assoc., Washington, D.C.

Hart, B., and J. Rosenstein. 1964. Examining language behavior of deaf children. Volta Rev. 66: 679–682.

Hartung, J. 1972. A review of procedures to increase verbal imitation skills and functional speech in autistic children. J. Speech Hear. Disord. 35: 203–217.

Heider, F., and G. Heider. 1941. Comparison of sentence structure of deaf and hearing children. Volta Rev. 43: 364–406, 536–564, 599–628.

Heider, F., G. Heider, and J. Stykes. 1941. A study of the spontaneous vocalizations of fourteen deaf children. Volta Rev. 43: 10–14.

Hess, L. 1972. The development of transformational structures in a deaf child and a normally hearing child over a period of five months. Unpublished master's thesis, University of Cincinnati, Cincinnati, Oh.

Hester, M. 1964. Manual communication. In Report of the Proceedings of the International Congress on Education of the Deaf and the 41st Meeting of the Convention of American Instructors of the Deaf, pp. 211–221. U.S. Government Printing Office, Washington, D.C.

Hodges, R., and E. Rudorf. (eds.). 1972. Language and Learning to Read. Houghton and Mifflin, Co., New York.

Hoemann, H. 1972. The development of communication skills in deaf and hearing children. Child Dev. 43: 990–1003.

Hoemann, H. 1976. The transparency of meaning of sign language gestures. Sign Lang. Stud. 7: 151–161.

Holland, A. 1975. Language therapy for children: Some thoughts on context and content. J. Speech Hear. Disord. 40: 514–523.

Holm, V., and L. Kuntze. 1969. Effect of chronic otitis media on language and speech development. Pediatrics 43: 833–839.

Holmes, D. 1972. The use of structured imitation in the assessment of deaf children's syntax. Unpublished doctoral dissertation, Syracuse University Syracuse, New York.

Holzman, M. 1974. The verbal environment provided by mothers for their very young children. Merrill-Palmer Quart. 20: 31–42.

Hornby, P. 1974. Surface structure and presupposition. J. Verb. Learn. Verb. Behav. 13: 530–538.

Horton, K. 1974. Infant intervention and language learning. In R. Schiefelbusch and L. Lloyd (eds.), Language Perspectives—Acquisition, Retardation, and Intervention, pp. 469–491. University Park Press, Baltimore.

Hubbell, R. 1977. On facilitating spontaneous talking in young children. J. Speech Hear. Disord. 42: 216–230.

Huey, E. 1968. The Psychology and Pedagogy of Reading. MIT Press, Cambridge, Ma. (Originally published 1908.)

Huey, E. 1970. Language, perception, and reading. In A. Blumenthal (ed.), Language and Psychology, pp. 147–156. John Wiley and Sons, New York. Originally published in 1908.

Hughes, J. 1974. Acquisition of a non-vocal 'language' by aphasic children. Cognition 3: 41–55.

Hughes R. 1961. Verbal conceptualization in deaf and hearing children. Except. Child. 22: 517–522.

Huttenlocher, J. 1964. Children's language: Word-phrase relationship. Science 143: 264–265.

Huttenlocher, J. 1974. The origins of language comprehension. In R. Solso (ed.), Theories in Cognitive Psychology: The Loyola Symposium, pp. 331–368. John Wiley and Sons, New York.

Huttenlocher, J., K. Eisenberg, and S. Strauss. 1968. Comprehension: Relation between perceived actor and logical subject. J. Verb. Learn. Verb. Behav. 7: 527–530.

Huttenlocher, J., and S. Strauss. 1968. Comprehension and a statement's relation to the situation it describes. J. Verb. Learn. Verb. Behav. 7: 300–304.

Huttenlocher, J., and S. Weiner. 1971. Comprehension of instruction in varying contexts. Cog. Psychol. 2: 369–385.

Ivimey, G. 1976. The written syntax of an English deaf child: An exploration in method. Br. J. Disord. Commun. 11: 103–120.

Jackendoff, R. 1972. Semantic Interpretation in Generative Grammar. MIT Press, Cambridge, Ma.

Jacobs, R., and P. Rosenbaum. 1968. English Transformational Grammar. Blaisdell, Waltham, Ma.

Jacobson, M. 1975. Brain development in relation to language. In E. Lenneberg and E. Lenneberg (eds.), Foundations of Language Development, Vol. 1, pp. 105–121. Academic Press, New York.

Jaffe, J., D. Stern, and J. Peery. 1973. 'Conversational' coupling of gaze behavior in prelinguistic human development. J. Psycholinguist. Res. 2: 321–330.

Jakobson, R. 1968. Child Language, Aphasia, and Phonological Universals. Mouton, The Hague.

Jakobson, R., and M. Halle. 1956. Fundamentals of Language. Mouton, The Hague.

James, P. 1974. The James Language Dominance Test: English/Spanish. Learning Concepts, Austin, Texas.

Jarvella, R., and J. Lubinsky. 1975. Deaf and hearing children's use of language describing temporal order among events. J. Speech Hear. Res. 18: 58–73.

Jeffree, D., K. Wheldall, and P. Mittler. 1973. Facilitating two-word utterances in two Down's Syndrome boys. Am. J. Mental Def. 78: 123–127.

Johnson, E. 1948. The ability of pupils in a school for the deaf to understand various methods of communication. Am. Ann. Deaf 93: 194–213.

Johnson, H. 1975. The meaning of *before* and *after* for preschool children. J. Exp. Child Psychol. 19: 88–99.

Jones, L., M. Goodman, and J. Wepman. 1963. The classification of parts of speech for the characterization of aphasia. Lang. Speech 6: 94–107.

Jones, M. 1976. A longitudinal investigation into the acquisition of question formation in English and American Sign Language by three hearing children with deaf parents. Unpublished doctoral dissertation, University of Illinois, Urbana, Il.

Jones, M. H. 1972. Learning to process visually-coded symbolic information. In R. Hodges and E. Rudorf (eds.), Language and Learning to Read, pp. 117–130. Houghton and Mifflin Co., New York.

Jones, M. H. 1973. Some thoughts on perceptual units in language processing. In K. Goodman (ed.), The Psycholinguistic Nature of the Reading Process, pp. 41–57. Wayne State University Press, Detroit.

Juenke, D. 1971. An application of a generative-transformational model of linguistic description of hearing impaired subjects in the generation and expansion stages of language development. Unpublished master's thesis, University of Cincinnati, Cincinnati, Oh.

Kaplan, E., and G. Kaplan. 1971. The prelinguistic child. In J. Eliot (ed.), Human Development and Cognitive Processes, pp. 358–381. Holt, Rinehart, and Winston, New York.

Katz, J. 1972. Semantic Theory. Harper and Row Publishers, New York.

Katz, J. and J. Fodor. 1963. The structure of a semantic theory. Language 39: 170–210.

Katz, J., and P. Postal. 1964. An Integrated Theory of Linguistic Descriptions. MIT Press, Cambridge, Ma.

Kavanagh, J., and I. Mattingly (eds.), 1972. Language by Ear and by Eye: The Relationship between Speech and Reading. MIT Press, Cambridge, Ma.

Kaye, K. 1976. Infants, effects upon their mothers' teaching strategies. In J. Glidewell (ed.), The Social Context of Learning and Development. Gardner Press, New York.

Kaye, K. 1977. Toward the origin of dialogue. In H. Schaffer (ed.), Studies in Mother-Infant Interaction, pp. 89–117. Academic Press, London.

Keller, L. 1944. Hearing survey in Detroit schools. Except. Child. 11: 168–173.

Kempson, R. 1975. Presupposition and the Delimitation of Semantics. Cambridge University Press, Cambridge, England.

Kent, L., D. Klein, A. Falk, and H. Guenther. 1972. A language acquisition program for the retarded. In J. McLean, D. Yoder, and R. Schiefelbusch (eds.), Language Intervention with the Retarded, pp. 151–190. University Park Press, Baltimore.

Kiefer, F. 1973. On presuppositions. In F. Kiefer and N. Ruwet (eds.), Generative Grammar in Europe. Reidel, Dordrecht, Netherlands.

Kimball, J. 1973. Seven principles of surface structure parsing in natural language. Cognition 2: 15–47.

Kintsch, W. 1972. Notes on the structure of semantic memory. In E. Tulving and W. Donaldson (eds.), Organization of Memory, pp. 247–308. Academic Press, New York.

Kintsch, W. 1974. The Representation of Meaning in Memory. Lawrence Erlbaum Assoc., Hillsdale, N. J.

Kirk, S., J. McCarthy, and W. Kirk. 1968. Illinois Test of Psycholinguistic Abilities. University of Illinois Press, Urbana.

Klima, E., and U. Bellugi, 1966. Syntactic regularities in the speech of children. In J. Lyons and R. Wales (eds.), Psycholinguistic Papers, pp. 183–208. Edinburgh University Press, Edinburgh.

Kobashigawa, B. 1969. Repetitions in a mother's speech to her child. Working Paper No. 14, Language Behavior Research Laboratory, University of California, Berkeley, Ca.

Kolers, P. 1973a. Reading temporally and spatially transformed text. In K. Goodman (ed.), The Psycholinguistic Nature of the Reading Process, pp. 27–40. Wayne State University Press, Detroit.

Kolers, P. 1973b. Three stages of reading. In F. Smith (ed.), Psycholinguistics and Reading, pp. 28–49. Holt, Rinehart, and Winston, New York.

Kolers, P., and M. Katzman. 1966. Naming sequentially presented letters and words. Lang. Speech 9: 84–95.

Koplin, J., P. Odom, R. Blanton, and J. Nunnally. 1967. Word association test performance of deaf subjects. J. Speech Hear. Res. 10: 126–132.

Kramer, P. 1977. Young children's free responses to anomalous commands. J. Exp. Child Psychol. 24: 219–234.

Kretschmer, R. E. 1976. Judgments of grammaticality by 11, 14, and 17 year old hearing and hearing impaired youngsters. Unpublished doctoral dissertation, University of Kansas, Lawrence, Ks.

Kretschmer, R. R. 1972a. A study to assess the play activities and gesture output of hearing handicapped pre-school children. Final Report, Project No. 45-2109, Office of Education, Bureau of Education for the Handicapped.

Kretschmer, R. R., 1972b. Transformational linguistic analysis of the written language of hearing impaired and normal hearing students. Unpublished doctoral dissertation, Teachers College, Columbia University, New York City.

Kretschmer, R. R. 1974. Auditory training for the preschool child. In K. Donnelly (ed.), Interpreting Hearing Aid Technology. Charles C Thomas Publishers, Springfield, Il.

Kretschmer, R. R. Comparison of the spontaneous written language of hearing and deaf children. In preparation.

Kretschmer, R., and L. Kretschmer (eds.). 1973. Language Development Outline: A Guide for Clinicians and Teachers of Language Impaired Children. Department of Special Education, University of Cincinnati, Cincinnati, Oh.

Labelle, J. 1973. Sentence comprehension in two age groups of children as related to pause position or the absence of pauses. J. Speech Hear. Res. 16: 231–237.

Lahey, M., and L. Bloom. 1977. Planning a first lexicon: Which words to teach first. J. Speech Hear. Disord. 42: 340–350.

Landes, J. 1975. Speech addressed to children: Issues and characteristics of parental input. Lang. Learn. 25: 355–379.

Langacker, R. 1973. Language and Its Structure. 2nd ed. Harcourt Brace Jovanovich, New York.

Langendoen, D. 1969. The Study of Syntax: The Generative-Transformational Approach to American English. Holt, Rinehart, and Winston, New York.

Langendoen, D. 1970. Essentials of English Grammar. Holt, Rinehart, and Winston, New York.

Larsen-Freeman, D. 1975. The acquisition of grammatical morphemes by adult ESL students. TESOL Quart. 9: 4–7.

Larsen-Freeman, D. 1976. An explanation for the morpheme acquisition order of second language learners. Lang. Learn. 26: 125–134.

Larson, G., and P. Summers. 1976. Response patterns of pre-school age children in the Northwestern Syntax Screening Test. J. Speech Hear. Disord. 41: 486–498.

Lawrence, J. 1971. A comparison of operant methodologies relative to language development in the institutionalized mentally retarded. Unpublished doctoral dissertation, Boston University, Boston, Ma.

Lawson, R. 1978. Patterns of communication in intermediate level classrooms of the deaf. Audiol. Hear. Educ. 4: 19–23+.

Lee, L. 1966. Developmental sentence types: A method for comparing normal and deviant syntactic development. J. Speech Hear. Disord. 31: 311–330.

Lee, L. 1969. Northwestern Syntax Screening Test. Northwestern University Press, Evanston, Il.

Lee, L. 1974. Developmental Sentence Analysis. Northwestern University Press, Evanston, Il.

Lee, L. 1977. Reply to Arndt and Byrne. J. Speech Hear. Disord. 42: 323–327.

Lee, L., and S. Canter. 1971. Developmental sentence scoring: A clinical procedure for estimating syntactic development in children's spontaneous speech. J. Speech Hear. Disord. 36: 315–338.

Lee, L., R. Koenigsknecht, and S. Mulhern. 1975. Interactive Language Development Teaching. Northwestern University Press, Evanston, Il.

Leech, G. 1974. Semantics. Penguin, Baltimore.

Lefevre, C. 1973. A multidisciplinary approach to language and to reading: Some projections. In K. Goodman (ed.), The Psycholinguistic Nature of the Reading Process, pp. 189–312. Wayne State University Press, Detroit.

Lenneberg, E. 1967. Biological Foundations of Language. John Wiley and Sons, New York.

Leonard, L. 1973. Teaching by the rules. J. Speech Hear. Disord. 38: 174–183.

Leonard, L. 1975a. The role of nonlinguistic stimuli and semantic relations in children's acquisition of grammatical utterances. J. Exp. Child Psychol. 19: 346–357.

Leonard, L. 1975b. Developmental considerations in the management of language disabled children. J. Learn. Disabil. 8: 44–49.

Leonard, L. 1975c. On differentiating syntactic and semantic features in emerging grammars: Evidence from empty form usage. J. Psycholinguist. Res. 4: 357–363.

Leonard, L. 1976. Meaning in Child Language. Grune and Stratton, New York.

Leonard, L., J. Bolders, and R. Curtis. 1977. On the nature of the children's judgments of linguistic features: Semantic relations and grammatical morphemes. J. Psycholinguist. Res. 6: 233–245.

Lewis, M.,and L. Cherry. 1977. Social behavior and language acquisition. In M. Lewis and L. Rosenblum (eds.), Interaction, Conversation, and the Development of Language, pp. 227–246. John Wiley and Sons, New York.

Libergott, J., and S. Swope. 1976. Learners' needs: Speech and language disabilities. In F. Withrow and C. Nygren (eds.), Language, Materials and Curriculum Management for the Handicapped Learner, pp. 68–85. Charles E. Merrill Publishing Co., Columbus, Oh.

Liberman, A. 1970. The grammar of speech and language. Cog. Psychol. 1: 301–323.

Liberman, A., F. Cooper, D. Shankweiler, and M. Studdert-Kennedy. 1967. Perception of the speech code. Psychol. Rev. 74: 431–459.

Lieberman, P. 1967. Intonation, Perception, and Language. MIT Press, Cambridge, Ma.

Liles, B., M. Shulman, and S. Bartlett. 1977. Judgments of grammaticality by normal and language disordered children. J. Speech Hear. Disord. 42: 199–209.

Limber, J. 1973. The genesis of complex sentences. In T. Moore (ed.), Cognitive Development and the Acquisition of Language, pp. 169–185. Academic Press, New York.

Limber, J. 1976. Unravelling competence, performance, and pragmatics in the speech of young children. J. Child Lang. 3: 309–318.

Ling, D. 1972. Rehabilitation of cases with deafness secondary to otitis media. In A. Glorig and K. Gerwin (eds.), Otitis Media-Proceedings of the National Conference-Callier Hearing and Speech Center, Dallas, Texas, pp. 249–253. Charles C Thomas Publishers, Springfield, Il.

Ling, D. 1976. Speech and the Hearing Impaired Child: Theory and Practice. Alexander Graham Bell Assoc., Washington, D.C.

Lipsitt, L. 1977. Sensory and learning processes of newborns: Implications for behavior diabilities. Paper presented at Conference on Early Intervention with Infants and Young Children. University of Wisconsin-Milwaukee, Milwaukee, Wi.

Lisker, L., and A. Abramson. 1964. A cross-language study of voicing in initial stops: Acoustical measurements. Word 20: 384–422.

Lloyd, P., and M. Donaldson. 1976. On a method eliciting true/false judgments from young children. J. Child Lang. 3: 411–416.

Longhurst, T., and J. File. 1977. A comparison of developmental sentence scores from head start children collected in four conditions. Lang. Speech Hear. Serv. Schools 8: 54–64.

Longhurst, T., and T. Schrandt. 1973. Linguistic analysis of children's speech: A comparison of four procedures. J. Speech Hear. Disord. 38: 240–249.

Lovell, K., and E. Dixon. 1967. The growth of the control of grammar in imitation, comprehension, and production. J. Child Psychol. Psychiatry 8: 31–39.

Lovell, K., H. Hoyle, and M. Siddall. 1968. A study of some aspects of the play and language of young children with delayed speech. J. Child Psychol. Psychiatry 9: 41–50.

Lowenbraun, S., and J. Affleck. 1970. The ability of deaf children to use syntactic cues in immediate recall of speechread materials. Except. Child. 36: 735–741.

Luterman, D. 1976. A comparison of language skills of hearing impaired children trained in a visual/oral method and an auditory/oral method. Am. Ann. Deaf 121: 389–393.

Lynch, J., and W. Bricker. 1972. Linguistic theory and operant procedures: Toward an integrated approach to language training for the mentally retarded. Ment. Retard. 12: 12–17.

McAloney, T. 1931. The Barry slate system. Volta Rev. 33: 530–542.

McCabe, A., J. Levin, and P. Wolff. 1974. The role of overt activity in children's sentence production. J. Exp. Child Psychol. 17: 107–114.

McCarr, J. 1972. The developmental use of transformational grammar. In Proceedings of the 45th Meeting of the Convention of American Instructors of the Deaf, pp. 668–689. U.S. Printing Office, Washington, D.C.

McCawley, J. 1968. The role of semantics in a grammar. In E. Bach and R. Harms (eds.), Universals in Linguistic Theory, pp. 124–169. Holt, Rinehart, and Winston, New York.

McCracken, G., and C. Walcott. 1963. Basic Reading Series. Basic Reading, Philadelphia.

MacDonald, J. 1976. Environmental language intervention. In F. Withrow and C. Nygren (eds.), Language, Materials, and Curriculum Management for the Handicapped Learner, pp. 13–33. Charles E. Merrill Publishing Co., Columbus, Oh.

MacDonald, J., and J. Blott. 1974. Environmental language intervention: The rationale for a diagnostic and training strategy through rules, context, and generalization. J. Speech Hear. Disord. 39: 244–256.

MacDonald, J., J. Blott, K. Gordon, B. Spiegel, and M. Hartmann. 1974. An experimental parent-assisted treatment program for preschool language-delayed children. J. Speech Hear. Disord. 39: 395–415.

MacGinitie, W. 1964. Ability of deaf children to use different word classes. J. Speech Hear. Res. 7: 141–150.

McIntire, M. 1974. A modified model for the description of language acquisition in a deaf child. Unpublished master's thesis, California State University, Northridge, Ca.

MacKay, D. 1976. On the retrieval and lexical structure of verbs. J. Verb. Learn. Verb. Behav. 15: 169–182.

McLean, L., and J. McLean. 1974. A language training program for nonverbal autistic children. J. Speech Hear. Disord. 39: 186–193.

MacNeilage, P. 1970. Motor control of serial ordering of speech. Psychol. Rev. 77: 182–196.

McNeill, D. 1970a. The Acquisition of Language: The Study of Developmental Psycholinguistics. Harper and Row Publishers, New York.

NcNeill, D. 1970b. Explaining linguistic universals. In J. Morton (ed.), Biological and Social Factors in Psycholinguistics pp. 53–60. University of Illinois, Press, Urbana.

McReynolds, L., and D. Engmann. 1974. An experimental analysis of the relationship of subject and object noun phrases. In L. McReynolds (ed.), Developing Systematic Procedures for Training Children's Language, pp. 30–46. Monogr. ASHA 18: December.

Marquardt, T., and J. Saxman. 1972. Language comprehension and auditory discrimination. J. Speech Hear. Res. 15: 382–389.

Marshall, W. 1970. Contextual constraint on deaf and hearing children. Am. Ann. Deaf 115: 682–689.

Martin, J. 1972. Rhythmic (hierarchical) versus serial structure in speech and other behavior. Psychol. Rev. 79: 487–509.

Mattingly, I., and J. Kavanagh. 1973. The relationships between speech and reading. U.S. Department of Health, Education, and Welfare, Public Health Service, National Institute of Health. DHEW Publication #(NIH) 73-475.

Mayberry, R. 1976. An assessment of some oral and manual language skills of hearing children of deaf parents. Am. Ann. Deaf 121: 507–512.

Meadow, K. 1968. Early manual communication in relation to the deaf child's intellectual, social, and communicative functioning. Am. Ann. Deaf 113: 29–41.

Mecham, M. 1959. Verbal Language Development Scale. Educational Test Bureau, Minneapolis, Mn.

Mehrabian, A., and M. Williams. 1971. Piagetian measures of cognitive development up to age two. J. Psycholinguist. Res. 1: 113–126.

Mellon, J. 1967. Transformational sentence-combining: A method for enhancing the development of syntactic fluency in English composition. Harvard R & D Center on Educational Differences, Report 1, Cambridge, Ma.

Menyuk, P. 1963a. A preliminary evaluation of grammatical capacity in children. J. Verb. Learn. Verb. Behav. 2: 429–439.

Menyuk, P. 1963b. Syntactic structures in the language of children. Child Dev. 34: 407–422.

Menyuk, P. 1964a. Alternation of rules in children's grammar. J. Verb. Learn. Verb. Behav. 3: 408–488.

Menyuk, P. 1964b. Comparison of grammar of children with functionally deviant and normal speech. J. Speech Hear. Res. 7: 109–121.

Menyuk, P. 1969. Sentences Children Use. MIT Press, Cambridge, Ma.

Menyuk, P. 1971. The Acquisition and Development of Language. Prentice-Hall, Englewood Cliffs, N.J.

Menyuk, P. 1974. Early development of receptive language: From babbling to words. In R. Schiefelbusch and L. Lloyd (eds.), Language Perspectives—Acquisition, Retardation, and Intervention, pp. 213–235. University Park Press, Baltimore.

Menyuk, P., and P. Looney. 1972. A problem of language disorder: Length versus structure. J. Speech Hear. Res. 15: 264–279.

Messer, S. 1967. Implicit phonology in children. J. Verb. Learn. Verb. Behav. 6: 609–613.

Miller, G. 1956. The magical number seven, plus or minus two: Some limits on our capacity for processing information. Psychol. Rev. 63: 81–97.

Miller, G. 1973. Some preliminaries to psycholinguistics. In F. Smith (ed.), Psycholinguistics and Reading, pp. 10–20. Holt, Rinehart, and Winston, New York.

Miller, G., and P. Johnson-Laird. 1976. Language and Perception. Harvard University Press, Cambridge, Ma.

Miller, J. 1973. Sentence imitation in pre-school children. Lang. Speech 16: 1–14.

Miller, J., and R. Chapman. 1975. Length variables in sentence imitation. Lang. Speech 16: 35–41.

Miller, J., and D. Yoder. 1972. A syntax teaching program. In J. McLean, D. Yoder, and R. Schiefelbusch (eds.), Language Intervention with the Retarded, pp. 191–211. University Park Press, Baltimore.

Miller, J., and D. Yoder. 1974. An ontongenetic language teaching strategy for retarded children. In R. Schiefelbusch and L. Lloyd (eds.), Language Perspectives—Acquisition, Retardation, and Intervention, pp. 505–528. University Park Press, Baltimore.

Miller, W., and S. Ervin. 1964. The development of grammar in child language. In U. Bellugi and R. Brown (eds.), The Acquisition of Language, pp. 929–934. Monog. Soc. Res. Child Dev. 29: No. 1.

Milon, J. 1974. The development of negation in English by a second language learner. TESOL Quart. 8: 137–143.

Miner, L. 1969. Scoring procedures for the length-complexity index: A preliminary report. J. Commun. Disord. 2: 224–240.

Moerk, E. 1972. Principles of interaction in language learning. Merrill-Palmer Quart. 18: 229–257.

Moerk, E. 1974. Changes in verbal child-mother interactions with increasing language skills of the child. J. Psycholinguist. Res. 3: 101–116.

Moerk, E. 1975a. Piaget's research as applied to the explanation of language development. Merrill-Palmer Quart. 21: 151–169.

Moerk, E. 1975b. Verbal interactions between children and their mothers during the preschool years. Dev. Psychol. 11: 788–794.

Moerk, E. 1977. Processes and products of imitation: Additional evidence that imitation is progressive. J. Psycholinguist. Res. 6: 187–202.

Moffitt, A. 1971. Consonant cue perception by twenty- to twenty-four week old infants. Child Dev. 42: 717–731.

Monroe, M., and B. Rogers. 1964. Foundations for Reading. Scott Foresman, Chicago.

Montgomery, G. 1966. The relationship of oral skills to manual communication in profoundly deaf adolescents. Am. Ann. Deaf 111: 557–565.

Morehead, D., and D. Ingram. 1973. The development of base syntax in normal and linguistically deviant children. J. Speech Hear. Res. 16: 330–352.

Morehead, D., and A. Morehead. 1974. From signal to sign: A Piagetian view of thought and language during the first two years. In R. Schiefelbusch and L. Lloyd (eds.), Language Perspectives—Acquisition, Retardation, and Intervention, pp. 153–190. University Park Press, Baltimore.

Morrison, A. 1970. An investigation of the utility of drawing as a means of expressing understanding of certain linguistic rules by hearing impaired and normal hearing adolescents. Unpublished master's thesis, University of Cincinnati, Cincinnati, Oh.

Morse, P. 1972. The discrimination of speech and non-speech stimuli in early infancy. J. Exp. Child Psychol. 14: 477–492.

Morse, P. 1974. Infant speech perception: A preliminary model and review of the literature. In R. Schiefelbusch and L. Lloyd (eds.), Language Perspectives—Acquisition, Retardation, and Intervention, pp. 19–53. University Park Press, Baltimore.

Muma, J. 1974. Language intervention: Ten techniques. Lang. Speech Hear. Serv. Schools 5: 7–17.

Murphy, C., and D. Messer. 1977. Mothers, infants, and pointing: A study of a gesture. In H. Schaffer (ed.), Studies in Mother-Infant Interaction, pp. 325–354. Academic Press, London.

Myklebust, H. 1954. Auditory Disorders in Children. Grune and Stratton, New York.

Myklebust, H. 1960. The Psychology of Deafness. Grune and Stratton, New York.

Myklebust, H. 1965. Development and Disorders of Written Language. Volume 1: Picture Story Language Test. Grune and Stratton, New York.

Natalicio, D., and L. Natalicio. 1969. 'The child's learning of English morphology' revisited. Lang. Learn. 19: 205–215.

Natalicio, D., and L. Natalicio. 1971. A comparative study of English pluralization by native and non-native speakers. Child Dev. 42: 1302–1306.

Needleman, H. 1977. Effects of hearing loss from early recurrent otitis media on speech and language development. In B. Jaffe (ed.), Hearing Loss in Children, pp. 640–649. University Park Press, Baltimore.

Neisser, N. 1967. Cognitive Psychology. Appleton-Century-Crofts, New York.

Nelson, K. 1973. Structure and strategy in learning to talk. Monogr. Soc. Res. Child Dev. 38: No. 1–2.

Nelson, K. 1974. Concept, word, and sentence: Interrelations in acquisition and development. Psychol. Rev. 81: 267–285.

Newcomer, P., and D. Hammill. 1976. Psycholinguistics in the Schools. Charles E. Merrill Publishing Co., Columbus, Oh.

Newfield, M., and B. Schlanger. 1968. The acquisition of English morphology by normal and educable mentally retarded children. J. Speech Hear. Res. 11: 693–706.

Newport, E., H. Gleitman, and L. Gleitman. 1977. Mother, I'd rather do it myself: Some effects and non-effects of maternal speech style. In C. Snow and C. Ferguson (eds.), Talking to Children, pp. 109–150. Cambridge University Press, Cambridge, England.

Nicolich, L. 1977. Beyond sensorimotor intelligence: Assessment of symbolic maturity through analysis of pretend play. Merrill-Palmer Quart. 23: 89–99.

Nix, G. 1975. Total communication: A review of the studies offered in its support. Volta Rev. 77: 470–494.

Northcutt, W. (ed.). 1977. Curriculum Guide: Hearing Impaired Children (0–3 Years) and Their Parents. Alexander Graham Bell Assoc., Washington, D.C.

Nottebohm, F. 1975. A zoologist's view of some language phenomena with particular emphasis on vocal learning. In E. Lenneberg and E. Lenneberg (eds.), Foundations of Language Development, Vol. 1, pp. 61–104. Academic Press, New York.

Nunnally, J., and R. Blanton. 1966. Patterns of word association in the deaf. Psychol. Rep. 18: 87–92.

Nurss, J., and D. Day. 1971. Imitation, comprehension, and production of grammatical structures. J. Verb. Learn. Verb. Behav. 10: 68–74.

Odom, P., and R. Blanton. 1967. Phrase-learning in deaf and hearing subjects. J. Speech Hear. Res. 10: 600–605.

Odom, P., R. Blanton, and J. Nunnally. 1967. Some 'cloze' technique studies of language capability in the deaf. J. Speech Hear. Res. 10: 816–827.

Oller, D. 1975. Simplification as the goal of phonological processes in child speech. Lang. Learn. 24: 299–303.

Oller, D. 1977. Infant vocalization and development of speech. Paper presented at Conference on Early Intervention with Infants and Young Children. University of Wisconsin-Milwaukee, Milwaukee, Wi.

Oller, D., L. Wieman, W. Doyle, and C. Ross. 1976. Infant babbling and speech. J. Child Lang. 3: 1–11.

Olsen, H. 1973. Linguistics and materials for beginning reading instruction. In K. Goodman (ed.), The Psycholinguistic Nature of the Reading Process, pp. 271–287. Wayne State University Press, Detroit.

Olson, D. 1977. From utterance to text: The bias of language in speech and writing. Harvard Educ. Rev. 47: 257–281.

O'Neill, M. 1973. The receptive language competence of the base structure rules of transformational-generative grammar. Unpublished doctoral dissertation, University of Pittsburgh, Pittsburgh, Pa.

Owrid, H. 1975. Studies in manual communication with hearing impaired children. Volta Rev. 77: 152–154.

Paraskevopoulos, J., and S. Kirk. 1969. The Development and Psychometric Characteristics of the Revised Illinois Test of Psycholinguistic Abilities. University of Illinois Press, Urbana.

Pawlby, S. 1977. Imitative interaction. In H. Schaffer (ed.), Studies in Mother-Infant Interaction, pp. 203–224. Academic Press, London.

Peck, R. 1972. Patterned language: A practical application of linguistic principles. In Proceedings of the 45th Meeting of the Convention of American Instructors of the Deaf, pp. 658–667. U.S. Printing Office, Washington, D.C.

Peckham, C., M. Sheridan, and N. Butlert. 1972. School attainment of seven-year-old children with hearing difficulties. Dev. Med. Child Neurol. 14: 592–602.

Pendergrass, R., and M. Hodges. 1976. Deaf students in group problem solving situations: A study of the interactive process. Am. Ann. Deaf 121: 327–330.

Perlman, C. 1973. An investigation of deaf and hearing children's ability to apply morphonemic rules to lexical and nonsense items. Unpublished master's thesis, University of Cincinnati, Cincinnati, Oh.

Peterson, C., F. Danner, and J. Flavell. 1972. Developmental changes in children's response to three indications of communication failure. Child Dev. 43: 1463–1468.

Petretic, P., and R. Tweney. 1977. Does comprehension precede production? The development of children's responses to telegraphic sentences of varying grammatical adequancy. J. Child Lang. 4: 201–209.

Pfuderer, C. 1969. Some suggestions for a syntactic characterization of baby-talk style. Working Paper No. 14, Language Behavior Research Laboratory, University of California, Berkeley, Ca.

Phillips, J. 1973. Syntax and vocabulary of mothers' speech to young children: Age and sex comparisons. Child Dev. 44: 182–185.

Piaget, J. 1926. The Language and Thought of the Child. Harcourt Brace Jovanovich, New York.

Piaget, J. 1951. Plays, Dreams, and Imitation in Childhood. W. W. Norton and Co., New York.

Piaget, J. 1952. The Origins of Intelligence in Children. W. W. Norton and Co., New York.

Piaget, J. 1954. The Construction of Reality in the Child. Basic Books, New York.

Piaget, J., and B. Inhelder. 1969. The Psychology of the Child. Basic Books, New York.

Pillsbury, W. 1897. The reading of words: A study in apperception. Am. J. Psychol. 8: 315–393.

Pisoni, D., and Sawusch, J. 1975. Some stages of processing in speech perception. In A. Cohen and S. Nooteboom (eds.), Structure and Process in Speech Perception, pp. 16–34. Springer-Verling, Heidelberg, Germany.

Premack, D., and A. Premack. 1974. Teaching visual language to apes and language-deficient persons. In R. Schiefelbusch and L. Lloyd (eds.), Language Perspectives—Acquisition, Retardation, and Intervention, pp. 347–376. University Park Press, Baltimore.

Presnell, L. 1973. Hearing-impaired children's comprehension and production of syntax in oral language. J. Speech Hear. Res. 16: 12–21.

Prutting, C., and J. Connolly. 1976. Imitation: A closer look. J. Speech Hear. Disord. 41: 412–422.

Prutting, C., T. Gallagher, and A. Mulac. 1975. The expressive portion of the NSST compared to a spontaneous language sample. J. Speech Hear. Disord. 40: 40–48.

Prutting, C., and N. Rees. 1977. Pragmatics of language: Applications to the assessment and remediation of communicative behaviors. Paper presented at the ASHA annual convention, Chicago.

Putnam, V., I. Iscoe, and R. Young. 1962. Verbal learning in the deaf. J. Comp. Physiol. Psychol. 55: 843–846.

Quigley, S. 1969. The Influence of Fingerspelling on the Development of Language, Communication, and Educational Achievement in Deaf Children. Institute for Research on Exceptional Children, University of Illinois, Urbana.

Quigley, S., D. Montanelli, and R. Wilbur. 1976. Some aspects of the verb system in the language of deaf students. J. Speech Hear. Res. 19: 536–550.

Quigley, S., D. Power, and M. Steinkamp. 1977. The language structure of deaf children. Volta Rev. 79: 73–84.

Quigley, S., N. Smith, and R. Wilbur. 1974. Comprehension of relativized sentences by deaf students. J. Speech Hear. Res. 17: 325–341.

Quigley, S., and F. Thomure. 1968. Some effects of hearing impairment on school performance. Institute of Research on Exceptional Children. University of Illinois, Urbana.

Quigley, S., R. Wilbur, and D. Montanelli. 1974. Question formation in the language of deaf students. J. Speech Hear. Res. 17: 699–713.

Quigley, S., R. Wilbur, and D. Montanelli. 1976. Complement structures in the language of deaf students. J. Speech Hear. Res. 19: 448–457.

Quigley, S., R. Wilbur, D. Power, D. Montanelli, and M. Steinkamp. 1976.

Syntactic Structures in the Language of Deaf Children. Institute for Child Behavior and Development, University of Illinois, Urbana.

Raffin, M. 1976. The acquisition of inflectional morphemes by deaf children using See Essential English. Unpublished doctoral dissertation, University of Iowa, Iowa City.

Ratusnik, D., and R. Koenigsknecht. 1975. Internal consistency of the Northwestern Syntax Screening Test. J. Speech Hear. Disord. 40: 59–68.

Read, C. 1975. Lessons to be learned from the preschool orthographer. In E. Lenneberg and E. Lenneberg (eds.), Foundations of Language Development, Vol. 2, pp. 329–346. Academic Press, New York.

Reay, E. 1946. A comparison between deaf and hearing children in regard to the use of verbs and nouns in compositions describing a short motion picture story. Am. Ann. Deaf 91: 453–491.

Reed, N. 1977. An analysis of comprehension levels of an ask/tell syntactic structure in a group of adolescents, aged ten to eighteen years. Unpublished master's thesis, University of Cincinnati, Cincinnati, Oh.

Rees, N. 1975. Imitation and language development: Issues and clinical implications. J. Speech Hear. Disord. 40: 339–350.

Reynell, J. 1969. Reynell Developmental Language Scales, Manual. National Foundation for Educational Research in England and Wales.

Risely, T., B. Hart, and L. Doke. 1972. Operant language development: The outline of a therapeutic technology. In R. Schiefelbusch (ed.), Language of the Mentally Retarded, pp. 107–123. University Park Press, Baltimore.

Risley, T., and N. Reynolds. 1970. Emphasis as a prompt for verbal imitation. J. Appl. Behav. Anal. 3: 185–190.

Roach, R., and C. Rosecrans. 1971. Verbal deficit in children with hearing loss. Except. Child 38: 395–399.

Romanik, S. 1976. An investigation into deaf children's use of the interrogative form. Austral. Teach. Deaf 17: 14–28.

Rosansky, E., J. Schumann, and H. Cancino. 1975. The acquisition of the English auxiliary by native Spanish speakers. TESOL Quart. 9: 4–6.

Ross, J. 1970. On declarative sentences. In R. Jacobs and Rosenbaum (eds.), Readings in English Transformational Grammar, pp. 222–272. Ginn and Co., Waltham, Ma.

Ross, J. 1975. Where to do things with words. In M. Cole and J. Morgan (eds.), Syntax and Semantics, Vol 3, pp. 233–256. Academic Press, New York.

Ruddell, R. 1973. The relation of regularity of grapheme-phoneme correspondences and of language structure to achievement in first-grade reading. In K. Goodman (ed.), The Psycholinguistic Nature of the Reading Process. Wayne State University Press, Detroit.

Rudell, R., and H. Bacon. 1972. The nature of reading: Language and meaning. In R. Hodges and E. Rudorf (eds.), Language and Learning to Read. Houghton Mifflin Co., Boston.

Ruder, K., P. Hermann, and R. Schiefelbusch. 1977. Effects of verbal imitation and comprehension training on verbal production. J. Psycholinguist. Res. 6: 59–72.

Rumbaugh, D., and T. Gill. 1976. Language and the acquisition of language-type skills by a chimpanzee. Ann. N.Y. Acad. Sci. 270: 90–123.

Rumbaugh, D., and T. Gill. 1977. Language and language-type communication: Studies with a chimpanzee. In M. Lewis and L. Rosenblum (eds.), Interaction,

Conversation, and the Development of Language, pp. 115–131. John Wiley and Sons, New York.

Rush, M. 1964. Programmed instruction for the language of directions. Am. Ann. Deaf 109: 356–358.

Ruwet, N. 1973. An Introduction to Generative Grammar. North-Holland Publishing Co., Amsterdam.

Ryan, E., and M. Semmel. 1969. Reading as a constructive language process. Read. Res. Quart. 5: 59–83.

Sachs, J., and J. Devin. 1976. Young children's use of age-appropriate speech styles. J. Child Lang. 3: 81–98.

Sacks, H., E. Schegloff, and G. Jefferson. 1974. A simplest systematics for the organization of turn-taking for conversation. Language 50: 696–735.

Sailor, W. 1971. Reinforcement and generalization of productive plural allomorphs in two retarded children. J. Appl. Behav. Anal. 4: 305–310.

Sailor, W., D. Guess, and D. Baer. 1973. Functional language for verbally deficient children. Ment. Retard. 11: 27–35.

Sailor, W., and T. Taman. 1972. Stimulus factors in the training of prepositional usage in three autistic children. J. Appl. Behav. Anal. 5: 183–190.

Salzinger, K., R. Feldman, J. Cowan, and S. Salzinger. 1965. Operant conditioning of verbal behavior of two young speech-deficient boys. In L. Krasner and L. Ullman (eds.), Research in Behavior Modification, pp. 82–105. Holt, Rinehart, and Winston, New York.

Sanders, L. 1971. The comprehension of certain syntactic structures by adults. J. Speech Hear. Disord. 14: 739–745.

Sarachan-Deily, A., and R. Love. 1974. Underlying grammatical rule structure of the deaf. J. Speech Hear. Res. 17: 689–698.

Scaife, M., and J. Bruner. 1975. The capacity for joint visual attention in the infant. Nature 253: 265–266.

Schaffer, H., G. Collis, and G. Parsons. 1977. Vocal interchange and visual regard in verbal and pre-verbal children. In H. Schaffer (ed.), Studies in Mother-Infant Interaction, pp. 291–324. Academic Press, London.

Schegloff, E. 1968. Sequencing in conversational openings. Am. Anthropol. 70: 1075–1095.

Schegloff, E., and H. Sacks. 1973. Opening up closings. Semiotica 8: 289–327.

Schiff, N. 1976. The development of form and meaning in the language of hearing children of deaf parents. Unpublished doctoral dissertation, Columbia University, New York.

Schiff, N., and I. Ventry. 1976. Communication problems in hearing children of deaf parents. J. Speech Hear. Disord. 41: 348–358.

Schlesinger, H., and K. Meadow. 1972. Sounds and Sign. University of California Press, Berkeley.

Schlesinger, I. 1971. Production of utterances and language acquisition. In D. Slobin (ed.), The Ontogenesis of Grammar, pp. 63–101. Academic Press, New York.

Schlesinger, I., and L. Namur. 1978. Current Trends in the Study of Sign Language of the Deaf. University Park Press, Baltimore.

Schulze, G. 1965. An evaluation of vocabulary development by thirty-two deaf children over a three year period. Am. Ann. Deaf 110: 424–435.

Schumaker, J., and J. Sherman. 1970. Training generative verb usage by imitation and reinforcement procedures. J. Appl. Behav. Anal. 3: 273–287.

Scroggs, C. 1975. The effects of expansion on the communication rate of hearing impaired students. Am. Ann. Deaf 120: 350–359.

Scroggs, C. 1977. Analyzing the language of hearing impaired children with severe-language acquisition problems. Am. Ann. Deaf 122: 403–406.

Searle, J. 1969. Speech Acts. Cambridge University, Cambridge, England.

Searle, J. 1975. Indirect speech acts. In M. Cole and J. Morgan (eds.), Syntax and Semantics, Vol. 3, pp. 59–82. Academic Press, New York.

Selinker, L., M. Swain, and G. Dumas. 1975. The inter-language hypothesis extended to children. Lang. Learn. 25: 139–152.

Sharf, D. 1972. Some relationships between measures of early language development. J. Speech Hear. Disord. 37: 64–74.

Shatz, M., and R. Gelman. 1973. The development of communication skills: Modifications in the speech of young children as a function of listener. Monogr. Soc. Res. Child Dev. 38(5): 1–37.

Sheldon, A. 1977. On strategies for processing relative clauses: A comparison of children and adults. J. Psycholinguist. Res. 6: 305–318.

Shields, J., A. McHugh, and J. Martin. 1974. Reaction time to phoneme targets as a function of rhythmic cues in continuous speech. J. Exp. Psychol. 102: 250–255.

Shipley, E., C. Smith, and L. Gleitman. 1969. A study in the acquisition of language: Free responses to commands. Language 45: 322–342.

Shriner, T. 1969. A review of mean length of response as a measure of expressive language development in children. J. Speech Hear. Disord. 34: 61–68.

Shuy, R. (ed.). 1965. Social Dialects and Language Learning. National Council of Teachers of English, Champlain, Il.

Shvachkin, N. 1973. The development of phonemic speech perception in early childhood. In C. Ferguson and D. Slobin (eds.), Studies of Child Language Development, pp. 91–127. Holt, Rinehart, and Winston, New York.

Silverman-Dresner, T., and G. Guilfoyle. 1972. Vocabulary Norms for Deaf Children. Alexander Graham Bell Assoc., Washington, D.C.

Simmons, A. 1962. A comparison of the type-token ratio of spoken and written language of deaf and hearing children. Volta Rev. 64: 117–121.

Simmons-Martin, A. 1976. Early intervention programs. In B. Bolton (ed.), Psychology of Deafness for Rehabilitation Counselors, pp. 125–136. University Park Press, Baltimore.

Sinclair, H. 1973. Language acquisition and cognitive development. In T. Moore (ed.), Cognitive Development and the Acquisition of Language, pp. 9–26. Academic Press, New York.

Sinclair, H., and J. Bronckart. 1972. SVO—A linguistic universal. J. Child Exp. Psychol. 14: 329–348.

Sinclair, H., and E. Ferriero. 1970. Comprehension, production, et repetition des phrases au mode passif. Arch. Psychol. 40: 1–42.

Skarakis, E., and C. Prutting. 1977. Early communication: Semantic functions and communicative intentions in the communication of the preschool child with impaired hearing. Am. Ann. Deaf 122: 382–391.

Slobin, D. 1973. Cognitive prerequisites for the development of grammar. In C. Ferguson and D. Slobin (eds.), Studies of Child Language Development, pp. 175–208. Holt, Rinehart, and Winston, New York.

Slobin, D., and C. Welsh. 1973. Elicited information as a research tool in developmental psycholinguistics. In C. Ferguson and D. Slobin (eds.), Studies in Child Language Development, pp. 485–497. Holt, Rinehart, and Winston, New York.

Smith, F. 1971. Understanding Reading: A Psycholinguistic Analysis of Reading and Learning to Read. Holt, Rinehart, and Winston, New York.

Smith, F. (ed.). 1973a. Psycholinguistics and Reading. Holt, Rinehart, and Winston, New York.

Smith, F. 1973b. Reading: The great fallacy. In F. Smith (ed.), Psycholinguistics and Reading, pp. 70–83. Holt, Rinehart, and Winston, New York.

Smith, F. 1973c. The efficiency of phonics. In. F. Smith (ed.), Psycholinguistics and Reading, pp. 84–90. Holt, Rinehart, and Winston, New York.

Smith, F. 1973d. Alphabetic writing: A language compromise? In F. Smith (ed.), Psycholinguistics and Reading, pp. 116–130. Holt, Rinehart, and Winston, New York.

Smith, F. 1973e. Twelve easy ways to make learning to read difficult. In F. Smith (ed.), Psycholinguistics and Reading, pp. 183–196. Holt, Rinehart, and Winston, 1973.

Smith, F. 1975. Comprehension and Learning. Holt, Rinehart, and Winston, New York.

Smith, F. 1977. Making sense of reading and of reading instruction. Harvard Educ. Rev. 47: 386–395.

Smith, F., and K. Goodman. 1973. On the psycholinguistics method of teaching reading. In F. Smith (ed.), Psycholinguistics and Reading, pp. 177–182. Holt, Rinehart, and Winston, New York.

Smith, F., and D. Holmes. 1973. The independence of letter, word, and meaning identification in reading. In F. Smith (ed.), Psycholinguistics and Reading, pp. 50–69. Houghton Mifflin Co., Boston.

Smith, L. 1972. Comprehension performance in oral deaf and normal hearing children at three stages of language development. Unpublished doctoral dissertation, University of Wisconsin, Madison, Wi.

Snow, C. 1972. Mothers' speech to children learning language. Child Dev. 43: 549–565.

Snow, C. 1977. The development of conversation between mothers and babies. J. Child Lang. 4: 1–22.

Snow, C., A. Arlman-Rupp, Y. Hassing, J. Jobse, J. Joosten, and J. Vorster. 1976. Mothers' speech in three social classes. J. Psycholinguist. Res. 5:1–20.

Snow, C., and C. Ferguson. (eds.). 1977. Talking to Children. Cambridge University Press, Cambridge, England.

Snyder, L., T. Lovitt, and J. Smith. 1975. Language training for the severely retarded: Five years of behavior analysis research. Except. Child. 43: 7–15.

Snyder, L., and J. McLean. 1976. Deficient acquisition strategies: A proposed conceptual framework for analyzing severe language deficiency. Am. J. Ment. Def. 81: 338–349.

Solly, G. 1975. Tests of comprehension of spoken language for use with hearing impaired children. Teach. Deaf 73: 74–85.

Spence, C. 1973. Relational concepts in the language and thought of deaf and hearing preschool children. Unpublished doctoral dissertation, University of Washington.

Stanton, A. 1976. A qualitative assessment of comprehension and imitation in language-delayed pre-school children in comparison with normal children of the same age. Br. J. Disord. Commun. 11: 63–71.

Stark, J., R. Rosenbaum, D. Schwartz, and A. Wilson. 1973. The nonverbal child: Some clinical guidelines. J. Speech Hear. Disord. 38: 59–71.

Stark, R., J. Heinz, and C. Wright-Wilson. 1976. Vowel utterances of young infants. J. Acoustic. Soc. Am. 60(1): S43.

Stark, R., S. Rose, and M. McLagen. 1975. Features of infant sounds: The first eight weeks of life. J. Child Lang. 2: 205–222.

Steinkamp, M., and S. Quigley. 1976. Assessing deaf children's written language. Volta Rev. 78: 10–18.

Stockwell, R., P. Schachter, and B. Partee. 1973. The Major Syntactic Structures of English. Holt, Rinehart, and Winston, New York.

Stoutenburgh, G. 1971. A psycholinguistic approach to study the language deficits in the language performance of deaf children. Unpublished doctoral dissertation, Syracuse University, Syracuse, N.Y.

Strawson, P. 1964. Intention and convention in speech acts. Philosoph. Rev. 73: 439–460.

Stremel, K. 1972. Language training: A program for retarded children. Ment. Ret. 12: 47–49.

Streng, A. 1972. Syntax, Speech, and Hearing. Grune and Stratton, New York.

Strickland, R. 1962. The language of elementary school children. Indiana Univ. School Educ. Bull. 38: 1–131.

Strohner, H., and K. Nelson. 1974. The young child's development of sentence comprehension: Influence of event probability, non-verbal context, syntactic form, and strategies. Child Dev. 45: 567–576.

Stuckless, E., and J. Birch. 1962. A programmed approach to written language development in deaf children. Volta Rev. 64: 415–417.

Stuckless, E., and J. Birch. 1966. The influence of early manual communication on the linguistic development of deaf children. Am. Ann. Deaf 111: 452–460.

Studdert-Kennedy, M. 1974. The perception of speech. In T. Sebeok (ed.), Current Trends in Linguistics, Vol. 12, pp. 2349–2386. Mouton, The Hague.

Studdert-Kennedy, M. 1975. Speech perception. In N. Lass (ed.), Contemporary Issues in Experimental Phonetics, pp. 243–293. Charles C Thomas Publishers, Springfield, Il.

Tatham, S. 1970. Reading comprehension of materials written with selected oral language patterns: A study at grades two and four. Read. Res. Quart. 5: 415–483.

Taylor, L. 1969. A language analysis of the writing of deaf children. Unpublished doctoral dissertation, Florida State University, Tallahassee, Fl.

Teece, C. 1976. Language and play: A study of the relationship between functions and structures in the language of five year old children. Lang. Speech 19: 179–192.

Terman, L., and M. Merrill. 1960. Stanford-Binet Intelligence Scale. 3rd rev. ed. Houghton and Mifflin Co., Boston.

Tervoort, B. 1970. The understanding of passive sentences by deaf children. In G. Flores d'Arcais and W. Levelt (eds.), Advances in Psycholinguistics, pp. 166–173. North-Holland Press, Amsterdam.

Tervoort, B. 1975. Developmental Features of Visual Communication. North-Holland Press, Amsterdam.

Thomas, E. 1958. A system of sentence structure for the development of language for the deaf. Am. Ann. Deaf 103: 510–523.

Thompson, W. 1936. An analysis of errors in written compositions by deaf children. Am. Ann. Deaf 81: 95–99.

Thorndike, E. 1970. Reading as reasoning: A study of mistakes in paragraph reading. Read. Res. Quart. 6: 425–434. (Originally published in 1917.)

Todd, P. 1976. A case of structural interference across modalities in second-language learning. Word 27: 102–118.

Trantham, C., and J. Pedersen. 1976. Normal Language Development: The Key to Diagnosis and Therapy for Language-Disordered Children. Williams and Wilkins, Baltimore.

Trehub, S. 1973. Infant's sensitivity to vowel and tonal contrasts. Dev. Psychol. 9: 91–96.

Trehub, S., and M. Rabinovitch. 1972. Auditory-linguistic sensitivity in early infancy. Dev. Psychol. 6:74–77.

Trevarthen, C. 1977. Descriptive analyses of infant communication behavior. In H. Schaffer (ed.), Studies in Mother-Infant Interaction, pp. 227–270. Academic Press, London.

Turnure, C. 1971. Response to voice of mother and stranger by babies in the first year. Dev. Psychol. 4: 182–190.

Turnure, J., N. Buium, and M. Thurlow. 1976. The effectiveness of interrogatives for promoting verbal elaboration productivity in young children. Child Dev. 47: 851–855.

Twardosz, S., and D. Baer. 1973. Training two severely retarded adolescents to ask questions. J. Appl. Behav. Anal. 6: 655–661.

Tweney, R., and H. Hoemann. 1973. The development of semantic associations in profoundly deaf children. J. Speech Hear. Res. 16: 309–318.

Tweney, R., H. Hoemann, and C. Andrews. 1975. Semantic organization in deaf and hearing subjects. J. Psycholinguist. Res. 4: 61–73.

Tyack, D., and R. Gottsleben. 1974. Language Sampling, Analysis, and Training: A Handbook for Teachers and Clinicians. Consulting Psychological Press, Palo Alto, Ca.

Uzgiris, I., and J. Hunt. 1975. Assessment in Infancy: Ordinal Scales of Psychological Assessment. University of Illinois, Urbana.

Valian, V., and R. Wales. 1976. What's what: Talkers help listeners hear and understand by clarifying sentential relations. Cognition 4: 155–176.

Vanderheiden, D., W. Brown, P. MacKenzie, S. Reinen, and C. Schiebel. 1975. Symbol communication for the mentally handicapped. Ment. Retard. 13: 34–37.

Vanderheiden, G., and D. Harris-Vanderheiden. 1976. Communication techniques and aids for the nonvocal severely handicapped. In L. Lloyd (ed.), Communication Assessment and Intervention Strategies. University Park Press, Baltimore.

Vellutino, F. 1977. Alternative conceptualization of dyslexia: Evidence in support of a verbal deficit hypothesis. Harvard Educ. Rev. 47: 334–354.

Vernon, M., and S. Koh. 1969. Early manual communication and deaf children's achievement. Am. Ann. Deaf 115: 529–536.

Vernon, M., and S. Koh. 1970. Effects of oral preschool compared to early manual communication on education and communication in deaf children. Am. Ann. Deaf 116: 569–574.

Vicker, B. 1974. Nonoral Communication System Project. University of Iowa Press, Iowa City.

Waldon, E. 1963. A study of the spoken and written language of children with impaired hearing. Unpublished doctoral dissertation, Ohio State University, Columbus, Oh.

Walter, J. 1955. A study of the written sentence construction of a group of profoundly deaf children. Am. Ann. Deaf 100: 235–252.

Walter, J. 1959. Some further observations on the written sentence construction of profoundly deaf children. Am. Ann. Deaf 104: 282–285.

Walter, Sr. M. 1959. The Fitzgerald Key on wheels. Am. Ann. Deaf 104: 366–371.

Walton, L. 1972. A description of the linguistic environments and the syntactic output of ten black hearing-impaired adolescents. Unpublished master's thesis, University of Cincinnati, Cincinnati, Oh.

Warden, D. 1976. The influence of context on children's use of identifying expressions and references. Br. J. Psychol. 67: 101–112.

Waryas, C., and K. Ruder. 1974. On the limitations of language comprehension procedures and an alternative. J. Speech Hear. Disord. 39: 44–52.

Wasserman, M. 1976. Interpreting semantic structure in utterances of hearing impaired children: Given varying degrees of linguistic and paralinguistic information. Unpublished master's thesis, University of Cincinnati, Cincinnati, Oh.

Watson, D., and A. Pickles. 1957. Home training. In A. Ewing (ed.), Educational Guidance and the Deaf Child. Alexander Graham Bell Assoc., Washington, D.C.

Watt, W. 1970. On two hypotheses concerning psycholinguistics. In J. Hayes (ed.), Cognition and the Development of Language, pp. 137–220. John Wiley and Sons, New York.

Weber, R. 1969. A linguistic analysis of first-grade reading errors. Read. Res. Quart. 5: 427–451.

Weener, P. 1971. Language structure and the free recall of verbal messages by children. Dev. Psychol. 5: 237–243.

Weiner, P. 1972. The perceptual level functioning of dysphasic children: A follow-up study. J. Speech Hear. Res. 15: 423–438.

Weir, R., and R. Venezky. 1973. Spelling-to-sound patterns. In K. Goodman (ed.), The Psycholinguistic Nature of the Reading Process, pp. 185–199. Wayne State University Press, Detroit.

Wells, G. 1974. Learning to code experience through language. J. Child Lang. 1: 243–269.

West, J., and J. Weber. 1974. A linguistic analysis of the morphemic and syntactic structures of a hard-of-hearing child. Lang. Speech 17: 68–79.

Wheeler, A., and B. Sulzer. 1970. Operant training and generalization of a verbal response form in a speech-deficient child. J. Appl. Behav. Anal. 3: 139–147.

Whitehurst, G., and G. Novak. 1973. Modeling, imitation training and the acquisition of sentence phrases. J. Exp. Child. Psychol. 16: 332–345.

Whitehurst, G., and R. Vasta. 1975. Is language acquired through imitation? J. Psycholinguist. Res. 4: 37–59.

Wilbur, R. 1976. The linguistics of manual language and manual systems. In L. Lloyd (ed.), Communication Assessment and Intervention Strategies, pp. 425–500. University Park Press, Baltimore.

Wilbur, R. 1977. An explanation of deaf children's difficulty with certain syntactic structures in English. Volta Rev. 79: 85–92.

Wilbur, R. 1978. American Sign Language and Sign Systems: Research and Applications. University Park Press, Baltimore.

Wilbur, R., and M. Jones. 1974. Some aspects of the bilingual/bimodal acquisition of Sign and English by three hearing children of deaf parents. In M. LeGaly, R. Fox, and A. Bruck (eds.), Proceedings of the Tenth Regional Meeting, Chicago Linguistic Society, Chicago.

Wilbur, R., D. Montanelli, and S. Quigley. 1976. Pronominalization in the language of deaf students. J. Speech Hear. Res. 19: 120–140.

Wilbur, R., and S. Quigley. 1975. Syntactic structures in the written language of deaf children. Volta Rev. 77: 194–203.

Wilbur, R., S. Quigley, and D. Montanelli. 1975. Conjoined structures in the language of deaf students. J. Speech Hear. Res. 18: 319–335.

Wilcox, J., and H. Tobin. 1974. Linguistic performance of hard-of-hearing and normal hearing children. J. Speech Hear. Disord. 17: 286–293.

Williams, R. 1977. Play behavior of language handicapped and normal speaking preschool children. Unpublished doctoral dissertation, University of Cincinnati, Cincinnati, Oh.

Wing, G. 1887. The theory and practice of grammatical methods. Am. Ann. Deaf 32: 84–92.

Winslow, L. 1973. Learning to see a language: Development of the language of signs. Unpublished honor thesis, Harvard University, Cambridge, Ma.

Wolf, T. 1977. Reading reconsidered. Harvard Educ. Rev. 47: 411–429.

Wolff, S. 1977. Cognition and communication patterns in classrooms for deaf students. Am. Ann. Deaf 122: 319–327.

Woodward, J. 1971. Variation in American Sign Language syntax: Agent-beneficiary directionality. In R. Fasold and R. Shuy (eds.), Analyzing Variation in Language. Georgetown University Press, Washington, D.C.

Woodward, J. 1973a. Some characteristics of pidgin sign English. Sign Lang. Stud. 2: 37–46.

Woodward, J. 1973b. Inter-rule implications in American Sign Language. Sign Lang. Stud. 2: 47–56.

Woodward, J. 1976. Black Southern signing. Lang. Soc. 5: 211–218.

Wulbert, M., S. Inglis, E. Kriegsmann, and B. Mills. 1975. Language delay and associated mother-child interactions. Dev. Psychol. 11: 61–70.

Yule, W., M. Berger, and P. Howlin. 1975. Language deficit and behavior modification. In N. O'Connor (ed.), Language, Cognitive Deficits, and Retardation, pp. 209–223. Butterworths, London.

Zlatin, M. 1975. Explorative mapping of the vocal tract and primitive syllabification in infancy. Purdue University Center Publications, No. 5, West Lafayette, Ind.

Zlatin, M. 1976. Language acquisition: Some acoustic and interactive aspects of infancy. Final Report, U.S. Department of Health, Education and Welfare, NE-G-00-3-0077.

Author Index

Subject Index

Notes

Notes

Notes

Notes

Notes

Notes

Notes

Notes

Notes